Life and Letters in France

Life and Letters in France
General Editor
Austin Gill CBE, MA
Marshall Professor of French,
University of Glasgow

Other Volumes

The Seventeenth Century
W D Howarth MA

The Nineteenth Century
A W Raitt MA, D Phil

Life and Letters in France

The Eighteenth Century

Richard Fargher
Fellow of St Edmund Hall, Oxford

Charles Scribner's Sons New York

A - 8.71 (I)

Printed in Great Britain by Richard Clay (The Chaucer Press), Ltd,
Bungay, Suffolk
Library of Congress Catalog Card Number 77-166297
SBN 684-12617-6 (college paper)
SBN 684-12616-8 (trade cloth)

Contents

List of Plates

Acknowledgments

My thanks are due to the General Editor of the series, to Mr Donald Sutherland, Librarian of the Taylor Institution, Oxford, and to many other colleagues who have been generous with help and advice. I owe a special debt of gratitude to Mrs A. M. Barnes, Reader in French Literature at Oxford, Fellow of St Anne's College, and to John McManners, Professor of History at Leicester University. Mrs Barnes, whose *Jean Le Clerc et la République des Lettres* is a standard work on eighteenth-century intellectual life, devoted many hours to reading the drafts of my chapters. Her critical insight and constructive enthusiasm were of the greatest value to me. Professor McManners allowed me to draw freely on his vast and vivid knowledge of eighteenth-century French social history, guided me through the intricacies of current historical research, and prevented me from making a number of errors. Those which remain are my own. By her patient but pertinacious refusal to agree that arguments were clear when they might have been put more clearly, my wife has ensured that the book is as readable as we could together make it. She also corrected the proofs.

R.F.

For permission to reproduce photographs, the author makes grateful acknowledgment to The Wallace Collection (Plate I): the Musée d'Art et d'Histoire, Geneva (Plate II); the Alte Pinakothek, Munich (Plate III); the Nationalmuseum, Stockholm (Plate IVa); the Staatliche Museen, Berlin-Dahlem (Plate IVb); The Bowes Museum, Barnard Castle, Durham (Plate V); the Musée Calvet, Avignon (Plate VI); the Ashmolean Museum (Plate VIIa); The Barber Institute of Fine Arts (Plate VIIb); and the Musée de Versailles (Plate VIII).

Preface

The type of commentary presented in this series is not meant to serve as an alternative to, and still less to compete with, the close analytical study known as *l'explication de textes*. It is intended rather as a complement, fulfilling a need which teachers of French literature in this country are acutely aware of, and which *la lecture expliquée* on the usual lines cannot conveniently satisfy. Our pupils are not equipped, like those brought up in French schools, with the knowledge of French history, political, social, economic and cultural, which should be brought to the understanding and appreciation of French authors. On that side of their study they need help which a method devised for teaching French literature in France does not afford. It is to the familiar problem of how best to give this help that the *Life and Letters in France* series suggests an answer. How good an answer, experience must decide, but *a priori* the method has some promising advantages. It places the historical facts not in an historian's arrangement, but in perspectives directly relevant to the study of literature. Also, since the historical commentary is directed to the explanation of particular passages, the literary usefulness of a knowledge of history (about which students are often sceptical) is constantly illustrated.

The extent to which the understanding of literature is thus sharpened and deepened by systematic attention to what is conveniently called historical background is variable, of course. It depends a good deal on the nature of the works studied. The kind of passage selected for commentary naturally reflects that fact. The passages are varied enough to show that the method is appropriate to many different kinds of work, but that is not to say that they represent adequately the variety of French literature at any period in its history. Nor, on the other hand, do the commentaries in any of the volumes attempt to cover, taken together, all the main aspects of background for the century concerned. It was desirable to aim at diversity, but it would have been foolish to try to be complete.

That, in bare outline, is what the authors of the different volumes have attempted. They are all French tutors. That is a fair guarantee, I hope, that they have kept firmly in view the practical aim of teaching our compatriots to read French literature with profit and enjoyment. It is as tutors also that they particularly wish to guard against two possible misunderstandings. First, what is proposed here is a technique for teaching and learning; it has nothing to do with examining. Secondly, the concern for historical aspects of the study of literature which characterises this series does not signify that those are the aspects in which all or any of us are most interested, or as teachers would stress most. The commentaries themselves make it quite clear, I believe, that their authors are very much alive to the strictly literary qualities of the passages they are discussing, though for the moment they are studying them from another point of view.

A.G.

Reading List

[Books on individual authors are given in the notes at the end of chapters]

I. POLITICAL, SOCIAL, AND ECONOMIC HISTORY

C. B. A. Behrens, *The Ancien Régime* (London, 1967)

A. Cobban, *A History of Modern France*, Vol. I: 1715–1799 (London, 1957)

J. Godechot, *Les Révolutions. 1770–1789* (Paris, 1963)

F. C. Green, *The Ancien Régime. A Manual of French Institutions and Social Classes* (Edinburgh, 1958)

J. Lough, *An Introduction to Eighteenth-Century France* (London, 1960)

J. McManners, *French Ecclesiastical Society Under the Ancien Régime* (Manchester, 1960)

—, *The French Revolution and the Church* (London, 1969)

R. Mandrou, *La France au XVIIᵉ et XVIIIᵉ siècles* (Paris, 1967)

R. Mousnier, E. Labrousse, and M. Bouloiseau, *Le XVIIIᵉ siècle. L'Epoque des 'lumières' – Histoire générale des civilisations*, Vol. V (4ᵉ édition, Paris, 1963)

E. Préclin and V. L. Tapié, *Le XVIIIᵉ siècle* (Paris, 1952)

P. Sagnac, *La Formation de la société française moderne*, Vol. II (Paris, 1946)

H. Sée, *La France économique et sociale au XVIIIᵉ siècle.* Bibliographie mise à jour par J. A. Lesourd (Paris, 1967)

Livre et Société dans la France du XVIIIᵉ siècle. G. Bollème, J. Ehrard, F. Furet, D. Roche, J. Roger. Post-face d'A. Dupront, Professeur à la Sorbonne. *Civilisations et Sociétés*, I (Paris, La Haye, 1965)

II. HISTORY OF LITERATURE, THOUGHT, TASTE

A. Adam, *Le Mouvement philosophique dans la première moitié du XVIIIᵉ siècle* (Paris, 1967)

A. Chérel, *De Télémaque à Candide* (Paris, 1933, 1958)

L. G. Crocker, *An Age of Crisis. Man and World in Eighteenth-Century French Thought* (Baltimore, 1959)

—, *Nature and Culture, Ethical Thought in the French Enlightenment* (Baltimore, 1963)

J. Ehrard, *L'Idée de nature en France dans la première moitié du XVIIIᵉ siècle* (Paris, 1963)

J. Fabre, *Lumières et Romantisme* (Paris, 1963)

O. E. Fellows and N. L. Torrey, *The Age of Enlightenment. An Anthology of Eighteenth-Century French Literature* (New York, 1942)

P. Gay, *The Party of Humanity. Studies in the French Enlightenment* (London, 1964)

—, *The Enlightenment: An Interpretation*. Vol. I: *The Rise of Modern Paganism*; Vol. II: *The Science of Freedom* (London, 1967, 1969)

J.-M. Goulemot and M. Launay, *Le Siècle des lumières* (Paris, 1968)

G. R. Havens, *The Age of Ideas. From Reaction to Revolution in eighteenth-century France* (New York, 1955)

R. Laufer, *Style rococo, style des 'lumières'* (Paris, 1963)

M. Leroy, *Histoire des idées sociales en France*. Vol. I. *De Montesquieu à Robespierre* (Paris, 1946)

R. Mauzi, *L'Idée du bonheur dans la littérature et la pensée françaises au XVIIIe siècle* (Paris, 1960)

G. May, *Le Dilemme du roman au XVIIIe siècle* (Paris, 1963)

R. Mercier, *La Réhabilitation de la nature humaine 1700–1750* (Villemomble, 1960)

D. Mornet, *Le Romantisme en France au XVIIIe siècle* (Paris, 1912)

—, *Les Origines intellectuelles de la Révolution française* (Paris, 1933)

V. Mylne, *The Eighteenth-Century Novel. Techniques of Illusion* (Manchester, 1965)

R. R. Palmer, *Catholics and Unbelievers in Eighteenth-Century France* (New York, 1961)

R. Pomeau, *L'Europe des lumières. Cosmopolitisme et unité européenne au XVIIIe siècle* (Paris, 1966)

J. Seznec, *Essais sur Diderot et l'antiquité* (Oxford, 1957)

J. S. Spink, *French Free-Thought from Gassendi to Voltaire* (London, 1960)

J. Starobinski, *L'Invention de la liberté* (Geneva, 1964)

Paul van Tieghem, *Le Sentiment de la nature dans le préromantisme européen* (Paris, 1960)

Ph. van Tieghem, *Les Influences étrangères sur la littérature française 1550–1880* (Paris, 1961)

—, *Petite Histoire des grandes doctrines littéraires en France* (Paris, 1946)

Introduction

The 1787 edition of the *Nouvelle Description des environs de Paris*, by J. A. Dulaure, describes in detail the country estate at Franconville (twenty kilometres north-west of Paris on the Pontoise road), which had recently been laid out on modern lines by its progressive owner, the comte d'Albon. Nature was not insulted in this happy abode by formal alleys, artificial watercourses or clipped trees, nor were there boundary-walls emphasising private property: all was open and unencumbered, in token of 'the candour and trustfulness possessed by all honest souls', such as the local villagers, who were encouraged to use the estate for their own merry-making, on the recreation ground specially provided for them. Exhibits in the library testified to the count's interest in classical antiquity; his fondness for modern literature was demonstrated by a grove with statues, representing 'the First Kiss of Love, the tender, passionate scene so ardently described in Rousseau's novel *La Nouvelle Héloïse*'. A temple in the classical style, dedicated to the Dying Christ, was equipped with a relic of the True Cross, an eleventh-century chalice, statues to Love and Fidelity on either side of the altar, and, as an act of homage to God, the balloon which had made an ascent from the garden on 16 January 1784. Among other attractions in the grounds were: an obelisk fifty feet high, erected by the count for his beloved and virtuous wife; an open-air salon of friendship, with white doves; a Lyceum Portico with busts of Montaigne and Rousseau; a lake, with statues of Seneca and Cato; a statue to the god Priapus at the bottom of the kitchen garden; monuments to the Dutch doctor Boerhaave and the Swiss scientist Haller; a Devil's bridge with inscriptions from the *Roman de la Rose*; the tomb of the count's friend, the Protestant pastor A. Court de Gébelin; pyramids in honour of two of the count's ancestors, both Marshals of France; a monument to the agricultural economist the marquis de Mirabeau, author of *L'Ami des hommes* and other works; a Swiss village with cows, and chalets inhabited by the count and his wife; a statue of Pan, with goat-house; monuments to William Tell and to the American republican scientist Benjamin

Franklin; a Mast of Liberty bearing the date 1782 – the year in which a Treaty of Peace was negotiated in Paris between Britain and the now victorious American revolutionaries; a cavern, in reminiscence of the Revd Edward Young, author of *Night Thoughts on Life, Death and Immortality*; a mock-medieval feudal keep, with Gothick windows, as described by the latest fashionable poets, but not, as in the bad old days, inhabited by a wicked baron, 'Scourge of his vassals, terror of the land'.

In all this, Dulaure remarks, we see 'the scholar, the scientist, the connoisseur, the man of letters and good taste, the virtuous and tender-hearted citizen, the friend of nature and mankind'.[1] Whether a more appropriate description might not be 'the naïve, pompous and more than faintly ludicrous representative of an Edenic world where virtue and happiness were considered attainable by all men, and the monster Sade was still safely locked up', is a matter of opinion. Comte d'Albon himself never needed to ask such a question, for he died in 1789. What his taste in garden ornaments undoubtedly reveals, however, is the many-sidedness of eighteenth-century culture, where modernity and tradition, intellectual inquiry and emotionalism, religion and science, egalitarianism and aristocratic self-assertion, cosmopolitanism and patriotism, artificiality and a yearning for naturalness, all inextricably mingle together.

This diversity, so evident in the literature of the period, will be illustrated by the passages commented on in this volume. One of the main achievements of eighteenth-century studies during the 1950s and 1960s has been to show how inadequate was the traditionally accepted view of eighteenth-century literature as a conflict between 'sensibility' and 'reason', or between the 'classicism' inherited from the previous century, and the 'pre-romanticism' which, allegedly, superseded it. There is now widespread acceptance, in France, of the critical school which 'explains' the eighteenth century in terms of economic processes, and of class-rivalries between 'the ascendant bourgeoisie' and 'the nobles'. When handled with discrimination, this method of approach can deepen our understanding of the literature of the period; but its results are derisory when it is imposed upon literary texts crudely, arbitrarily, or to the exclusion of all else. The commentaries in this volume take account of recent scholarship, without, it is hoped, credulously relying on any one current school of thought.

'Sensibility' is frequently taken to imply swooning lovers, copious tears, mawkish moralising, faithful friends and servants, or frenzy such

as that of Claire in *La Nouvelle Héloïse*, biting the chair-legs in grief
at Julie's death. It is expressed sometimes in melodramatic gush bedewed
with dots and dashes, sometimes in poetic language that can still move
the reader today. 'Pre-romanticism' is held to mean 'sensibility'
(neither term being at all rigorously defined), together with a hetero-
geneous collection of things such as enjambement, imitations of
Shakespeare, Richardson, Ossian, etc., tombs, country churchyards,
horrors, the sea, suicides, stage-directions, medievalism, Rousseau,
primitivism, fate, melancholia, occultism, storms, monks, cataracts,
ruins, mountains, the moon, and imitations of *The Sorrows of Young
Werther*. But it is also recognised today that this whole trend is not
unconnected with the sensualist philosophy of Locke, with the rehabilitation of passion as the stimulus to action, with escape or revulsion from
an artificial, over-intellectualised society, and with the pride, anguish,
exultation and terror of eighteenth-century man, who, having renounced
the old beliefs about God and the universe, is at once master of his own
fate, rationally moulding the world to his desire, and an insignificant
speck in Nature, whether Nature be regarded as a machine functioning
according to eternal laws fixed by an inscrutable Creator, or as blind
matter in constant ferment of change.

The notion that, in literature and the arts, the first half of the century
was essentially different from the 'pre-romantic' second half is hardly
borne out by the facts. 'Pre-romanticism' of a sort already co-exists
with classicism in the *Cours de peinture par principes* of Roger de Piles,
published in 1708 and again in 1766 and 1791. Though the true basis
of aesthetic pleasure is perfection, de Piles argues, accurate, formal
perfection is often insipid unless accompanied by enthusiasm, which
carries the soul even higher than the sublime, of which it is the source.
As de Piles's eighteenth-century English translator puts it, 'men of a
fiery genius easily give in to enthusiasm, because their imagination is
almost always upon the stretch'; by conscious mental effort, less fervid
souls can achieve enthusiasm of a more ordered kind. But even with
faults, enthusiasm will 'always be preferred to a correct mediocrity,
because it ravishes the soul, without giving it time to examine anything,
or to reflect on particulars'. Idealised nature and classical scenes are
admirable if well executed, puerile if not. Representations of wild,
unadorned nature, on the other hand, give pleasure even though the
painter's technique is imperfect; such scenes 'cheer the imagination
by the novelty and beauty of their form, even when the local colouring
is but modestly performed'. Rocks and waterfalls 'give an infinite

pleasure, and seem to have a soul which animates them'; 'mountains that
are high, and covered with snow, are very proper to produce extra-
ordinary effects . . . which are advantageous to the painter, and pleasing
to the spectator'. De Piles in no way belittles the temples and palaces
which adorn heroic paintings, but he delights in rustic landscape
paintings with thatched cottages and ruined towers, so suggestive of
wildness, magic and desolation:

> Buildings in general are a great ornament in landscape, even when they
> are Gothick, or appear uninhabited and partly ruinous: they raise the
> imagination by the use they are thought to be designed for; as appears
> from ancient towers, which seem to have been the habitations of fairies,
> and are now retreats for shepherds and owls.[2]

Throughout the century, painting and art-criticism often anticipated
literature proper, especially in a fondness for landscapes and seascapes.
But it would be possible to extract a 'pre-romantic' manifesto on poetry
and drama from the abbé Dubos's *Réflexions critiques sur la poésie et sur
la peinture*, first published in 1719, in Paris. Dubos already has some
inkling of romantic *ennui*, 'a dull, listless reverie, during which the
mind finds positive pleasure in nothing'. Hugolian ideas about realism
and local colour in painting and poetry have already occurred to him:
'depict as they actually were the localities where the action took place';
'poetic verisimilitude demands also that nations be portrayed with their
garb, their weapons and their banners'. He sees cultural borrowings
between peoples as ordained by Providence; if English tragedies contain
too much spectacle, French tragedies have too little. Like de Piles, he is
very willing to accept violation of the classical rules; regularity is not
the yard-stick for judging poems, nor is poetry a matter of orthodox
prosody: 'There are fine poems without verse, and fine verses without
poetry.' The best poem is that which moves and interests us most,
'which so delights us that we fail to observe the majority of its faults'.
A materialist determinist, Dubos rejects any absolute, universally
valid aesthetic criterion. A man's 'spiritual soul' functions by aid of his
physical organs, which are conditioned by the air and climate of the
country he inhabits. Abstract moral causes are thus subsidiary to
physical causes, which explain the differences between nations and
epochs:

> From what I have set forth, it is more than probable that the peculiar
> genius of each people depends on the quality of the air which it breathes.
> The lack of geniuses, and types of mind required for certain things,
> which is observable among some nations, may rightly be explained by

the climate. Likewise, it is to the changes which take place in the air of a country that we must attribute the variations that occur in the customs and genius of its inhabitants.... How can we fail to believe that physical factors determine moral ones?

Since everything is relative to physical circumstances of place and time, there can be no fixed and absolute aesthetic values. Just as the Paris Academy of Sciences and the Royal Society of London have replaced arbitrary systems by objective experimentation, so too, in literature, he argues, one should not judge a work before allowing oneself to experience the emotions which it arouses. Sentiment is consequently a better guide to literary appreciation than abstract reasoning: reason, here, 'must accept the judgment pronounced by sentiment'. Common experience indicates that we have within us a 'sixth sense', whose organs are invisible, but whose function is aesthetic appraisal. The heart moves without our deliberation; instinctive emotional reaction, not ratiocination, is what poetry must be assessed by: 'If there is any topic where reason must remain silent in the face of experience, assuredly it is in the questions which may be asked about the beauty of a poem.'

Dubos is in numerous ways typical of the Enlightenment – that body of eighteenth-century thinkers who, casting aside reverence for established authority, and calling all things into question, nevertheless believed in their hearts and minds that man, in acquiring knowledge about himself and the world around him, would be enabled to destroy or mitigate the gloomy horrors which still beset society. The son of a merchant, Dubos proclaims that true loftiness consists in 'nobility of heart and high-mindedness', and not in the haughty arrogance, narrowness and vice so often found in high places. His interest in Nature extends to improved methods of stock-breeding in northern England, and the yields of flax in foreign countries. He is convinced that Reason leads to knowledge and enlightenment in literature, as in science and in all else:

> The progress achieved in the art of reasoning, which has already brought about so many discoveries in the natural sciences, is an abundant fount of fresh enlightenment. This is already spreading to literature, where it will abolish ancient prejudices, just as it has abolished them in the natural sciences. Enlightenment will permeate the various trades and professions, and is already dawning among all classes of society.

It is by analogy with natural science that Dubos, equating feeling with the experimental method, proclaimed the superiority of sentiment over

B

reason in literature. He none the less believed that the sceptical, inquir-
ing, analytical, rationalistic tone of the age was incompatible with great
literature as the seventeenth century had understood it. Unable to
divine what would take its place, he, like Voltaire after him, asserted that
'the philosophic spirit' would prove fatal to the creative imagination.
And so, in spite of his satisfaction at the imminent decay of the classical
rules, as far as literature was concerned this forward-looking abbé took
refuge in the past. He professed to find ancient literature more sublime
than modern, Homer superior to Virgil, and the Old Testament superior
to Homer. The Paris censor pronounced his book to be 'full of learned
research and sound, judicious observations'.[3]

It is not only in treatises, however, that 'pre-romantic' attitudes are
visible before 1750. Bloodshed and violence underlie the elegance in
Montesquieu's novel *Lettres persanes*; Roxane, dying with the dignity
of a Racinian heroine, declares to her tyrant the licitness of her passionate
emancipation:

> I feel the near approaches of death; the poison is working in my
> veins. For what should I do here, since the only man that made life
> agreeable is no more? I am dying, my ghost is upon the wing. . . . No:
> I have lived in servitude, but still I was free: I reformed thy laws by
> those of Nature, and my mind still kept itself independent. Doubtless
> this language seems new to thee: is it possible, after I have overwhelmed
> thee with grief, I should likewise force thee to admire my courage?
> But it is done: the poison consumes me: my strength forsakes me: my
> pen drops from my hand: I feel even my very hatred decay: I am dying.[4]

The heroes of Prévost's novels – wanderers, outlaws, legislators, rebels –
are tormented by nearly all conceivable forms of anguish and despair.
Prévost himself learned much from *Les Illustres Françoises* by Robert
Chasles (1713) – a work whose importance was overlooked by manuals of
literary history because no text was readily available until F. Deloffre
published his edition in 1959. Even Voltaire's Zadig (1748), enlightened
reformer and victim of injustice, alternates between direst woe and the
study of natural philosophy:

> With a mind agitated by these fatal reflections, his eyes covered with
> a veil of grief, the paleness of death on his countenance, and his soul
> plunged in the blackest despair, he continued his journey towards
> Egypt. Zadig directed his course by the stars. . . . He reflected with
> admiration on those vast globes of light which appear to our eyes no
> more than faint sparks, while the earth, which in reality is but an
> imperceptible point in nature, seems to our fond imaginations far
> more grand and noble. He then reflected on the whole race of mankind,

and considered them, truly, as insects that devour each other, on an atom of earth. The idea seemed greatly to alleviate his misfortunes, by making him retrace the nothingness of his own being, and even that of Babylon. His capacious soul now soared into infinity, and contemplated, while detached from her earthly partner, the immutable order of the universe. But the moment he returned to himself, and again searched into his own heart, he began to consider that Astarte might possibly have died for him; the universe vanished from his sight, and he beheld nothing throughout all nature, but Astarte dying, and Zadig unfortunate. As he gave himself up to this flux and reflux of sublime philosophy and distressing sorrow, he insensibly arrived on the frontiers of Egypt; and his faithful attendant. . . .[5]

The two intimately linked currents of 'reason' and 'emotion', which exist side by side, though in varying proportions, in most of the writers of the age, both become more vigorously aggressive during the second half of the century. Denunciations of allegedly 'unreasonable' and pernicious practices in religion and government are more numerous and impassioned with the campaigns of Voltaire and d'Holbach, while 'emotional' traits find expression in the masterpieces of those two propagandists for social reform, Diderot and Rousseau, as well as in a spate of lesser writers, and in ever more translations from English and German. Has this upsurge anything to do with developments in the social, political and economic life of the age, and with non-literary strivings towards progress and renovation? That the literature of the Enlightenment had practical implications for society was self-evident to the established authorities who tried, not very successfully, to quell or control it. The very terms 'bourgeois tragedy', 'bourgeois drama', indicate a desire by some section of the middle class to claim for itself a moral dignity hitherto reserved in literature for kings and nobles. Rousseau's *Discours sur l'inégalité* may seem to be no more than classical rhetoric and perfervid nostalgia; but the notes which comprise one-third of that work contain invective against speculators on the corn market, and against voluptuaries who depopulate the countryside in order to consume products of the luxury industries and overseas trade. One of the best introductions to a sociological study of eighteenth-century literature was written in 1799 – Mme de Staël's *De la littérature considérée dans ses rapports avec les institutions sociales*. Her contemporary the vicomte de Bonald hated most of what Mme de Staël stood for, but he too regarded literature as the reflection of society.

It would, of course, be unprofitable to seek in the great literature of the period a direct and passive reflection of life as it actually was. Even the most 'realistic' art is the result of selection and interpretation by the artist, and even in those works which at first sight come closest to a depiction of the everyday world, there is embellishment, exaggeration, or falsification.[6] There are, for example, valid reasons for believing that conversation was not as kindly or sparkling as Marivaux makes out, that peasant life was not so alluringly poetic as our Restif de la Bretonne passage suggests, and that financiers and textile manufacturers were less saintly than those in our Beaumarchais extract. It is to the social historian, not the literary critic, that we must go for an authentic account of society. In the commentaries which follow, an attempt has been made to assess, in the light of present-day historical research, the accuracy of the 'life' depicted by the selected authors, and, also, to see how far a knowledge of history can aid our appreciation of literature proper. (The commentary on Chénier will, it is hoped, demonstrate that this latter approach is a valid one for students of literature.) But, just as a single page of Voltaire permits a more vivid and immediate insight into his personality than might possibly be afforded by whole masses of biographical documentation, so, in the literature of the age, we can see at first hand the aspirations of various social groups, and the reactions of exceptionally gifted men to life as they knew it, or wanted to present it, or dreamed that it might be. Literary and historical studies can collaborate, to their mutual advantage, in their effort to understand the 'life' and the 'letters' of past ages.

Brilliant specialists in eighteenth-century literature have investigated the links between the culture of the period and the economic processes which were transforming society. Thus, J. Ehrard, in his indispensable book *L'Idée de nature en France dans la première moitié du XVIIIᵉ siècle* (1963), sifts out those ideas, attitudes and beliefs which the as yet relatively conformist and unaggressive middle class developed or adopted in order to assert, justify, enhance or cloak its own ambitions. R. Laufer, in *Style rococo, style des 'lumières'* (1963), explains the gay, witty, ironic, polished style typical of the century, as the product of unresolved tensions between feudal–aristocratic and capitalist–bourgeois interests.[7] J. Starobinski, in *L'Invention de la liberté* (1964), portrays the aristocracy as a doomed class which, having lost the responsibilities that justified its privileges, is left with the pursuit of pleasure as its sole aim. The bourgeois, by contrast, are energetic, forward-looking, proud of their money and the pleasures it brings, and justifying their commercial success by professions of high moral virtue. Consequently, Professor Starobinski would have us believe, the pre-romantic obsessions with darkness, despair and annihilation are aristocratic in origin, whereas the bourgeois ethos is one of hope, vigour, victory and 'bliss was it in that dawn to be alive'.[8]

Clearly, the hazards of such interpretations are as great as their fascination. The fact that most trends in the period can be traced back to previous centuries, or to foreign writers, does not in itself invalidate sociological explanations: there is usually some reason why certain ideas are taken over and not others. But even the eighteenth-century novel, the form most generally agreed to be middle class in orientation, needs considerable processing before it can be fitted into systems of allegedly bourgeois ideology. Mme de Miran in *La Vie de Marianne* is an aristocrat who, in the name of God and Reason, gives her son permission to marry an orphan of unknown origin. M. Ehrard, propounding the principle that 'the social status of the characters in a novel does not necessarily coincide with the novel's ideological content', makes Mme de Miran the expression of bourgeois sentimentality[9] – as though even middle-class mothers, then or now, were best pleased when their sons threw themselves away on penniless adventuresses picked up in the street. Mme de Tourvel, wife of a nobleman, in *Les Liaisons dangereuses*, is a virtuous, high-minded, passionate, and penitent adulteress. To Professor Laufer, since 'a considerable part of the enlightened nobility has been won over to the ideology of the rising bourgeoisie', she is the mouthpiece of middle-class values against the vicious, cruel, cynical and depraved aristocracy.[10] By these arguments, *La Princesse de Clèves* would be a bourgeois manifesto. But, in fact, though modern scholarship has given us statistics about the class distribution of subscribers to the *Encyclopédie* and members of certain provincial academies, it is unlikely that any eighteenth-century ecclesiastical archives will yield percentage tables of the relative incidence of love, pity, chastity and fornication among nobles and commoners respectively.

Themes, styles and attitudes in literature, like fashions in so many other things, do indeed tend to spill over class barriers, even where these are rigidly defined. Aristocratic forms of taste inherited from the seventeenth century were aspired to by many middle-class writers in the eighteenth. There is no evidence, on the other hand, that the emotionalism of the petit-bourgeois Jean-Jacques Rousseau was less pleasing to duchesses than to middle-class ladies. Jacob-Nicolas Moreau, enemy of the philosophes, librarian to Marie-Antoinette, author of a manual on absolute monarchy commissioned by the Dauphin for the future Louis XVI, uses in his *Vérités morales*[11] the same treacly, sentimental style as does the philosophe Marmontel in the middle-class *Contes moraux* with which he regaled aristocrats. Classical tragedy during the century served as a tribute to the past glories of the monarchy, a vehicle for philosophe propaganda and sentiment, then as a major means of expression for republican severity and fervour. In 1785 Robespierre (a bourgeois who signed himself *de Robespierre*) published a eulogy of the sanctimonious, clericalist playwright Gresset, recommending his works as suitable for family reading. In 1787, he was admitted to an Arras literary society called the Rosati, which indulged in *vin rosé*, song, serious discussion, and frivolous verses modelled on those of the slothful, libidinous, parasitical aristocrat Chaulieu.[12] In 1794, the *de* now dropped from his name, the Jacobin dictator Robespierre was practising the aristocratic seventeenth-century art-form known as the *portrait* in a speech consigning to the guillotine his colleague Fabre d'Eglantine, a republican, journalist, pretty poet, and imitator of Molière.[13] It is obvious that eighteenth-century literature and taste cannot be fitted into any tidy pattern of development.

The traditional view of the philosophes as a united band conspiring to overthrow the Ancien Régime has long since been exploded. Except in moments of exasperation, they wanted to reform it gradually, from within. Church, monarchy and established institutions still had a powerful hold on men's minds. Though irksome restrictions existed, and even increased as the century progressed, the differences between aristocracy and the rich bourgeoisie became less significant. Already in the *Lettres persanes* (with irony, it is true), Montesquieu declared that

> Liberty and Equality reign at Paris. Birth, virtue, nay even the greatest services in war, do not lift a man above the crowd in which he is confounded. Jealousy about rank is here unknown. They say the chief man in Paris is he that has the best horses to his coach.[14]

Robespierre in 1785 appears heartily to desire the integration into the aristocracy of the bourgeois élite: posterity will remember with gratitude, he pompously declares, those monarchs who add lustre to the nobility by bestowing titles on talented men of common birth.[15] The ultimate lack of clear-cut distinctions, and a deep-rooted emotional attachment to the old order, sometimes lead to a curious evasiveness even in such 'advanced' writers as Rousseau and Diderot. For a supreme example of that hypocrisy which Continentals tend to regard as peculiarly English, we need look no further than M. de Voltaire taking communion in the little chapel which he built for the villagers just inside the main entrance to his country estate. All things considered, the Age of Ambiguity would be no more misleading a title for the century than the Age of Reason.

Some present-day historians so play down the idea of a nobles-versus-bourgeois conflict (for example, they consider the fiscal privileges enjoyed by the nobles to have been often a relatively trifling matter), that one wonders where all the revolutionary bourgeois hatred of the aristocrats came from, and why writers in the 1790s used such phrases as 'the odious vestiges of feudalism'. Professor Cobban, opposing the French Marxist view, went so far as to suggest that the word 'bourgeoisie' should not be used at all in discussions about late eighteenth-century France.[16] But it is not surprising that historians should fail to agree on such matters. In his *Treatise on Tolerance*, Voltaire bids us be chary of them:

> The trouble with historians is that nearly all of them overstate their case, just as all controversialists explain away the errors of which their opponents accuse them. Let us believe neither the Paris doctors of theology nor the Amsterdam preachers.[17]

In other words, it would be unwise for us to believe uncritically either those who seem to regard eighteenth-century literature primarily as a weapon in a socio-economic struggle that has lessons for the present, or, on the other hand, those who, for reasons good and bad, dismiss all sociological interpretation as irrelevant to the enjoyment of works of art.

It is clear that much eighteenth-century literature was *littérature engagée*. From the moment they appeared, the great works were praised or blamed for moral, political, social, religious or partisan reasons as well as (sometimes) on aesthetic grounds. A standard nineteenth-century view of Enlightenment literature was published three days before Christmas, 1800, by Chateaubriand, at a moment in his career when he considered becoming a propagandist for throne, altar and counter-revolution:

> I am filled with holy wrath when the authors of the eighteenth century are likened to the writers of the seventeenth. . . . How paltry and petty they seem to me, the majority of these eighteenth-century men, who, instead of that infinite harmony which supplied the keynote for the eloquence of geniuses such as Racine and Bossuet, use the scale of a narrow philosophy which subdivides the soul into degrees and minutes, reducing the whole Universe, God included, to a mere abstraction of nothingness.[18]

Voltaire had already said much the same thing, more succinctly: 'Reason has done harm to literature as it has to religion: it has emaciated it'; 'much has been written in this century, there were men of genius in the previous one'.[19] As far as the continuation of seventeenth-century literature is concerned, they were right: there were no worthy successors to Corneille, Racine, Molière, La Fontaine, Bossuet. It is in the minor genres – prose fiction, pamphlets, correspondence, dialogues, autobiography and the like – that the new age expressed itself to perfection: in the taut, lucid, mocking style of Voltaire, in the full-blooded yet infinitely subtle harangues by which Diderot makes himself our contemporary, in the lyricism, savageness or brooding of Rousseau. The alleged superficiality of the century has been much exaggerated: neither *Du Contrat social* nor the *Paradoxe sur le comédien* yield much to the hasty reader. And no one who has studied *De l'Esprit des lois* would call that work frivolous. Indeed, whether they are superficial or not, authors as different as Prévost, Rousseau, d'Holbach and Condorcet are sententious, not gay: it often seems as if that much-vaunted sense of the ridiculous was the quality least evident in the eighteenth century. Count d'Albon was by no means exceptional in his elaborate pomposity. Victorian seriousness had begun to exist long before the arrival of black tall hats.

Eighteenth-century French literature offers a wide variety of forms and styles. There are countless good aesthetic reasons for studying it. But what it uniquely gives us is the picture of men who, with a medley of sentiment and reason, irony and faith, realism and illusion, took stock of what was wrong in society and set out to right it. There were many doctrinal differences among the philosophes, but it is their essential beliefs which are expressed in Thomas Jefferson's draft for the American Declaration of Independence:

> We hold these truths to be sacred and undeniable, that all men are created equal and independent, that from that equal creation they derive rights inherent and inalienable, among which are the preservation of life, and liberty, and the pursuit of happiness.

The greatness of the century lies in its conviction that freedom, tolerance and humanity can conquer darkness and oppression.

The ideals of the French Enlightenment were soon submerged in strife and bloodshed. By 1799 the modern world had begun. Their intelligence and scepticism notwithstanding, there is something appealingly innocent about those eighteenth-century writers who did not live to see the Revolution.

NOTES

1 J. A. Dulaure, *Nouvelle Description des environs de Paris*, seconde édition (Paris, 1787), I, pp. 254–75.

2 *Cours de peinture par principes*. Composé par Mr de Piles (Paris, 1708), pp. 114–24, 200–22. *The Principles of Painting*. Translated into English by a Painter (London, 1743), pp. 71–7, 127–36.

3 Abbé J.-B. Dubos, *Réflexions critiques sur la poésie et sur la peinture* (Paris, 1719), I, pp. 7, 247–50, 275–80, 371–4, 593–4, 679–85; II, pp. 10, 18, 72, 136–40, 175, 225–30, 272, 287–360, 422–41, 470, 528, and *Privilège* of 25 Sept. 1718.

4 *Lettres persanes*, Lettre CLXI. *Persian Letters*. Translated by Mr Ozell (London, 1722), Letter CL.

5 *Zadig*. Voltaire, *Romans et Contes*, ed. H. Bénac (Paris, 1958), pp. 23–4. *Zadig, or, the Book of Fate*. Translated from the French of M. de Voltaire by Francis Ashmore, Esq. (London, 1780), pp. 18–19.

6 See, for example, J. Rustin, 'Mensonge et vérité dans le roman français du XVIIIe siècle', *Revue d'histoire littéraire de la France*, 1969, No. 1, pp. 13–38.

7 Laufer, op. cit., pp. 12–38. 'For as long as the Ancien Régime is threatened by bourgeois capitalism but resists it, and the bourgeois and aristocratic ideologies inextricably contaminate one another, the conditions for rococo style exist. . . . The great art of the century was the one which expressed, indirectly, of course, the contradiction which was resolved only by the Revolution, that between feudalism and the bourgeoisie.'

8 Starobinski, op. cit., p. 54, *Philosophie et mythologie du plaisir*. It is true that M. Starobinski prefaces this part of his argument by the remark 'Presenting it somewhat diagrammatically', and puts his verbs in the conditional.

9 Ehrard, op. cit., p. 313, n.

10 Laufer, op. cit., pp. 137–8.

11 Moreau's *Vérités morales et philosophiques* (Paris, 1785) opens with an effusive, lachrymose dedication to the 'dear and respectable half of himself', i.e. his wife. He had attacked the philosophes as evil, malevolent poisoners in *Les Cacouacs*, an article which appeared in the *Mercure de France* in October 1756, and was reprinted, with additional material, as *Nouveau mémoire pour servir à l'histoire des Cacouacs* (Amsterdam, 1757). On his manual of 1764, the *Leçons de morale, de politique et de droit public . . . d'après les vues de Monseigneur le Dauphin pour l'instruction des princes, ses enfants*, and the twenty-one-volume enlargement of it which the future Louis XVIII admired, see J. Godechot, *La Contre-Révolution* (Paris, 1961), pp. 18–19.

12 *Œuvres de Maximilien Robespierre, Société des études robespierristes*, Tome Premier, ed. E. Lesueur (Paris, 1912), pp. 96–114, 193, 209–19. Lesueur quotes from the diploma in verse given to Robespierre on his admission to the Rosati by the society's chaplain, one abbé Berthier:

> Nous qui, l'esprit toujours joyeux,
> Savons, dans une aimable orgie,
> Ramener les siècles heureux
> De la badine poésie.

13 'Rules for behaviour, and no virtues; talents, and emptiness of soul; cunning in the art of portraying men, more cunning still in that of deceiving them, he had, perhaps, studied them only in order to exhibit them with success upon the stage; he wished to set them in action, for his own advantage, upon the stage of the Revolution: well enough acquainted with the chief *dramatis personae* of all the political parties . . . because he had served or deceived them all. . . .' Robespierre, *Textes choisis*, ed. J. Poperen, vol. III (Paris, 1958), pp. 138–9.

14 Lettre LXXXVIII. *Persian Letters*. Translated by Mr Ozell (London, 1722), Letter LXXXVI.

15 *Œuvres*, ed. Lesueur, I, p. 113. (From Robespierre's *Eloge de Gresset*.)

16 For a brief discussion of Professor Cobban's contention that the eighteenth-century bourgeoisie was not a homogeneous class, that it did not abolish 'feudalism' of its own free will, that its members owned much land, that its leaders did not come from business and industry, that the Revolution set back rather than hastened economic progress in France, see J. McManners, *Lectures on European History 1789–1914* (Oxford, 1966), pp. 22–3.

17 Voltaire, *Mélanges*, ed. J. van der Heuvel, Pléiade (Paris, 1961), p. 641.

18 Chateaubriand, *Œuvres complètes*, Garnier (Paris, s.d.), III, p. 655–6: 'Lettre au Citoyen Fontanes sur la deuxième édition de l'ouvrage de Mme de Staël.' Par l'auteur du *Génie du Christianisme. Mercure de France*, 22 décembre 1800.

19 *Précis du siècle de Louis XV* (Moland, XV, p. 434); *Notebooks*, ed. T. Besterman (Geneva, 1952), p. 365.

1 · Chaulieu (1639–1720)

Réponse aux deux épîtres de l'abbé Courtin (written 1703.

    Abbé, dont le discours flatteur,
    Qu'avec grâce ta Muse étale,
    Vient par un murmure enchanteur
    Tâcher d'endormir ma morale,
    Tu crois qu'avec avidité
    Déjà l'amour-propre enchanté
    Avale la délicatesse
    D'un poison si bien apprêté:
    Je sens, malgré ma vanité,
    Que je dois à ta politesse
    Beaucoup plus qu'à la vérité.
    Il faut avouer sa faiblesse,
    J'en conviens, puisque tu le veux.
    Né sensible et voluptueux,
Source où tous mes défauts ont pris leur origine
    Soit bien traité, soit malheureux,
    J'ai vécu souvent amoureux;
    Toujours d'humeur si libertine
    Dans l'engagement que j'ai pris,
    Qu'au mépris des pasteurs fidèles
    Mon amour eut toujours des ailes
Aussi bonnes du moins que celui de Cloris.
    Ovide, que je pris pour maître
    M'apprit qu'il faut être fripon;
    Abbé, c'est le seul moyen d'être
    Autant aimé que fut Nason:
    Catulle m'en fit la leçon.
    Pour Tibulle, il était si bon
    Que je crois qu'il aurait dû naître
    Sur les rivages du Lignon;
    Et là, qu'on l'eût placé peut-être
    Entre la Fare et Céladon.
L'amour fut-il jamais fait pour être durable?
C'est le feu d'un éclair, un peu solide bien;
C'est un songe enchanteur, un fragile lien
Que ne forme et ne rompt rien qui soit raisonnable.
Le Père des Héros, ce Dieu si redoutable

Que la victoire suit partout dans les combats,
  Avait beau paraître estimable,
  Sa maîtresse ne laissa pas
De découvrir à nu ses plus secrets appas
  Au berger qui parut aimable
  A la femme de Ménélas.
  Chez moi tous les amusements
  Ont encore une libre entrée;
  Mais fût-ce une chaîne dorée,
  J'en hais tous les attachements.
  Pour toi, qu'un teint vif et fleuri,
  Et la perruque bien poudrée,
  Flattent d'être le favori
  Encor de quelque mijaurée;
  Goûte l'erreur des passions,
Etends tout au plus loin les bornes du bel âge:
  La moindre de tes actions
  Vaudra bien mieux que la plus sage
  De toutes mes réflexions.
Moi, qui sens qu'à grands pas la vieillesse s'avance,
  Et qui, par mille changements,
  Connais déjà la décadence
  Qu'apporte le nombre des ans,
  Dans une douce nonchalance
Je jouis du printemps, du soleil, d'un beau jour;
Je vis pour moi, content que ma seule indolence
Me tienne lieu de biens, de fortune et de cour.
  Si j'ai du goût pour quelque belle,
J'y trouve du plaisir, et n'en crains point de maux;
  Je ne veux que boire avec elle,
  Et me moquer de mes rivaux.
Revenu des erreurs, après de longs détours
  Comme moi, vous aurez recours
Quelque jour aux leçons de la philosophie,
Qui ne déçut jamais le sage qui s'y fie,
Et dont j'ai si souvent éprouvé le secours.
C'est elle qui me fait avec tranquillité
Regarder fixement le terme de la vie,
Occupé seulement du soin de ma santé,
De goûter à longs traits ma chère liberté
Qu'une foule d'erreurs m'a si longtemps ravie;
L'avenir sur mon front n'excite aucun nuage,
  Et bien loin de craindre la mort,
  Tant de fois battu par l'orage,
  Je la regarde comme un port
Où je n'essuierai plus tempête ni naufrage.

Les Derniers Libertins, ed. F. Lachèvre (Paris, 1924), pp. 160–1.

The abbé Courtin, twenty years younger than the abbé de Chaulieu, had long been his companion in debauch. But now, by reason of age and gout, Chaulieu is able to dispense with Courtin's services as a purveyor of pretty girls:

> Bien connaissais d'officieux talents
> Que sur ta bonne et facile nature
> Avait enté, dès tes plus jeunes ans,
> Ce gentil Dieu qu'on appelle Mercure;
> Dieu des fripons, des ribleurs et ribauds,
> Dieu, qui mieux est, d'autres rimes en *aux*,
> Dont je faisais autrefois grande mise,
> Mais qu'entre Abbés je n'ose plus nommer,
> Tant par respect que l'on doit à l'Eglise
> Que pour raison que de leur entremise
> N'ai le besoin qui me les fit aimer.[1]

Intrigued by Chaulieu's new-found peace, Courtin sends him two Epistles, seeking his advice on the art of happiness. Chaulieu, Courtin says, is the perfect Epicurean philosopher:

> Fidèle ami, fidèle à ton maître Epicure
> Dans le parfait repos mettant tout ton bonheur,
> Tu suis les lois de la sage nature,
> Et braves les périls sans connaître la peur.

He wants to know whether the love which he, Courtin, feels for the fair Sylvie is compatible with the 'sage et tranquille volupté' of which Chaulieu is so perfect an exemplar.

Chaulieu begins his *Réponse* by rejecting so flattering a tribute: he also, he declares, has known the agitations of love. The word *sensible* which he uses here had not yet acquired the solemn, portentous meaning it was to have by Rousseau's time, and most of Chaulieu's love poetry had been cavalier in tone:

> Venez me voir, objet rare et divin,
> Venez me voir, mon aimable Catin,

though he did, in *Perfection d'Amour*, express an intensity of passion transcending mere libertinage:

> Par l'excès du plaisir nos forces suspendues,
> Nos corps entrelacés, nos âmes confondues,
> Ont goûté de concert les plaisirs les plus doux,
> Inconnus aux mortels moins amoureux que nous.

In his advice to Courtin, however, he chooses to treat love with that

flippant detachment which was to be characteristic of such writers as
Crébillon fils.

Chloris, in the second alexandrine of the *Réponse*, is Flora, bride of
Zephyrus. So, 'Aussi bonnes du moins que celui de Cloris' means:
Chaulieu's love has winged from flower to flower as freely as did Flora's
lover, the Wind. Flora's marriage (the Romans celebrated her feast on
May-day with sexual revelry) is described by P. Ovidius Naso in Book V
of his *Fasti*; but it was Ovid's *Ars Amatoria* which Chaulieu, like
André Chénier, used as a manual of seduction. Catullus wrote out-
spokenly of his mistress Lesbia. Tibullus's poems are more restrained:
so Chaulieu would place him between Céladon, the timid faithful
shepherd of *L'Astrée*, and Chaulieu's debauchee friend and fellow-poet,
the marquis de La Fare, who had translated Tibullus's first Elegy. The
lady who displayed her naked charms was Aphrodite, wife of Hephaestus
but mistress of Ares, the god of war. The shepherd Paris awarded her the
golden apple as the most beautiful of the goddesses; in return, he
received Helen of Troy, wife of Menelaus. But no such explanations
would be necessary for Chaulieu's readers. Gentlemen knew the classics,
and the seventeenth-century use of them for burlesque or erotic purposes
continued, with modifications, throughout the eighteenth. Boucher
painted nymphs and goddesses to titillate jaded philanderers; the
sculptor Claude-Michel Clodion specialised in bas-reliefs and terracotta
groups of satyrs and nymphs; and as late as 1788 even David, whose
austere classicism reflected republican ideals of virtue, painted a *Loves
of Paris and Helen* which could almost serve as an illustration to Chaulieu's
lines.

After this Greek and Latin interlude, with its reiteration that all women
are wantons, Chaulieu urges the fat, periwigged[2], forty-four-year-old
abbé Courtin to love while he yet may, even though she prove faithless
and break his heart. Chaulieu's own lusts are quenched; his emotions
are no longer violent. The 'maux' he no longer fears are refusal and
infidelity, which tormented him in the days when frequent love-affairs
– 'une foule d'erreurs' – disturbed his peace. But there are still pleasures
left to beguile him: nature in the sunshine, wine, converse with pretty
girls. (Chaulieu was to write a charming epistle, tinged with bitterness
at the inexorability of human decay, on his unconsummated love for
Mlle de Launay.) The continuance of enjoyment which he urges on
Courtin: 'Etends tout au plus loin les bornes du bel âge', is paralleled
by his own determination to 'goûter à longs traits ma chère liberté'.
This striving for pleasure, as well as the 'lessons of philosophy' which

console him – not the eighteenth-century philosophes' gospel of action, but an epicurean stoicism that taught ease, comfort, detachment, acceptance of approaching death, disbelief in any torment beyond the grave – are typical of Chaulieu's outlook.

In one poem only, *Réflexion sur la maxime d'Epicure: Sapiens non accedat ad Rempublicam*, he urges men to serve their country:

> Il faut pour son pays un entier dévouement,
> Et l'on doit rigoureusement
> Compte de ses talents à la chose publique.

For the rest, he stands by his advice to the chevalier de Bouillon: better 'folâtrer, dessus l'herbette', and die

> au sortir d'un repas
> Ou des bras de sa maîtresse

than lose your leg in battle and hobble around waiting for a hero's funeral. (Frédéric-Jules de la Tour d'Auvergne, chevalier de Bouillon, was an apt pupil: he resigned from the Navy and initiated the Bals de l'Opéra.) Chaulieu believed in a Creator of the world who daily enlightened him (whether by grace or sunshine is not made clear), a 'bienfaisant' and 'pitoyable' God, who will not punish men for following the promptings of Nature.

> Dans le fond de mon cœur je lui bâtis un temple;
> Prosterné devant lui, j'adore sa bonté.

He appears to have retained some idea of a life after death: 'Un asile assuré dans le sein de mon Dieu.' Holy Writ is not entirely absent from his verses: one half stanza elegantly paraphrases part of Psalm CXIV:

> Mer vaste, vous fuyez!
> Et toi, Jourdain, pourquoi dans tes grottes profondes
> Retournant sur tes pas, vas-tu cacher tes ondes?

But his real Gospel, the one he preached in 1700 to his patroness the duchesse de Bouillon, is a simplified version of Epicurus, 'that noble mind' who

> Affranchit les mortels d'une indigne terreur,
> Et bannit, le premier, de la machine ronde,
> Les enfants de la peur, le mensonge et l'erreur.

Like Pascal's Montaigne, Chaulieu 'ne pense qu'à mourir mollement'.

The existence of unedifying clerics like Courtin and Chaulieu was one of the prices the eighteenth-century Gallican church had to pay for its great riches and for the *feuille des bénéfices* – the system whereby, since the concordat of 1516, the King had the right to nominate the abbot or abbess of more than a thousand of the richest French abbeys. The *abbés commendataires*, as the abbots appointed in this way were called, received one-third or more of the revenues of the abbey of which they were the nominal head, and ranked just below a bishop in honorific rights. They were supposed to be ordained priest within a year of appointment, but in practice often went no further than minor orders, an ecclesiastical costume, and abstention from holy matrimony. There were numerous other benefices, of major and minor financial value, to which the right of nomination was held by *seigneurs*, heads of religious orders, universities, and the like.[3] The title abbé was thus extended to the holders of even minor benefices for which – as for the abbots – the minimum ecclesiastical requirement was to be tonsured. In some cases even young boys, whose families had the right sort of connections, were tonsured, given the costume and title of abbé, and provided with a living. Abbés were so prominent in society that the term became a normal form of address for priests generally, even for the poorest parish clergy whose basic stipend (*portion congrue*) was raised in 1786 to 700 livres for a *curé*, and 350 livres for a *vicaire*.[4]

The rich abbés are mocked by Voltaire in the fifth of his *Lettres philosophiques*:

> Cet être indéfinissable, qui n'est ni ecclésiastique ni séculier, en un mot, ce que l'on appelle un abbé, est une espèce inconnue en Angleterre; les ecclésiastiques sont tous ici réservés et presque tous pédants. Quand ils apprennent qu'en France de jeunes gens connus par leurs débauches, et élevés à la prélature par des intrigues de femmes, font publiquement l'amour, s'égaient à composer des chansons tendres, donnent tous les jours des soupers délicats et longs, et de là vont implorer les lumières du Saint-Esprit et se nomment hardiment les successeurs des apôtres, ils remercient Dieu d'être protestants.

But it was ungenerous of Voltaire to attack these scandalous prelates, for to them he owed his initiation into aristocratic high life, the art of verse, and disrespect for authority, human and divine. His godfather (father, according to those who questioned Mme Arouet's virtue), François-Maurice de Castagnéry, abbé de Châteauneuf, prior of Saint-Paul-en-Chablais, abbé de Beaugency, introduced him to the Temple, the Paris headquarters of the Grand Prior in France of the Knights of Malta, Philippe de Vendôme, the illegitimate great-grandson of Henri IV, and a distinguished general of Louis XIV in the war against William of

PLATE I   J.-A. Watteau (1684–1721): *Les Charmes de la vie* (1716)

PLATE II   N.-N. Coypel (1690–1734): *Alliance de Bacchus et Vénus* (1726)

Orange. The Grand Prior gathered round him a free-thinking, pleasure-loving group of laymen and clerics which became known as the Société du Temple.[5] One of them, the abbé de Bussy-Rabutin (who in 1723 became bishop of Luçon, where he administered his diocese strictly and pursued Jansenists), was famous for his social graces. Président Hénault describes him as

> le modèle de ce qu'on appelait la bonne compagnie, et que l'on ne retrouve guère dans ce temps. . . . Un esprit naturel, une gaieté douce, toujours nouveau, racontant mieux qu'homme du monde, le ton de la vieille cour, et quelle cour! Des plaisanteries fines, délicates, flatteuses, sans aucune fadeur, vous laissant toujours content de vous . . . , plein d'anecdotes qu'il ne rappelait qu'à propos. . . . Gourmand, il en est mort; mais gourmand, comme il était tout le reste, sans qu'il fût plus cela qu'autre chose.

Another member of the group, the abbé Servien, was less edifying, but not without a sense of propriety: he truthfully replied 'Monsieur, je ne suis pas prêtre' to a person complaining that 'ce bougre de prêtre' had trodden on his foot. Servien openly mocked the King at the Opera, and was exiled, then, in 1714, imprisoned. Voltaire wrote an *Epître à M. l'abbé Servien, prisonnier au château de Vincennes*, in which the three Graces, weeping,

> Redemandaient au Destin en colère
> Le tendre abbé qui leur servait de père.[6]

The abbé François Courtin, son of an ambassador, was given the abbey of Mont-Saint-Quentin when only nineteen years old: there is no reason to doubt Saint-Simon's statement that Courtin 'took orders because of sloth and debauchery'. His friend the abbé Guillaume Amfrie de Chaulieu, on the other hand, waited until he was sixty before settling down exclusively to gout, revelry, women and verse. Of ancient English and Norman nobility, according to his own claims, he went with the marquis de Béthune in 1675 on a mission to John Sobieski, King of Poland, and travelled with the King to the Ukraine. Unsuccessful in the attempt to have himself appointed Polish chargé d'affaires in Paris, he next attached himself to the duc de Vendôme, the Grand Prior's brother, in the hope of becoming a cardinal-statesman. Instead, he acquired benefices: Saint-Georges-en-l'Ile d'Oléron and three other priories, then, in 1682, the abbey of Aumale. Though there is no evidence that he actually resided at Aumale, he was involved in lawsuits about maintenance of the fabric[7] – loose masonry made the choir dangerous – and it is probable that he had a hand in the sale of lead

C

stolen from old coffins. He seems to have resigned this unjust stewardship in 1697 or 1698; in 1699 he relinquished his appointment as financial
administrator to the duc de Vendôme, who awarded him a pension of
6,000 livres. His benefices brought him in 30,000 livres a year. (In the
middle of the century, 15,000 livres was considered not quite enough to
enable one to live in Paris in grand style.[8]) Hénault describes the gay
suppers, with song, at Chaulieu's apartments in the Temple. In a letter
of 1716 Voltaire, himself exiled to the estates of their mutual friend the
duc de Sully, addresses Chaulieu as his master, recalls the help which
Chaulieu, Bussy and Vendôme have given him with his tragedy *Œdipe*,
and promises to follow Chaulieu's advice on how to deal with the Regent.
Chaulieu, for his part, flatteringly writes to Voltaire about 'la secte
des philosophes, où vous avez la bonté de m'associer de votre autorité'.[9]
When Chaulieu died in 1720, Voltaire's *Epître* to the duc de Sully
lamented the passing of an age:

> Sa perte au Parnasse est funeste.
> Presque seul il était resté
> D'un siècle plein de politesse.[10]

Voltaire's *Epître à Uranie*, of about 1722, with its epicurean deism,
abolition of Hell, and stoic acceptance of death, is so similar in form and
content to Chaulieu that when it was published in 1732 Voltaire could
convincingly pass it off as Chaulieu's own:

> Tu veux donc, belle Uranie,
> Qu'érigé par ton ordre en Lucrèce nouveau
> Devant toi, d'une main hardie,
> Aux superstitions j'arrache le bandeau;
> Que j'expose à tes yeux le dangereux tableau
> Des mensonges sacrés dont la terre est remplie,
> Et que ma philosophie
> T'apprenne à mépriser les horreurs du tombeau
> Et les terreurs de l'autre vie.[11]

Voltaire's definitive verdict on Chaulieu the *poète négligé* (that is, a writer
of more or less spontaneous verse, not polished and corrected according to Boileau's prescription) is given in the *Temple du Goût* of 1733. The
god mentioned is the god of taste, in whose temple the dead poets are
judged:

> Je vis arriver en ce lieu
> Le brillant abbé de Chaulieu,
> Qui chantait en sortant de table.
> Il osait caresser le dieu
> D'un air familier, mais aimable.

> Sa vive imagination
> Prodiguait, dans sa douce ivresse,
> Des beautés sans correction,
> Qui choquaient un peu la justesse,
> Mais respiraient la passion. ...

Le dieu aimait fort tous ces messieurs, et surtout ceux qui ne se piquaient de rien: il avertissait Chaulieu de ne se croire que le premier des poètes négligés, et non pas le premier des bons poètes.[12]

In spite of his debt to them, however, Voltaire was right to disapprove of these abbés. The smug, libidinous, parasitic old reprobate Chaulieu was, indeed, a disgrace to his cloth and to society. One can understand why, in the 1790s, comte Joseph de Maistre saw the horrors of the Revolution as divine punishment for the evil selfishness of a whole century of *privilégiés*. Without knowing it, merely by existing, the unaggressive, sybaritic, unbelieving Société du Temple was part of that process of subversion which, within the very fabric and institutions of the Ancien Régime, brought authority and tradition into disrepute. Ironically, it was from a prison in the Temple on the morning of 21 January 1793 that citizen Capet, formerly Louis XVI, was carted off to execution.

But at least Chaulieu was not a Tartuffe. There is even a child-like trustfulness about him:

> Malgré tous mes défauts, qui ne m'aurait aimé?
> J'étais pour mes amis l'ami le plus fidèle.

Pacific, hospitable, rich enough not to be greedy of filthy lucre, he seems never to have questioned the rightness of a system which made life so pleasant for him:

> Ainsi je ne crains point qu'un Dieu dans sa colère
> Me demande les biens ou le sang de mon frère,
> Me reproche la veuve, ou l'orphelin pillé,
> Le pauvre par ma main de son champ dépouillé,
> Le viol du dépôt, ou l'amitié trahie,
> Ou par quelques forfaits la fortune envahie.

Even in the presence of brutal horror, his cheerfulness prevailed: his *Epître à son altesse sérénissime Mgr le duc de Vendôme sur la charge de général des galères que le roi lui donna en 1694* depicts the criminals, aboard their vessels, singing sweet harmonies in praise of the new General who will make their life a merry one:

> Je le vois: sur sa galère
> Ce Général est monté;
> Déjà son humanité
> Dans le sein de la misère
> Fait renaître la gaieté:
> Ce demi-Dieu secourable
> Vient, dans un séjour affreux,
> D'un arrêt irrévocable
> Consoler ces malheureux,
> Sûrs que son cœur pitoyable
> De leurs maux se touchera,
> Et que, sensible à leurs peines,
> Ne pouvant briser leurs chaînes,
> Sa main les relâchera.[13]

(Presumably he had never heard of the Huguenot *galériens pour la foi*, who found in their tribulations an intensification of spiritual life.[14]) The appalling winters that moved the good abbé Massillon to wrath against the luxurious rich were, to Chaulieu, merely an exercise in stoico-epicureanism:

> Au milieu cependant de ces peines cruelles,
> De notre triste hiver compagnes trop fidèles,
> Je suis tranquille et gai. Quel bien plus précieux
> Puis-je espérer encore de la bonté des Dieux?

Such moral blindness doubtless explains many things in the eighteenth century. But this insouciance, together with his apparent freedom from any religious or metaphysical *Angst*, did enable Chaulieu to make brilliant use of the poetic technique which Chapelle had taught him:

> Cet Esprit délicat, comme moi libertin
> Entre les amours et le vin,
> M'apprit, sans rabot et sans lime
> L'art d'attraper facilement
> Sans être esclave de la rime,
> Ce tour aisé, cet enjouement,
> Qui seul peut faire le sublime.

Sublime, hardly. But at least one of his poems, *Louanges de la vie champêtre, A Fontenay, ma maison de campagne*, of 1707, has a permanent appeal.[15] (Deprived of its movingly restrained opening lines, and chastely docked of its conclusion: 'Mais je vois revenir Lisette . . .', it can be read in the *Oxford Book of French Verse*.) Its themes – *Beatus ille*, shepherds' pipes, streams and meadows, rural pleasures soon to be relinquished for an ancestral grave beneath the trees loved by the poet in his childhood – were to become increasingly important as the century

progressed. Delille mentions these 'vers pleins d'une si douce mélancolie' in the notes to *Les Jardins*. Even Chateaubriand uses *A Fontenay*
as a text for meditation on the soul's infinite yearnings.[16]

The word *philosophie*, in Chaulieu's sense of indolence, withdrawal
from public life, continued to be used right up to the end of the old
régime.[17] But even in his own day, Chaulieu's passivity was becoming
anachronistic. The abbé de Saint-Pierre, only twenty years his junior,
was symptomatic of the new age.[18] It is difficult to imagine what any
church could do with Chaulieu today, were he to return from his sleepy
Elysium. The abbé de Saint-Pierre, with his handsome sons, his
projects for peace, morality via legislation, 'le paradis aux bienfaisants',
reforms all round, and the biggest pleasures for the biggest numbers,
would fit almost perfectly into a London canonry. In his ignorance of
modern science also, Chaulieu was out of touch with his age. Though
he paraphrased Virgil's 'Felix qui potuit rerum cognoscere causas', his
inquiries seem to have stopped short at vague musings about Copernicus:

> Je contemple à loisir cet amas de lumière,
> Ce brillant tourbillon, ce globe radieux,
> Et cherche s'il parcourt en effet sa carrière,
> Ou si, sans se mouvoir, il éclaire les cieux.

This survivor from the world of La Fontaine continued to attract
readers in the eighteenth century. Editions of his poems appeared in
1724, 1731, 1733, 1740, 1757, 1774, 1777. Diderot quotes him, in about
1777.[19] Four years before the Revolution, Robespierre was sentimentalis-
ing over him: 'Tendre Chaulieu, puissé-je être à jamais privé du plaisir
de lire vos écrits, si j'osais entreprendre d'obscurcir votre gloire.'[20]

Through their influence on their disciple Voltaire, Chaulieu and his
circle ensured that something of the seventeenth-century aristocratic
charm and gaiety survived to leaven the often laborious portentousness
of eighteenth-century philosophe writings. Of course, Voltaire moved
in other circles too. R. Naves, in *Le Goût de Voltaire*, asserts that the
Société du Temple was merely 'son péché de jeunesse, le centre de sa
vie d'étudiant', and that he learned more from visiting the salon of the
Duchesse du Maine at Sceaux.[21]

It would certainly be wrong to take Chaulieu as typical of the French
clergy, for in the Church of the period can be found the same contradictions and contrasts – riches and poverty, immorality and godliness,
privilege and injustice, enlightenment and obscurantism – which mark
the whole life of the nation during the century. It was not only voluptuous idlers who became clerics: the wealth and prestige of the Church

made it an attractive career for intelligent, ambitious, and not necessarily irreligious young men. Of the authors represented in this volume, four – Chaulieu, Massillon, Prévost, Delille – were ecclesiastics. Gresset was an apprentice Jesuit until that order expelled him. Rousseau offered himself as a candidate for the priesthood, but was wisely rejected by the authorities at the seminary where he was being trained.[22] Diderot was tonsured shortly before he was thirteen, and wore the costume of an abbé for two years; though the plan for him to succeed his uncle as canon fell through, he again seriously considered taking holy orders during a pious phase he went through in his late teens.[23] Chateaubriand was tonsured in December 1788, so that he might become rich as a member of the celibate order of the Knights of Malta:

> Comme Mme de Chateaubriand était une véritable sainte, elle obtint de l'évêque de Saint-Malo la promesse de me donner la cléricature. . . .
> Je me mets à genoux, en uniforme, l'épée au côté, aux pieds du prélat; il me coupa deux ou trois cheveux sur le sommet de la tête; cela s'appela tonsure, de laquelle je reçus lettres en bonnes formes. Avec ces lettres, 200 mille livres de rentes pouvaient m'échoir, quand mes preuves de noblesse auraient été admises à Malte: abus, sans doute, dans l'ordre ecclésiastique, mais chose utile dans l'ordre politique de l'ancienne constitution. Ne valait-il pas mieux qu'une espèce de bénéfice militaire s'attachât à l'épée d'un soldat qu'à la mantille d'un abbé, lequel aurait mangé sa grasse prieurée sur les pavés de Paris?[24]

As R. R. Palmer has shown in *Catholics and Unbelievers in Eighteenth-Century France*, the clerical apologists for religion were by no means lacking in mental vigour. And though bishoprics were bestowed for high birth, not holiness, by no means all the bishops were as cynical and depraved as Talleyrand, the brilliantly intelligent absentee bishop of Autun. There was, for example, Mgr François de Belsunce de Castelmorin, who ministered heroically to his flock at Marseilles during the 1720 plague. (His name is perpetuated in Pope's *Essay on Man*[25] and in the *Petit Larousse Illustré*.) All things considered, the eighteenth-century French bishops were not such a disgrace: 'These consecrated noblemen brought to their task both the vices and virtues of their race; a few were immoral, many were luxurious and non-resident, a few were deeply pious, most were decent and dignified and a number of them showed remarkable administrative ability.'[26]

The good *curé* is a common enough character in eighteenth-century literature. Restif de la Bretonne, for example, sings the praises of his two saintly brothers. But there is ample evidence from less dubious sources that virtue, piety, sincerity and conscientiousness were not lacking among the parochial clergy. If there were apostates in the French Church at the time of the Revolution, there were also confessors and martyrs. The Englishmen whom Voltaire met in the 1720s were shocked at the immorality of worldly abbés. During the persecutions in the 1790s, thirty-one French bishops and more than 10,000 French priests took temporary refuge in England. The English were impressed by their piety and seemly behaviour.[27]

NOTES

1 Apart from those mentioned in notes 9, 13 and 15 below, all the quotations from Chaulieu and from Courtin are taken from F. Lachèvre, *Les Derniers Libertins* (Paris, 1924), pp. 145–98. The 'rimes en *aux*' are, presumably, 'maquereaux', meaning pimps. The passage in which they occur is written in 'style marotique', i.e., in imitation of Clément Marot (1496–1544). Cf. Boileau: 'Imitez de Marot l'élégant badinage'.

2 According to J.-B. Thiers, *Histoire des Perruques* (Avignon, 1777; original edition 1689), p. 25, foppish, fashionable abbés took to wearing wigs in the 1660s, and were the first ecclesiastics so to do.

3 On abbés, see M. Marion, *Dictionnaire des institutions de la France au XVIIe et XVIIIe siècles* (Paris, 1923), and F. C. Green, *The Ancien Régime* (Edinburgh, 1958), pp. 61–2.

4 P. Sagnac, *La Formation de la société française moderne* (Paris, 1946), II, p. 215. The parish clergy considered the *congrue* insufficient to live on. (The poor clergyman in Goldsmith's *The Deserted Village*, of 1770, was 'passing rich with forty pounds a year'. 700 livres was less than thirty pounds sterling.)

5 See G. Desnoiresterres, *Voltaire et la société française au XVIIIe siècle* (Paris, 1871), vol. 1, pp. 10, 39, 89–112, 205, 230–31. There are articles on Bouillon, Bussy-Rabutin, Châteauneuf, Chaulieu and Courtin in the *Dictionnaire de Biographie Française* (Paris, still in process of publication). The quotations from Hénault are from *Mémoires du Président Hénault*, ed. Baron de Vigan (Paris, 1855), pp. 98, 416–18.

6 Voltaire tells the 'bougre de prêtre' story in the *Sottisier* (*Œuvres*, ed. Moland), vol. 32, p. 570. There are verse Epistles of Voltaire to or about the abbés Servien, Bussy, Chaulieu and Courtin in vol. 10, pp. 216, 237, 240. Cf. ibid., p. 220, 'Epître à Monsieur l'abbé de *** qui pleurait la mort de sa maîtresse', which urges him to get a new one: 'Et la véritable sagesse / Est de savoir fuir la tristesse / Dans les bras de la volupté.'

7 J. McManners, *French Ecclesiastical Society under the Ancien Régime* (Manchester, 1960), p. 77, points out that there were disadvantages in being given abbeys: 'Taking into account repairs, litigation and fluctuations of income, even sinecures in eighteenth-century France were something of a gamble.'

8 F. Bluche, *Les Magistrats du Parlement de Paris au XVIIIᵉ siècle* (Paris, 1960, p. 152.

9 *Œuvres de Chaulieu* (La Haye. Chez Gosse Junior, 1777), vol. 2, p. 168.

10 *Œuvres*, ed. Moland, vol. 10, p. 249. See Ch. IV, below, for similar laments on the decline of *politesse* at the end of the century.

11 Ibid., vol. 9, pp. 358–62.

12 Voltaire, *Mélanges*, Pléiade (Paris, 1961), pp. 148–9.

13 *Œuvres de Chaulieu*, ed. cit., vol. 1, p. 169.

14 E. G. Léonard, *Histoire Générale du Protestantisme*, vol. 3 (1964), pp. 63–4.

15 *Œuvres de Chaulieu*, ed. cit., vol. 1, pp. 33–4.

16 *Mémoires d'Outre-Tombe*, Pléiade, vol. II (Paris, 1964), p. 923.

17 Cf. Ch. VII, *Le Philosophe*, below. P. Grosclaude, *Malesherbes. Témoin et interprète de son temps* (Paris, 1961), pp. 413, 519, shows that, for public-spirited men in the second half of the century, *philosophie* was considered wicked if it meant wilful avoidance of responsibilities.

18 On the abbé de Saint-Pierre, see A. Chérel, *De Télémaque à Candide* (Paris, 1958), pp. 155–9. Rousseau in *Emile*, ed. F. et P. Richard (Paris, s.d.), pp. 229–30, tells how the abbé made it his civic duty to beget children.

19 *Œuvres esthétiques*, ed. P. Vernière (Paris, 1959), p. 824: 'Qu'est-ce qu'un poète négligé? C'est celui qui sème de temps en temps de la prose lâche et molle à travers de beaux vers; il est *semi-poeta*.'

20 Robespierre, *Œuvres*, ed. E. Lesueur (Paris, 1912), vol. I, p. 96 (*Eloge de Gresset*, published at the end of 1785 with the date 1786).

21 *Le Goût de Voltaire* (Paris, s.d.), pp. 153–5: 'Sceaux voit régner l'élégance féminine et la préciosité; c'est là que paradoxalement Voltaire trouve ses premiers conseillers pour la poésie tragique et la poésie épique, Malezieu, Polignac, Conti; c'est là probablement qu'il passe les heures les plus enivrantes de sa jeunesse, partagé entre les fêtes galantes, les représentations théâtrales et le travail poétique... On sait que jusqu'en 1750, malgré bien des traverses, il restera fidèle à la société de la duchesse du Maine, à laquelle il doit une de ses plus charmantes inspirations, *Zadig*.'

22 *Confessions*, Livre III: 'J'étais destiné à être le rebut de tous les états. . . . Aussi l'évêque et le supérieur se rebutèrent-ils, et on me rendit à madame de Warens comme un sujet qui n'était pas même bon pour être prêtre, au reste assez bon garçon, disait-on, et point vicieux.'

23 F. Venturi, *Jeunesse de Diderot* (Paris, 1939), pp. 21–9. Diderot's only brother became a priest, and one of his two sisters a nun.

24 *Mémoires d'Outre-Tombe*, ed. cit., vol. I (Paris, 1966), pp. 158–9.

25 *Essay on Man*, Epistle V:

> Oh, blind to truth, and God's whole scheme below,
> Who fancy bliss to vice, to virtue woe!
>
> .   .   .   .   .
>
> Why drew Marseilles' good bishop purer breath,
> When nature sicken'd, and each gale was death?

26 J. McManners, *French Ecclesiastical Society* . . ., p. 196. See ibid., Chapters I–III, VI–VII, XII–XIV for the part played by the Church in the ordinary

daily life of Frenchmen, the intellectual and cultural interests of the clergy, the virtues and failings of a cross-section of the *curés*, and the clergy's reactions to reform. On the French clergy from the eve of the Revolution to the restoration of the Church by Napoleon in 1802, see J. McManners, *The French Revolution and the Church* (London, 1969).

27 A. Latreille, *L'Eglise Catholique et la Révolution Française* (Paris, 1946), I, pp. 187–9.

II · Massillon (1663-1742)

FROM the *Sermon pour le quatrième dimanche de Carême. Sur l'Aumône* (1709)

Et certes, dites-moi: tandis que les villes et les campagnes sont frappées de calamités; que des hommes créés à l'image de Dieu, et rachetés de tout son sang, broutent l'herbe comme des animaux, et, dans leur nécessité extrême, vont chercher à travers les champs une nourriture que la terre n'a pas faite pour l'homme, et qui devient pour eux une nourriture de mort; auriez-vous la force d'y être le seul heureux? Tandis que la face de tout un royaume est changée, et que tout retentit de cris et de gémissements autour de votre demeure superbe, pourriez-vous conserver au dedans le même air de joie, de pompe, de sérénité, d'opulence? et où serait l'humanité, la raison, la religion? Dans une république païenne, on vous regarderait comme un mauvais citoyen; dans une société de sages et de mondains, comme une âme vile, sordide, sans noblesse, sans générosité, sans élévation; et dans l'Eglise de Jésus-Christ, sur quel pied voulez-vous qu'on vous regarde? eh! comme un monstre indigne du nom chrétien que vous portez, de la foi dont vous vous glorifiez, des sacrements dont vous approchez, de l'entrée même de nos temples où vous venez, puisque ce sont là les symboles sacrés de l'union qui doit être parmi les fidèles.

Cependant la main du Seigneur est étendue sur nos peuples dans les villes et dans les campagnes; vous le savez, et vous vous en plaignez: le ciel est d'airain pour ce royaume affligé; la misère, la pauvreté, la désolation, la mort, marchent partout devant vous. Or, vous échappe-t-il de ces excès de charité, devenus maintenant une loi de discrétion et de justice? prenez-vous sur vous-même une partie des calamités de vos frères? vous voit-on seulement toucher à vos profusions et à vos voluptés, criminelles en toute sorte de temps, mais barbares et punissables même par les lois des hommes en celui-ci? Que dirai-je? ne mettez-vous pas peut-être à profit les misères publiques? ne faites-vous pas peut-être de l'indigence comme une occasion barbare de gain? n'achevez-vous pas peut-être de dépouiller les malheureux, en affectant de leur tendre une main secourable? et ne savez-vous pas l'art inhumain d'apprécier les larmes et les nécessités de vos frères? Entrailles cruelles! dit l'Esprit de Dieu, quand vous serez rassasié, vous vous sentirez déchiré; votre félicité fera elle-même votre supplice; et le Seigneur fera pleuvoir sur vous sa fureur et sa guerre.

Mes frères, que la présence des pauvres devant le tribunal de Jésus-Christ sera terrible pour la plupart des riches du monde! que ces accusateurs seront puissants! et qu'il vous restera peu de chose à répondre, quand ils vous reprocheront qu'il fallait si peu de secours pour soulager leur indigence, qu'un seul jour retranché de vos profusions aurait suffi pour remédier aux besoins d'une de leurs années; que c'est leur propre bien que vous leur refusiez, puisque ce que vous aviez de trop leur appartenait; qu'ainsi vous avez été non-seulement cruels, mais encore injustes en le leur refusant; mais enfin que votre dureté n'a servi qu'à exercer leur patience, et les rendre plus dignes d'immortalité, tandis que vous alors, dépouillés pour toujours de ces mêmes biens que vous n'avez pas voulu mettre en sûreté dans le sein des pauvres, n'aurez plus pour partage que la malédiction préparée à ceux qui auront vu Jésus-Christ souffrant la faim, la soif, la nudité dans ses membres, et qui ne l'auront pas soulagé: *Nudus eram, et non cooperuistis me.* (MATTH., xxv, 43.)

Œuvres de Massillon (Paris, Chez Firmin Didot frères) 1838, I, pp. 371–2.

Blenheim 1704, Ramillies 1706, the siege of Toulon in 1707, Oudenarde 1708, and Lille occupied by the Dutch – the defeated armies of Louis le Grand could no longer keep the frontiers inviolate. Then came the coldest winter in living memory, and with it, famine. On 17 January 1709 the Princess Palatine, sister-in-law of the King, reported to her German correspondents that, in spite of huge fires, the royal family shivered in their apartments. On the 19th she wrote that people were dying from the cold, partridges were frozen dead in the fields, theatres and law-courts were closed. On 2 February, she announced that 24,000 people had died in Paris; transport was difficult, since either there were no sledges or the French did not know how to use them. On 9 February wolves prowling near Marly; the courier from Alençon and his horses had been eaten by them. On 2 March she recounted the sad story of a woman apprehended for stealing a loaf: when the police went to the house they found three starving children, and the corpse of the father, who had hanged himself in despair.[1]

It was against this background of disaster that the fashionable preacher Massillon delivered his sermon on almsgiving at Notre-Dame on the fourth Sunday in Lent, 10 March 1709.[2] He must also have known that Lesage's play *Turcaret*, produced at the Comédie Française on 14 February, was a bitter attack on the alleged rapacity, heartlessness, cynicism and brutality of the financiers and tax-farmers who, according to popular belief, were a main cause of the miseries of the people.

10 March was, however, too early for word to have reached Massillon of the crisis at Lyons, where, by the end of the month, the ex-Huguenot financier Samuel Bernard had gone bankrupt, and, with him, the national exchequer.[3]

Since so much of the finest eighteenth-century literature is secular, if not actually anti-Christian in content, literary historians have tended to overlook the immense importance which Catholic teaching and practice continued to have for Frenchmen. A lay attitude is assumed to be present everywhere. In the case of Massillon, it is customary to allege that he soft-pedalled Christianity. Gustave Lanson sounds positively apostolic as he complains:

> Son pire défaut est ce qui l'a fait préférer de Voltaire, de La Harpe et des Encyclopédistes, entre tous les prédicateurs. Il efface le dogme, il cite à peine l'Ecriture, sa prédication est toute morale, toute philosophique, presque laïque. Si l'on excepte les formules traditionnelles, rien n'y sent le chrétien.

But already in the 1680s Fénelon, in his *Dialogues sur l'éloquence*, stated of preachers generally that 'on s'attache trop aux peintures morales, et on n'explique pas assez les principes de la morale évangélique'. A century later Louis XVI, a monarch more renowned for piety than wit, is supposed to have remarked at the end of a Lenten course of sermons in 1781: 'Si l'abbé Maury nous avait parlé un peu de religion, il nous aurait parlé de tout.'[4] It is worth considering whether Massillon did in fact speak only as a lay moralist in this sermon preached during the 1709 hunger, and whether the doctrine of Christian charity continued to remain alive during the century.

His text, John, VI, 11, is from the Gospel for the day, on the feeding of the five thousand. Part I[5] demonstrates the dangers rich men incur by eluding their duty to feed the poor. The communism of the primitive church no longer exists, but the superfluous wealth that the rich spend on pomp, pleasure and wicked luxury[6] is not theirs; it is 'le fonds et l'héritage des pauvres; vous n'en êtes que le dépositaire, et ne pouvez y toucher sans usurpation et sans injustice'. Newly ennobled families in particular should give: their wealth has doubtless been unjustly acquired, and in any case it is unseemly for them to spend as much as great aristocrats. If wealth is not used to succour God's afflicted people, the poor, He will transfer it to some more faithful guardian, and – as is written in the Book of Esther, IV, 14 – 'thou and thy father's house shall be destroyed'. God does not demand the relinquishment of all possessions. Even profiteers from war and disaster – 'vous qui ne devez peut-être qu'aux malheurs publics et à des gains odieux et suspects l'accroissement de votre fortune' – may retain their riches, provided that they are not barbarous to their brethren, or to the mother reduced to selling her daughter's virtue for bread. Charity will avert the wrath of God, and it is the poor, rather than the saints, who can unlock the door to Heaven. In the early Church, there was not 'any among them that lacked' (Acts, IV, 34); today, rich men buy titles and dignities in order to cover up their humble origin. If only they would regularly set aside a fixed proportion of their money for the poor, the present 'monstrueuse disproportion' between opulence and indigence would give way to 'la paix, l'allégresse, l'heureuse égalité des premiers chrétiens'. But people give arbitrarily or not at all, forgetting their duty as 'membre de Jésus-Christ, frère d'un chrétien affligé'. Then comes the extract printed above, which brings Part I of the sermon to an end.

Part II gives rules for the exercise of charity: it should not be proud, ostentatious, harsh, humiliating, insulting, capricious, sporadic or inquisitorial. Landowners, whose pomp and luxury are 'les fruits de la sueur et des travaux de tant d'infortunés qui habitent vos terres et vos campagnes', should succour their needy tenants, instead of cruelly extorting their feudal dues.[7] Massillon's arguments become recognisably 'eighteenth-century'. He plays upon his audience's *sensibilité*, and, anticipating Rousseau, contrasts their tears at theatrical performances with their stony-heartedness in real life; 'Ame inhumaine! avez-vous donc laissé toute votre sensibilité sur un théâtre infâme? le spectacle de Jésus-Christ souffrant dans un de ses membres n'offre-t-il rien qui soit digne de votre sensibilité?' He returns three times more to the theme which novelists and painters were to find so intriguing – the 'jeune personne . . . sur le bord d'un précipice . . ., que le sexe et l'âge exposent à la séduction et dont vous pourriez préserver l'innocence'.[8] He emphasises the pleasurable emotions to be derived from being 'miséricordieux', 'humain', 'bienfaisant', arguing that these are qualities inherent in human nature, 'des sentiments d'humanité dont nous ne saurions nous dépouiller qu'en nous dépouillant de la nature même!' But he subordinates all this to his theme of man's relationship with God. He again threatens the uncharitable with financial ruin and the extinction of their line, whereas the ready giver will lay up treasure for himself even in this world: 'Le succès de vos entreprises sera l'affaire de Dieu même; vous aurez trouvé le moyen de l'intéresser à votre fortune.' To balance the vision of eternal damnation which had concluded the first part, the second ends with the prospect of Judgment Day, and the

eternal bliss promised to the charitable in Matthew, xxv, 34–40:
'Come, ye blessed of my father. . . .'

There is nothing unorthodox or startlingly new in all this. The argument that, since property is stewardship, it is mortal sin to withhold alms from the needy, goes back at least as far as St Thomas Aquinas. The statements in Part I that communism was practised by natural man and the early Church is less positive than Gratian's dictum: 'Communis enim usus omnium, quae in hoc mundo, omnibus hominibus esse debuit', which was well known in the Middle Ages. And Holy Scripture – of which Massillon in this sermon at any rate is less sparing than Lanson makes out – is full of strictures upon the rich.

In the context of the 1709 famine and defeats, however, the old ideas take on a vivid actuality. The first sentence of our extract is more than a mere reminiscence of La Bruyère, and the horrors of present facts truthfully reported are heightened by the theological affirmation that men are 'créés à l'image de Dieu et rachetés de son sang'.[9] Are the complacent pomp and opulence which Massillon condemns in his hearers a little too evident in his own style? Perhaps; but he is bound by the rules of the genre he is using, and is aware that a congregation of rich bourgeois and nobles ('vous qui, dans un quartier, tenez le premier rang, ou par vos biens ou par votre maison') must be addressed with rotund formality, even when they are in imminent danger of Hell. His reference to the virtuous pagan is brief – self-identification with citizens of Ancient Republics had not yet become a mania with Frenchmen. He lays more stress on the standards required of the *honnête homme* – the 'âme vile . . .' sounds like a description of Turcaret. But it is the Christian vocabulary which gives the last sentence of the paragraph its fullness and rhythmic effect.

The hand of the Lord in the second paragraph should refer to the military disasters: Massillon has already asserted that the lack of bread is due to rich men's cupidity. But whatever its precise point, this threnody of doom, death and desolation is poetically moving. It is followed by a renewed exhortation to charity, and a hint that legal punishment may overtake those who too blatantly flaunt their ill-gotten riches. For in spite of its repeated 'peut-être' and the negative interrogative, the sentence 'Que dirai-je . . .' accuses landowners and/or merchants of exploiting the shortage, callously calculating how much profit they can extort. (Present-day historians confirm this allegation that the famine was largely caused by speculators: when the mild winter of 1709–10 gave prospects of a good harvest and a fall in prices, the grain cornered

in 1709 emerged from concealment.)[10] The last sentence of this paragraph, mainly about punishment after death, but with a hint of the here-
and-now and the possible ravaging of property by invading armies, is full
of biblical reminiscences, Job XX in particular. The third paragraph
urges escape from eternal damnation by even a modest reimbursement
of the paupers' own money. The patience of the poor was, indeed,
remarkable; but Massillon cannot have been unaware that riots and
uprisings by peasants and town-dwellers had occurred throughout
the reign, and that the hangman was used to suppress them.[11]

Tradition says that his audience was moved to tears. What more
practical effects his oratory had, I have failed to discover. Boileau, in a
letter of 15 May 1709, noted that 'Il n'y a point de semaine où l'on ne
joue trois fois l'opéra avec une fort grande abondance de monde, et
jamais il n'y eut tant de plaisirs, de promenades et de divertissements'.[12]
In any case, Massillon had the highest biblical authority for believing
that the poor would be always with him.

One may regret that, when scourging seigneurial exactions and
businessmen's machinations, he did not also attack the system of taxation which, as much as anything else, was responsible for the peasants'
miseries. He knew that a juster system could be devised, for in 1707
Vauban's *Dîme Royale* had presented to the King precise plans for fiscal
reform. Doubtless such matters were forbidden to Massillon in his
Paris pulpit: when bishop of Clermont (Clermont-Ferrand), he did
protest to Louis XV's minister Fleury about the iniquitous taxation of
the Auvergnat peasants.[13]

For the rest, his denunciations in the *Sermon sur l'Aumône* are not
wholly dissimilar from those made by another preacher, Jean Meslier,
parish priest of Etrépigny, a poor village in the Ardennes:

> Vous étonnez-vous, pauvres peuples, que vous avez tant de mal et
> tant de peines dans la vie? C'est que vous portez seuls tout le poids du
> jour et de la chaleur, comme ces laboureurs dont il est parlé dans une
> parabole de l'Evangile, c'est que vous êtes chargés, vous et tous vos
> semblables, de tout le fardeau de l'Etat; vous êtes chargés non seule-
> ment de tout le fardeau de vos rois et de vos Princes, qui sont vos
> premiers tyrans, mais vous êtes encore chargés de toute la Noblesse,
> de tout le Clergé, de toute la Moinerie, de tous les gens de justice, de
> tous les gens de guerre, de tous les maltôtiers, de tous les gardes de sel
> et de tabac, et enfin de tout ce qu'il y a de gens fainéants et inutiles
> dans le monde. Car ce n'est que des fruits de vos pénibles travaux
> que tous ces gens-là vivent, eux et tous ceux et celles qui les servent.
> Vous fournissez par vos travaux non seulement tout ce qui est nécessaire

à leur subsistance, mais encore tout ce qui peut servir à leurs divertissements et à leurs plaisirs.[14]

There indeed is a style more vigorous than Massillon's. But we do not
know whether the passage ever actually formed part of one of Meslier's
sermons. His writings did not begin to circulate – and then only clandestinely – until after his death in 1733.

Poverty continued to exist throughout the century. Rousseau, in
note (i) of De l'Inégalité, described 'les campagnes abandonnées, les
terres en friche, et les grands chemins inondés de malheureux citoyens
devenus mendiants ou voleurs, et destinés à finir un jour leur misère
sur la roue ou sur un fumier'. The Committee on Mendicity of the Constituent Assembly reported that in forty-two departments one-ninth
of the population was indigent, and in six departments one-fifth.
Until the Revolution abolished them, ancient endowments and current
benefactions continued to finance hospitals and homes run by nuns.
Bishops and clergy encouraged alms-giving, and frequently led the
way in generosity. Massillon devoted most of his episcopal income to
charities in his diocese. During the 1789 food shortage at Angers, nearly
half the total sum raised for the official relief fund was contributed by
clergy. Local parishes organised soup-kitchens in many towns. Robespierre, in July 1793, described with approval how,

> Dans le grand hiver de 1788, le curé de Sainte-Marguerite, à Paris,
> employa avec le plus grand succès, une recette composée d'un mélange
> de plusieurs espèces d'aliments; il fit vivre fort sainement une multitude
> immense de malheureux, et la portion d'un homme fait n'allait pas à
> trois sous par jour.[15]

Since private charities under Church auspices were patently inadequate
and often inefficient, there was an increasing demand for lay control of
religious charitable institutions, and, of course, of their endowments.
Men like Turgot and Necker proposed that the State should assume
responsibility for pauper relief. Already under Louis XIV the civil
authorities had instituted hôpitaux généraux where beggars were put to
work. In the second half of the eighteenth century, the Government
set up poor-houses.[16]

In the 1790s the religious orders were suppressed, and the Church
lands sold off by the Government to private citizens. But the new, lay,
republican welfare services proved at least as inadequate as those they
replaced. Catholic and counter-revolutionary propagandists accused the
lay administrators and nurses of infamous peculation, and of murdering

PLATE III   J.-B. Greuze (1725–1805): *La Vertu chancelante (c. 1775)*

PLATE IVa   F. Boucher (1703–70): *La Toilette de Vénus* (1746)

PLATE IVb   J.-F. de Troy (1679–1752): *La Déclaration d'amour* (1731)

in their beds the indigent sick and the orphaned children.[17] The ex-abbé Delille, in his poem *La Pitié*, written in 1799, inveighed against the bloody revolutionaries who had stolen the paupers' crust and destroyed the Catholic hospitals,

Des maux de l'indigence, ô refuges pieux!
Où des saints fondateurs la charité sublime
Consacrait la richesse ou rachetait le crime.
Je ne vois plus ces sœurs dont les soins délicats
Apaisaient la souffrance ou charmaient le trépas,
Qui pour le malheur seul connaissant la tendresse,
Aux besoins du vieil âge immolaient leur jeunesse.
Leurs toits hospitaliers sont fermés aux douleurs,
Et la tendre pitié s'enfuit les yeux en pleurs;
Le pauvre des bienfaits voit la source tarie,
Et l'enfant vient mourir sur le seuil de la vie.

When this poem was published in Paris in 1803, the First Consul Bonaparte had already reinstalled the Sisters of Charity as hospital nurses. But the Church property was to remain in lay hands.

It is possible that the philosophe writers who, throughout the eighteenth century, sought to replace medieval notions of charity by new economic doctrines, were themselves motivated in their desire to do good by the Christian traditions in which they had been nurtured. Even the *Encyclopédie* article on religious foundations proclaims, along with Massillon, that 'le pauvre a des droits incontestables sur l'abondance du riche; l'humanité, la religion nous font également un devoir de soulager nos semblables dans le malheur'.[18] But the biblical text most appropriate to their teaching is St Paul's 'This we commanded you, that if any would not work, neither should he eat'. The abbé de Saint-Pierre, the eighteenth-century proto-apostle of *bienfaisance*, urged rich men to put their money into productive industry: 'Faire travailler une grande quantité d'ouvriers pour la plus grande utilité publique, voilà où doit se placer la magnificence pour mériter des louanges.'[19] Montesquieu, in *De l'Esprit des lois*, announced that 'un homme n'est pas pauvre parce qu'il n'a rien, mais parce qu'il ne travaille pas'. Monasteries and charitable endowments inspire a spirit of laziness, which breeds poverty: commerce and industry flourished in England as a result of the suppression of the monasteries. The State should look after the indigent aged, sick and orphans, who should all be made to do appropriate work: 'il (l'état) donne aux uns les travaux dont ils sont capables; il enseigne les autres à travailler, ce qui fait déjà un travail'. The State should also give prompt relief to workmen who are in temporary distress through

D

fluctuations in trade and commerce. Montesquieu offers two reasons why this help should be given: 'Soit pour empêcher le peuple de souffrir, soit pour éviter qu'il ne se révolte.'[20] Turgot likewise, in his *Encyclopédie* article 'Fondation', denounced the indiscriminate charity of religious houses, whereby 'la race des citoyens industrieux est remplacée par une populace vile, composée de mendiants vagabonds, et livrés à toutes sortes de crimes'. Every able-bodied man should earn his own living: the remedy for pauperism is a completely free, competitive economy:

> Ce que l'Etat doit à chacun de ses membres, c'est la destruction des obstacles qui les gêneraient dans leur industrie, ou qui les troubleraient dans la jouissance des produits qui en sont la récompense'.[21]

Turgot's friend Malesherbes opposed the idea of any tax to finance poor relief. This should be left to private enterprise, since private charity is best exercised in making the poor work: one must not nourish 'le mendiant valide sans travail'.[22] Condorcet produced figures for tontines, friendly societies and insurances, whereby the thrifty poor could provide for their old age.[23] And, cleverer than the curé of Sainte-Marguerite, the philanthropic Idéologues in 1800 were collecting money for paupers' soup which was not merely presumed nourishing but guaranteed nasty, and still only cost 25 francs per 120 portions.[24]

The word *sensibilité* acquired many meanings during the eighteenth century. The work-house was the philathropists' answer to Massillon's 'offrons du moins des cœurs sensibles à leurs misères'. After all, it was better than death by famine and poisonous fern.

NOTES

1 *Lettres de Madame Palatine*. Club du meilleur livre (1961), pp. 250–54.
2 1709 is the date given by Massillon's nephew, Joseph Massillon, prêtre de l'Oratoire, in his edition of his uncle's sermons published in 1745 (vol. 3, pp. 250–5). Easter Sunday fell on 31 March in 1709. The fourth Sunday in Lent would therefore have been 10 March. The Princess Palatine first reports rioting in Paris in a letter of 7 April, when she writes that market-women killed a *commissaire* in the Place Maubert because of the high price of bread. On 12 August, she wrote that from 4 a.m. until midday a crowd of 4,000, assembled at the Porte Saint-Martin, looted bakeries and stoned the troops sent to keep order. The mob eventually dispersed with cries of 'Vive le roi et du pain'. (*Lettres*, pp. 256–64.) Cf. G. Walter, *Histoire des paysans de France* (Paris, 1963), pp. 302, 516. Marlborough's bloody victory at Malplaquet was won on 11 September.
3 Bernard had abjured Protestantism in 1685, after Louis XIV's thugs had

ransacked his house at Chennevières, but he became the main banker for the Huguenot exiles. He recovered from his 1709 bankruptcy, and married off his daughter and grand-daughter to members of illustrious aristocratic families. (P. Sagnac, *La Formation de la société française moderne*, I, pp. 213–14; II, 59–60.) For a technical account of the financial and monetary crisis of 1709, see H. Lüthy, *La Banque protestante en France de la Révocation de l'Edit de Nantes à la Révolution*, vol. I (1959), pp. 29, 197–202, 223. After Bernard's crash, the Controller-General of Finances tried in vain to raise a loan from Genevan bankers on the security of the crown jewels. On 26 August he wrote to the King: 'La situation présente des affaires est si mauvaise qu'elle cause à ceux qui la connaissent de justes inquiétudes sur les événements malheureux que l'on peut appréhender. Depuis quatre mois, toute la circulation de l'argent est cessée. Les peuples ne paient point la taille ni la capitation. . . . Nulle ressource à espérer des banquiers.' The King had his gold and silver melted down to help the treasury.

4 M. Leroy, *Histoire des idées sociales en France*, vol. I, p. 197.

5 The accepted method of constructing a sermon, which Massillon here follows fairly closely, was: 'Un texte de l'Ecriture d'où un premier exorde tire, parfois avec subtilité, l'énoncé du sujet dont l'exposition est mise sous la protection de la Vierge par l'*Ave Maria*. Un second exorde contient la division et le plan. Le sermon est divisé en deux ou trois points, la division est justifiée par des raisons intrinsèques et des raisons de circonstance. Chaque point est divisé en deux ou trois parties. Chaque partie comprend un exposé de la doctrine tirée d'un texte de l'Ecriture, que l'orateur commente par une citation d'un Père de l'Eglise et corrobore par un raisonnement. De cette vérité dogmatique, brièvement présentée, découle la morale qui a deux aspects: ce que commande la morale évangélique, ce que font les lâches chrétiens. Les points épuisés, le sermon se termine par une brève exhortation.' (J. Calvet, *La Littérature religieuse de François de Sales à Fénelon*, Paris, 1938, pp. 414–15.)

6 Massillon, in his 'Oraison funèbre de Louis le Grand, roi de France', again denounces luxury as the cause of poverty: 'Le luxe, toujours le précurseur de l'indigence, en corrompant les mœurs, tarit la source de nos biens.' (*Œuvres de Massillon*, Paris, Didot, 1838, vol. I, p. 673.) But in the same sermon he anticipates Diderot and the abbé Raynal by his admiration for commerce and civil engineering: 'La navigation, plus florissante que sous tous les règnes précédents, étendit notre commerce dans toutes les parties du monde connu . . . un canal miraculeux par la hardiesse et les travaux incompréhensibles de l'entreprise, rapprocha ce que la nature avait séparé par des espaces immenses.' (Ibid., pp. 673–4.)

7 'Ah! c'est pour exiger de ces malheureux vos droits avec barbarie; c'est pour arracher de leurs entrailles le prix innocent de leurs travaux, sans avoir égard à leur misère, au malheur du temps que vous nous alléguez, à leurs larmes souvent et à leur désespoir: que dirai-je? c'est peut-être pour opprimer leurs faiblesses, pour être leur tyran, et non pas leur seigneur et leur père. O Dieu, ne maudissez-vous pas ces races cruelles, et ces richesses d'iniquités?'

8 Cf. the repentant seducer Climal in Marivaux's *Marianne*; the preservation of Julie's virtue by the *bienfaisant* comte de *** in Duclos's novel (see Ch. VI

below); Greuze's picture 'La Vertu chancelante', painted in the 1770s
(Fig. No. 235 in *France in the Eighteenth Century*, Royal Academy of Arts
Winter Exhibition 1968, p. lxxxii). In his sermon 'Sur le Bonheur des justes',
Massillon links the insipid, sentimental aspects of eighteenth-century
literature with the violent, orgiastic currents, and describes something that
already sounds like Romantic *mal du siècle*: 'Les spectacles, ne trouvant
presque plus dans les spectateurs que des âmes grossièrement dissolues, et
incapables d'être réveillées que par les excès les plus monstrueux de la
débauche, deviennent fades . . .'; 'Essayez tous les plaisirs; ils ne guériront
pas ce fond d'ennui et de tristesse que vous traînez partout avec vous.'
(*Œuvres*, 1838, I, pp. 9, 16.)

9 The 'nourriture de mort' was presumably bread made of dried ferns.
P. de Saint Jacob, *Les Paysans de la Bourgogne du Nord au dernier siècle de
l'Ancien Régime* (Paris, 1960), quotes from the *Chronique* of a canon of
Beaune: 'La plupart mourait en chemin au coin des buissons, les autres
ordinairement pauvres, vivaient de pain de fougère séchée au four, ce qui a
causé une mortalité si terrible parmi ce menu peuple que les villages sont
demeurés déserts et abandonnés.' This was in 1709. On the 1693 famine,
Saint Jacob quotes: 'Le pauvre peuple vit avec du pain de racines de fougère
. . . réduits à manger de l'herbe dans les prés comme des bêtes et à mourir
la plupart dans les rues et dans les grands chemins' (pp. 178, 192–6).

10 Writing of the 1693 famine, Saint Jacob (op. cit., pp. 178–9) explains the
relationship between high taxation, bad winters, speculation and famine:
'Cette grande disette est intéressante en ce qu'elle permet de saisir le pro-
cessus qui, jusqu'à la Révolution, restera celui de toutes les crises. D'abord,
une montée de fiscalité [increased taxation], essentielle et déterminante
pour une large part, ravageait les maigres économies paysannes. Dans le
malaise d'argent, une mauvaise récolte détermine le choc générateur de la
crise. Immédiatement, cette insuffisance crée la panique, renforce la spéculation et exagère la pénurie. Les prix grandissent en flèche devant le besoin
général et la faiblesse des moyens. La rareté des grains ne prend toute son
importance que dans un climat favorable [i.e. to crisis]; la crise des subsis-
tances est souvent commandée par celle des ressources pécuniaires et
l'ampleur de la spéculation, plus que par la baisse de la production.' Of the
1709 famine, Saint Jacob states: 'La disette était moins affaire de pénurie
que de répartition. Des spéculateurs affamaient le peuple.' (pp. 195–6.) Cf.
Sagnac, op. cit., vol. I, pp. 158–60, 204–7.

11 R. Mandrou, *La France au XVIIᵉ et XVIIIᵉ siècles*, pp. 38–48, column 3;
P. Sagnac, op. cit., vol. I, pp. 220–1.

12 Quoted by G. Walter, op. cit., p. 305.

13 See F. Godefroy, *Massillon, Œuvres choisies* (Paris, 1868), vol. I, pp. 30
et seq. The somewhat tentative 'progressive' remarks which occur here and
there in Massillon's works show that it was not only the philosophes who
were critical of the authorities. Thus, in his funeral oration on Louis XIV,
he denounced the St Bartholomew massacre, and, though rejoicing at
Louis's suppression of heresy, deplored the violence used, cast doubt on
the value of forced conversions, and pointed out the economic and military
disadvantages of the Revocation of the Edict of Nantes. He frequently

inveighed against the horrors of war. And, as a good Gallican, he made at least one oblique reference to the Papal concept of liberty: 'Mais qui ne sait combien la religieuse soumission qu'on doit à tout ce qui part de ce trône auguste, et les hommages éternels dont le pontife est environné, le familiarisent peu avec une liberté chrétienne, et des discours qui ne sont pas faits pour louer?' (*Œuvres de Massillon*, 1838, vol. I, p. 679; vol. II, pp. 452; 146 – 'Sermon pour le jour de Saint Bernard'.)

14 Jean Meslier, *Testament*, ed. Rudolf Charles (Amsterdam, 1864), vol. II, pp. 223–4, quoted by J. Ehrard, *L'Idée de nature en France* . . ., p. 521 n. On the bitter resentment the peasants felt about having to pay feudal dues and tithes, in addition to the high state taxes, see Tocqueville, *L'Ancien Régime*, Bk II, ch. 1.

15 Robespierre, *Textes choisis*, ed. J. Poperen (Paris, 1957), vol. 2, p. 180. Robespierre denounced the economic theories of the liberal philosophes: 'Cette espèce de philosophie pratique qui, réduisant l'égoïsme en système, regarde la société humaine comme une guerre de ruse, le succès comme la règle du juste et de l'injuste, la probité comme une affaire de goût ou de bienséance, le monde comme le patrimoine des fripons adroits' (ibid., vol. 3, pp. 170–1).

16 See J. McManners, *French Ecclesiastical Society under the Ancien Régime*, pp. 93–102, 233–5; H. Sée, *La France économique et sociale au XVIIIᵉ siècle*, pp. 167–74.

17 E.g. the Royalist–Catholic fortnightly review *Les Annales philosophiques, morales et littéraires, ou suite des Annales catholiques*, 1800, vol. 1, pp. 106–13, article 'Les Hospices'.

18 Article 'Fondation', by Turgot, in the *Encyclopédie*, vol. 7 (Paris, 1757), pp. 72–5. The article concludes by saying that the State has the incontestable right to use the endowments of ancient foundations for new objects, or, better still, suppress the foundations altogether, since public utility is the supreme law.

19 *Ouvrages de politique* (Amsterdam, 1733–40), vol. V, p. 41. Quoted by J. Ehrard, op. cit., p. 533.

20 *De l'Esprit des lois*, XXIII, 29, Pléiade ed., vol. 2, pp. 712–13.

21 Turgot's article was written before 1757. When Intendant at Limoges in 1770 he wrote 'Le soulagement des hommes qui souffrent est le devoir de tous, et toutes les autorités se réuniront pour y concourir' (H. Sée, op. cit., p. 171).

22 P. Grosclaude, *Malesherbes. Témoin et interprète de son temps* (Paris, 1961), p. 348.

23 *Esquisse d'un tableau historique des progrès de l'esprit humain*, ed. O. H. Prior (Paris, 1933), pp. 189, 213.

24 Their review, *La Décade philosophique*, made frequent appeals for subscriptions to *soupes à la Rumford* throughout 1800, and published a report on the *Comité central des soupes économiques* in January 1803. It assured its readers that the soup would not 'tenter la sensualité' of the paupers.

III · Montesquieu (1689-1755)

FROM *Lettres persanes* (published 1721)
(Lettre CVI)

Paris est peut-être la ville du Monde la plus sensuelle, et où l'on raffine le plus sur les plaisirs; mais c'est peut-être celle où l'on mène une vie plus dure. Pour qu'un homme vive délicieusement, il faut que cent autres travaillent sans relâche. Une femme s'est mise dans la tête qu'elle devait paraître à une assemblée avec une certaine parure; il faut que, dès ce moment, cinquante artisans ne dorment plus et n'aient plus le loisir de boire et de manger: elle commande, et elle est obéie plus promptement que ne serait notre monarque, parce que l'intérêt est le plus grand monarque de la Terre.

Cette ardeur pour le travail, cette passion de s'enrichir, passe de condition en condition, depuis les artisans jusques aux grands. Personne n'aime à être plus pauvre que celui qu'il vient de voir immédiatement au-dessous de lui. Vous voyez à Paris un homme qui a de quoi vivre jusqu'au Jour du Jugement, qui travaille sans cesse et court risque d'accourcir ses jours pour amasser, dit-il, de quoi vivre.

Le même esprit gagne la Nation: on n'y voit que travail et qu'industrie. Où est donc ce peuple efféminé dont tu parles tant?

Je suppose, Rhedi, qu'on ne souffrît dans un royaume que les arts absolument nécessaires à la culture des terres, qui sont pourtant en grand nombre, et qu'on en bannît tous ceux qui ne servent qu'à la volupté ou à la fantaisie; je le soutiens: cet état serait un des plus misérables qu'il y eût au Monde.

Quand les habitants auraient assez de courage pour se passer de tant de choses qu'ils doivent à leurs besoins, le Peuple dépérirait tous les jours, et l'Etat deviendrait si faible qu'il n'y aurait si petite puissance qui ne pût le conquérir.

Il me serait aisé d'entrer dans un long détail et de te faire voir que les revenus des particuliers cesseraient presque absolument, et, par conséquent, ceux du Prince. Il n'y aurait presque plus de relation de facultés entre les citoyens; on verrait finir cette circulation de richesses et cette progression de revenus qui vient de la dépendance où sont les arts les uns des autres: chaque particulier vivrait de sa terre et n'en retirerait que ce qu'il lui faut précisément pour ne pas mourir de faim. Mais, comme ce n'est pas quelquefois la vingtième partie des revenus d'un état, il faudrait que le nombre des habitants diminuât à proportion, et qu'il n'en restât que la vingtième partie. Fais bien attention jusqu'où vont les revenus de l'industrie. Un fonds ne produit annuellement à son maître que la vingtième partie de sa valeur; mais, avec une pistole de couleur, un peintre fera un tableau qui lui en vaudra cinquante. On en peut dire de même des orfèvres, des ouvriers en laine, en soie, et de toutes sortes d'artisans.

De tout ceci, on doit conclure, Rhedi, que, pour qu'un prince soit puissant, il faut que ses sujets vivent dans les délices; il faut qu'il travaille à leur procurer toutes sortes de superfluités, avec autant d'attention que les nécessités de la vie.

> *Œuvres complètes*, ed. Roger Caillois. Bibliothèque de la Pléiade (Paris, 1956), I, pp. 288–90.

The grave Président de Montesquieu could be as charmless as any twentieth-century economist when he chose. There is, for example, in the *Pensées détachées que je n'ai pas mises dans mes ouvrages*, a singularly unalluring statistical passage comparing the tax revenue and the national debt of England and France in the year 1733.[1] But one of the many luxuries demanded by polite society in the first half of the eighteenth century was the pleasure of intellectual activity without the laborious effort normally considered essential to the pursuit of knowledge. Fontenelle's *Entretiens sur la pluralité des mondes* (1686) had already presented Copernican astronomy and an initiation into scientific principles under the guise of conversation with an attractive young marquise walking by moonlight through the park of her country estate. Sixty-two years later, in *De l'Esprit des lois*, Montesquieu attempted to camouflage his arid researches into the theory of commerce, monetary systems and international trade, by evoking the neo-classic grace and semi-poetic imaginativeness of the rococo quest for enjoyment:

> Vierges du mont Piérie, entendez-vous le nom que je vous donne? Inspirez-moi. Je cours une longue carrière; je suis accablé de tristesse et d'ennui. Mettez dans mon esprit ce charme et cette douceur que je sentais autrefois et qui fuit loin de moi. Vous n'êtes jamais si divines que quand vous menez à la sagesse et à la vérité par le plaisir.
>
> Mais, si vous ne voulez point adoucir la rigueur de mes travaux, cachez le travail même; faites qu'on soit instruit, et que je n'enseigne pas; que je réfléchisse, et que je paraisse sentir; et lorsque j'annoncerai des choses nouvelles, faites qu'on croie que je ne savais rien, et que vous m'avez tout dit. . . .
>
> Divines Muses, je sens que vous m'inspirez, non pas ce qu'on chante à Tempé sur les chalumeaux, ou ce qu'on répète à Délos sur la lyre; vous voulez que je parle à la raison; elle est le plus parfait, le plus noble et le plus exquis de nos sens.[2]

In fact, the Genevan pastor Jacob Vernet, who saw *De l'Esprit des lois* through the press, prevailed on Montesquieu to delete this Invocation to the Muses from Book 20 of the Fourth Part, for which it was intended, and the work appeared without it. A similar awareness of a mid-century trend towards seriousness was manifested by Voltaire in 1752, when Micromégas dismisses Fontenellian preciosity with the tart rebuke 'Je ne veux point qu'on me plaise; je veux qu'on m'instruise'.

In the *Lettres persanes*, however, Montesquieu was so durably successful in capturing the effervescent, frivolous tone of the 1720s, that modern readers frequently fail to notice, in letter CVI, the outlines of an economic theory which by the end of the century had developed into liberal *laissez-faire* doctrine, and still underlies the Western consumer society of our own day.

According to the traditional arguments, summarised by Montesquieu in the previous letter, luxury implied vice, sloth, softness, and the decay of empires. Deliberately avoiding moral objections, Letter CVI applauds the pleasure-loving, luxurious life of rich Parisians. By the use of paradox and antithesis (*plaisirs . . . vie dure*, etc.), and the hypothetical example of a rush order for a social function, the first paragraph conjures up the feverish activity of couturiers, jewellers, embroiderers, coiffeurs and the like, all intent on making money. The neat aphorism 'l'intérêt est le plus grand monarque de la terre' presses home the notion that the motive-force of society is self-interest and the desire for profit, more powerful in their effect than the decrees of the Oriental despots whom the Persian travellers in Paris had tremblingly obeyed. The second paragraph broadens from the specific example to the whole of Paris, from the highest aristocrats to the artisan classes. Christian moralists had denounced covetousness, and, in word at least, proclaimed the message given by St Paul in chapter VI of his First Epistle to Timothy:

> And having food and raiment let us be therewith content. But they that will be rich fall into temptation and a snare, and into many foolish and hurtful lusts, which drown men in destruction and perdition. For the love of money is the root of all evil: which while some coveted after, they have erred from the faith, and pierced themselves through with many sorrows. But thou, O man of God, flee these things.

In order that he should be ever mindful of the Christian attitude to poverty, Montesquieu's parents had chosen a beggar as one of his god-fathers. Here, however, adopting the standpoint of an impartial observer such as a visiting Persian might conceivably be, Montesquieu equates the lust for money with a virtue, hard work, and clinches his point with the witticism about the immensely rich man who shortens his life in order to have the wherewithal to live.

Turning from Paris to the whole of France, Montesquieu now counters the traditional arguments against luxury: far from causing national decadence and military defeat, it promotes a vigorous and healthy economy. ('Industrie' here means manufacturing processes and the 'ensemble des opérations qui concourent à la production et à la circulation des richesses'.) The remainder of the passage attempts to prove that the nation would perish if it permitted only those trades necessary for agriculture – metal-workers, blacksmiths, cutlers, wheelwrights, potters, coopers, tanners, harness-makers, etc. – and abolished 'luxury', that is, banned the making of all products which, though not necessary to sustain life, provide pleasure and satisfaction for the body or the mind, and have come to be regarded as necessities. It is highly improbable that Montesquieu really possessed the statistical details which he says it would have been so easy for him to include. Indeed, since the first editions say *centième partie*, and *vingtième partie* only appeared in the last edition of the *Lettres persanes* prepared by Montesquieu, one suspects that the figure is somewhat arbitrary. The insertion of *quelquefois* further suggests that he is not giving guaranteed information.

What is 'easy' about the paragraph is the way he explains that, if the luxury trades were banished, and landowners produced only enough for their bare subsistence, money would cease to circulate, the national income would drop by 95 per cent, and 95 per cent of the population would disappear. The speed of the argument prevents the reader from asking what authority Montesquieu has for his statements, and the terms *relation de facultés, circulation de richesses, progression de revenus,* provide the pleasurable feeling that one is well versed in technicalities of economics. The three terms mean approximately the same thing: circulation of money; this was considered by economists of the period to be as essential to the body politic as is the circulation of the blood (discovered by William Harvey in the previous century) to the life of the human body. The vision of mass starvation or emigration which would result from the banning of luxury is contrasted with the high profits and prosperity produced by manufacture. Landed property (*un fonds*) brings in only 5 per cent per annum of its purchase value, whereas a painter can make 4,900 per cent profit on a picture for which the raw material, paint, cost him only one *pistole* (10 francs). Similar percentages, Montesquieu suggests, are made by goldsmiths, clothiers, silk-weavers and various other sorts of craftsmen. (There is nothing odd

in the inclusion of painters in this list of artisans: it was not until the
Romantic period that artists claimed the right to be idolised as beings
apart.) Since the reader knows that, in addition to colours, an artist has
to buy canvas, brushes, etc., Montesquieu is again indicating that he does
not intend the sums to be taken literally. In any case, fine ladies and
gentlemen are above such details. Anticipating any incipient tedium, and
at the same time suggesting that his cavalier treatment of the subject
has in fact been a profound discussion, he rounds off his argument with
the balanced and alliterative paradox, so flattering to his rich readers,
that sumptuous pleasures mean national greatness, and that even the
monarch must toil and strive to ensure a plentiful supply of exquisite
frivolities.

The ideas in this letter were not at all new. In the seventeenth century,
libertins had extolled pleasure, and moralists had argued (on a human
level only, of course, and without reference to the workings of divine
grace) that vice and virtue were both inextricably linked with self-
interest, the basis for men's actions. In Saint-Evremond's opinion,
abstinence from pleasure was a great sin, and luxury was socially useful
in circulating money. Bayle maintained that a Christian society,
living frugally in apostolic simplicity, would have no money and no
soldiers: avarice and ambition are good for trade; moderate luxury
provides a livelihood for the lower classes; present prosperity is what
matters, not some alleged process of decadence, and a wicked man may,
in terms of economics, be a good citizen.[3] The scandalous paradox that
'vices' were essential to a thriving economy was given wide European
notoriety by *The Fable of the Bees, or Private Vices, Public Benefits*,
published in 1714 by the London Dutchman Bernard de Mandeville:

> Luxury
> Employed a million of the poor,
> And odious pride a million more.
> Envy itself, and vanity
> Were ministers of industry;
> Their darling folly, fickleness,
> In diet, furniture, and dress,
> That strange, ridiculous vice, was made
> The very wheel that turned the trade.[4]

In 1721, however, such ideas had been given a new significance in
France by the shameless speculation, quick fortunes, and sudden ruin,
associated with the *Système* of John Law, the Scotsman who, with the
Regent's support, established a bank which in 1717 acquired the monopoly of trade with Louisiana, the West Indies and Canada, and in 1719

absorbed the French companies trading with the East Indies, China and Africa. Law took over the royal debt, set about reorganising the collection of taxes, allowed the shares in the Mississippi Company to reach grotesquely inflated prices, became Controller-General of Finances, and went spectacularly bankrupt in October 1720. It was not only the banking and monetary system which collapsed: the scandalous frenzy for easy profits, in which great aristocrats had revealed themselves no better than the shadiest adventurers, made a mockery of the whole social and moral structure on which the monarchy was based. Though the currency fell in value during the years 1717–20, the income from land did not rise. (Montesquieu's estimate of 5 per cent per annum of the purchase price is not far from the figure of 4 per cent arrived at for the year 1726 by the nineteenth-century historian G. d'Avenel.) Industrial enterprises, on the other hand, were doing well. Montesquieu's own financial situation at the time was not of the healthiest since, apart from his *charge* in the Bordeaux Parlement, his income was derived largely from his vineyards.[5]

There were, then, personal financial reasons why the land-owning nobleman Montesquieu might question the desirability of a commercial, industrial economy such as he had so enthusiastically outlined in letter CVI. He also had moral and political grounds for doubting whether unbridled self-interest was, in fact, so conducive to national prosperity. Letters XII and XIII, on the Troglodytes, are, in part, a literary exercise on the theme of the Golden Age which, from classical antiquity onwards, had haunted the minds of successive generations; but it is partly, also, in disgust at the France of 1720 that Montesquieu escapes into this imaginary idyllic community of shepherds and husbandmen living in virtuous frugality, free from the evils of ambition, cupidity, riches and soft living. His moral fervour, so absent from letter CVI, inspires the sombre eloquence of letter CXLVI, which consists of noble and sustained invective against John Law and the speculators who have brought such vileness and degradation to France. Cruel, fraudulent profiteers, brazenly disregarding all standards of humanity, have reduced their fellow-men to despair, ruination and the grave:

> J'y ai vu une nation, naturellement généreuse, pervertie en un instant, depuis le dernier des sujets jusqu'aux plus grands, par le mauvais exemple d'un ministre. . . . J'ai vu naître soudain, dans tous les cœurs, une soif insatiable des richesses. J'ai vu se former en un moment une détestable conjuration de s'enrichir, non par un honnête travail et une généreuse industrie, mais par la ruine du Prince, de l'Etat et des

concitoyens. . . . Quel plus grand crime que celui que commet un ministre lorsqu'il corrompt les mœurs de toute une nation, dégrade les âmes les plus généreuses, ternit l'éclat des dignités, obscurcit la vertu même, et confond la plus haute naissance dans le mépris universel?

In this passage there is already a hint of the distinction, which later eighteenth-century writers were to make, between the 'bad' and sterile luxury upon which the ill-gotten gains of financiers and courtiers were squandered, and the 'good' luxury which resulted from the productive hard work of thrifty, honest citizens.

For the remainder of his life, after the *Lettres persanes*, Montesquieu continued to occupy himself with the debate on luxury, never coming to a definitive conclusion. He continually oscillates between praise of trade, commerce, industry, and condemnation of the evils which, he believes, are implicit in a self-seeking society where the ancient ideals of the landed nobility no longer command respect. His bland assurance, in letter CVI, that hard work produces affluence for all, is countered, in the *Pensées*, with a reflection that the common people are so ground down by excessive taxes that they lack the opportunity to become rich.[6] Virtuous frugality and rural simplicity, so remote from the luxurious civilisation of Paris, continue to attract him, and he holds up as models of happiness the communism of Plato's Republic, of Sparta, and of the Jesuit state in Paraguay.[7] Then, turning from Utopia to his own country, he argues that in France 'luxury' is necessary: it is essential for the rich to spend money on superfluities in order that the poor may live; all classes will thereby benefit, and even the yeoman will have an opportunity to enjoy more than the barest necessities of life.[8] Dubious none the less about the idle frivolity of the French upper classes, he contrasts them with a free, proud, independent, prosperous, well-governed island people, who, less conscious than the French of the difference between lords and commoners, have an altogether more serious attitude to the possession and spending of money. Here is part of Montesquieu's eulogy of England, which (as he himself does not live in a land of liberty and a free Press), he does not name, and speaks of only in the conditional tense:

> On n'y estimerait guère les hommes par des talents ou des attributs frivoles, mais par des qualités réelles; et de ce genre il n'y en a que deux: les richesses et le mérite personnel.
> Il y aurait un luxe solide, fondé, non sur le raffinement de la vanité, mais sur des besoins réels; et l'on ne chercherait guère dans les choses que les plaisirs que la nature y a mis.
> On y jouirait d'un grand superflu, et cependant les choses frivoles y seraient proscrites . . .

Comme on serait toujours occupé de ses intérêts, on n'aurait point cette politesse qui est fondée sur l'oisiveté; et réellement on n'en aurait pas le temps.[9]

Nevertheless, in spite of his admiration for the middle-class, commercial achievements of England, he regards the commercial spirit as degrading and corrupting:

Le cœur des habitants des pays qui vivent de commerce est entièrement corrompu: ils ne vous rendront pas le moindre service, parce qu'ils espèrent qu'on le leur achètera.[10]

Half a century before Edmund Burke's lament that 'the age of chivalry is gone, that of sophisters, economists and calculators has succeeded, and the glory of Europe is extinguished for ever', Montesquieu was reluctantly but realistically adjusting himself to the fact that the traditional ideals of the French aristocracy no longer had much significance in the reign of Louis XV:

Il y a apparence que ce qu'on appelle valeur héroïque va se perdre en Europe. . . . Cet esprit de gloire et de valeur se perd peu à peu parmi nous. La philosophie a gagné du terrain. Les idées anciennes d'héroïsme et les nouvelles de chevalerie se sont perdues. . . . La philosophie et j'ose dire un certain bon sens ont gagné trop de terrain dans ce siècle-ci pour que l'héroïsme y fasse désormais une grande fortune; . . . Chaque siècle a son génie particulier . . .; et c'est l'esprit de commerce qui domine aujourd'hui. Cet esprit de commerce fait qu'on calcule tout. Mais la gloire, quand elle est toute seule, n'entre que dans les calculs des sots.[11]

On the problem of luxury, as on most other topics, Montesquieu sets the tone for the age. His arguments for and against commerce are taken up and expanded, over and over again, by the many writers who, in the second half of the century, carried on the discussion without ever producing conclusive arguments on one side or the other. A comprehensive analysis of the debate on luxury could only be produced after years of work by an economic historian who was also a sociologist and a literary critic. Certain things are, however, reasonably clear. One of these is that, though the men of letters engaged in the controversy were themselves often confused or self-contradictory about the issues they discussed, and tended to see them in terms of Sparta, Ancient Rome or primitive societies, their arguments were not, on the whole, moral abstractions only, but reactions to contemporary social and economic realities. French overseas trade quadrupled between 1715 and 1789. During the same period, the population increased from sixteen or seventeen million to about twenty-six million: yet, though the urban population expanded, at the end of the Ancien Régime all but approximately two million Frenchmen still lived in the country or in small country towns. In spite of periodic famines and price fluctuations, the years 1730 to 1778 were a time of agricultural prosperity and an upward trend in the price of corn, with the result that, for nobles and bourgeois alike, land was an attractive form of investment. Yet the poor peasants remained, on the whole, poor: the surplus profits from agriculture went, largely, to the landowners and rich bourgeoisie, and it was to satisfy their requirements that the whole economy was geared. The mark of the privileged classes was to 'live nobly', that is, to live in magnificently furnished houses, to provide custom for artists and the manufacturers of such luxuries as silk, porcelain, silverware and mirrors, and to be the main consumers of the luxury colonial imports which (combined with the slave-trade), brought prosperity to the ship-owners and merchants of towns like Bordeaux. By nineteenth-century standards, the economy was backward and primitive. France was still essentially an agricultural nation, big factories had hardly begun to exist, and industrial capitalism was found only in an embryonic form.[12]

Various writers attacked luxury with widely different intentions. Sometimes the attacks expressed the purely negative animosity felt by bourgeois or the poorer nobility against rich parvenus or the court; sometimes they were voiced by the self-assertive and morally self-righteous middle class, critical of the allegedly dissolute, spendthrift aristocracy, and anxious to accumulate capital and to reform the national economy; elsewhere the anti-luxury arguments reflected the desire of enlightened and progressive landowners to improve their estates instead of frittering away money on sterile pomp.

Jean-Jacques Rousseau's early pronouncements on the subject, in his *Epître à M. Bordes* written about 1741, were in favour of the luxury industries. As a 'fier républicain que blesse l'arrogance', he began this Epistle by evoking the frugality and happy simplicity of ancient times, but then, dismissing such opinions as empty rhetoric, went on to praise the city of Lyons and its

> innocente industrie
> Qui sait multiplier les douceurs de la vie,
> Et, salutaire à tous dans ses utiles soins,
> Par la route du luxe apaise les besoins.
> C'est par cet art charmant que sans cesse enrichie
> On voit briller au loin ton heureuse patrie [13]

Rousseau had already left Lyons when, in 1744, the silk workers who had come out on strike had to be persuaded to resume the charming art of their innocent industry by the forces of law and order, which tortured the strike leaders, then executed them or gave them life sentences in the galleys. His conversion to anti-luxury opinions may have owed something to the influence of his friend the abbé G. B. de Mably, brother of J. B. de Mably who was provost marshal at Lyons and Rousseau's employer there from 1740 to 1741. In his *Parallèle des Romains et des Français* of 1740, the abbé de Mably had been in favour of riches, abundance, arts and industry. In his *Observations sur l'histoire de la Grèce*, however, published in 1749, Mably eulogises Sparta, where, he argues, Lycurgus had banned everything not necessary to subsistence, abolished gold and silver money, instituted communal feeding and education, and rid his country of depravity, corruption, civil inequality, tyranny, avarice and wars of conquest. Montesquieu's arguments against luxury in his *Considérations sur les causes de la grandeur des Romains et de leur décadence*, and in the parts of *De l'Esprit des lois* devoted to democracies, were, doubtless, one of Mably's sources, and Rousseau's. Mably, like Rousseau, was temperamentally averse to compliance with the accepted standards of polite society. But there were wider reasons why, around 1750, anti-luxury opinions were in vogue. Though less disastrous than the wars of Louis XIV, the costly War of the Austrian Succession ended in 1748 without advantage to France; the attempted reform of the tax system in 1749, and the imposition of the *vingtième*, a tax on all incomes without exception, was bitterly opposed by the nobility, the Church, and the court *dévot* party centred round the Queen; meanwhile, Mme de Pompadour, official mistress of Louis XV since 1745, was evoking widespread dissatisfaction by her profuse expenditure on buildings, fêtes, ornamentation, works of art and luxuries of all kinds.

It was against this background that the Academy of Dijon in 1750 awarded its prize to Rousseau, and the *proxime accessit* to an essay by Grosley which was also opposed to luxury. In his *Discours sur les Sciences et les Arts*, Rousseau invokes the authority of Ancient Greece and Rome to support his pleas for frugality and austerity. He has also read modern economists, and been shocked by what he has found:

Je sais que notre philosophie, toujours féconde en maximes singulières, prétend, contre l'expérience de tous les siècles, que le luxe fait la splendeur des états; mais après avoir oublié la nécessité des lois somptuaires, osera-t-elle nier encore que les bonnes mœurs ne soient essentielles à la durée des empires, et que le luxe ne soit diamétralement opposé aux bonnes mœurs? Que le luxe soit un signe certain de richesses; qu'il serve même si l'on veut à les multiplier: Que faudra-t-il conclure de ce paradoxe si digne d'être né de nos jours; et que deviendra la vertu, quand il faudra s'enrichir à quelque prix que ce soit? Les anciens politiques parlaient sans cesse de mœurs et de vertu; les nôtres ne parlent que de commerce et d'argent. ... Ils évaluent les hommes comme des troupeaux de bétail. Selon eux, un homme ne vaut à l'état que la consommation qu'il y fait.[14]

With the economic system, Rousseau rejected eighteenth-century French civilisation as a whole; its wit, elegance, *politesse* and charm now seemed a vicious fake, hateful to him in his quest for sincerity and truth:

Aujourd'hui que des recherches plus subtiles et un goût plus fin ont réduit l'art de plaire en principes, il règne dans les mœurs une vile et trompeuse uniformité. ... Les soupçons, les ombrages, les craintes, la froideur, la réserve, la haine, la trahison se cacheront sans cesse sous ce voile uniforme et perfide de politesse, sous cette urbanité si vantée que nous devons aux lumières de notre siècle.

The Dijon Academy declined in 1754 to award a prize to Rousseau's second *Discours*, where he denounces even more vehemently the hypocritical wickedness of a society based on competition and self-interest:

Etre et paraître devinrent deux choses tout à fait différentes, et de cette distinction sortirent le faste imposant, la ruse trompeuse, et tous les vices qui en sont le cortège. ... Enfin, l'ambition dévorante, l'ardeur d'élever sa fortune relative, moins par un véritable besoin que pour se mettre au-dessus des autres, inspire à tous les hommes un noir penchant à se nuire mutuellement, une jalousie secrète d'autant plus dangereuse que, pour faire son coup plus en sûreté, elle prend souvent le masque de la bienveillance: en un mot, concurrence et rivalité d'une part, de l'autre opposition des intérêts, et toujours le désir caché de faire son profit aux dépens d'autrui.[15]

Rousseau's rancour and intensity are his own; but by attacking vice and luxury he was following a dominant trend of the time. In 1736 Voltaire's *Le Mondain* had caused a scandal by contrasting the squalid amours of Adam and Eve in Eden with the refined delights available to rich men in the real earthly paradise, Paris.[16] There are no grounds for thinking that Voltaire ever abandoned this view. In 1745, however, in Part VII of his *Discours sur l'homme*,[17] he acknowledges that nowadays

Le nom de la vertu retentit sur la terre;
On l'entend au théâtre, au barreau, dans la chaire,

and concludes his poem with a eulogy, not of luxury and riches, but of philanthropy – *bienfaisance*, that eighteenth-century substitute for Christian ethics – which could be practised so much more efficaciously by the rich than by the poor. Mandeville's cynical association of vice with trade had become out of date; progressive writers could now not only foster virtue by castigating the sterile luxury of the vicious and parasitic rich, but could sanctify wealth by advocating uses of it which were morally as well as economically beneficial.

For Diderot, the luxury displayed by nobles and *fermiers-généraux* is in every respect pernicious. Its degrading effect on the art of the nation is exemplified by Boucher, who paints 'indecencies for a noble's dressing-room', prostituting his talent to titillate the depraved taste of bored voluptuaries:

> Je ne sais que dire de cet homme-là. La dégradation du goût, de la composition, des caractères, de l'expression, du dessin, a suivi pas à pas la dépravation des mœurs. . . . Je n'ose dire que cet homme ne sait vraiment ce que c'est que la grâce; j'ose dire qu'il n'a jamais connu la vérité; j'ose dire que les idées de délicatesse, d'honnêteté, d'innocence, de simplicité, lui sont devenues presque étrangères; j'ose dire qu'il n'a pas vu un instant la nature. . . . Eh bien, mon ami, c'est au moment où Boucher cesse d'être un artiste, qu'il est nommé premier peintre du roi.[18]

To counter such upper-class wickedness, Diderot advocates the senti-mental moral attitudinizing of the painter Greuze, and its theatrical counterpart, the *drame bourgeois*; then, realising the hollowness of both these forms, takes as model the austere republican virtue of classical antiquity, so pointing the way to David and the heroic period of the French Revolution. Diderot's social and economic views are a compen-dium of mid-century reformist ideas, about which, in his capacity as editor of the *Encyclopédie*, it was his duty to be informed. Luxury is only pernicious, his argument went, if it is the prerogative of a minority battening on the wealth of the nation. If, however, the surplus wealth from agriculture were used to provide solid comforts and enjoyments for a wider section of the nation, such 'luxury' would betoken public happiness and prosperity. In order to achieve this eminently desirable 'good luxury', Diderot propounds a whole plan of liberal reform: the encouragement and improvement of agriculture, recognised as the primary source of national wealth; economies in wasteful expenditure by the Court; a check on the accumulation of wealth by the Church; fair assessment of taxes according to wealth, the abolition of exemptions

E

for the privileged, and the suppression of the system whereby the *fermiers-généraux* acquired immense riches at the expense of the nation; entry into offices of state by merit and competition, not purchase or privilege; freedom of speech and of the Press; the abolition of the guilds and other restrictions on free enterprise; free internal and foreign trade, subject to government supervision, so that prices could find a natural level. In spite of his detestation of upper-class vice, the jovial Diderot did not favour puritanical dourness. Like Montesquieu in the *Lettres persanes*, he too thought that the monarch should procure pleasures for his people, but insisted that they should be more equitably distributed:

> Mais lorsque le talent et la vertu mèneront à quelque chose, lorsque la nation entière aura toute l'aisance que chaque condition comporte, lorsqu'il n'y aura d'inégalité entre les fortunes que celle que l'industrie et le bonheur doivent y mettre, lorsque j'aurai anéanti toutes ces corporations où l'on ne peut entrer sans argent, et qu'on doit regarder comme autant de privilèges exclusifs qui condamnent des milliers de citoyens industrieux à mourir de faim ou à entrer dans une prison; lorsque j'aurai encouragé l'agriculture, la mère nourrice de tout un empire; lorsque j'aurai des citoyens riches, que feront ces citoyens de leur or? L'or ne se mange pas. Ils l'emploieront à multiplier leurs jouissances. Et quelles sont ces jouissances? Celles de tous les sens. J'aurais donc des poètes, des philosophes, des peintres, des statuaires, des magots de la Chine, en un mot tout le produit d'un autre luxe, tous ces vices charmants qui font le bonheur de l'homme dans ce monde-ci et sa damnation éternelle dans l'autre. . . . Mais je m'épargnerai, du moins, tous ceux d'entre ces vices que la misère, le goût du faste et l'indigence produisent. Cela deviendra ce que cela pourra. Je ne me mêlerais que de faire durer l'aisance et le bonheur, quelles qu'en puissent être les suites.[19]

Much the same programme, but with a great emphasis on the bourgeois virtues of thrift, temperance and the productive use of capital, was put forward by Diderot's rich friend the baron d'Holbach. Aggressively and consciously middle class, d'Holbach saw the accession of Louis XVI in 1774, and the appointment of the philosophe Turgot to the post of Contrôleur-Général, as the beginning of a liberal era. In his *Ethocratie, ou le Gouvernement fondé sur la morale*, d'Holbach appeals to the young king to abolish extravagance and unjust privileges. Idlers are dangerous, vicious and perverse; the nobles, 'cette troupe oisive et corrompue qui demande des plaisirs continuels' and who glory in their barbaric and Gothic ignorance, should take up useful activities, such as the improvement of their agricultural estates. For though commerce is important, 'the soil is the basis of national felicity', and agriculture must take precedence over manufacture and trade. Where the commercial spirit reigns supreme, freedom, morals and happiness are in danger; thus, England is 'the abode of corruption, discord, venality, melancholy, boredom'. *La Morale universelle, ou les Devoirs de l'homme fondés sur la nature*, also of 1776, similarly denounces England for its exclusive concern with money, but the book also holds that the desire for riches and material well-being is a source of national prosperity. Though vain ostentation and spendthrift lavishness are bad, a seemly outlay on luxury is proper for those who can afford it. Thus, rich men are foolish if they emulate the magnificence of monarchs, but are entitled to fine houses and furniture, carriages, servants, good food and the like, if they can safely afford such things. What is necessary expenditure for the rich is reprehensible extravagance for the poor. Drunkenness and debauch are especially wicked when indulged in by those of small means, and the poor, for whom thrift must be a major virtue, should abstain from such luxuries as tobacco and theatre-going. As for the rich and great – let them be citizens instead of sybarites; instead of spending money on parks and hunting-forests, which remove land from cultivation, they should help the industrious and respectable poor by putting more land under tillage, draining marshes, or constructing canals for the expeditious transport of merchandise. Idleness makes bad citizens, hard work good and virtuous ones: 'La vraie philosophie doit toujours annoncer des mœurs innocentes et sévères; grave, sans être ni triste ni farouche, elle ne doit jamais se prêter aux dérèglements des hommes'.[20] D'Holbach's education, title and fortune had been provided for him by his uncle, a minor German tax-official who had made a fortune in Paris at the time of the John Law scandals.[21] But d'Holbach in 1776 is far removed from the frivolous world of the *Lettres persanes*.

D'Holbach inclines, on the whole, to the Physiocratic doctrine with its emphasis on agriculture as the main source of French prosperity.[22] For an apotheosis of commerce, we must turn to the *Histoire philosophique et politique des établissements et du commerce des Européens dans les deux Indes*, a curious hotch-potch of anticlerical and liberal propaganda published under the name of the abbé Raynal, but in which Diderot and others had a hand. Wickedness, tyranny and oppression, this book appears to suggest, are the product of illiberal commercial systems, which must and will be abolished. Thus, it urges the people of India to revolt against the British East India Company:

Non, non; il faut que tôt ou tard justice soit faite. S'il en arrivait autrement, je m'adresserais à la populace; je lui dirais: Peuples, dont les rugissements ont fait trembler tant de fois vos maîtres, qu'attendez-vous? Pour quel moment réservez-vous vos flambeaux et les pierres qui pavent vos rues? Arrachez-les.

Monopoly is destructive and wasteful, but in a free economy the profit motive is the spur to endeavour and progress:

Désir de jouir, liberté de jouir, il n'y a que ces deux ressorts d'activité, que ces deux principes de sociabilité parmi les hommes.

When it is unhampered and unshackled, as Nature intended it to be, commerce will bring liberty, prosperity, virtue and happiness to the whole earth:

La société universelle existe pour l'intérêt commun et par l'intérêt réciproque de tous les hommes qui la composent. De leur communication, il doit résulter une augmentation de félicité. Le commerce est l'exercice de cette précieuse liberté, à laquelle la nature a appelé tous les hommes, a attaché leur bonheur, et même leurs vertus. Disons plus, nous ne les voyons libres que dans le commerce; ils ne le deviennent que par les lois qui favorisent réellement le commerce; et ce qu'il y a d'heureux en cela, c'est qu'en même temps qu'il est le produit de la liberté, il sert à la maintenir.

Thus, far from being the root of all evil, love of money becomes a means of human regeneration. In a hymn of praise to commerce, 'the motive force of the world', the *Histoire philosophique* looks to a future when the whole globe is opened up to free enterprise, and when human wickedness, which from the days of Noah has brought destruction upon the earth, will give place to the felicities of economic and commercial expansion, in conformity with God's purposes for mankind:

ouvrir, en un mot, toutes les sources de la population et de la volupté pour les verser par mille canaux sur la face du monde. C'est alors peut-être que la Divinité contemple avec plaisir son ouvrage et ne se repent pas d'avoir fait l'homme.[23]

The economic ideas of the philosophe party in the final years of the century are recorded in their review *La Décade philosophique, littéraire et politique*, which appeared three times a month from 29 April 1794, until 21 September 1807, when Napoleon suppressed it. Written for the professional, administrative and commercial middle class ('Equality, Liberty, Property' was the motto it proposed for France in its number of 11 December 1799), *La Décade* attacked wasteful, unproductive extravagance, and campaigned for free enterprise, competition, thrift, the ideas of Adam Smith, and the application of science to technological progress. Its chief spokesman on economic matters, J.-B. Say, echoed Rousseau in his condemnation of 'luxury':

> Un des principes les plus faux en économie politique . . . est celle qui prétend qu'un homme est utile à l'état en proportion de ce qu'il consomme. . . . Le luxe et la misère marchent toujours ensemble.[24]

But by precept and example, Say pointed the way to nineteenth-century industrialism. In 1803 he published his *Traité d'économie politique*; in 1806, he established a cotton-mill, with two hundred employees, in a former convent at Auchy, in the Pas-de-Calais.[25] These latter-day philosophes were uneasily aware that the overthrow of king and nobles had not yet solved the problems of inequality, and that the suppression of Babeuf's communist plot in 1797 had not permanently removed the danger of proletarian revolt.[26] What more immediately threatened them, however, in the early years of the nineteenth century, was counter-revolution by the former privileged classes of the Ancien Régime, anxious to recover their property and power, and to dispossess the republican purchasers of the Church estates. It was in the hope of setting up a romantic, mock-medieval kingdom, where nobles and Church were dominant, the peasants attached like serfs to the soil, and the bourgeois debarred from high office, that the vicomte de Bonald, also echoing Rousseau's fulminations against luxury, denounced the liberal school of economics, and proclaimed that the concentration of power in the hands of the commercial classes meant the decay of morals and the end of Christian civilisation.[27]

NOTES

1 *Œuvres complètes*, Pléiade, I, pp. 1512–13. *Pensées*, 2027/259.

2 Ibid., II, pp. 584–5.

3 A. Morize, *L'Apologie du luxe au XVIIIᵉ siècle et 'Le Mondain' de Voltaire* (Paris, 1909), pp. 34–65; R. Shackleton, *Les Lumières et l'action politique en Angleterre (Utopie et institutions au XVIIIᵉ siècle*, ed. P. Francastel, Paris, La Haye, 1963), pp. 79–80.

4 Ed. F. B. Kaye (Oxford, 1924), I, p. 25.

5 R. Shackleton, *Montesquieu. A Critical Biography* (Oxford, 1961), pp. 81, 200–8.

6 *Œuvres*, ed. cit., I, p. 1512. *Pensées*, 2025/1640.

7 Ibid., II, p. 269, *De l'Esprit des lois*, IV, 6.

8 Ibid., p. 336. VII, 4.

9 Ibid., p. 581. XIX, 27.
10 Ibid., I, p. 864. *Voyages. Hollande.*
11 Ibid., I, pp. 1305–7. *Pensées*, 1226–8/760–1, 810.
12 A. Cobban, *A History of Modern France* (London, 1961), vol. I, pp. 36–59; H. Lüthy, *La Banque protestante en France de la Révocation de l'Edit de Nantes à la Révolution* (vol. II, Paris, 1961), pp. 20–30, 737; J. Ehrard, *L'Idée de nature en France dans la première moitié du XVIIIe siècle* (Paris, 1963), pp. 575–606; G. V. Taylor, *Types of Capitalism in Eighteenth-century France* (*English Historical Review*, vol. 79, 1964), pp. 478–97. Some of the main findings of E. Labrousse (*Esquisse du mouvement des prix et des revenus au XVIIIe siècle*, Paris, 1932) are summarised by J. Lough, *An Introduction to Eighteenth-Century France* (London, 1960), pp. 8–11, 28, 65–7.
13 *Œuvres*, Pléiade, ed. B. Gagnebin et R. Raymond, vol. II, pp. 1130–3.
14 Ed. G. R. Havens (New York, 1946), pp. 134–5. The economists to whom Rousseau here refers are Sir William Petty, *An Essay in Political Arithmetick*, of which a French translation appeared in London in 1686, and J.-F. Melon, *Essai politique sur le commerce* (Nouvelle édition augmentée, s.l., 1736).
15 Ed. Vaughan, J.-J. Rousseau, *Political Writings* (Oxford, 1962), I, pp. 178–9.
16 *Mélanges*, Pléiade, pp. 203–6. The first edition of *Le Mondain* ended with the line: 'Le Paradis terrestre est à Paris'.
17 Ibid., pp. 236–9.
18 Diderot, *Les Salons* (Salon de 1765), ed. R. Desné (Paris, 1955), pp. 86–7; J. Seznec et J. Adhémar (Oxford, 1960), pp. 75–6.
19 *Mémoires pour Catherine II*, ed. P. Vernière (Paris, 1966), pp. 145–60. See also J. Proust, *Diderot et l'Encyclopédie* (Paris, 1962), pp. 453–91, and J. Seznec, *Diderot: Sur l'art et les artistes* (Paris, 1967), pp. 73–83, 191–4.
20 *Ethocratie, ou Le Gouvernement fondé sur la morale* (Amsterdam, 1776; Milan, 1967), pp. 51–4, 123, 144, 149, 253, 266–7, 275; *La Morale universelle* (Paris, L'An IV de la République française), vol. I, pp. xxvi–vii, 35, 104–5, 110, 143; vol. II, pp. 44, 103, 108, 174–8, 256, 180–93, 266–8; vol. III, pp. 116, 247; selections from d'Holbach in R. Desné, *Les Matérialistes français de 1750 à 1800* (Paris, 1965). On the unfavourable impressions d'Holbach formed of England during his visit there in 1765, see Diderot, *Lettres à Sophie Volland*, ed. A. Babelon (Paris, 1938), vol. II, pp. 72–6, 83–5.
21 Lüthy, op. cit., vol. I, pp. 338–42.
22 For a brief summary of the ideas of the physiocrats, see Cobban, op. cit., pp. 88, 100. The standard work on them is by G. Weulersse, *Le Mouvement physiocratique en France de 1756 à 1770* (Paris, 1910); *La Physiocratie à la fin du règne de Louis XV* (Paris, 1959). The word physiocracy means government by nature.
23 Raynal, *Histoire philosophique* . . ., Paris, A. Costes & Cie., 1820, Bk III, Ch. LXIX, pp. 381–2; Bk V, Ch. XXIV, pp. 156–9; Bk XIX, Ch. VI, p. 232. It was first published in 1772.
24 J.-B. Say, *Olbie, ou Essai sur les moyens de réformer les mœurs d'une nation* (Paris, An VIII), note V, pp. 123–4.

25 Say's descendants founded the well-known firm of sugar refiners. But the
    most famous of the capitalists who wrote for *La Décade* is P.-S. Dupont
    (known as Dupont de Nemours because he represented Nemours at the
    Estates General). He emigrated to the U.S.A. in 1799, returned to Paris in
    1802, became President of the Paris Chamber of Commerce, and went back
    to America in 1815. Meanwhile, in 1802, his son Eleuthère-Désiré Dupont
    established a gunpowder factory, Eleutherian Mills, near Wilmington,
    Delaware, from which developed the great chemical firm of Du Pont.
    'Eleutherian' was one of the titles of Zeus, in his capacity as protector of
    political liberty.

26 E. g. *La Décade*, An XII, 10 Frimaire (December 1803), p. 398, says that the
    continual war between rich and poor will lead to an upheaval, unless there
    are speedy efforts to 'favoriser partout, sans violence, une plus égale répar-
    tition des biens de la nature et des jouissances de la société.'

27 Bonald, *Considérations politiques sur l'argent*, an article published in the
    Mercure de France in September 1806, and reprinted in Bonald, *Mélanges
    littéraires, politiques et philosophiques* (Paris, 1819), vol. I, pp. 212–247.

IV · Prévost (1697-1763)

FROM *Cleveland* (Vols. I–IV, published 1731)

Ils étaient tous dans cette religieuse disposition, lorsqu'ils se rendirent l'après-midi à l'assemblée. J'y fus charmé de leur zèle jusqu'à verser des larmes de joie. Fanny et Madame Riding, qui voulurent être témoins de ce pieux spectacle, en furent aussi attendries que moi. Ils écoutèrent mes discours avec une respectueuse attention. Je leur proposai le plan que j'avais formé, je réglai le temps et l'ordre des assemblées; je leur découvris avec les plus vives expressions, et sous les plus fortes images, la grandeur du Maître qu'ils allaient servir, ce qu'ils devaient attendre de sa bonté s'ils le servaient fidèlement, et de sa colère s'ils oubliaient jamais les engagements qu'ils allaient prendre. Malgré leur grossièreté, je leur fis comprendre, qu'indépendamment des plaisirs et des récompenses que je promettais après la vie à leur fidélité, la religion qu'ils embrassaient serait d'un extrême avantage pour le bien de la nation et pour le soutien des lois que j'avais établies; qu'après l'obligation d'honorer le Dieu tout-puissant, elle ne leur en imposait point d'autre que celles que je leur avais déjà prescrites; c'est-à-dire, de s'aimer les uns les autres, et de contribuer de tout leur pouvoir au bien public et particulier. Je les exhortai surtout à la reconnaissance pour les faveurs continuelles qu'ils recevaient du Souverain Etre. C'est lui, leur dis-je, qui vous a donné la naissance, qui vous conserve, qui vous fournit libéralement tout ce qui vous plaît et qui vous est utile. Ne sentez-vous pas qu'il faut aimer celui qui vous comble ainsi de ses bienfaits? O bons Abaquis! la nature vous a donné un cœur, apprenez à en faire usage; et si vous êtes sensibles à quelque chose, soyez-le à ses faveurs que vous éprouvez continuellement.

Ce bon peuple était dans un silence qui exprimait son consentement et son admiration. Je remarquai que la plupart tournaient leurs yeux vers le Ciel, lorsqu'ils m'entendaient prononcer le nom de Dieu, comme s'ils eussent cherché à le voir dans le lieu où je leur avais dit qu'il faisait son séjour, et qu'il était sur son trône à les observer et à juger de la sincérité de leur hommage. Enfin je renouvelai leur attention, en leur parlant de la prière que j'avais composée pour eux, et les ayant exhortés à me suivre de cœur, je la prononçai à haute voix, les yeux et les bras levés. Ils imitèrent tous ma posture. Je dois le confesser, un sentiment de joie délicieuse se répandit dans mon âme, en finissant le dernier acte de cette auguste cérémonie. Peut-être le Ciel ne reçut-il jamais d'hommage plus sincère que celui qui lui était rendu dans ce moment par des cœurs simples où régnait la droiture et l'innocence; et j'ai toujours regardé comme une des plus glorieuses et des plus fortunées circonstances de ma vie, la part que je puis m'attribuer à ce grand changement.

> Le Philosophe Anglais, ou Histoire de Monsieur Cleveland, Fils Naturel de Cromwell, écrite par lui-même. Traduite de l'anglais. A Amsterdam et à Leipzig. Chez Arkstée et Merkus. MDCCXLIV. Tome Troisième. Livre 4e, pp. 226–9

To escape death at the hands of his cruel father Oliver Cromwell, Cleveland takes up residence while still a boy in the caverns of Rumney Hole, in Devonshire. There he meets Viscount Axminster, also a fugitive from the tyrant, and falls in love with Axminster's daughter Fanny. All three, together with Mrs Riding, a lady from the vicinity, set sail from Topsham to join the exiled King Charles II in France. Axminster and his party eventually go to America to rally support for the King, but by one of those malevolent blows of fate which unremittingly assail him, Cleveland is prevented from accompanying them. After numerous adventures and misfortunes, including a sojourn in a communist Huguenot colony near St Helena, he eventually finds them, naked except for grass skirts, prisoners of the Abaqui tribe somewhere in the region of the Appalachians. Axminster gives his daughter Fanny in marriage to Cleveland, according to the rites of Nature and the Abaqui sun-cult, then goes off in search of civilisation, leaving his squire Mr Youngster with Mr and Mrs Cleveland and Mrs Riding. Cleveland becomes ruler over the six thousand Abaquis, who have sworn allegiance to him by the sun, and with Mr Youngster he drills them into an army which may be of use to King Charles. Meanwhile, he plans to give them a better religion, and wonders 'par quel stratagème nous pourrions en imposer à ce peuple crédule et grossier'. The miracle is forthcoming. Mooi, a leading Savage with an affection for Fanny, has been insulted by Mr Youngster, and plots revolt, his oath of allegiance notwithstanding. Cleveland announces to the tribe that Heaven will strike the perjurer dead. Mr Youngster lets an explosive booby-trap down Mooi's chimney (Prévost is bad on Indian local colour); Mooi is killed; the tribe accepts the new religion. This teaches that there is one God, whose throne is above the clouds, who is visible in the wonders and gifts of nature, and who rewards and punishes human deeds. The liturgy consists of one short prayer, to be said daily by both sexes at home, and by heads of families in rotation at compulsory public worship in a field every third day. There are no mysterious ceremonies, since these degenerate into superstition and idolatry, and no temples, since these produce 'un redoublement d'ignorance et de ténèbres'.

Cleveland apologises to his readers for his pious deceit:

> Peut-être trouvera-t-on quelque chose d'irrégulier, ou du moins de trop humain dans les moyens que j'employai: mais je crois ma conduite justifiée par mes intentions, surtout à l'égard d'un peuple grossier qui ne pouvait être ébranlé d'une autre manière.[1]

It is conceivable that Prévost introduces Mooi's murder as a satire on the supernatural origins claimed by Judaism, Christianity and Mohammedanism. Those of his readers in the 1730s who were familiar with clandestine philosophe literature would doubtless so have interpreted it.[2] But, in the context of the novel, such an interpretation would probably be wrong. Cleveland's scorn for the benighted savages whom he plans to use against the Cromwellian forces does not in the least prevent him from believing that he is doing God's will in the best interests of the savages themselves:

> La vérité de ma réponse, le ton peut-être dont je la prononçai, ou plutôt la bonté infinie de Dieu qui voulait tirer ces pauvres Sauvages de leur aveuglement, leur dessilla si entièrement les yeux, qu'ils me parurent transportés de joie de se trouver tout à coup au milieu de la lumière.[3]

It would be anachronistic to turn Cleveland's murderous and hypocritical deceit into an attack by Prévost on English colonialism. Throughout the book, Cleveland indulges in 'innocent stratagems' which reflect the tortuousness and dishonesty of Prévost himself. This lack of straightforwardness may be the result of Prévost's false position as a runaway priest and monk, who had posed as a protestant layman, been thwarted in his attempt to marry an English heiress, and then lived in concubinage with a Dutchwoman.[4] Whatever the reason, his novels are full of moral and intellectual ambiguity.[5]

Ils in the first sentence refers to the Abaqui chiefs who, convinced by Cleveland's exposition of the new religion, are now gathered together in a field with the people for the inaugural ceremony. The submissiveness of 'ce bon peuple' to Cleveland is emphasised throughout the passage ('respectueuse attention', 'son consentement et son admiration', etc.), just as the series of verbs ('je proposai', 'je réglai', etc.) conveys his masterfulness. The Abaquis may possess 'droiture' and 'innocence', but they are not presented as Noble Savages whom Europeans should take as a model; Cleveland and the two ladies have already tried to educate them in matters of sexual modesty, conjugal fidelity, duty towards children:

> Nous prenions toutes nos mesures de concert et avec délibération, et le but commun de nos soins était de délivrer les Abaquis de tout ce qui les avait ravalés jusqu'alors au-dessous de la qualité d'Hommes.[6]

The ideal stage of human development, according to this part of *Cleveland*, is midway between savagery and European civilisation, which is corrupted by softness, luxury, ambition and avarice. Some nations, Cleveland asserts,

> sont en quelque sorte au-delà de leur condition naturelle, et les autres sont au-dessous; et les Européens et les Américains [i.e. the Indians] sont ainsi de vrais barbares, par rapport au point dans lequel ils devraient se ressembler pour être véritablement hommes.[7]

It is to this stage that he wishes to raise the Abaquis. What, if anything, Prévost is here trying to tell his contemporaries through the mouth of his English hero is obscure. In Part V of the *Mémoires et Aventures d'un homme de qualité*,[8] published in 1731, he had fulsomely extolled the free, Protestant, commercial, scientific, self-confident civilisation of England, and he continued, by his journalism and translations, to be one of the main purveyors of English culture in France.

One consequence of the eighteenth-century reaction against the allegedly immoral aristocracy, and of the search for an ethical system to replace the discredited authority of the Church, was a self-righteous striving after a pleasurable form of social virtue. And since it was generally accepted that all knowledge came through the senses, and that the more a man was able to feel, the more potential he had, 'sensibility' came to be regarded as a mark of excellence, and – by those who found satisfaction in the new moralising trend – as a sign of virtue. People self-consciously gloated over their own good deeds, or the good deeds of others, or – if no good deeds of any sort were to hand – over imaginary scenes of hypothetical philanthropy. This lust for vicarious virtue is exemplified by Fanny and Mrs Riding, who are 'attendries' by the pious spectacle which they insist on witnessing. Cleveland himself, who has stage-managed the whole affair, is moved by it, and even in retrospect feels a glow of moral self-satisfaction. (Are the words *sincère, sincérité, droiture, innocence*, in the second paragraph, an unconscious disavowal by the apostate priest Prévost of any guilt in deserting Christianity?)

Some eighteenth-century writers managed to combine the glorification of passion, an unbridled indulgence in sentimentality, and a subtle sense of the ridiculous. No such combination exists in *Cleveland*: no one ever laughs; wit, irony and the intentionally comic are absent. It may none the less be a sign of some rudimentary satirical awareness in Prévost that, although Cleveland describes the new posture for the worship which he has invented ('les yeux et les bras levés'), he does not vouchsafe to his readers the text of his new prayer.

Though, as the century progressed, atheism tended to replace deism in advanced philosophe circles, deism remained very much alive. Voltaire and Rousseau both believed in God, and both believed that religion was necessary to society. The French Republic formally proclaimed its adherence to deist beliefs on Whit Sunday, 1794, when Robespierre officiated at the Fête de l'Etre Suprême – an open-air ceremony not very different, in its essentials, from the one engineered by Cleveland.

The new religion brings little benefit to the Abaquis. The army of two thousand men, which Cleveland has raised and with which he is going in search of Axminster, is decimated by sickness: the survivors are roasted and eaten by the tigrish Rouinton savages, in a four-day cannibal orgy. Mrs Riding and Fanny's baby daughter Cécile are also thought to have been roasted. (In fact, they are preserved, so that, years later, Cleveland shall be prevented at the last moment from consummating an incestuous love with which Cécile is likewise inflamed and from which she dies.)

Woes without number afflict Cleveland: he is an accursed wanderer, 'le seul individu de ma malheureuse espèce'. In vain he seeks, like the philosophes,

> non seulement de travailler à mon bonheur et à ma perfection, mais de me rendre utile, autant qu'il m'était possible, au bonheur des autres, car ces deux obligations touchent presque également un homme raisonnable et vertueux, qui sent qu'il est fait pour la société, et qu'il doit par conséquent aux autres presque autant qu'à lui-même.[9]

By Book VI, Plato, Seneca, and the divines of the Protestant academy of Saumur have all proved vain: possessed by 'une horreur invincible de la vie', he decides to exterminate himself and his little sons:

> O Dieu! pourquoi permettiez-vous que je les misse au monde? Un

homme aussi infortuné que moi n'est-il pas une espèce de monstre dans la société des autres hommes? Comment votre sagesse et votre bonté peuvent-elles souffrir que la race s'en perpétue?[10]

But then the voice of nature speaks: 'Il n'y a sagesse ni folie, qui puisse endurcir contre les sentiments de la nature'; 'tous les mouvements de la nature sont droits.' He turns for comfort to a tolerant, rational religion, neither Protestant nor Catholic, which teaches love of God and of his creatures. The French Catholic clergy are portrayed as intolerant persecutors, who kidnap his sons in order to convert them. Cleveland himself falls into the clutches of an evil, malicious, scheming Jesuit, referred to as 'le J.' Renewed and varied calamities continue to beset Cleveland. We are still in volume IV, published in 1731.

When Dom Prévost returned to France in 1734, he made his peace with the Church, but not with the Benedictines, from whom he had absconded. The *lettre de cachet* issued against him in 1728 remained in force. In January 1735, at the request of Fontenelle, a reconciliation was effected between Prévost and his order through the good offices of the bishop of Luçon, who was M. de Bussy, the former habitué of the *société du Temple*.[11]

Volume VI, written 'pour nourrir ma tristesse, et pour en inspirer à tous les cœurs sensibles qui sont capables de s'attendrir et de s'affliger avec moi', appeared in 1738. 'Le J.', now referred to as 'le ★★★', is eventually shown to be totally unrepresentative of his innocent and virtuous Society, for which Cleveland expresses boundless admiration.[12] In volume VII (1739), Cleveland consorts with 'materialist philosophes', who explain to him that religion is only for the common people:

> Les sentiments que je vous propose sont aujourd'hui ceux de tous les honnêtes gens. On abandonne au peuple toutes les vieilles chimères. Ce frein est nécessaire pour les contenir. La convenance des choses, le goût de l'ordre, et les lois de la société, sont les seules règles de l'homme d'honneur et du philosophe.[13]

But the pleasure of associating with this 'distinguished sect', which numbers high-born persons and ecclesiastics among its adherents, proves as unsatisfying to Cleveland as does the life of ease, luxury and culture which his riches allow him to pursue in Paris. New and hitherto unimaginable woes assail him. At last, realising that he has found only bitterness 'dans tout ce qui passe au monde pour le comble de la félicité', he is converted to Christianity by Lord Clarendon. It is an easy sort of Christianity:

> Ici l'on m'offrait une face riante et dont les charmes seuls étaient d'abord

un soulagement pour mon imagination: des grâces intérieures, des
secours invisibles, des faveurs constantes qui n'avaient besoin que d'être
demandées pour être obtenues, une liaison anticipée de l'esprit et du
cœur avec un ordre supérieur à la nature, et pour dernière perspective
une éternité de bonheur et d'amour'.[14]

Its dogmas, referred to only in general terms, are presented as easily
acceptable: 'Le chemin est court jusqu'à la conviction de toutes les
autres parties de la vérité auxquelles le parfait repos du cœur est attaché.'
This very humane, moderate religion has no objection to moderate
participation in the joys and duties of society, and finds nothing sinful
in innocent sensual pleasures with woman, 'le plus parfait ouvrage de la
nature'.[15] As Fanny has become a Catholic (after all, though one of her
grandfathers was governor of New England, the other was governor of
Cuba), it is presumably into the Church of Rome that Cleveland is
received. But with typical prevarication, Prévost does not say so.

The author of *Manon Lescaut* cannot be fitted into any neat scheme of
eighteenth-century literary or intellectual development. Lanson opines
that 'l'abbé Prévost est peut-être l'écrivain qui a le mieux traduit les
premières langueurs romantiques de l'âme française'.[16] But 'langueurs'
is an inadequate word to describe Cleveland's hellish woes. Professor
Mauzi would have us believe that Prévost was 'l'une des consciences les
plus lucides de son siècle et l'un des plus efficaces pourfendeurs
d'illusions', 'la seule conscience tragique, avec Rousseau, d'une
époque où les euphories artificielles savaient admirablement endormir
ou masquer le malaise des âmes'.[17]

In spite of the facile sentimentality, the assertions that the voice of
nature is always sound, and the easy religion with which the novel ends,
Cleveland offers no explanation or solution for the problem of suffering.
Unlike some of the romantic poets, the hero is unwilling to regard sexual
love as a justification for existence in this world and the next: he dismisses as 'les imaginations d'un honnête et simple ecclésiastique' the
good Père Recteur's assurances that Cécile's passion was a form of
sanctitude:

> un cœur digne de Dieu même, par l'ardeur de ses sentiments . . . déjà
> moins semblable à une créature mortelle qu'à ces bienheureux esprits
> dont la substance est toute composée d'amour, son dernier soupir
> n'avait été que l'élancement passionné d'une amante qui se précipite
> dans le sein qu'elle aime, pour y rassasier à jamais la fureur qu'elle
> a d'aimer et d'être aimée.[18]

And he does not depart from his early belief that human wickedness
springs from 'the corruption which is common to all men'.[19]

It is certainly a fact that Cleveland depicts a nightmare universe of violence and horror, inhabited by victims predestined to suffer, but in whom the boundaries between sorrow and joy are as blurred as those between innocence and guilt. To determine how original, and even, perhaps, how sincere Prévost was in choosing to depict such a universe, it would be necessary to determine what, if anything, he owed to the numerous novels of malediction, darkness and terror which – as Professor Fabre points out – had been written throughout the seventeenth and early eighteenth centuries.[20] The horrors of the twentieth century, together with the diffusion of knowledge about psycho-analytic techniques, produced a revival of interest in that eighteenth-century literature of violence and morbidity which found its extreme expression in the marquis de Sade. Reading Cleveland is an odd experience. But there is no reason why one should have to be solemn about the book. After all, Prévost made it so long-winded not because he needed all those pages for artistic self-expression, but because he needed the money which those pages brought in. The passage selected is a fair enough specimen of his narrative style. Some of the anguished introspective passages display greater subtlety:

> Qu'on y fasse attention, une véritable joie a les mêmes symptômes qu'une excessive douleur. Elle excite les larmes, elle ôte l'usage de la voix, elle cause une délicieuse langueur, elle attache l'âme à considérer la cause de ses émotions; et de deux hommes transportés l'un de joie et l'autre de douleur, je ne sais lequel souffrirait le plus volontiers qu'on lui arrachât le sentiment dont il jouit.[21]

And the novel contains elements of a sociology of emotion:

> Les grands ne connaissent point l'effet des passions violentes. Soit que la facilité qu'ils ont à les satisfaire les empêche d'en ressentir jamais toute la force, soit que leur dissipation continuelle serve bientôt à l'adoucir, ils ignorent ces tempêtes de l'âme, qui ébranlent la raison jusque dans ses fondements, et qui agissent quelquefois sur le corps avec plus de furie que tous les maux extérieurs auxquels on attribue les plus redoutables effets.[22]

But there are limits to Prévost's variety in depicting grief. Book II (1731) ends with a prayer by Cleveland (and, one suspects, by Prévost) for strength to tell the tale:

> Mon nom était écrit dans la page la plus noire et la plus funeste du livre des destinées; il y était accompagné d'une multitude d'arrêts terribles, que j'étais condamné à subir successivement. . . . O Dieu, qui m'as donné la force de les supporter, donne-m'en assez maintenant pour les rappeler à ma mémoire.[23]

Book III begins 'J'entre dans la mer immense de mes infortunes'.
And so on, right until 1739, when, after yet another of Cleveland's
'innocent artifices' (he says he is going to Rouen but in fact embarks
for England), Book XV ends with the promise, mercifully unfulfilled,
that 'les événements de sa vie chrétienne seront donnés un jour au
public'.

NOTES

1 Ed. cit., t. III, livre 4, p. 204. Rousseau's Legislator, in *Du Contrat social*,
   II, vii, also claims divine authority for the system he imposes on the unre-
   generate people: 'Voilà ce qui força de tous temps les pères des nations de
   recourir à l'intervention du ciel et d'honorer les dieux de leur propre
   sagesse, afin que les peuples, soumis aux lois de l'Etat comme à celles de la
   nature et reconnaissant le même pouvoir dans la formation de l'homme et
   dans celle de la Cité, obéissent avec liberté, et portassent docilement le joug
   de la félicité publique.'
2 See J. S. Spink, *French Free Thought from Gassendi to Voltaire* (London,
   1960), pp. 301, 313.
3 Ed. cit., t. III, livre 4, p. 225.
4 *L'Abbé Prévost. Colloque d'Aix-en-Provence 1963* (Aix-en-Provence, 1965),
   pp. 1–9: F. Deloffre, *Les Fiançailles anglaises de l'abbé Prévost*. See also
   H. Roddier, *L'Abbé Prévost. L'Homme et l'œuvre* (Paris, 1955).
5 See E. Beaumont, *Abbé Prévost and the Art of Ambiguity*, *The Dublin
   Review*, vol. 229, no. 468, Second Quarter, 1955, pp. 164–75; J. Sgard,
   Prévost Romancier (Paris, 1968), Ch. I, 'Ambiguïté de Prévost'.
6 Ed. cit., t. III, livre 4, p. 230.
7 Ibid., p. 231.
8 *Edition critique* par Mysie E. I. Robertson (Paris, 1927). This volume –
   which, among other things, is a guide-book to London and the southern
   counties as Prévost knew them in the 1720s – is one of the key texts for the
   study of anglomania. It is fairly short and very readable.
9 *Cleveland*, ed. cit., t. III, livre 5, p. 186.
10 Ibid., t. IV, livre 6, p. 65.
11 *Colloque d'Aix-en-Provence*, p. 16: J. Sgard, *L'Apostasie et la réhabilitation
   de l'abbé Prévost*.
12 Ed. cit., t. V, livre 8, p. 21; t. VI, livre 11, pp. 154, 233–42; livre 12,
   pp. 337–47. Vol. VI of the original edition is vol. V of the ed. cit.
13 Ibid., t. VII, livre 14, pp. 100–1.
14 Ibid., livre 15, p. 382.
15 Ibid., pp. 397–401.
16 *Histoire de la littérature française*, 12e édition (1912), p. 1193.
17 R. Mauzi, *L'Idée du bonheur dans la littérature et la pensée françaises au
   XVIIIe siècle* (Paris, 1960, 725 pp.), pp. 10, 261. Professor Mauzi remarks

on p. 10 of his thesis that 'Quand on connaît *Cleveland* et *La Nouvelle Héloïse*, il reste peu à découvrir sur le XVIIIe siècle'!

18 Ed. cit., t. VII, livre 15, pp. 322–5.
19 Ibid., t. I, livre 2, p. 275.
20 *Colloque d'Aix-en-Provence*, pp. 41–54: J. Fabre, *L'Abbé Prévost et la tradition du roman noir*. In his introduction to the volume Professor Fabre claims that Prévost is one of the creators of the eighteenth-century *European* novel: 'Il est évident que la promotion et le renouvellement du roman en Europe ont été un des faits décisifs de la littérature au 18e siècle, et non moins évident que l'abbé Prévost en a été à la fois l'initiateur et l'un des principaux artisans.' (Pp. xxvi–xxvii.)
21 Ed. cit., t. III, livre 4, p. 97.
22 Ibid., t. V, livre 8, p. 57.
23 Ibid., t. I, livre 2, p. 315.

F

V · Marivaux (1688–1763)

FROM *La Vie de Marianne ou les Aventures de madame la comtesse de* ***
Part IV, published 1736

Marianne is a beautiful, intelligent, penniless girl of about sixteen. There is evidence, but no legal proof, that she is the daughter of high-born foreigners murdered by bandits when she was a baby. She had been brought up by a country priest and his sister who, though well-bred, did not belong to fashionable Parisian society. Now she is in the care of a noblewoman, Mme de Miran, whose son, Valville, has fallen in love with Marianne and offered her his hand. Mme de Miran has consented to the marriage, which she describes as shocking to accepted social convention, but not to God or reason. To prepare Marianne's acceptance by aristocratic circles, Mme de Miran takes her to a dinner-party (held shortly after 1 p.m.) in the Paris mansion of her friend Mme Dorsin. There are present: Mme de Miran, Mme Dorsin, Marianne, Valville, and three or four other persons whose name and sex are not given. These unnamed persons are told that Marianne is the daughter of a provincial lady who is a friend of Mme de Miran. The company dining is the choicest and best which Mme de Miran knows. Mme Dorsin is on friendly terms with the highest in the land, 'des gens puissantes qui ont du crédit ou des dignités, et qui composent ce qu'on appelle le grand monde'.

Marivaux left this novel unfinished – partly, no doubt, because it would have been unrealistic to have married an adventuress to a rich young nobleman, facile and conventional to have produced proof of her high birth, and emotionally unsatisfying to have disposed of her in a convent or by marriage to a suitor less eligible than Valville. We do know, however, that Marianne has made good socially, for it is she herself, now the comtesse de ***, in her fifties, who narrates the events of her youth.

Nous arrivâmes alors, et nous entrâmes chez Mme Dorsin; il y avait trois ou quatre personnes avec elle.

'Ah! la voilà donc enfin! vous me l'amenez, dit-elle à Mme de Miran en me voyant. Venez, Mademoiselle, venez que je vous embrasse, et allons nous mettre à table; on n'attendait que vous.' Nous dînâmes. Quelque novice et quelque ignorante que je fusse en cette occasion-ci, comme l'avait dit Mme de Miran, j'étais née pour avoir du goût, et je sentis bien avec quelles gens je dînais.

Ce ne fut point à force de leur trouver de l'esprit que j'appris à les distinguer; pourtant, il est certain qu'ils en avaient plus que d'autres, et que je leur entendais dire d'excellentes choses, mais ils les disaient avec si peu d'effort, ils y cherchaient si peu de façon, c'était d'un ton de conversation si aisé et si uni, qu'il ne tenait qu'à moi de croire qu'ils disaient les choses les plus communes. Ce n'était point eux qui y mettaient de la finesse, c'était de la finesse qui s'y recontrait; ils ne sentaient pas qu'ils parlaient mieux qu'on ne parle ordinairement; c'étaient seulement de meilleurs esprits que d'autres, et qui par là tenaient de meilleurs discours qu'on n'a coutume d'en tenir ailleurs, sans qu'ils eussent besoin d'y tâcher, et je dirais volontiers sans qu'il y eût de leur faute; car on accuse quelquefois les gens d'esprit de vouloir briller; oh! il n'était pas question de cela ici; et, comme je l'ai déjà dit, si je n'avais pas eu un peu de goût naturel, un peu de sentiment, j'aurais pu m'y méprendre, et je ne me serais aperçue de rien.

Mais, à la fin, ce ton de conversation si excellent, si exquis, quoique si simple, me frappa.

Ils ne disaient rien que de juste et que de convenable, rien qui ne fût d'un commerce doux, facile et gai; j'avais compris le monde tout autrement que je ne le voyais là (et je n'avais pas tant de tort): je me l'étais figuré plein de petites règles frivoles et de petites finesses polies; plein de bagatelles graves et importantes, difficiles à apprendre, et qu'il fallait savoir sous peine d'être ridicule, toutes ridicules qu'elles sont elles-mêmes.

Et point du tout; il n'y avait rien ici qui ressemblât à ce que j'avais pensé, rien qui dût embarrasser mon esprit ni ma figure, rien qui me fît craindre de parler, rien au contraire qui n'encourageât ma petite raison à oser se familiariser avec la leur; j'y sentis même une chose qui m'était fort commode, c'est que leur bon esprit suppléait aux tournures obscures et maladroites du mien. Ce que je ne disais qu'imparfaitement, ils achevaient de le penser et de l'exprimer pour moi, sans qu'ils y prissent garde; et puis ils m'en donnaient tout l'honneur.

Enfin ils me mettaient à mon aise; et moi qui m'imaginais qu'il y avait tant de mystère dans la politesse des gens du monde, et qui l'avais regardée comme une science qui m'était totalement inconnue et dont je n'avais nul principe, j'étais bien surprise de voir qu'il n'y avait rien de particulier dans la leur, rien qui me fût si étranger; mais seulement quelque chose de liant, d'obligeant et d'aimable.

Il me semblait que cette politesse était celle que toute âme honnête, que tout esprit bien fait trouve qu'il a en lui dès qu'on la lui montre.

Romans, ed. by Marcel Arland. Bibliothèque de la Pléiade (Paris, 1949), pp. 246–8.

This passage gives an account of what polite French conversation was like in the best French society of the early eighteenth century. Marianne is struck by its ease, spontaneity, effortlessness and subtlety; all join in at the same level; it is not laboured or thought out in advance;

there is nothing stiff, self-conscious or affected about these *honnêtes gens*. What they talk about is not stated – but obviously, since the inexperienced Marianne takes part, it can be nothing erudite, or even about the latest books, plays or philosophic ideas, since she is ignorant of these.[1] Everything said is within the range of her own natural good sense.

Naturalness, suitably rectified by art, was a quality to which the age of Watteau and Marivaux aspired. Rousseau was to reject French civilisation as a perversion of all that was good and natural. Marivaux, far from wishing to destroy society, proclaims its rightness by presenting his depiction of it as the very reflection of 'nature':

> A l'égard du genre de style et de conversation . . . ce n'est pas moi que j'ai voulu copier, c'est la nature, c'est le ton de la conversation en général que j'ai tâché de prendre.[2]

Like many of Marivaux's contemporaries, Marianne believes that she possesses an instinctive sentiment and a spontaneous intuition, which coincide with reason, or even replace it. Marivaux himself defined 'sentiment' as 'un instinct qui nous conduit et qui nous fait agir sans réflexion';[3] by the 1740s, it had become a commonplace to regard 'sentiment' as a truer guide and light than ratiocination. But even 'rationalists' such as Fontenelle, whom Marivaux encountered in the salon of Mme de Lambert, in no way excluded the emotional, the apparently irrational, the *je ne sais quoi*: they merely tried, as Marianne does in this passage, to analyse such manifestations of 'nature'.[4]

The consideration with which Marianne is treated was not a sentimental invention of Marivaux. A major characteristic of the eighteenth-century quest for happiness was an insistence on the pleasures of generosity, humanity, kindliness. Treatises on *politesse* in the first half of the century teach how to avoid cruel mockery and offence to the susceptibilities of others.[5] The Suffolk squire Arthur Young, who at Bagnères-de-Luchon in 1787 shared the company of 'persons of the first fashion in the Kingdom' – dukes and duchesses, countesses, bishops, army officers and the like – remarked on

> the advantages of an unaffected and polished society, in which an invariable sweetness of disposition, mildness of character, and what in England we emphatically call *good temper*, eminently prevails: – seeming to arise – at least I conjecture it, from a thousand little nameless and peculiar circumstances; not resulting entirely from the personal character of the individuals, but apparently holding of the national one.[6]

Conversation was an art-form, like music or the dance, valued for its own sake by the pleasure-loving society of which it was the expression. In addition, it was a badge of rank, a means to social advancement, and a way of glossing over the divisions between various sections of aristocracy and middle class. Marivaux, the analyser of amorous subtleties, was also a realistic chronicler of society – a society less fluid, it is true, than that depicted by Balzac, but one in which it was increasingly possible to make one's way. He contrasts the conversation of the great with that of the diverse representatives of the lower orders: Parisian shopkeepers, cabbies, or with the nauseatingly cringing smugness of an aspirant to petit-bourgeois respectability.[7] Jacob, in *Le Paysan Parvenu*, rises from farmer's son to financier, passing through a lower middle-class milieu in which the grocer keeps his distance from the ex-footman, and the daughter of a farmer-become-shopkeeper plays the lady in front of a man whose father still ploughs fields. At the point where Marivaux leaves that novel unfinished also, Jacob is being mocked by young lordlings to whom he has been introduced as an equal, but who know from his speech and posture that he is a fraud:

> Il est vrai aussi que je n'avais point passé par assez de degrés d'instruction et d'accroissements de fortune pour pouvoir me tenir au milieu de ce monde avec la hardiesse requise. J'y avais sauté trop vite: je venais d'être fait *monsieur*; encore n'avais-je pas la subalterne éducation des messieurs de ma sorte, et je tremblais qu'on ne connût à ma mine que ce monsieur-là avait été Jacob. Il y en a qui, à ma place, auraient eu le front de soutenir cela, c'est-à-dire, qui auraient payé d'effronterie; mais qu'est-ce qu'on y gagne? Rien. Ne voit-on pas bien alors qu'un homme n'est effronté que parce qu'il devrait être honteux?[8]

In due course, Jacob will learn how to pass as a fine gentleman. One dinner-party is enough to launch Marianne, because – in addition to having natural poise – she has been brought up by the gentlemanly curé and his sister. Her ability to converse does not of itself guarantee her ascent to nobleman's wife – nobleman's mistress is all that one lady deems her fit for[9] – but it does make possible her integration into the aristocracy.

Montesquieu remarks on the importance of the social graces in winning approval:

> Il est de l'utilité publique que les hommes aient du crédit et de l'ascendant sur l'esprit les uns des autres: chose à laquelle on ne parviendra jamais par une humeur austère et farouche.[10]

Mme de Staël outlines a whole sociology of Ancien Régime *politesse*. The King himself, she argues, being no despot but merely First Gentleman of the Realm, strengthened his authority by seeking to flatter his nobles. Ability to charm and flatter was the means to high office under the monarchy; the ruling classes, in their turn, bestowed preferment upon those best versed in the art of pleasing. Thus, from the courtiers downwards, ambitious men – aristocrats, bourgeois, artists, writers – vied with one another in attractiveness of talk and manner:

> La flatterie qui sert à l'ambition exige beaucoup plus d'esprit et d'art que celle qui ne s'adresse qu'aux femmes: ce sont toutes les passions des hommes et tous les genres de vanité qu'il faut savoir ménager, lorsque la combinaison du gouvernement et des mœurs est telle, que les succès des hommes entre eux dépendent de leur talent mutuel de se plaire, et que ce talent est le seul moyen d'obtenir les places éminentes du pouvoir ... La cour voulait plaire à la nation, et la nation à la cour; la cour prétendait à la philosophie, et la ville au bon ton. Les courtisans venant se mêler aux habitants de la capitale, voulaient y montrer un mérite personnel, un caractère, un esprit à eux; et les habitants de la capitale conservaient toujours un attrait pour les manières brillantes des courtisans. Cette émulation réciproque ne hâtait pas les progrès des vérités austères et fortes; mais il ne restait pas une idée fine, une nuance délicate, que l'intérêt ne fît découvrir ... Ce n'était ni par le travail, ni par l'étude qu'on parvenait au pouvoir en France: un bon mot, une certaine grâce, était souvent la cause de l'avancement le plus rapide.... Quand l'amusement est non seulement permis, mais souvent utile, une nation doit s'attendre en ce genre à ce qu'il peut y avoir de plus parfait.

The elegant speech and manners adopted by the uppermost classes to identify their own members and detect interlopers were imitated by those outside these classes; and since there were no rigidly defined barriers between one class or group and the next, a whole process of social manoeuvring was expressed in subtleties of word and gesture:

> Les rapports des différentes classes entre elles étaient aussi très propres à développer en France la sagacité, la mesure et la convenance de l'esprit de société. Les rangs n'y étaient pas marqués d'une manière positive, et les prétentions s'agitaient sans cesse dans l'espace incertain que chacun pouvait tour à tour ou conquérir ou perdre. Les droits du tiers état, des parlements, de la noblesse, la puissance même du roi, rien n'était déterminé d'une façon invariable; tout se passait pour ainsi dire en adresse de conversation.[11]

Mme de Staël's assertion that class boundaries in the Ancien Régime were not rigidly defined coincides with the views held by modern historians.[12] In spite of the 'feudal reaction' at the end of the Ancien

Régime, and the restrictions limiting the 'honours of the Court' and commissions in the Army to those with documentary proof that their blood was of ancient blueness, there was a certain equality, cemented by a common social behaviour[13], among those who by birth, money, office or talent formed what was regarded as good society. Marivaux describes a salon where such equality reigned:

> Il n'était point question de rangs ni d'états chez elle [Mme Dorsin]; personne ne s'y souvenait du plus ou du moins d'importance qu'il avait; c'étaient des hommes qui parlaient à des hommes . . .; des intelligences entre lesquelles il ne s'agissait plus des titres que le hasard leur avait donnés ici-bas, et qui ne croyaient pas que leurs fonctions fortuites dussent plus humilier les unes qu'enorgueillir les autres.[14]

But, as Mme de Staël points out, polite conversation 'effaçait les distances sans en détruire aucune'[15]: even within upper-class society, the differences remained. Charles-Louis de Secondat, baron de la Brède et de Montesquieu, debated with himself on how to address great aristocrats.[16] The millionaire art-patron M. de la Poupelinière moved in the highest circles: 'Jamais bourgeois n'a mieux vécu en prince, et les princes venaient jouir de ses plaisirs'. But observers remarked on the carefully calculated degree of deference and independence which he showed to his distinguished visitors. Voltaire, who had been beaten up on an aristocrat's orders, then imprisoned and exiled, consorted all his life with great lords, and was celebrated for the nice blend of familiarity and respect with which he handled them.[17] Men of letters less eminent than he might dream that they were social equals of the nobles they conversed with; but they knew that the Bastille awaited those who really forgot their place.[18]

Callousness and insolence, as well as 'an invariable sweetness of disposition', existed in polite circles. The underling whom Valville's relatives offer to Marianne as a husband has not been allowed to develop human dignity; he is

> un pauvre petit homme sans conséquence, dont le métier était de ramper et d'obéir, à qui même il n'appartenait pas d'avoir reçu du cœur, et à qui on pouvait dire: Retirez-vous, sans lui faire injure.[19]

Count Alexandre de Tilly, who had been a page to Queen Marie-Antoinette, was an expert at sensing the gradations between Court and Paris, Paris and good provincial societies. He could recognise, underneath the differences, a common striving towards grace and elegance. He exploited his own charm to seduce women whom he later abandoned. He threatened to murder a bourgeois creditor who pressed for payment, tried to beat an offending coachman to death, insulted the coachman's master, who was a mere provincial Intendant, and bullied, then patronised and sneered at, a minor official whose services he required.[20]

The anglophile Montesquieu opined that, since Englishmen never committed discourtesies, they did not need to make a show of courteous words, and, in any case, had better things to occupy their time.[21] Anglo-Saxons who flounder amid the nimble flippancies of French conversation may also console themselves by the thought that even in the eighteenth century, when the art was at its peak, not all Frenchmen were good at it. At least we can do better than Blaise the tiler and 'Malbrough' the old soldier whom Restif de la Bretonne cites as not untypical of rustic taciturnity: as they began walking home from Auxerre, 'Malbrough' said to Blaise: 'Fine cornfield'; Blaise's answer, 'Nice and green', was not ready until they were back at their village, twenty miles further on.[22] The Swiss Jean-Jacques Rousseau, though more articulate than his Irish contemporary Goldsmith, 'who wrote like an angel and talk'd like poor Poll', gives as one of his chief reasons for fleeing society the certainty that he would always make a fool of himself at polite assemblies.[23] Even among the most elegant Parisians, the high art of conversation sometimes fell flat. Montesquieu complains that serious discussion has been sacrificed to idle chit-chat in which the most empty-headed young woman can join: 'Plaire dans une conversation vaine et frivole est aujourd'hui le seul mérite.' The whole subject-matter, he laments, is silly tittle-tattle, or the latest scandal about the fatuous promiscuities of an insignificant group of fashionable people. With rueful satisfaction, he recounts how he heard two hundred and twenty-five times in the course of three weeks the same pointless bit of gossip which was occupying the attention of 'le monde poli'.[24] According to Marmontel, Montesquieu himself lacked spontaneity, and was a little too anxious to say his piece, while Marivaux had the reputation of being touchy, awkward, and altogether too ready to display his delicate perceptivity.[25] It was for his supposed financial genius, not his conversation, that Mme de Staël's father, the Swiss banker Necker, was called in to save France from bankruptcy. He was noteworthy for his taciturnity at his wife's receptions. Mme Necker herself, lacking the skill of French hostesses, was unable to make the conversation go, and would look accusingly at her guests during awkward silences.[26]

It is customary for works on eighteenth-century literature to stress the importance of the literary salons – those of the duchesse du Maine,

Mme de Lambert, Mme de Tencin, Mme du Deffand, Mme Geoffrin and the rest. As far as discussion on religion or politics was concerned, these literary hostesses seem, in the main, to have sedulously avoided anything dangerously 'advanced', and the contribution of their salons to the development of philosophic ideas would appear to have been minimal.[27] That men of letters did frequent these salons, that reputations, and valuable contacts, were made there, and that much eighteenth-century literature is still readable today because it is stamped by the grace, wit, lightness and elegance fostered by the salons, is undeniable. It is also probable, as Montesquieu and Mme de Staël allege, that profundity, originality, sincerity and vigour were in some cases stifled by the writers' dread of being ridiculed as eccentrics. Arthur Young (who gave as one reason for the ineffectualness of French gentlemen the fact that they ate no breakfast, changed for dinner which took place soon after noon, and then, in their silk breeches and silk stockings, with powdered heads, and hats under their arms, were no good for anything but conversation with the ladies) found aristocratic conversation as insipid as it was amiable:

> All vigour of thought seems so excluded from expression, that characters of ability and of inanity meet nearly on a par: tame and elegant, uninteresting and polite, the mingled mass of communicated aside has powers neither to offend nor instruct; where there is much polish of character there is little argument; and if you neither argue nor discuss, what is conversation?

Morellet's view was that, though authors who had too little intercourse with the *gens du monde* become pedantic and heavy, those who spent too much time with them became affected and impoverished in style and thought. D'Holbach was certain that the disadvantages more than outweighed the gain: 'Pour plaire aux gens du monde, l'homme de lettres doit être frivole, badin, superficiel, et ne jamais parler raison'.[28] In addition to the literary and social salons there were, of course, throughout the century, more serious gatherings devoted to erudition, or political, scientific and religious discussion.[29] At the philosophe conventicles organised by d'Holbach, truth, not wit or grace, was the professed aim. The philosophe Helvétius, according to Marmontel and Morellet, was a dull conversationalist; and if his writings are anything to go by, so was d'Holbach too, in spite of the lively and stimulating talk of his visitors Diderot and the abbé Galiani.[30] Denouncing the so-called witty conversation of aristocratic circles as idle, tasteless, jaded, insipid, rancorous and hateful, d'Holbach – already heralding the grave, sententious bourgeois of the nineteenth century – demands that conversation be serious, thoughtful, well informed, directed towards the useful as well as the agreeable, and inspired by goodness of heart and benevolence to one's fellow men.[31]

Yet, in spite of allegations that polite society was shallow and inane, we find, throughout the century, nostalgia for standards of excellence said to be no longer attained. Voltaire saw in the death of Chaulieu the passing of seventeenth-century urbanity; Hénault lamented the extinction of M. de Bussy, 'le modèle de ce qu'on appelle la bonne compagnie, et que l'on ne retrouve guère dans ce temps'.[32] In 1799 Mme de Staël proclaimed that, with the disappearance of the old monarchy, the whole charm and loveliness of the old society would eventually become less than a memory in the graceless, oafish France of the Republic. By 1810, she is wistfully recalling the delights of Paris, from which Napoleon has exiled her:

> Il me semble... que Paris est la ville du monde où l'esprit et le goût de la conversation sont le plus généralement répandus; et ce qu'on appelle le mal du pays, ce regret indéfinissable de la patrie, qui est indépendant des amis qu'on y a laissés, s'applique particulièrement à ce plaisir de causer que les Français ne retrouvent nulle part au même degré que chez eux.... Le genre de bien-être que fait éprouver une conversation animée ne consiste pas précisément dans le sujet de cette conversation; les idées ni les connaissances qu'on peut y développer n'en sont pas le principal intérêt; c'est une certaine manière d'agir les uns sur les autres, de se faire plaisir réciproquement et avec rapidité, de parler aussitôt qu'on pense, de jouir à l'instant de soi-même, d'être applaudi sans travail, de manifester son esprit dans toutes les nuances par l'accent, le geste, le regard, enfin de produire à volonté comme une sorte d'électricité qui fait jaillir des étincelles, soulage les uns de l'excès même de leur vivacité, et réveille les autres d'une apathie pénible.[33]

But it is Mme de Staël herself who says that the sort of conversation she is describing cannot be conveyed by the printed page.[34] Plays, novels, correspondence, memoirs, philosophical dialogues can, perhaps, give us an inkling of what it was like. The whole of La Vie de Marianne is in conversational form.[35] So, too, is much of Crébillon's fiction; but we suspect that what we find there is a quintessence, or else a travesty, of the real thing. Alexandre de Tilly maintained that the licentious novels of the second half of the century, taken by foreigners and the lower orders as a true picture of aristocratic life, are no true reflection of 'la plus grande compagnie de France', and that even Les Liaisons dangereuses, despite authentic touches, gives a false impression.[36] The refined snobberies, the elusive shibboleths, are hidden from us. So were they too, in all probability, from the bourgeois philosophes and professional men of letters. The literary salons to which they were admitted – often on a different day of the week from the nobility and gentry – were not the main expression of aristocratic social life, which has left no adequate record: 'Les salons littéraires sont à tort considérés comme l'essentiel de la vie de société à la fin de l'ancien régime. Les réunions proprement aristocratiques restent ignorées.'[37] In volume III of the collected works ascribed to a minor satirical writer, F.-A. Chevrier (published 'A Londres. Chez l'éternel Jean Nourse. L'an de la Vérité 1774'), an article entitled 'De la bonne compagnie' tells how Lord *** came to Paris in search of the best society. An English earl, who had spent five years in Paris on the same quest, told him, on the authority of a reliable Frenchman, that la bonne compagnie was a mythical entity which all sought, but none discovered. Lord *** renounced his inquiry and returned to England. As far as recapturing the full and authentic tone, spirit, content and electrical spark of eighteenth-century French conversation is concerned, we must be content to do likewise.

NOTES

1 Marivaux is supposed to have modelled Mme de Miran on Mme de Lambert whose salon he frequented. R. Shackleton, in *Montesquieu. A Critical Biography* (Oxford, 1961), p. 58, states: 'Duty, taste, love, friendship, happiness: such were the topics discussed in Madame de Lambert's apartment in the Hôtel de Nevers. They were simple moral problems, calling for no especial competence or experience, but rather for a clear mind and good will.'

2 *Avertissement* to *Les Serments indiscrets. Théâtre Complet* (Pléiade, 1961), p. 817. See J. Ehrard, *L'Idée de nature en France dans la première moitié du XVIIIᵉ siècle* (Paris, 1963), pp. 266; 311–12.

3 *Le Spectateur français. Romans* (Pléiade, 1949), p. 914.

4 Ehrard, op. cit., pp. 262–88; R. Mercier, *La Réhabilitation de la nature humaine 1700–1750* (Villemomble, 1960), pp. 131, 370–5.

5 R. Mauzi, *L'Idée du bonheur dans la littérature et la pensée françaises au XVIIIᵉ siècle* (Paris, 1960), p. 583. Cf. Montesquieu, *Pensées* 619–26 (1270–7), *Œuvres* (Pléiade, 1956), vol. 1, pp. 1144–9.

6 *Arthur Young's Travels in France* (London, 1909), p. 39.

7 *La Vie de Marianne*, ed. cit., pp. 101–3, 174–5, 149–54, 329–33.

8 *Le Paysan parvenu. Romans* (Pléiade, 1949), pp. 655–7, 673–4, 774–6, 789–91.

9 Ed. cit., p. 337.

10 *Pensées* 619 (1270). *Œuvres* (Pléiade), vol. 1, p. 1145.

11 *De la littérature considérée dans ses rapports avec les institutions sociales,*

I, XVIII, ed. P. Van Tieghem (Genève; Paris, 1959), pp. 262–70; *De l'Allemagne*, I, XI, ed. S. Balayé (Paris, 1968), pp. 105–6.

12 For details of the homogeneousness of the nobility, the absence of rigid division between *noblesse d'épée* and *noblesse de robe*, the ways of becoming ennobled, and the no-man's-land where nobility and rich bourgeoisie interpenetrated, see F. Bluche, *Les Magistrats du Parlement de Paris au XVIIIᵉ siècle* (Paris, 1960); F. Bluche, P. Durye, *L'Anoblissement par charges avant 1789* (*Les Cahiers nobles*, 23, 24, 1962); A. Goodwin, 'French eighteenth-century nobility', *Bulletin of the John Rylands Library*, vol. 47 (Manchester, 1965); C. B. A. Behrens, *The Ancien Régime* (London, 1967). M. Reinhard, 'Elite et noblesse dans la seconde moitié du XVIIIᵉ siècle', in the *Revue d'histoire moderne et contemporaine*, vol. III (1956), shows that it was possible for successful professional men – doctors, surgeons, engineers, painters, architects, etc. – to become nobles.

13 A. Goodwin, op. cit., points out that there were loop-holes in the 1759 regulations limiting the 'honours of the Court' to those with proof of nobility back to 1400, and in the restriction, in 1781, of direct military commissions to those with four generations of noble birth.

14 *La Vie de Marianne*, ed. cit., p. 257. Cf. A. de Tocqueville, *L'Ancien Régime*, II, viii, ed. G. W. Headlam (Oxford, 1904), p. 88: 'A la fin du XVIIIᵉ siècle, on pouvait encore apercevoir, sans doute, entre les manières de la noblesse et celles de la bourgeoisie, une différence . . . mais au fond, tous les hommes placés au-dessus du peuple se ressemblaient; ils avaient les mêmes idées, les mêmes habitudes, suivaient les mêmes goûts, se livraient aux mêmes plaisirs, lisaient les mêmes livres, parlaient le même langage. Ils ne différaient plus entre eux que par les droits.' Voltaire and André Chénier are examples of bourgeois who made valuable friendships with nobles at school: on the importance of the 'old school tie' see Bluche, op. cit., p. 246.

15 *De la littérature*, ed cit., p. 266.

16 *Pensées* 625 (1276), ed. cit., p. 1148: 'A l'égard des Grands, autrefois, on n'avait qu'à conserver la liberté. Aujourd'hui, il est difficile d'allier la familiarité où tout le monde vit, avec les égards qu'il faut faire sortir de cette familiarité.'

17 Marmontel, *Mémoires* (Paris, 1819), vol. 1, pp. 184–92, 221.

18 E.g., ibid., pp. 321–32, where Marmontel describes his eleven days in the Bastille for his lack of respect to the duc d'Aumont. On the imprisonment of Voltaire and Diderot, and the social status of writers, see J. Lough, *An Introduction to Eighteenth Century France* (London, 1960), pp. 260–71, 308–11.

19 *La Vie de Marianne*, ed. cit., p. 349.

20 *Mémoires du comte Alexandre de Tilly*, ed. C. Melchior-Bonnet (Paris, 1965), pp. 103, 232, 289, 291. Of his love-affairs he writes (p. 71): 'Jai souvent affecté le jargon du sentiment et l'attitude de la mélancolie pour pallier la luxure et faire plus d'honneur au plaisir'.

21 *Œuvres* (Pléiade), vol. 1, p. 883 (*Notes sur l'Angleterre*), p. 1335, *Pensées*, 1428 (780).

22 *Monsieur Nicolas* (Paris, 1883), p. 128.

23 *Confessions,* ed. J. Voisine (Paris, 1964), p. 127–9: 'J'aimerais la société comme un autre, si je n'étais sûr de m'y montrer non seulement à mon désavantage, mais tout autre que je suis.'

24 *Pensées,* 860 (1062), 1193 (107), ed. cit., vol. 1, pp. 1234, 1300.

25 Marmontel, op. cit., vol. 1, pp. 183–4, describes the salon of Mme de Tencin: 'Je m'aperçus bientôt qu'on y arrivait préparé à jouer son rôle, et que l'envie d'entrer en scène n'y laissait pas toujours à la conversation la liberté de suivre son cours facile et naturel. C'était à qui saisirait le plus vite, et comme à la volée, le moment de placer son mot, son conte, son anecdote, sa maxime ou son trait léger et piquant; et pour amener l'à-propos, on le tirait quelquefois d'un peu loin. Dans Marivaux, l'impatience de faire preuve de finesse et de sagacité perçait visiblement. Montesquieu, avec plus de calme, attendait que la balle vînt à lui, mais il l'attendait. ... Fontenelle seul la laissait venir sans la chercher. . . . Helvétius, attentif et discret, recueillait pour semer un jour.' Hénault, *Mémoires* (Paris, 1855), p. 411, describes Marivaux as 'un peu pointilleux, par la délicatesse de son amour-propre'. For conflicting eighteenth-century views on Montesquieu as a conversationalist, see R. Shackleton, op. cit., pp. 381–2.

26 Marmontel, op. cit., vol. 2, p. 114. Morellet, *Mémoires* (Paris, 1822), vol. 1, p. 154, says, however, of the Necker salon: 'La conversation y était bonne, quoiqu'un peu contrainte par la sévérité de Mme Necker. ... Mais en matière de littérature on causait agréablement, et elle en parlait elle-même fort bien.'

27 For an extreme view that the literary salons had no influence on ideas, see A. Adam, *Le Mouvement philosophique dans la première moitié du XVIIIe siècle* (Paris, 1967), p. 13. On scholarly as well as literary salons, etc., see R. Shackleton, op. cit., pp. 55–61, 178–90, and L. Gossman, *Medievalism and the Ideologies of the Enlightenment* (Baltimore, 1968), pp. 44–70.

28 Montesquieu, *Pensées* 860 (1062), ed. cit. p. 1234; Staël, *De la littérature,* ed. cit., p. 267; Young, op. cit., pp. 38–40; Morellet, op. cit., vol. 2, p. 129; d'Holbach, *La Morale universelle, ou les Devoirs de l'homme fondés sur la nature,* of 1776, ed. Paris, L'An IV de la République française, vol. 2, p. 229.

29 For the Club de l'Entresol, see R. Shackleton, op. cit., pp. 63–6, and for the meetings and discussions of the Académie des Inscriptions et des Belles-Lettres, see index to L. Gossman, op. cit. The social and ideological signific-ance of the provincial learned societies is discussed by D. Roche in *Livre et société dans la France du XVIIIe siècle,* ed. A. Dupront (Paris, La Haye, 1965), pp. 93–184.

30 P. Gay, *The Enlightenment: An Interpretation* (London, 1967), p. 16, points out that in 1779 Horace Walpole wrote that 'the philosophes' except for Buffon, are solemn, arrogant, dictatorial coxcombs – I need not say superlatively disagreeable'.

31 Op. cit., vol. 1, pp. 288–9: 'Ce qu'on appelle le grand monde n'est le plus souvent composé que de personnes très vaines, qui croient réciproquement ne se rien devoir; qui, privées d'instruction, ne portent dans la société que de la raideur, de la sécheresse, du dégoût; . . . il n'y a que l'amitié franche et sincère, la science, la vertu, qui puissent donner de la vie au commerce des hommes'; vol. 2, p. 229. Morellet, op. cit., vol. 1, p. 133, gives vivid

descriptions of the stimulating conversation chez d'Holbach: 'C'est là qu'il fallait entendre la conversation la plus libre, et la plus animée, et la plus instructive qui fût jamais; quand je dis libre, j'entends en matière de philosophie, de religion, de gouvernement, car les plaisanteries dans un autre genre en étaient bannies.'

32 Hénault, op. cit., p. 416–7.
33 *De la littérature*, ed. cit., pp. 301–7; *De l'Allemagne*, ed. cit., I, xi, pp. 101–2.
34 *De la littérature*, p. 307: 'Le temps fera disparaître les hommes qui sont encore des modèles en ce genre, et l'on finira par en perdre le souvenir; car il ne suffit pas des livres pour se le rappeler. Ce qui est plus fin que la pensée ne peut être appris que par l'habitude.' Forty years later, if Flaubert's testimony can be relied on, the conversation of the middle-class celebrities who filled the salons was dull, dreary, platitudinous: 'la misère des propos se trouvait comme renfoncée par le luxe des choses ambiantes; mais ce qu'on disait était moins stupide que la manière de causer, sans but, sans suite et sans animation' (*L'Education Sentimentale*, ed. E. Maynial, Paris, 1954, p. 130). Barbey d'Aurevilly was in raptures at Astolphe de Custine's conversation because it was a relic of the departed glory: 'Il cause comme un homme qui a connu Mme de Staël et qui a gardé les parfums de cette rose de feu de la causerie' (cited by A. M. Rubino, *Alla ricerca di Astolphe de Custine*, Roma, 1968, p. 23).
35 On novels in conversational form, see Vivienne Mylne, *The Eighteenth-Century Novel. Techniques of Illusion* (Manchester, 1965), p. 105 ff.
36 Op. cit., pp. 91–2, 176–7. Cf. Sénac de Meilhan, *L'Emigré*, Pléiade, Romanciers du XVIIIᵉ siècle, II (Paris, 1965), pp. 1564–5.
37 Bluche, *Les Magistrats . . .*, p. 334.

VI . Duclos (1704–1772)

FROM *Les Confessions du comte de* *** (published 1741)

Mon admiration et mon respect augmentaient chaque jour pour Mme de Selve. Ses sentiments me faisaient rougir des miens; mais ils ne me corrigeaient pas. Ce n'était pas la raison qui devait me ramener et me guérir de mes erreurs; il m'était réservé de me dégoûter des femmes par les femmes mêmes. Bientôt je ne trouvai plus rien de piquant dans leur commerce. Leur figure, leurs grâces, leur caractère, leurs défauts même, rien n'était nouveau pour moi. Je ne pouvais pas faire une maîtresse qui ne ressemblât à quelqu'une de celles que j'avais eues. Tout le sexe n'était plus pour moi qu'une seule femme pour qui mon goût était usé, et ce qu'il y avait de singulier, c'est que Mme de Selve reprenait à mes yeux de nouveaux charmes. Sa figure effaçait tout ce que j'avais vu, et je ne concevais pas que j'eusse pu lui préférer personne. L'habitude, qui diminue le prix de la beauté, ajoute au caractère, et ne sert qu'à nous attacher. D'ailleurs, mon inconstance pour Mme de Selve lui avait donné occasion de me montrer des vertus que je croyais au-dessus de l'humanité, et que mon injustice avait fait éclater.

Mme de Selve reprit tous ses droits sur mon cœur, ou plutôt ce n'étaient plus ces mouvements vifs et tumultueux qui m'avaient d'abord entraîné vers elle avec violence, et qui étaient ensuite devenus la source de mes erreurs. Ce n'était plus l'ivresse impétueuse des sens. Un sentiment plus tendre, plus tranquille et plus voluptueux remplissait mon âme; il y faisait régner un calme qui ajoutait encore à mon bonheur en me laissant la liberté de le sentir.

Je n'avais jamais cessé de voir Mme de Selve. Mes visites, que j'avais suspendues pendant quelque temps lorsque je voulais lui dérober la connaissance de mes infidélités, redevinrent plus fréquentes aussitôt qu'elles ne furent plus contraintes. Bientôt je ne trouvai de douceur que chez elle. Insensiblement, et sans que je m'en aperçusse distinctement, le dégoût me détacha du monde que la dissipation m'avait fait rechercher.

Ed. by Marguerite du Cheyron in *Romanciers du XVIIIe siècle*, Bibliothèque de la Pléiade (Paris, 1965), vol. 2, p. 300.

Most eighteenth-century French novelists sought to make their fictions plausible by passing them off as genuine memoirs, correspondence or first-hand narration. Duclos shows some originality in calling his novel *Confessions*. The comte, who writes his life-story as a moral lesson for a young relative, is a rich man with estates in Brittany. When there is a war, he defends France with his sword because this is 'l'unique profession de la noblesse française comme elle en était l'origine'.[1] But in times of peace, his sole occupation is to amuse himself, and the chief amusement is amorous intrigue with the equally idle wives or widows of other aristocrats. He moves, for the most part, in a closed society; almost all the young Madames de —, whom he sees at Versailles, in the Parisian town houses or country châteaux, have been to bed with various of the young or middle-aged men who, like him, have nothing else to do. The classic description of this milieu is given by Crébillon *fils* in his gay little novel *La Nuit et le Moment*:

> Jamais les femmes n'ont mis moins de grimaces dans la société; jamais l'on n'a moins affecté la vertu. On se plaît, on se prend. S'ennuie-t-on l'un avec l'autre? on se quitte avec tout aussi peu de cérémonie que l'on s'est pris. Revient-on à se plaire? on se reprend avec autant de vivacité que si c'était la première fois qu'on s'engageât ensemble. On se quitte encore, et jamais on ne se brouille. Il est vrai que l'amour n'est entré pour rien dans tout cela; mais l'amour, qu'était-il, qu'un désir que l'on se plaisait à s'exagérer, un mouvement des sens, dont il avait plu à la vanité des hommes de faire une vertu? On sait aujourd'hui que le goût seul existe; et si l'on se dit encore qu'on s'aime, c'est bien moins parce qu'on le croit, que parce que c'est une façon plus polie de se demander réciproquement ce dont on sent qu'on a besoin. Comme on s'est pris sans s'aimer, on se sépare sans se haïr, et l'on retire du moins, du faible goût que l'on s'est mutuellement inspiré, l'avantage d'être toujours prêts à s'obliger.[2]

There was general agreement that the routine was boring. The serious provincial Montesquieu mocks not only the sexual promiscuity of Parisian high society, but the tedium resulting from it. His Persian traveller relates:

> Je fus, il y a quelques jours, d'un souper que des femmes firent à la campagne. Dans le chemin, elles disaient sans cesse: 'Au moins, il faudra bien nous divertir'.
> Nous nous trouvâmes assez mal assortis, et, par conséquent, assez sérieux. 'Il faut avouer, dit l'une de ces femmes, que nous nous divertissons bien: il n'y a pas aujourd'hui dans Paris une partie si gaie que la nôtre.' Comme l'ennui me gagnait, une femme me secoua et me dit: 'Eh bien! ne sommes-nous pas de bonne humeur? – Oui,

lui répondis-je en bâillant; je crois que je crèverai à force de rire.'
Cependant la tristesse triomphait toujours des réflexions, et, quant à
moi, je me sentis conduit de bâillement en bâillement dans un sommeil
léthargique, qui finit tous mes plaisirs.[3]

The hero of *La Nuit et le Moment*, on the other hand, resignedly carries
on the game with as much resilience and good humour as he can command:

Comment voulez-vous qu'on fasse? On est dans le monde, on s'ennuie,
on voit des femmes qui, de leur côté, ne s'y amusent guère: on est
jeune; la vanité se joint au désœuvrement. Si avoir une femme n'est
pas toujours un plaisir, du moins c'est toujours une sorte d'occupation.[4]

Of course, religion might have been one cure for the *vide de l'âme*
which, it would appear from the novels and memoirs of the century,
the worldlings' pleasures could not fill. Centuries earlier, St Augustine
in his own *Confessions* had proclaimed that the peace of God was the
only solution for man's spiritual unease. According to Pascal, the pursuit
of pleasure proved the misery of man without God. Bossuet had said
that Louis XIV's ex-mistress La Vallière 'trouva en soi un vide infini
que Dieu seul pouvait remplir'. Malebranche saw in man's restlessness
and dissatisfaction a yearning for the divine.[5] Chateaubriand was to
say something very similar in *Le Génie du Christianisme*. But for roués
of the eighteenth century, the religious life had little attraction. The
comte de Tilly (whose *Mémoires* are believed to be genuine) did visit
the Trappist monastery near Mortagne-au-Perche to see if it did him
any good, but three days there was as much as he could stand:

En entrant dans la solitude de ce cloître, mon imagination espérait
des sites sauvages et tout le sombre cortège de la mélancolie. . . . Je
ne fus intéressé que par l'histoire d'un religieux, le seul qui eût,
si je puis dire, un visage romantique, et empreint de ces grandes
peines qui fondent dans l'âme l'amour de la solitude et la haine du
siècle.[6]

There were easier ways available to escape boredom, as the baron points
out in Poinsinet's play *Le Cercle, ou La Soirée à la mode* (1764):

Je me sens un certain vide dans l'âme; enfin je veux me marier.
J'épouserai quelque personne honnête qui m'aimera, qui en aura l'air,
au moins; je tâcherai d'en avoir bien vite une couple d'enfants, dont
l'éducation sera l'amusement, la consolation de mes vieux jours; en
formant leur cœur je jouirai du mien; cela m'animera, m'occupera; car
il faut s'occuper: j'en ai plus besoin qu'un autre, et je ne conçois pas
qu'un homme oisif puisse être vertueux. . . . Les plaisirs honnêtes
ennuient bientôt un homme qui peut se livrer à tous; l'esprit s'y
habitue, les sens s'émoussent, le cœur se blase, le goût s'endort, et ce
n'est plus que les excès qui les réveillent.[7]

G

Escape into sentiment – the deliberate, calculated, cold-blooded cult
of innocence, virtue, simplicity, emotion from whatever source – is the
subject of many novels and plays of the century. The frenzied search
for new thrills is as manifest in the calculated artlessness of that fake-
innocent pastoral *Paul et Virginie*[8] as it is in the vengeance exacted by
the passionate and jealous villainess of *Les Liaisons dangereuses*.
The comte de *** opts for escape into virtue, and not into excess or
perversions. Instead of consigning a beautiful but penniless girl of sixteen to one of the 'soupers de liberté' where he and his fellows drearily
try to find with prostitutes a spontaneity lacking in ladies, he enables
her to marry her virtuous suitor. The good deed costs him nothing:
the couple not only prove excellent agents for him on his Brittany estates,
but provide a pleasure which he has not hitherto experienced – con-
templation of the bliss enjoyed by these innocent spouses, and the
knowledge that he has been able to bestow happiness by beneficence:

> Je n'ai jamais senti dans ma vie de plaisir plus pur que celui d'avoir
> fait leur bonheur. L'auteur d'un bienfait est celui qui en recueille le
> fruit le plus doux. Il semblait que leur état se réfléchît sur moi. Tous
> les plaisirs des sens n'approchent pas de celui que j'éprouvais. Il faut
> qu'il y ait dans le cœur un sens particulier et supérieur à tous les
> autres.[9]

For the first time, he is lucidly aware of something more satisfying than
debauch:

> Je trouvai un vide dans mon âme que tous mes faux plaisirs ne pouv-
> aient remplir; leur tumulte m'étourdissait au lieu de me satisfaire,
> et je sentis que je ne pouvais être heureux si mon cœur n'était véritable-
> ment rempli. L'idée de ce bonheur me rendit tous mes autres plaisirs
> odieux et, pour me dérober à leur importunité, je résolus d'aller à la
> campagne chez un de mes amis qui me priait depuis longtemps de le
> venir voir dans une terre qu'il avait à quelques lieues de Paris.[10]

His emptiness is filled by Mme de Selve, a beautiful, virtuous, intelligent,
strong-minded, affectionate widow of twenty-three, whom he makes
'maîtresse absolue de mon sort et de ma conduite'. Though unwilling
to marry him yet, she eventually becomes his mistress in the other sense
of the word, when he is about to leave her to fight in the wars. For the
first time, he knows the joys of true love. Though approaching forty,
he is like a young romantic hero in his *ivresses voluptueuses* and *plaisirs
inexprimables* – pleasures which he holds to be completely innocent when
experienced by both partners:

> Mme de Selve se calma et me dit en m'embrassant tendrement qu'elle

ne se reprocherait jamais d'avoir tout sacrifié à mes désirs, tant qu'elle serait sûre de mon cœur, dont la fidélité ou l'inconstance la rendrait la plus heureuse ou la plus malheureuse des femmes. Mes serments, mes transports et l'amour dissipèrent toutes ses craintes; j'obtins mon pardon et nous le scellâmes par les mêmes caresses qui un moment auparavant m'avaient rendu criminel, et qui deviennent également innocentes et délicieuses quand deux amants les partagent. Etat heureux où les désirs satisfaits renaissent d'eux-mêmes.[11]

France does not go to war, and his rapture lasts for a whole year. He yearns for an eternity of emotional joy with his mistress:

Pourquoi faut-il qu'un état aussi délicieux puisse finir? Ce n'est point une jeunesse inaltérable que je désirerais; elle est souvent elle-même l'occasion de l'inconstance. Je n'aspire point à changer la condition humaine; mais nos cœurs devraient être plus parfaits, la jouissance des âmes devrait être éternelle.[12]

But, of course, it becomes tedious. He longs for the social activities of which he is deprived by isolation with Mme de Selve. He takes another mistress whom he does not love, and decides, after all, that 'le plaisir imite un peu l'amour'. Then, in its turn, this turbulent life of pleasure becomes boring again; his admiration for Mme de Selve increases when she utters no reproach at his infidelities, but herself remains faithful.

Paragraph one of the passage is devoid of the grandiloquence and melodrama which characterise Alfred de Musset's lamentations on the bitter fruits of sin. Duclos expresses with economy, simplicity and intensity the bleak horrors of satiety. He is, at this point, in the tradition of the seventeenth-century moralists, just as his style, in the penultimate sentence of the first paragraph, is an echo of the *maximes*. The titled ladies who are successively 'eues' (this monosyllable was the technical term for the process) by relays of lovers inhabit an ordered, ceremonious world. The plebeian girl saved from prostitution is called Julie; the Christian names of Mme de Selve are not divulged.

The second paragraph depicts *sensibilité* as the panacea for sick souls. The comte's is filled by a calmly voluptuous feeling, as different from frenzied passion as it is from stoic ataraxia. The emotion which he savours and assesses in tranquillity is not the product of his reason; but rational analysis of this emotion is part of the pleasure it provides. By the 1740s, the cult of mildly emotional affection, considered more alluring than the fires of lust, seems to have been developed as a sort of spiritual aphrodisiac for the bored and jaded.[13] Sentiment and the idea of virtue ('au-dessus de l'humanité' if possible) were luxurious refinements for the emotional titillation of rich voluptuaries.[14]

Religion *is* mentioned in the novel: early in his military career the comte enjoyed the embraces of a noble Spanish adulteress, as superstitious as the grossly ignorant Spanish clergy themselves; then, on his return to France, he had as his mistress a lady whose ostentatious piety was a cover for eroticism, and who replaced him by her spiritual adviser. But the amours of the comte and Mme de Selve take place in a completely secular atmosphere. Mme de Selve is his only salvation: she is all wisdom, all virtue, all sweetness. She is also very intelligent. Though not in the least unfeminine, or domineering, or insensitive to physical pleasure, she meets him on equal terms; he even refers to her as though she were a man: 'Je trouvai en elle l'ami le plus sûr.'[15] There is a current of feminism in the eighteenth century, from Roxane – the strong-minded, sexually enterprising young woman in the *Lettres persanes*[16] – right up to Mme de Staël, who was not only highly conscious of her body, but fought hard for women's right to have minds. Duclos's approval of emancipated women is made clear in the ending of the 1767 edition of the *Confessions*:

> La célèbre Ninon de Lenclos, amante légère, amie solide, honnête homme et philosophe, se plaignait de la bizarrerie et de l'injustice du préjugé à cet égard. 'J'ai réfléchi, disait-elle, dès mon enfance, sur le partage inégal des qualités qu'on exige dans les hommes et dans les femmes. Je vis qu'on nous avait chargées de ce qu'il y avait de plus frivole, et que les hommes s'étaient réservé le droit aux qualités essentielles; dès ce moment, je me fis homme.' Elle le fit, et fit bien.[17]

Once Mme de Selve is convinced that the comte's distaste for promiscuity has made fidelity possible for him, she accepts his hand, and they retire to one of his country estates. They have no wish to visit Paris:

> Eh! qu'y ferions-nous? le monde est inutile à notre bonheur, et ne ferait que nous trouver ridicules. Nous sommes de plus charmés de notre solitude. Je trouve l'univers entier avec ma femme, qui est mon amie. Elle est tout pour mon cœur, et ne désire pas autre chose que de passer sa vie avec moi. Nous vivons, nous sentons, nous pensons ensemble.
>
> Nous jouissons de cette union des cœurs, qui est le fruit et le principe de la vertu. Ce qui m'attache le plus à ma femme, c'est que je lui dois cette vertu précieuse, et sans doute elle me chérit comme son ouvrage.[18]

Here we are not far from the tone of the *comédie larmoyante* and *drame bourgeois*, with their analytical definitions of moral concepts, and their shrill cries that happiness, virtue made easy, and the assurance that one has a feeling heart, are all much the same thing. The comte and his wife enjoy dispassionate bliss for a whole year. And then Duclos decides it is time for the novel to end.

The *Confessions* were thought by contemporaries to be a *roman à clef*. Whether the pair existed or not, escape into the countryside, and the innocent pleasures of matrimony, were common enough themes in literature of the period.[19] The notion of *le vide de l'âme* – with or without sentiment as a cure – continued throughout the century and merged into romantic gloom. The comte de Tilly exemplifies the development from *vide de l'âme* to *mal du siècle*:

> J'ai vu cet univers; son vide m'a suivi partout; j'ai connu les rois, les peuples, visité les nations; j'ai éprouvé ce qu'il y a de plus actif dans les affections humaines; en dernière analyse, il n'y a rien . . ., j'ai senti plus que jamais ce vide immense qui nous ceint de tous les côtés, et dont l'idée seule doit assouvir la faim des honneurs pendant la vie, et étancher la soif de la renommée après la mort.[20]

But nihilistic melancholy was only one not very important facet of the transformation of Europe which we call 'romanticism', and there are more significant things in the eighteenth century than the pointless ennui of effete aristocrats. The comte and Mme de Selve, withdrawn from life and existing only for themselves, do not even take an interest in their estates or provide work by entertaining. John Locke found in the human mind something that he called 'uneasiness', and his French translators 'inquiétude', which impelled man to activity.[21] Voltaire did not brood over *ennui*; he regarded it as something to be driven away by pleasant and useful occupations.[22] Duclos himself maintained that man is improvable by education, that passions are a motive force, that we have a duty to society, and that the aim of society is not epicurean aristocratic lethargy but the greatest good of the greatest number:

> Le meilleur des gouvernements n'est pas celui qui fait les hommes les plus heureux, mais celui qui fait le plus grand nombre d'heureux.

> On ne saurait trop s'attacher à corriger ou régler les passions qui rendent les hommes malheureux, sans les avilir; et l'on doit rendre de plus en plus odieuses celles qui, sans les rendre malheureux, les avilissent et nuisent à la société, qui doit être le premier objet de notre attachement.[23]

There is no evidence that Duclos intended his novel to be an attack on the nobility. The rich son of a bourgeois manufacturer and merchant, he associated with noblemen, and received a court appointment as historiographer royal. Partly, no doubt, to bolster up his own position, he proclaimed that 'la classe générale des gens du monde et la bourgeoisie opulente se ressemblent plus au fond qu'on ne le suppose'.[24] None the less, he deplores the fact that rich merchants turn their sons into nobles: 'De bons citoyens et d'excellents bourgeois, ils deviennent de plats anoblis.'[25] He goes out of his way to praise financiers.[26] He contrasts the jovial vigour of shopkeepers' wives with the tired boredom of fine ladies.[27]

The ideal society of this professional man of letters appears to be one in which aristocrats have the same sound, respectable, sensible standards as the middle class:

> La bonne compagnie est indépendante de l'état et du rang, et ne se trouve que parmi ceux qui pensent et qui sentent, qui ont les idées justes et les sentiments honnêtes.[28]

The lords and ladies depicted in the *Confessions du comte de* *** do not, on the whole, satisfy these requirements.

NOTES

1 *Confessions du comte de* ***, ed. cit., p. 284.
2 C.-P. J. de Crébillon fils, *La Nuit et le Moment* (1755), ed. P. Lièvre (Paris, 1929), p. 17.
3 Montesquieu, *Lettres Persanes*, CX (*Œuvres*, ed. Pléiade, vol. I, p. 294).
4 Crébillon fils, ibid., p. 96.
5 *L'Abbé Prévost. Colloque d'Aix-en-Provence*, 1963 (Aix-en-Provence, 1965) pp. 155–72: J. Deprun, *Thèmes malebranchistes dans l'œuvre de Prévost*. M. Deprun concludes that Prévost transmits to the eighteenth century 'la tradition d'une certaine sensibilité augustinienne'.
6 *Mémoires du comte Alexandre de Tilly pour servir à l'histoire des mœurs de la fin du xviiie siècle*, ed. C. Melchior-Bonnet (Paris, 1965), p. 224. Tilly, born in 1764 of an ancient Norman family, became page to Queen Marie-Antoinette at the age of fourteen, was commissioned into the Dragoons at the age of eighteen, emigrated during the Revolution, began his memoirs in Berlin in 1801, committed suicide in Brussels in 1816. He was a notorious rake.
7 *Le Cercle, ou La Soirée à la mode*, comédie épisodique en un acte et en prose par M. Poinsinet (Paris, MDCCLXIV), Sc. V, pp. 28–9.
8 M. J. Fabre strongly defends *Paul et Virginie* in Chapter 8 of *Lumières et romantisme* (Paris, 1963), and M. R. Mauzi (*Paul et Virginie*, Garnier-Flammarion, 1966, p. 24) finds it positively out of this world. Etiemble (*Romanciers du XVIIIe siècle*, Pléiade, II, p. xxxi) says 'Je ne puis le supporter'.
9 *Confessions*, ed. cit., pp. 268–75. 'Rien ne m'a donné une plus vive image du bonheur parfait que l'union et les transports de ces jeunes amants' (pp. 274–5).
10 Ibid., p. 275.
11 Ibid., p. 286.

12 Ibid., p. 286.
13 See R. Mercier, *La Réhabilitation de la nature humaine*, p. 372; J. Ehrard, *L'Idée de nature en France*, p. 553. On innocent pleasure in country retirement, see Mercier, pp. 99–100.
14 Pococurante, in *Candide*, Chapter 25, is 'bien las des dames de la ville' and prefers 'deux filles jolies et proprement mises', but he has not yet discovered the joys of virtue. Marmontel (*Mémoires*, Paris, 1819, vol. 1, p. 184) attributes the unhappiness of the *fermier-général* and art patron La Popelinière to Mme de la Popelinière's lack of wifely virtue: 'Une maison voluptueuse, dont les arts, les talents, tous les plaisirs honnêtes semblaient avoir fait leur séjour, et dans cette maison le luxe, l'abondance, l'affluence de tous les biens, tout cela corrompu par la défiance et la crainte, par les tristes soupçons et par les noirs chagrins!' Mme Geoffrin employed Marmontel to amuse *grands seigneurs* and their ladies at her *soupers intimes* by reading his nauseatingly sentimental *Contes moraux* to them: '... tous les moyens que je pouvais avoir d'être amusant et d'être aimable .... Ce qui me ravissait moi-même, c'était de voir de près les plus beaux yeux du monde donner des larmes aux petites scènes touchantes où je faisais gémir la nature ou l'amour' (ibid., pp. 315–16).
15 *Confessions*, ed. cit., p. 284.
16 *Lettres Persanes*, CLXI (ed. cit. p. 372): 'Comment as-tu pensé que je fusse assez crédule pour m'imaginer que je ne fusse dans le Monde que pour adorer tes caprices? que, pendant que tu te permets tout, tu eusses le droit d'affliger tous mes désirs? Non! J'ai pu vivre dans la servitude, mais j'ai toujours été libre: j'ai réformé tes lois sur celles de la Nature, et mon esprit s'est toujours tenu dans l'indépendance.'
17 *Confessions*, ed. cit., p. 1930.
18 Ibid., p. 301.
19 In his *Lettres Athéniennes* (published 1771) Crébillon *fils* mocks those who retreat into nature to cure their *vide d'âme*: 'Dans l'ennui de votre âme, vous avez attribué au lever de l'aurore, au murmure des ruisseaux, au silence de la solitude, aux exercices rustiques, aux chants des oiseaux, plus de charmes que tout cela n'en a peut-être.' (Quoted by L. Versini in *Prévost. Colloque d'Aix-en-Provence 1963*, p. 240: 'Thèmes empruntés à Prévost par le roman français').
20 *Mémoires*, ed. cit., pp. 278–9.
21 *An Essay concerning Human Understanding*, Bk 2, Ch. 21 (*Works of John Locke*, London, MDCCXIV), pp. 105–6: 'Good and Evil, present and absent, 'tis true, work upon the Mind: but that which immediately determines the Will, from time to time, to every voluntary Action, is the Uneasiness of Desire, fix'd on some absent Good; either negative, as Indolence to one in Pain; or positive, as Enjoyment of Pleasure. ... When a Man is perfectly content with the State he is in, which is when he is perfectly without any Uneasiness, what Industry, what Action, what Will is there left, but to continue in it?'
22 E.g., *Sur les Pensées de M. Pascal*, XXIII (Pléiade, *Mélanges*, pp. 118–19).
23 Duclos, *Considérations sur les Mœurs*, ed. F. C. Green (Cambridge, 1946), pp. 192, 194.

24 Ibid., p. 109.
25 *Confessions*, ed. cit., p. 236.
26 Ibid., pp. 253–4; *Considérations sur les Mœurs*, Ch. X, 'Sur les gens de fortune'.
27 *Confessions*, ed. cit., p. 236.
28 *Considérations sur les Mœurs*, ed. cit., p. 110. He excluded the 'bas peuple, qui n'a que des idées relatives à ses besoins, et qui en est ordinairement privé sur tout autre sujet' (p. 109).

VII · Anonymous

FROM *Le Philosophe* (published 1743)

L'entendement que l'on captive sous le joug de la foi, devient incapable des grandes vues que demande le gouvernement, et qui sont si nécessaires pour les emplois publics. On fait croire au superstitieux que c'est un être suprême qui l'a élevé au-dessus des autres: c'est vers cet être et non vers le public que se tourne sa reconnaissance. Séduit par l'autorité que lui donne son état, et à laquelle les autres hommes ont bien voulu se soumettre pour établir entre eux un ordre certain, il se persuade aisément qu'il n'est dans l'élévation que pour son propre bonheur, et non pour travailler au bonheur des autres. Il se regarde comme la fin dernière de la dignité qui, dans le fond, n'a d'autre objet que le bien de la république et des particuliers qui la composent.

J'entrerais volontiers ici dans un plus grand détail; mais on sent assez combien la république doit tirer d'utilité de ceux qui, élevés aux grandes places, sont pleins des idées de l'ordre et du bien public et de tout ce qui s'appelle humanité, et il serait à souhaiter qu'on en pût exclure tous ceux qui, par le caractère de leur esprit ou par leur mauvaise éducation, sont remplis d'autres sentiments.

Le philosophe est donc un honnête homme qui agit en tout par raison, et qui joint à un esprit de réflexion et de justesse les mœurs et les qualités sociables.

De cette idée il est aisé de conclure combien le sage insensible des stoïciens est éloigné de la perfection de notre philosophe. Nous voulons un homme, et leur sage n'était qu'un fantôme: ils rougissaient de l'humanité, et nous en faisons gloire; nous voulons mettre les passions à profit; nous voulons en faire un usage raisonnable et, par conséquent, possible, et ils voulaient follement anéantir les passions et nous abaisser au-dessous de notre nature par une insensibilité chimérique. Les passions lient les hommes entre eux, et c'est pour nous un doux plaisir que cette liaison. Nous ne voulons ni détruire nos passions, ni en être tyrannisés; mais nous voulons nous en servir et les régler.

Le Philosophe, ed. H. Dieckmann (Saint-Louis, 1948), pp. 58–60.

Le Philosophe, an anonymous text of about four and a half thousand words, was first made available to the modern reader in 1948 by Professor Herbert Dieckmann. It was probably written in the 1730s, and was published, clandestinely, in 1743 in a volume entitled *Les Nouvelles Libertés de penser*. It was reprinted repeatedly during the eighteenth century from 1745 to 1797. The imprint of the 1745 edition impertinently attributed it to the Jesuits: 'A Trévoux. Aux dépens de la Société de Jésus.' According to Voltaire a copy of it was 'dans le portefeuille de tous les curieux'. Diderot gave an expurgated version of t in the *Encyclopédie*, and Voltaire published another in 1773, in connection with his *Lois de Minos*. These two versions are printed alongside the 1743 text in Professor Dieckmann's edition, where the significance of *Le Philosophe* is examined against the background of seventeenth- and early eighteenth-century thought.

The text opens with a description of what constitutes a philosophe. Rejection of all revealed religions, and the recognition that 'nul être suprême n'exige de culte des hommes' is not enough to merit the title. The philosophe is a man who, while wishing to act in accordance with his own free will, understands the causes which determine his actions, and submits to the control of reason. He acts always after deliberation; though in the midst of darkness, reason is his light, and not – as followers of St Augustine believe – divine grace. He knows that all ideas come to him through the senses; that from observation and experience he can acquire knowledge, though his knowledge is necessarily limited by his senses and such extensions of them as telescopes; that he is a material substance, capable of thought; that thought is a physical sense, like sight and hearing. Though he does not scorn brilliant flashes of intuition, the method he relies on is deliberate, logical examination. His chief concern is not abstract speculation but practical issues of how to live in society. He does not regard himself as an exile in this vale of tears, assailed by the Enemy; on the contrary, this world is his paradise; 'Il veut jouir en sage économe des biens que la nature lui donne.' Society is the only God he recognises: the worship he offers Society is probity, scrupulous attention to duty, and 'un désir sincère de n'en être pas un membre inutile ou embarrassant'. Those who, instead of being determined by reason, are ruled by fanaticism and superstition become the prey of their uncontrolled passions. Setting themselves an unattainable standard of virtue, they betray their God, feel guilty, and betray their fellow men. Hopes of Heaven and fears of Hell are ineffectual moral aids: 'Le frein de la religion est bien faible.'[1]

Condemned criminals are always superstitious or ignorant men, never philosophes: 'Les passions tranquilles du philosophe peuvent bien le porter à la volupté, mais non pas au crime: sa raison cultivée le guide et ne le conduit jamais au désordre.' His incentives to act justly are powerful ones: his own self-satisfaction and the knowledge that crime will exclude him from the pleasure of society: 'Il est pétri, pour ainsi dire, avec le levain de l'ordre et de la règle; il est rempli des idées du bien de la société civile.' Reason, habit, thought have so conditioned and attuned him that he is incapable of wrong-doing. All men derive pleasure from the esteem of their fellows and the obligations of friendship. It is in the philosophe that such sentiments are strongest. Offences against society are incompatible with his principles: 'L'expérience fait voir tous les jours que, plus on a de raison et de lumière, plus on est sûr et propre pour le commerce de la vie.'[2] At this point in the text the writer invokes the authority of the Ancients, and quotes the maxim 'Que les peuples seront heureux quand les rois seront philosophes, ou quand les philosophes seront rois'. The *superstitieux* (still not defined, but equated earlier in the text with the *fanatique*) is unfit to rule because (1) his gaze is fixed on the next world, and he therefore has no real interest in his fellow men, (2) the economic and social doctrines taught by religion are, in spite of 'les interprétations qu'on a été obligé de leur donner', contrary to the requirements of a happy and flourishing state.[3]

The passage printed above then occurs. It asserts that the unquestioning acceptance of Christian doctrine makes a man unsuitable for high office of state. The 'que l'on captive' and 'on fait croire' in the first paragraph are, presumably, directed against clerical influence at Court. Bishops had, indeed, taught that monarchs derive their power from God alone. This doctrine had been the basis of Bossuet's *Politique tirée des propres paroles de l'Ecriture Sainte*, which he began to write in 1678 for the instruction of the Dauphin:

> Dieu est la sainteté même, la bonté même, la puissance même, la raison même. En ces choses est la majesté de Dieu. En l'image de ces choses est la majesté du Prince. Elle est si grande, cette majesté, qu'elle ne peut être dans le Prince comme dans sa source; elle est empruntée de Dieu qui la lui donne pour le bien de ses peuples, à qui il est bon d'être contenus par une force supérieure.[4]

But Bossuet, Fénelon and Massillon had also emphasised that monarchs should rule in the interests of their people, and not for their own pleasure. The author of *Le Philosophe* is careful, in the second paragraph of the passage, to suppress this fact and suggest the opposite. There is, however, a certain tentativeness in the way he implies that only philosophes should be responsible for the education of princes, and that only philosophes should wield political power. The phrase 'à laquelle les autres hommes ont bien voulu se soumettre' (an echo of Voltaire's 'où le peuple est assez bon pour le souffrir' in letter VI of the *Lettres philosophiques*) is not a firm statement that sovereignty lies with the people. The hypothetical 'J'entrerais volontiers ici dans un plus grand détail' may (as in the passage from the *Lettres persanes*) be a polite formula, explaining that he does not wish to bore the reader. It may also indicate that, even in a clandestine pamphlet, the author is unwilling to condemn outright the hereditary monarchy of France based on divine right and subject to clerical influence. The conditional and subjunctive 'il serait à souhaiter qu'on pût exclure' are, likewise, the opposite of trenchant. The education of heirs to the throne is implied in paragraph 3, but not openly mentioned.

Can the writer of this pamphlet really have been proposing, in the years before 1743, that the monarchy should turn from the Church and seek the guidance of atheist philosophes? It is certainly a fact that, a little later, the philosophes strove to get their ideas accepted at Court. (Mme de Pompadour had links with them.) In 1762, Voltaire wrote that 'les frères doivent toujours respecter la morale et le trône'[5] – in other words, the alliance of throne with altar should be replaced by one with a militant, organised philosophe party. That individuals and society could be perfected by education was, of course, one of the main philosophe tenets. Diderot, in 1769, contrasted the upbringing of middle-class children with that of princes, and regretted that no Hell existed to punish the (presumably ecclesiastical) tutors who corrupted the innocence of their royal pupils:

> Je souffre mortellement de ne pouvoir croire en Dieu. Ah Dieu! souffrirais-tu et les monstres qui nous dominent et ceux qui les ont formés, si tu étais quelque chose de plus qu'un vain épouvantail des nations?[6]

During the first half of the century, however, philosophe writings tended to disclaim any active political role. In his *Lettres philosophiques* (which the Parlement de Paris condemned to be burned as 'propres à inspirer le libertinage le plus dangereux pour la religion et l'ordre de la société civile'), Voltaire says that, unlike the theologians, 'qui ont porté le flambeau de la discorde dans leur patrie', thinking men, who are in a tiny minority, would never dream of overthrowing anything.[7]

Montesquieu, in Book XII, chapters 11–13, of *De l'Esprit des lois*, states that thought, written or spoken, is totally different from action, and therefore cannot legally be held seditious. Rousseau, in the second paragraph of *Du Contrat social*, disclaims any active role as a politician. Almost certainly, to its author, the political content of *Le Philosophe* could be little more than speculation – an echo of conversation on such matters in 'advanced' circles.[8] Nevertheless, in his *Considérations sur les Mœurs* of 1750, Duclos makes a distinction between what is impossible and what is merely difficult to achieve:

> Ce n'est point ici une idée de république imaginaire: d'ailleurs, ces sortes d'idées sont au moins d'heureux modèles, des chimères, qui ne le sont pas totalement, et qui peuvent être réalisées jusqu'à un certain point. Bien des choses ne sont impossibles que parce qu'on s'est accoutumé à les regarder comme telles. Une opinion contraire et du courage rendraient souvent facile ce que le préjugé et la lâcheté ugent impraticable.
>
> Peut-on regarder comme chimérique ce qui s'est exécuté? Quelques anciens peuples, tels que les Egyptiens et les Spartiates, n'ont-ils pas eu une éducation relative à l'état, et qui en faisait en partie la constitution?[9]

And there already existed a European monarch who encouraged the philosophes to regard him as one of themselves. On 22 May 1740, a few days before his accession to the throne, Frederick the Great wrote to Christian von Wolf that philosophers must be the preceptors of the universe and the masters of princes: what philosophers thought and discovered, monarchs would put into practice.[10]

The first three paragraphs of the passage are omitted from the version in the *Encyclopédie* and *Les Lois de Minos*. Paragraph four is described in a footnote as *Définition du philosophe*: it summarises the defence of philosophy so far made in the text, with its emphasis on social probity guaranteed by sound judgment and rational control. *Honnête homme* had various meanings already in the seventeenth century, according to the various social classes or groups of which it was used. Here, though it does signify social status and manner, it is primarily (in answer to attacks on the alleged wickedness of libertine philosophes) an affirmation of moral integrity.

The last paragraph dissociates the philosophe from the stoic ideal of ataraxia – detachment or impassivity. This ideal (which, combined with epicureanism, was to Chaulieu the only true wisdom), continued to be one connotation of the word philosophe throughout the eighteenth century. Voltaire, in the dedicatory epistle to *L'Orphelin de la Chine*

(1755), speaks of his retirement 'au pied des Alpes, et vis-à-vis des neiges éternelles, et où je devais n'être que philosophe'. The philosophes generally, however, stress the importance of activity and involvement. The best-known early statement of this comes in Voltaire's *Lettres philosophiques*: 'L'homme est né pour l'action, comme le feu tend en haut et la pierre en bas. N'être point occupé et n'exister pas est la même chose pour l'homme.' The passions are the driving-force of life: 'L'homme . . . est pourvu de passions pour agir, et de raison pour gouverner ses actions.' But reasoning power itself is linked to the physical senses, and 'ceux qui sont le mieux organisés sont ceux qui ont les passions les plus vives'. Far from being sinful, self-love and the desire for pleasure are implanted in man by God, and are the necessary basis of society: 'Il est aussi impossible qu'une société puisse se former et subsister sans amour-propre, qu'il serait impossible de faire des enfants sans concupiscence, de songer à se nourrir sans appétit, etc.'[11]

This doctrine of activity, pleasure and rational control is implicit in the final paragraph of our passage; but as the writer has previously accused the non-rational *superstitieux* of acting solely on the impulse of his passions, he is now obliged to emphasise the philosophe's rationality, and minimise the importance of passion. Later philosophes often went much further in extolling the passions. Already in 1746, Diderot, the translator and disciple of Shaftesbury, proclaimed in the *Pensées philosophiques* that great passions, elevating the soul to great things, are the source of sublimity in life, literature, painting and sculpture.[12] By the 1750s, when Diderot has come to reject the idea of a universe operating according to fixed and regular laws, and sees the whole of nature as a process of turbulent change and modification of matter in movement, he also comes more and more to glorify human energy in action, and to belittle the notion of order and control. For Helvétius, in *De l'Esprit* (1758), it is no longer faith that moves mountains, but the human energy of intensely passionate individuals:

> Ce sont les passions qui, fixant fortement notre attention sur l'objet de nos désirs, nous le font considérer sous des aspects inconnus aux autres hommes, et qui font en conséquence concevoir et exécuter aux héros ces entreprises hardies qui, jusqu'à ce que la réussite en ait prouvé la sagesse, paraissent folles, et doivent réellement paraître telles à la multitude.
> Voilà pourquoi, dit le cardinal de Richelieu, l'âme faible trouve de l'impossibilité dans le projet le plus simple, lorsque le plus grand paraît facile à l'âme forte: devant celle-ci les montagnes s'abaissent, lorsqu'aux yeux de celle-là les buttes se métamorphosent en montagnes.

Ce sont en effet les fortes passions qui, plus éclairées que le bon sens, peuvent seules nous apprendre à distinguer l'extraordinaire de l'impossible, que les gens sensés confondent presque toujours ensemble, parce que, n'étant point animés de passions fortes, ces gens sensés ne sont jamais que des hommes médiocres: proposition que je vais prouver, pour faire sentir toute la supériorité de l'homme passionné sur les autres hommes, et montrer qu'il n'y a réellement que les grandes passions qui puissent enfanter les grands hommes.[13]

Rousseau similarly, in *La Nouvelle Héloïse*, states what by the 1760s had become a commonplace:

la sublime raison ne se soutient que par la même vigueur de l'âme qui fait les grandes passions, et l'on ne sert dignement la philosophie qu'avec le même feu qu'on sent pour une maîtresse.[14]

Le Philosophe's moderate defence of the passions lacks any such lyrical qualities. Its atheism, too, lacks the glorification of man's efforts to master his own destiny which is visible in Diderot, and which Chénier exultantly sings in his unfinished epic *Hermès*:

La religion tombe et nous sommes sans maître;
Sous nos pieds à son tour elle expire; et les cieux
Ne feront plus courber nos fronts victorieux.[15]

Already in the *Lettres philosophiques*, Voltaire had found a connection between physical desire, self-love, passion, and the economic well-being of the individual and society:

C'est l'amour de nous-même qui assiste l'amour des autres; c'est par nos besoins mutuels que nous sommes utiles au genre humain; c'est le fondement de tout commerce; c'est l'éternel lien des hommes. Sans lui, il n'y aurait pas eu un art inventé, ni une société de dix personnes fondée; c'est cet amour-propre que chaque animal a reçu de la nature qui nous avertit de respecter celui des autres. La loi dirige cet amour-propre et la religion le perfectionne. Il est bien vrai que Dieu aurait pu faire des créatures uniquement attentives au bien d'autrui. Dans ce cas les marchands auraient été aux Indes par charité, et le maçon eût scié de la pierre pour faire plaisir à son prochain. Mais Dieu a établi les choses autrement. N'accusons point l'instinct qu'il nous donne, et faisons-en l'usage qu'il commande.

Human greatness is shown by activity, not idleness:

Et n'est-il pas plaisant que des têtes pensantes puissent imaginer que la paresse est un titre de grandeur, et l'action, un rabaissement de notre nature?[16]

Similarly, *Le Philosophe*'s modified eulogy of the passions leads (and this concludes the pamphlet) to praise of activity. To be a true philosophe, a man must live above mere subsistence-level,

> Il lui faut, outre le nécessaire précis, un honnête superflu nécessaire à un honnête homme, et par lequel seul on est heureux: c'est le fond des bienséances et des agréments.[17]

The philosophe's paradise consists of social intercourse with one's fellows in an atmosphere of ease, comfort and refined pleasures. Poverty, therefore, banishes a man from this paradise. The traditional teaching of the Church had – in theory if not in practice – honoured poverty. Bossuet preached a famous sermon *Sur l'éminente dignité des pauvres dans l'église*. The new philosophy taught that poverty is due to indolence, and that indolence is a vice. The philosophe will always help his fellow in distress, but he will not admit him as a social equal unless he works hard and makes money.[18]

As she lies dying, Julie in *La Nouvelle Héloïse* thanks God that she was born 'dans une honnête fortune et non dans les grandeurs du monde qui corrompent l'âme, ou dans l'indigence qui l'avilit'.[19] *Le Philosophe* likewise opts for the middle class. He abhors the great nobles:

> La plupart des grands, à qui les dissipations ne laissent pas assez de temps pour méditer, sont féroces envers ceux qu'ils ne croient pas leurs égaux[20]

and has no wish to be among the ignorant, superstitious common people. With his desire to 'jouir en sage économe des biens que la nature lui offre', his concern for practical matters, his emphasis on 'probity', and his detestation of idleness, he gives the text a smug, complacent, 'bourgeois' tone, more in harmony with the eighteenth century of Benjamin Franklin than with that of the young Voltaire or Mme de Pompadour. The style is polished and correct. But it is as devoid of wit as it is of poetry. Voltaire asserted that 'on n'est de bonne compagnie qu'à proportion qu'on a de la coquetterie dans l'esprit'.[21] Rivarol said of himself: 'Je fais descendre les idées du ciel, pour embellir les soupers de la bonne compagnie.'[22] The *honnêtes gens* with whom the author[23] of *Le Philosophe* had enough money to associate were clearly – if his style is anything to go by – not 'bonne compagnie' of this sort, nor is his tract written for those 'gens du monde' who wanted, above all else, to be amused. *Le Philosophe* is not in the least amusing. But in this respect it is not untypical of philosophe literature. The sprightliness of Voltaire was an exception, even in the eighteenth century.

NOTES

1 Cf. Voltaire, *Notebooks*, ed. T. Besterman (Geneva, 1952), p. 313: 'La religion n'est point un frein, c'est au contraire un encouragement au crime'. After 1750 Voltaire came to regard religion as socially necessary, and atheism as a danger to morality.

2 Duclos similarly, in *Considérations sur les Mœurs* (1750), abolishes the idea of sin, and regards ignorance as the cause of crime: 'Qu'on apprenne aux hommes à s'aimer entre eux, qu'on leur en prouve la nécessité pour leur bonheur. . . . Pour les rendre meilleurs, il ne faut que les éclairer: le crime est toujours un faux jugement' (ed. F. C. Green, Cambridge, 1939, pp. 10–11). If Professor Green was right in saying that Duclos was not a philosophe (pp. xi–xiii), and if Louis XV had really read the *Considérations* before pronouncing it to be 'l'ouvrage d'un honnête homme' (p. x), philosophe ideas on ethics must have achieved very wide acceptance by the middle of the century.

3 In the penultimate chapter of *Du Contrat social* Rousseau regards Christianity as incompatible with good government, for reasons not dissimilar to those of *Le Philosophe*.

4 Livre V, article iv.

5 Letter to Damilaville, 30 January, 1762. Quoted by R. Derathé, 'Les Philosophes et le despotisme', pp. 69–70 of *Utopie et Institutions au XVIIIe siècle*, ed. P. Francastel (Paris, La Haye, 1963).

6 *Œuvres*, Assézat, VIII, pp. 452–3.

7 Lettre XIII (Pléiade, *Mélanges*, p. 42).

8 A. Dupront, in the *Post-Face* to *Livre et société dans la France du XVIIIe siècle* (Paris, La Haye, 1965), speaks of 'cet univers folliculaire et pamphlétaire, intermédiaire entre l'univers du livre, des mécanismes scolaires et de la parole discutée et non écrite' (p. 232). According to Professor Dupront, books played a far smaller role than is generally imagined in the spread of new attitudes: 'Plutôt que d'être l'aliment énergétique de la dynamique révolutionnaire, le livre, actif ou passif aux rayons des bibliothèques et dans l'esprit de la société qui en use, auteurs et lecteurs réunis en leur monde étroit, garde une massivité grave, celle d'une culture fortement traditionnelle, nullement explosive, et où les valeurs neuves s'introduisent avec discrétion. Le livre est un outil de choix de la société des lumières, mais le flambeau ne passe encore que dans un petit nombre de mains' (p. 233).

9 Ed. cit., p. 21. Cf. p. 22: 'Il me semble qu'il y a une certaine fermentation de raison universelle qui tend à se développer, qu'on laissera peut-être se dissiper, et dont on pourrait assurer, diriger et hâter les progrès par une éducation bien entendue.'

10 Derathé, op. cit., p. 70. On the philosophes and enlightened despots, see J. Fabre, *Stanislas-Auguste Poniatowski et l'Europe des Lumières* (Paris, 1952), and pp. 142–61 of J.-M. Goulemot et M. Launay, *Le Siècle des lumières* (Paris, 1968).

11 *Sur les Pensées de M. Pascal*, nos. XXIII, III, XI (Pléiade, *Mélanges*, pp. 119, 106–7, 113).

H

12 On Diderot and Shaftesbury, see F. Venturi, *Jeunesse de Diderot* (Paris, 1939), pp. 46–70; 344–58.
13 Discours Troisième, Ch. VI: 'De la puissance des passions', ed. G. Besse (Paris, 1959), p. 144; Chérel, *De Télémaque à Candide*, pp. 204–10, discusses *De l'Esprit*, which he describes as 'une des sources les plus certaines de l'élan et de la pensée romantiques'. Cf. also the article 'Génie' in Diderot, *Œuvres esthétiques*, ed. P. Vernière, Classiques Garnier, pp. 9–20.
14 Seconde Partie, Lettre II, ed. Mornet, vol. II, p. 249 and n.
15 *Œuvres complètes*, Pléiade, ed. G. Walter, p. 393.
16 Ed. cit., nos. XI, XXIV, pp. 113, 119. In 1776 d'Holbach wrote: 'Le désir des richesses n'est que le désir des moyens de subsister commodément, et d'engager les autres à concourir à notre félicité particulière. Cette passion, bien dirigée, est la source de l'industrie, du travail, de l'activité nécessaire à la vie sociale' (*La Morale Universelle, ou les Devoirs de l'homme fondés sur la nature*. Paris, L'An IV de la République Française. T. I, Ch. VII: 'De l'utilité des passions'). Cf. J. Ehrard, *L'Idée de nature en France dans la première moitié du XVIIIᵉ siècle* (Paris, 1963), p. 382: 'Au XVIIIᵉ siècle l'apologie pour l'amour-propre et les passions est liée, sur le plan des faits, au développement du capitalisme commercial, et sur le plan des idées, à la naissance du libéralisme économique'.
17 *Le Philosophe*, p. 60.
18 Ibid., p. 62.
19 Sixième Partie, Lettre XI, ed. cit., vol. IV, p. 309.
20 *Le Philosophe*, p. 44.
21 *Notebooks*, ed. cit., p. 216.
22 *Esprit de Rivarol* (Paris, 1808), p. XXXIX.
23 Voltaire said that *Le Philosophe* was written by C. C. Dumarsais (1676–1756). Professor Dieckmann thinks this improbable. Dr A. W. Fairbairn, of the University of Newcastle upon Tyne, will present new evidence for Dumarsais's authorship in a future number of *Studies on Voltaire and the Eighteenth Century*, ed. Th. Besterman.

VIII · Gresset (1709–1777)

FROM *Le Méchant* (performed 1745)
(Act IV, scene iv)

The scene is the country château of Géronte, probably in Picardy. Apart from the
servants, all the characters in the play are nobles. Géronte and Valère's mother
have arranged a marriage between Valère and Géronte's niece Chloé. Partly to
possess himself of Géronte's money, but mainly because his chief delight is to do
evil, Cléon, a Parisian roué of mature years, has persuaded his protégé Valère
not to marry Chloé. Ariste, the friend of Géronte and of Valère's mother, opens
Valère's eyes to Cléon's malevolence.

VALÈRE
Je ne le verrais plus si ce que vous pensez
Allait m'être prouvé: mais on outre les choses;
C'est donner à des riens les plus horribles causes:
Quant à la probité, nul ne peut l'accuser;
Ce qu'il dit, ce qu'il fait, n'est que pour s'amuser.

ARISTE
S'amuser, dites-vous? Quelle erreur est la vôtre!
Quoi! vendre tour-à-tour, immoler l'une à l'autre
Chaque société, diviser les esprits,
Aigrir les gens brouillés, ou brouiller des amis,
Calomnier, flétrir des femmes estimables,
Faire du mal d'autrui ses plaisirs détestables;
Ce germe d'infamie et de perversité
Est-il dans la même âme avec la probité?
Et parmi vos amis vous souffrez qu'on le nomme?

VALÈRE
Je ne le connais plus s'il n'est point honnête homme:
Mais il me reste un doute; avec trop de bonté
Je crains de me piquer de singularité:
Sans condamner l'avis de Cléon, ni le vôtre,
J'ai l'esprit de mon siècle, et je suis comme un autre.
Tout le monde est méchant; et je serais partout
Ou dupe, ou ridicule, avec un autre goût.

ARISTE
Tout le monde est méchant? oui, ces cœurs haïssables,
Ce peuple d'hommes faux, de femmes, d'agréables,
Sans principe, sans mœurs, esprits bas et jaloux,
Qui se rendent justice en se méprisant tous.
En vain ce peuple affreux, sans frein et sans scrupule,
De la bonté du cœur veut faire un ridicule:
Pour chasser ce nuage, et voir avec clarté
Que l'homme n'est point fait pour la méchanceté,
Consultez, écoutez, pour juges, pour oracles,
Les hommes rassemblés; voyez à nos spectacles,
Quand on peint quelque trait de candeur, de bonté,
Où brille en tout son jour la tendre humanité,
Tous les cœurs sont remplis d'une volupté pure,
Et c'est là qu'on entend le cri de la nature.

Le Théâtre choisi du XVIIIᵉ siècle. Classiques Garnier
(Paris, s.d.), II, pp. 249–50.

The *Nouvelles libertés de penser* of 1743, in which *Le Philosophe* was
first published, also contained an anonymous *Traité de la liberté*,
believed to have been written by Fontenelle. This treatise maintains
that human beings do not possess free will: they are born with certain
propensities, which, in normal persons, can be modified by social
pressures:

Quant à la morale, ce système rend la vertu un pur bonheur, et le
vice un pur malheur; il détruit donc toute la vanité et toute la présomp-
tion qu'on peut tirer de la vertu, et donne beaucoup de pitié pour les
méchants, sans inspirer de haine contre eux: il n'ôte nullement
l'espérance de les corriger, parce qu'à force d'exhortations et
d'exemples, on peut mettre dans leur cerveau les dispositions qui les
déterminent à la vertu.

Some individuals, however, are so constituted that no education, laws,
rewards or punishments can correct them. These are monsters, who
must be exterminated:

Les criminels sont des monstres qu'il faut étouffer en les plaignant,
leur supplice en délivre la société, et épouvante ceux qui seraient
portés à leur ressembler.[1]

Gresset appears to have written his comedy on the basis of such ideas:

Je n'espère pas guérir les méchants invétérés, tout ce peuple de vieilles
beautés et de vieux freluquets qui se mange, se chante, se déchire. Les
monstres sont incurables, et ne sont pas faits pour rentrer dans la
nature. Mais si, par contraste à la méchanceté, j'ai bien peint la bonté,

la jeunesse s'éloignera peut-être de son contraire, la méchanceté.
J'aurai rendu service à ma patrie.[2]

By the end of the fifth act, Cléon has been revealed to everybody as a
monster:

> Qu'on ne m'en parle plus: c'est un fourbe exécrable,
> Indigne du nom d'homme, un monstre abominable.
> Trop tard pour mon malheur je déteste aujourd'hui
> Le moment où j'ai pu me lier avec lui.

But as the play is a comedy, the *méchant* cannot be exterminated according to the prescription in the *Traité de la liberté*. Social death, however,
is to be inflicted on him; Ariste will publicly inform society of his
crimes:

> Autant qu'il faut de soins, d'égards et de prudence
> Pour ne point accuser l'honneur et l'innocence,
> Autant il faut d'ardeur, d'inflexibilité
> Pour déférer un traître à la société;
> Et l'intérêt commun veut qu'on se réunisse
> Pour flétrir un méchant, pour en faire justice.
> J'instruirai l'univers de sa mauvaise foi
> Sans me cacher; je veux qu'il sache que c'est moi:
> Un rapport clandestin n'est pas d'un honnête homme;
> Quand j'accuse quelqu'un, je le dois, et me nomme.   (Act V, sc. iv)

Géronte, on the other hand, is born good; he cannot be wicked, even if
he wishes:

> Vous n'êtes pas méchant, et vous ne pouvez l'être.
> Quelquefois, je le sais, vous voulez le paraître;
> Vous êtes comme un autre, emporté, violent,
> Et vous vous fâchez même assez honnêtement:
> Mais au fond la bonté fait votre caractère,
> Vous aimez qu'on vous aime, et je vous en révère.   (Act I, sc. ii)

Valère, though he has been led astray by the wicked Cléon, is naturally
good, and amenable to education:

> Il est jeune, il peut être indiscret, vain, léger;
> Mais quand le cœur est bon, tout peut se corriger.   (Act IV, sc. vi)

Florise, similarly, is a fundamentally decent woman

> Qui veut être méchante, et n'en a pas l'étoffe.   (Act IV, sc. ix)

Though the virtuous people in the play are provincials, even in Paris
the wicked are depicted as a minority:

> par son succès bizarre,
> La méchanceté prouve à quel point il est rare.   (Act IV, sc. iv)

In Gresset's play *Sidnei* (1745), the hero describes humanity as fundamentally virtuous:

> Les hommes ne sont pas dignes de ce mépris:
> Il en est de pervers; mais dans tous les pays
> Où l'ardeur de m'instruire a conduit ma jeunesse,
> J'ai connu des vertus, j'ai trouvé la sagesse,
> J'ai trouvé des raisons d'aimer l'humanité,
> De respecter les nœuds de la société,
> Et n'ai jamais connu ces plaisirs détestables
> D'offenser, d'affliger, de haïr mes semblables.   (Act II, sc. ii)

'Le cri de la nature' which men utter when moved by moralising plays such as *Le Méchant* proves that they are naturally good.

Montesquieu in the *Lettres persanes* reflects the view, common in the first half of the eighteenth century, that goodness is something which normal men can easily attain:

> Ils leur faisaient surtout sentir que l'intérêt des particuliers se trouve toujours dans l'intérêt commun; que vouloir s'en séparer c'est vouloir se perdre; que la vertu n'est pas une chose qui doive nous coûter; qu'il ne faut point la regarder comme un exercice pénible, et que la justice pour autrui est une charité pour nous.[3]

In Letter LXXXIII he suggests that virtue is an instinct implanted in man by an eternally righteous God or Nature:

> Voilà, Rhedi, ce qui m'a fait penser que la Justice est éternelle et ne dépend point des conventions humaines; et, quand elle en dépendrait, ce serait une vérité terrible, qu'il faudrait se dérober à soi-même.
> Nous sommes entourés d'hommes plus forts que nous: ils peuvent nous nuire de mille manières différentes; les trois quarts du temps ils peuvent le faire impunément.
> Quel repos pour nous de savoir qu'il y a dans le cœur de tous ces hommes un principe intérieur qui combat en notre faveur et nous met à couvert de leurs entreprises!
> Sans cela nous devrions être dans une frayeur continuelle: nous passerions devant les hommes comme devant les lions, et nous ne serions jamais assurés un moment de notre bien, de notre honneur et de notre vie.[4]

Gresset appears to have read the *Lettres persanes*[5]. But he had no need to go either to Fontenelle or Montesquieu for his theories about good and evil: the Church itself taught that man was not totally corrupted at the Fall, and that goodness was, in certain respects, inherent in human nature.[6]

Gresset was well acquainted with such teachings: from 1726 to 1728 he was a Jesuit novice; he taught in Jesuit schools until 1734, when he began his formal theological training, and was given the chair of rhetoric at the Jesuit college of La Flèche. Before he had reached the stage of being ordained priest, he was expelled from the order – not, apparently, because of his charming mock-heroic poem *Vert-Vert* (1734) in which the convent parrot repeats to the nuns words that it has learned from bargees, but because of an attack on the Parlement in *La Chartreuse* (1735). He remained on the best of terms with Jesuits, and, though he lost his chair, influential friends procured for him a sinecure in the post office.[7]

The country gentry in *Le Méchant* are portrayed as good and happy. The picture of fashionable Parisian society is similar to that in the *Confessions du comte de ****[8]: promiscuity, artificiality, boredom, the search for amusement:

> Aujourd'hui dans le monde on ne connaît qu'un crime,
> C'est l'ennui; pour le fuir tous les moyens sont bons:
> Il gagnerait bientôt les meilleures maisons
> Si l'on s'aimait si fort; l'amusement circule
> Par les préventions, les torts, le ridicule:
> Au reste chacun parle et fait comme il l'entend.
> Tout est mal, tout est bien, tout le monde est content.
>
> (Act IV, sc. vii)

Cléon finds escape from ennui, not in *sensibilité* or *bienfaisance*, but in the deliberate pursuit of cruelty and wrong-doing.[9] He is the incarnation of evil – the forerunner of Lovelace in *Clarissa Harlowe* and the prototype of Valmont in *Les Liaisons dangereuses*. There is little gaiety in *Le Méchant*. Already, in his morose comedy *Sidnei* – with echoes from *Le Misanthrope* and a premonition of Lamartine – Gresset had expressed what we can justifiably assume to be his own disgust with fashionable society:

> Insensible aux plaisirs dont j'étais idolâtre,
> Je ne les connais plus, je ne trouve aujourd'hui
> Dans ces mêmes plaisirs que le vide et l'ennui:
> Cette uniformité des scènes de la vie
> Ne peut plus réveiller mon âme appesantie;
>
> . . .
>
> Dans le brillant fracas où j'ai longtemps vécu
> J'ai tout vu, tout goûté, tout revu, tout connu;
>
> . . .
>
> Le monde, usé pour moi, n'a plus rien qui me touche;
> Et c'est pour lui sauver un rêveur si farouche,
> Qu'étranger désormais à la société,
> Je viens de mes déserts chercher l'obscurité.   (Act II, sc. ii)

Voltaire alleged that Gresset the schoolmaster did not know how polite society behaved:

> Gresset, doué du double privilège
> D'être au collège un bel esprit mondain,
> Et dans le monde un homme de collège.

In fact, Gresset for years frequented the salon of his patron the duc de Chaulnes, and one reason for the success of *Le Méchant* was that the public tried to identify the characters with real people. Mme de Pompadour had the play performed at Versailles, and in 1748 he was elected to the Academy. One passage in his *discours de réception* – an attack on the 'esprits frivoles et superficiels' and a plea for 'l'essor et les succès de la raison et de l'esprit' – sounds like the manifesto of a bourgeois philosophe reformer. The scientific and philosophe movement in 1748 was conscious of its strength, and about to launch itself as a dominant force in society.[10] If Gresset had chosen to align himself with it, or if he had accepted Frederick the Great's invitation to go to Berlin, a profitable literary career would have been assured him. Instead, he retired to his native city of Amiens, used his influence to obtain royal letters patent for the establishment of an Académie des Sciences, des Belles Lettres et des Arts[11] at Amiens in 1750, and married the mayor's daughter in 1751. In 1754, in a speech at the Académie Française on the occasion of d'Alembert's admission to that body, he took it upon himself to attack worldly, absentee bishops who,

> regardant leur devoir comme un ennui, l'oisiveté comme un droit, leur résidence comme un exil, venaient promener leur inutilité parmi les écueils, le luxe ou la mollesse de la capitale, ou venaient ramper à la cour et y traîner de l'ambition sans talent, de l'intrigue sans affaires, et de l'importance sans crédit.

The King took this to imply that Gresset was a philosophe; Gresset, in horror at the imputation, fled back to Amiens to confer with his friend and spiritual adviser M. de la Mothe, the resident bishop.[12] In 1759 – the year after Rousseau quarrelled with the philosophes by attacking the theatre in his *Lettre sur les spectacles* – Gresset published a sanctimonious *Lettre sur la comédie*, bitterly regretting 'le scandale que j'ai pu donner à la religion par ce genre d'ouvrage'. In *Le Méchant* he had regarded sentimental, moralising comedy as a means of evoking the good, pure 'cri de la nature'. Now, all he credits the theatre with is 'le stérile mérite d'étonner un instant le désœuvrement et la frivolité, sans arriver jamais à corriger les vices'. Voltaire retorted that Gresset

flattered himself in supposing so poor a play as *Le Méchant* to be of much
service to the Devil.[13]

In 1774 Gresset delivered another harangue to the Académie Française. This time he attacked anglomania, lugubrious poetry, and the
flippancy, insincerity, emptiness and immorality of the fashionable
world. He called for a restoration of 'la bonne gaieté française', 'bonhomie', 'bonté', and the ancient standards of honour now regarded as
'sottise bourgeoise'. In 1777 Louis XVI granted him letters of nobility.
Marie-Antoinette paid the legal expenses. He died shortly after his
ennoblement.

In 1784 the Academy of Amiens offered a 12,000-franc prize for an
Eloge de Gresset. One of the unsuccessful competitors was the Arras
barrister Maximilien de Robespierre. Robespierre's essay applauded
Gresset for his friendship with the late bishop:

> Illustre prélat, recevez l'hommage de toutes les âmes honnêtes et
> sensibles.

It commended Gresset for defending religion at a time when the philosophes attacked it:

> C'est un grand spectacle de voir l'un des plus beaux génies dont le
> siècle s'honore, venger la religion et la vertu par son courage à suivre
> leurs augustes lois, et les défendre, pour ainsi dire, par l'ascendant de
> son exemple, contre l'attaque de tant de plumes audacieuses.

It praised him for his condemnation of contemporary society in his
reply to Suard's *Discours de réception* at the Académie Française on
4 August 1774:

> Ce fut sans doute pour le public une scène assez nouvelle de voir le
> directeur de l'Académie Française chargé de répondre à un Discours de
> réception qui contenait le plus magnifique éloge de ce siècle, ne pas
> appuyer le sentiment de l'orateur; ne pas enchérir sur son enthousiasme,
> mais trouver que ce siècle n'est pas le meilleur des siècles possibles;
> croire, en dépit de toutes les lumières dont il se vante, que le plus fortuné
> de tous les âges n'est pas celui, où un débordement de désolantes
> doctrines a renversé toutes les digues des passions, irritées par les
> énormes besoins du luxe, et s'élever, au nom de la raison et de la
> vérité, contre la corruption du goût et la dépravation des mœurs,
> auxquelles il trouvait une origine commune.[14]

Ariste, in *Le Méchant*, had declaimed about the necessity of punishing
evil-doers:

> Autant qu'il faut de soins, d'égards et de prudence
> Pour ne point accuser l'honneur et l'innocence,

> Autant il faut d'ardeur, d'inflexibilité
> Pour déférer un traître à la société;
> Et l'intérêt commun veut qu'on se réunisse
> Pour flétrir un méchant, pour en faire justice.

It is not inconceivable that when Robespierre sent men to the guillotine in the name of virtue, he remembered these lines, and the anonymous *Traité de la liberté* which called for the extermination of anti-social criminals. Gresset would certainly not have disavowed the attack Robespierre made on the Encyclopédistes and social corruption in his speech of 7 May 1794:

> Cette secte propagea avec beaucoup de zèle l'opinion du matérialisme qui prévalut parmi les grands et parmi les beaux esprits. On lui doit en grande partie cette espèce de philosophie pratique qui, réduisant l'égoïsme en système, regarde la société humaine comme une guerre de ruse, le succès comme la règle du juste et de l'injuste, la probité comme une affaire de goût et de bienséance, le monde comme le patrimoine des fripons adroits.[15]

Gresset was as mediocre a thinker as he was a dramatist. He does, however, illustrate the intricacy of eighteenth-century patterns of opinion. A devout and ultra-respectful admirer of throne and altar, he none the less reflects some aspects of Enlightenment thought. Though no one in the century was less of a rebel than he, by his denunciations of a corrupt and frivolous upper class he too, in a small way, helped to sap respect for established authority.

NOTES

1 *Nouvelles libertés de penser,* 1774 edition (A Londres. Chez l'éternel Jean Nourse. L'an de la Vérité 1774), pp. 207–8. On the *Traité de la liberté,* see Ira O. Wade, *The Clandestine Organization and Diffusion of Philosophic Ideas in France from 1700 to 1750* (Princeton, 1938), pp. 258–9; A. Adam, *Le Mouvement philosophique dans la première moitié du XVIIIe siècle* (Paris, 1967), p. 130: 'Ce traité . . . est de la façon la plus précise la source du déterminisme de Diderot. Celui-ci l'avait présent à l'esprit, il l'avait peut-être sur la table lorsqu'en 1756, il écrivait sa fameuse *Lettre à Paul Landois.*' The *Lettre* is in Diderot, *Correspondance,* ed. G. Roth, t. I, pp. 214–16.

2 P. Leroy, *Le Méchant. Notes sur un manuscrit de Gresset* (Paris, 1950), p. 18.

3 *Lettres Persanes,* XII (*Œuvres complètes,* Pléiade ed., I, p. 149).

4 Ibid., pp. 256–7. Cf. Lettre L., p. 203. Before concluding from these quotations that Montesquieu is guilty of what a reviewer in the *Times Literary Supplement* (16 July 1964, p. 633) called 'the puerility and superficiality which were characteristic of the Enlightenment', one should bear in mind that (1) the *Lettres Persanes* are a novel, not a final statement of Montesquieu's con-

sidered opinion; (2) only those who believe that capitalism was, and is, wholly evil, are entitled to dismiss as nonsense the idea that self-interest and private profit may spur men to produce good things for other people; (3) by 'virtue' Montesquieu means, not sanctity and sinlessness, but avoidance of what is commonly regarded as crime. Apart from time of war (when it is lawful for Christian men, at the commandment of the Magistrate, to murder and destroy), most of us do not find it excessively difficult to abstain from robbing and killing our neighbour, etc.; (4) evil is present in the *Lettres Persanes* from beginning to end: the smug Usbek is a cold-blooded tyrant; 'L'horreur, la nuit et l'épouvante règnent dans le sérail' (Lettre CLVI). The philosophes as a whole were more concerned with improving man by education, legislation and enlightened self-interest than with abstract discussion on the goodness or badness of human nature.

5 The arguments for suicide in Gresset's play *Sidnei*, Act II, sc. vi, appear to be taken from *Lettres persanes*, LXXVI.

6 On the acceptance by the Roman Catholic Church of the Molinist doctrine that when man fell from the state of innocence he only lost his supernatural gifts, but retained reason and the power to control his natural impulses and desires, which were not wicked in themselves, see R. R. Palmer, *Catholics and Unbelievers in Eighteenth Century France* (New York, 1961), pp. 31–3, 43–4, 51. Cf. A. Chérel, *De Télémaque à Candide*, Ch. 2: 'L'optimisme des Jésuites'; J.-F. Thomas, *Le Pélagianisme de J.-J. Rousseau* (Paris, 1956).

7 My information about Gresset's life is derived from A. A. Renouard, *Œuvres de Gresset* (Paris, 1811); L. N. J. J. de Cayrol, *Essai historique sur la vie et les ouvrages de Gresset* (Amiens, 1844); and J. Wogue, *J.-B.-L. Gresset. Sa vie. Ses œuvres* (Paris, 1894).

8 Duclos discusses *méchanceté* in Ch. VIII of his *Considérations sur les mœurs* (ed. F. C. Green, pp. 98–110).

9 The professional seducer ('l'homme à bonnes fortunes') is already described in the *Lettres persanes*, XLVIII (ed. cit., p. 201): 'Non, Monsieur, je n'ai d'autre emploi que de faire enrager un mari ou désespérer un père; j'aime à alarmer une femme qui croit me tenir et la mettre à deux doigts de ma perte.'

10 1746, *privilège* of the *Encyclopédie*; Condillac, *Essai sur l'origine des connaissances humaines*; 1748, Montesquieu, *De l'Esprit des lois*; La Mettrie, *L'Homme-machine*; 1749, Buffon, first books of *Histoire naturelle*; Diderot, *Lettre sur les aveugles*.

11 On the provincial academies, see G. Bollème, J. Ehrard, F. Furet, D. Roche, J. Roger, *Livre et société dans la France du XVIIIe siècle* (Paris, 1965), pp. 93–184, 'Milieux académiques provinciaux et société des lumières'.

12 M. de la Mothe was involved in the case of the chevalier de La Barre, who was arrested at Abbeville in October 1765, on a charge of insulting a Corpus Christi procession. In September, the bishop of Amiens had pronounced 'dignes des derniers supplices en ce monde, et des peines éternelles dans l'autre' the unidentified criminals who had defaced a crucifix on the bridge at Abbeville. In February 1766 an Abbeville court sentenced La Barre (who was now 20) to be burned. In June 1766 the Parlement de Paris rejected La Barre's appeal. The bishop of Amiens implored Louis XV to commute the sentence to life imprisonment, but the superstitious Louis

refused. On 1 July 1766, at Abbeville, after the routine torture had been administered, the chevalier de La Barre was beheaded, and his body burned along with a copy of Voltaire's *Dictionnaire philosophique*. This *cause célèbre* proved invaluable to French anticlerical propagandists, even though (as Chanoine L. Désers points out in *Le Chevalier de La Barre. La légende et la réalité*, Paris, 1922) it was lay courts which tried and sentenced La Barre, and the Assembly General of the Clergy called for clemency.

13 Voltaire, *Le Pauvre Diable, Œuvres*, ed. Moland, vol. 10, pp. 106–7. The *pauvre diable* was the Jansenist Abraham-Joseph de Chaumeix, whose *Préjugés légitimes contre l'Encyclopédie et essai de réfutation de ce dictionnaire* were published 1758–9. In March, 1759, the Conseil d'Etat withdrew the *privilège* of the *Encyclopédie*. Gresset's *Lettre*, which is dated 14 mai 1759, appeared at a moment when the *parti dévot* appeared to be in the ascendant.

14 Wogue, op. cit., pp. 330–2; Robespierre, *Œuvres*, ed. E. Lesueur (Paris, 1912), vol. I, pp. 106–10.

15 Robespierre, *Textes choisis*, ed. J. Poperen, vol. 3 (Paris, 1958), pp. 170–1.

IX · Rousseau (1712–1778)

FROM *La Nouvelle Héloïse* (published 1761)
(Part I, Letter XXVI)

Saint-Preux is the twenty-year-old private tutor to Julie, who is eighteen.
The couple have fallen in love, and exchanged one kiss, but know that Julie's
father, the Baron d'Etange, will never 'consentir à donner sa fille, son enfant
unique, à un petit bourgeois sans fortune'.[1] Consequently, the hot-blooded but
clear-headed Julie has sent her beloved away, for an indefinite time. She has
nevertheless just written to him, bemoaning her misery: 'Sens-tu combien un
cœur languissant est tendre, et combien la tristesse fait fermenter l'amour.'
From Meillerie on the Savoy side of Lake Geneva (whence, through a telescope
borrowed from the parish priest, he thinks he can descry the d'Etange château
on the Swiss side), Saint-Preux entreats her to elope with him.

Ah! si tu pouvais rester toujours jeune et brillante comme à présent,
je ne demanderais au Ciel que de te savoir éternellement heureuse, te
voir tous les ans de ma vie une fois, une seule fois; et passer le reste
de mes jours à contempler de loin ton asile, à t'adorer parmi ces rochers.
Mais hélas! vois la rapidité de cet astre qui jamais n'arrête; il vole et
le temps fuit, l'occasion s'échappe, ta beauté, ta beauté même aura
son terme, elle doit décliner et périr un jour comme une fleur qui
tombe sans avoir été cueillie; et moi cependant, je gémis, je souffre,
ma jeunesse s'use dans les larmes, et se flétrit dans la douleur. Pense,
pense, Julie, que nous comptons déjà des années perdues pour le
plaisir. Pense qu'elles ne reviendront jamais; qu'il en sera de même
de celles qui nous restent si nous les laissons échapper encore. O
amante aveuglée! tu cherches un chimérique bonheur pour un temps
où nous ne serons plus; tu regardes un avenir éloigné, et tu ne vois pas
que nous nous consumons sans cesse, et que nos âmes, épuisées
d'amour et de peines, se fondent et coulent comme l'eau. Reviens, il en
est temps encore, reviens, ma Julie, de cette erreur funeste. Laisse-là
tes projets et sois heureuse. Viens, ô mon âme, dans les bras de ton
ami, réunir les deux moitiés de notre être: viens à la face du ciel guide
de notre fuite et témoin de nos serments jurer de vivre et mourir l'un à
l'autre. Ce n'est pas toi, je le sais, qu'il faut rassurer contre la crainte
de l'indigence. Soyons heureux et pauvres, ah quels trésors nous aurons
acquis! Mais ne faisons point cet affront à l'humanité, de croire qu'il
ne restera pas sur la terre entière un asile à deux Amants infortunés.

J'ai des bras, je suis robuste; le pain gagné par mon travail te paraîtra plus délicieux que les mets des festins. Un repas apprêté par l'amour peut-il jamais être insipide? Ah! tendre et chère amante, dussions-nous n'être heureux qu'un seul jour, veux-tu quitter cette courte vie sans avoir goûté le bonheur?

Je n'ai plus qu'un mot à vous dire, ô Julie, vous connaissez l'antique usage du rocher de Leucate, dernier refuge de tant d'amants malheureux. Ce lieu-ci lui ressemble à bien des égards. La roche est escarpée, l'eau est profonde, et je suis au désespoir.

> *Julie, ou La Nouvelle Héloïse. Lettres de deux Amants, Habitants d'une petite Ville au pied des Alpes.* Recueillies et publiées par J.-J. Rousseau. Ed. Daniel Mornet (Paris, 1925), II, pp. 101–3.

This Romantic prose lyric, with its compulsive harmonies and plangent repetitions, is an expression of Rousseau's own unfulfilled longings. It is totally different from the ironic, destructive style of Voltaire, who – with that overdeveloped sense of the ridiculous which on occasion is as infuriating as Rousseau at his most humourless – remarked of the image 'nos âmes, épuisées d'amour . . .':

> Il peut être fort plaisant de voir couler une âme; mais pour l'eau, c'est d'ordinaire quand elle est épuisée qu'elle ne coule plus; je m'en rapporte à vous.[2]

Saint-Preux does not speak the language of court or salon. Indeed, the Baron d'Etange hardly regards him as a fellow human being at all, but as a thing, to be bought or got rid of at will:

> Dès qu'il a su que vous n'étiez pas noble, il a demandé ce qu'on vous donnait par mois.[3]

But Saint-Preux lays claim to a different sort of nobility, which is measured by the capacity to feel and to suffer, not by rank or birth. Striding from rock to rock in the wilderness, superior to the social distinctions which would stifle his virtuous passion for Julie, Saint-Preux glories in his emotions, and defiantly exults in his urge to encompass an infinity of grief:

> O Julie, que c'est un fatal présent du ciel qu'une âme sensible! Celui qui l'a reçue doit s'attendre à n'avoir que peine et douleur sur la terre. . . . Victime des préjugés, il trouvera dans d'absurdes maximes un obstacle invincible aux justes vœux de son cœur. Les hommes le puniront d'avoir des sentiments droits de chaque chose, et d'en juger par ce qui est véritable plutôt que par ce qui est de convention. Seul il suffirait pour faire sa propre misère, en se livrant indiscrètement aux

attraits divins de l'honnête et du beau, tandis que les pesantes chaînes
de la nécessité l'attachent à l'ignominie. Il cherchera la félicité suprême
sans se souvenir qu'il est homme: son cœur et sa raison seront incessam-
ment en guerre, et des désirs sans bornes lui prépareront d'éternelles
privations.[4]

He claims tragic grandeur for his despair by identifying himself with
lovers in classical antiquity who escaped their woes by jumping into the
waves from the rock of Apollo Leucadius.

'La roche est escarpée, l'eau est profonde, et je suis au désespoir'
is thus something more than a melodramatic phrase of moral blackmail.
In fact, Saint-Preux does not intend to submit to fate when this consists
merely of an obstinate Swiss baron. He stresses the shortness of youth,
the fleetingness of time, the sorrows of their mutual deprivation
('Pense, pense . . . perdues pour le plaisir') to convince Julie that she
must flee with him. The pleasures he promises her are not those vainly
sought by vicious, jaded, debauched nobles, but pure joys of virtuous
love, expressed partly in biblical language. Sexual passion, he has
already informed her, should be a source of heroic energy, not an excuse
for weakness or inaction:

l'amour véritable est un feu dévorant qui porte son ardeur dans les
autres sentiments, et les anime d'une vigueur nouvelle. C'est pour
cela qu'on a dit que l'amour faisait des Héros. Heureux celui que le sort
eût placé pour le devenir, et qui aurait Julie pour amante![5]

God, nature and their own free choice have ordained them to be man
and wife: the only impediment, barbaric, odious social prejudice, must
be swept aside:

Ces deux belles âmes sortirent l'une pour l'autre des mains de la
nature; c'est dans une douce union, c'est dans le sein du bonheur
que, libres de déployer leurs forces et d'exercer leurs vertus, elles
eussent éclairé la terre de leurs exemples. Pourquoi faut-il qu'un
insensé préjugé vienne changer les directions éternelles, et bouleverser
l'harmonie des êtres pensants? . . . Le lien conjugal n'est-il pas le plus
libre ainsi que le plus sacré des engagements? Oui, toutes les lois qui
le gênent sont injustes; tous les pères qui l'osent former ou rompre
sont des tyrans. Ce chaste nœud de la nature n'est soumis ni au pouvoir
souverain ni à l'autorité paternelle; mais à la seule autorité du père
commun qui sait commander aux cœurs, et qui leur ordonnant de s'unir,
les peut contraindre à s'aimer.[6]

Thus it would seem that, in Rousseau's opinion, the torments of
love are not something to be sought after or gloated over, but merely the
product of an unjust, unnatural society whose dictates are no longer

acceptable to valiant hearts. Already, in the *Discours sur l'Inégalité*, he had so explained the existence of star-crossed lovers and romantic suicides:

> Combien de mariages heureux, mais inégaux, ont été rompus ou troublés, et combien de chastes épouses déshonorées, par cet ordre des conditions toujours en contradiction avec celui de la nature! Combien d'autres unions bizarres formées par l'intérêt et désavouées par l'amour et par la raison! Combien même d'époux honnêtes et vertueux font mutuellement leur supplice pour avoir été mal assortis! Combien de jeunes et malheureuses victimes de l'avarice de leurs parents se plongent dans le vice, ou passent leurs tristes jours dans les larmes, et gémissent dans des liens indissolubles que le cœur repousse et que l'or seul a formés! Heureuses quelquefois celles que leur courage et leur vertu même arrachent à la vie, avant qu'une violence barbare les force à passer dans le crime ou dans le désespoir! Pardonnez-le moi, père et mère à jamais déplorables; j'aigris à regret vos douleurs; mais puissent-elles servir d'exemple éternel et terrible à quiconque ose, au nom même de la nature, violer le plus sacré de ses droits![7]

Saint-Preux implores Julie to accept bliss with him in some freer surroundings, where happiness is not measured by riches, and manual labour is not scorned. He offers her not only ecstatic joy, but, in addition, the satisfying routine of domesticity and good works within the community:

> Délices de l'amour, c'est alors que nos cœurs vous savoureraient sans cesse! Une longue et douce ivresse nous laisserait ignorer le cours des ans: et quand enfin l'âge aurait calmé nos premiers feux, l'habitude de penser et sentir ensemble ferait succéder à leurs transports une amitié non moins tendre. Tous les sentiments honnêtes nourris dans la jeunesse avec ceux de l'amour en rempliraient un jour le vide immense; nous pratiquerions au sein de cet heureux peuple, et à son exemple, tous les devoirs de l'humanité: sans cesse nous nous unirions pour bien faire, et nous ne mourrions point sans avoir vécu.[8]

Such a Utopia, he believes, already exists among the peasants of the Haut Valais, where the primitive virtues still hold sway, equality reigns, and money is of no importance:

> l'argent est fort rare dans le Haut Valais, mais c'est pour cela que les habitants sont à leur aise: car les denrées y sont abondantes sans aucun débouché au dehors, sans consommation de luxe au dedans, et sans que le cultivateur montagnard, dont les travaux sont les plaisirs, devienne moins laborieux. Si jamais ils ont plus d'argent, ils seront infailliblement plus pauvres. Ils ont la sagesse de le sentir, et il y a dans le pays des mines d'or qu'il n'est pas permis d'exploiter . . . les enfants en âge de raison sont les égaux de leurs pères, les domestiques

s'asseyent à table avec leurs maîtres; la même liberté règne dans les maisons et dans la république, et la famille est l'image de l'Etat.[9]

Other writers of the time besides Rousseau dealt with the theme of natural marriage, free from the vicious artificiality of social restrictions. In *La Basiliade*, of 1753, Morelly sang the innocence of sexual desire, and described with pathetic ludicrousness the mating, free from parental opposition, of two virtuous citizens of a society happier than his own:

> Tandis que ces heureux amants, oubliant le reste de l'Univers, semblables à ces précieux métaux que dissoud l'ardeur d'un feu violent coulent et s'unissent pour ne former qu'un corps; tandis que plus fortement liés que l'est le lierre à la plante qui le soutient et le nourrit, ils font des efforts pour devenir un même corps, ceux à qui ils doivent la vie, cachés derrière un arbre, les observent d'un œil curieux et content; ils sortent tout-à-coup pour applaudir à leur succès; le visage de ces Amants ne se couvre point d'une rougeur que répand la honte d'une action criminelle, la joie au contraire la plus vive y répand la sérénité.[10]

In his *Supplément au voyage de Bougainville, ou Dialogue entre A. et B. sur l'inconvénient d'attacher des idées morales à certaines actions physiques qui n'en comportent pas* (1772), Diderot – more radical than Rousseau in this as in many other respects – lyrically attacked the whole European tradition of marriage:

> Rien, en effet, te paraît-il plus insensé qu'un précepte qui proscrit le changement qui est en nous; qui commande une constance qui n'y peut être, et qui viole la liberté du mâle et de la femelle, en les enchaînant pour jamais l'un à l'autre; qu'une fidélité qui borne la plus capricieuse des jouissances à un même individu: qu'un serment d'immutabilité de deux êtres de chair, à la face d'un ciel qui n'est pas un instant le même, sous des antres qui menacent ruine; au bas d'une roche qui tombe en poudre; au pied d'un arbre qui se gerce; sur une pierre qui s'ébranle . . . Pauvre vanité de deux enfants qui s'ignorent eux-mêmes, et que l'ivresse d'un instant aveugle sur l'instabilité de tout ce qui les entoure.[11]

But Morelly's theories were not intended for immediate application in France, and Diderot not only set his Utopia in Tahiti, but declined to publish it at all. *La Nouvelle Héloïse*, on the other hand, purported to be the genuine correspondence of real people alive during the 1730s and 1740s.[12] Rousseau was not a citizen of Utopia, but an ex-lackey cohabiting with an ex-servant-girl. In spite of all its invective against the age of Louis XV, his novel could not, if it were to offer a convincing semblance of reality, uncompromisingly flout all accepted values. In the Saint-Preux whose heart and whose reason are incessantly at war, Rousseau expresses not only his own yearnings and revolt, but also his

I

sense of order and submission to established hierarchies. The whole
novel is a series of unreconciled contradictions about love, morality and
social status. Its ambiguities derive not merely from Rousseau's own
temperament and circumstances, but from the unresolved tensions in
pre-revolutionary French society.

By letter XXVIII, Julie, in revolt against the 'père barbare et
dénaturé' who wishes to marry her against her will ('Enfin, mon père m'a
donc vendue? il fait de sa fille une marchandise, une esclave'), has given
herself to her lover, Saint-Preux. But Rousseau will not commit himself
to any final, definitive answer to the question: is she, or is she not, a
fallen woman? Julie herself, when she has eventually married M. de
Wolmar, the middle-aged nobleman chosen by her father, professes to
find this marriage preferable even to marriage with Saint-Preux:

> Le Ciel éclaire la bonne intention des pères, et récompense la docilité
> des enfants . . . Quand avec les sentiments que j'eus ci-devant pour
> vous et les connaissances que j'ai maintenant, je serais libre encore, et
> maîtresse de me choisir un mari, je prends à témoin de ma sincérité
> ce Dieu qui daigne m'éclairer et qui lit au fond de mon cœur, ce n'est
> pas vous que je choisirais, c'est M. de Wolmar.[13]

Saint-Preux, the contemner of aristocrats, had taken as his bosom
friend Lord Edward Bomston. Lord Edward had offered Julie and
Saint-Preux (provided they got properly married in church), a retreat
on his Yorkshire estates:

> L'odieux préjugé n'a point d'accès dans cette heureuse contrée.
> L'habitant paisible y conserve encore les mœurs simples des premiers
> temps, et l'on y trouve une image du Valais.[14]

What he proposed for them, however, was not the manual labour and
dinners of herbs extolled by Saint-Preux, but a gentleman's residence,
complete with park, home farm, and a respectful tenantry.

Monsieur and Madame de Wolmar, enjoying a moderately large
income in their not excessively grandiose mansion at Clarens, like to
imagine that they have created a golden age of patriarchal simplicity,
and at wine-harvest time are graciously condescending to their equally
class-conscious farm-labourers:

> On dîne avec les paysans et à leur heure, aussi bien qu'on travaille avec
> eux. On mange avec appétit leur soupe un peu grossière mais bonne,
> saine et chargée d'excellents légumes. On ne ricane pas orgueilleuse-
> ment de leur air gauche et de leurs compliments rustauds: pour les
> mettre à leur aise on s'y prête sans affectation. Ces complaisances ne
> leur échappent pas; ils y sont sensibles, et voyant qu'on veut bien

sortir pour eux de sa place, ils s'en tiennent d'autant plus volontiers dans la leur.[15]

Even Saint-Preux, the 'petit bourgeois sans fortune', decides in the end that the prerogatives of rank take precedence over lovers' anguish. When Lord Edward proposes to marry a beautiful, cultivated, intelligent, faithful, pure-hearted ex-prostitute, Saint-Preux announces that 'tant que mon cœur battra, jamais Lauretta Pisana ne sera Ladi Bomston'. To preserve the respectability of the English peerage, he persuades the heroic creature to become a nun.[16]

Like Saint-Preux, Rousseau himself was the friend of noblemen as well as the plebeian in revolt; his own principles were, inevitably, coloured by the realities of the society in which he lived. *La Nouvelle Héloïse* reflects his double attitude of conformity and rebellion, of acceptance and escape. It heralds the smug complacency of the nineteenth century as well as the anguish and fervour of the Revolutionary and Romantic epochs. Claire, Julie's counsellor, says 'N'allons pas nous perdre dans le pays des chimères'. Julie herself eventually concludes that:

> Le pays des chimères est en ce monde le seul digne d'être habité, et tel est le néant des choses humaines, qu'hors l'Etre existant par lui-même, il n'y a rien de beau que ce qui n'est pas.[17]

Rousseau wrote his would-be realistic novel partly to prove that Christian marriage and bourgeois domesticity were preferable to frenzied passion and illicit unions, but it is only by dying that Julie can save herself from adultery:

> Vous m'avez crue guérie, et j'ai cru l'être. Rendons grâce à celui qui fit durer cette erreur autant qu'elle était utile; qui sait si me voyant si près de l'abîme, la tête ne m'eût point tourné? Oui, j'eus beau vouloir étouffer le premier sentiment qui m'a fait vivre, il s'est concentré dans mon cœur.[18]

This final avowal declares her love to be sinful; but her vision of Paradise is an eternity with Saint-Preux.

After 1762, with his main tasks completed, Rousseau began gradually to withdraw[19] into his own private world of introspection. Persecutions, real and imaginary, tormented him. His own nature, and his sickness, made him less and less able to compromise with the society whose evils he had denounced. His next masterpieces – the works which he wrote to justify himself to posterity, above the cries of his enemies, persecutors and slanderers – came from the *pays des chimères* of his diseased imagination. But these works revealed a new kind of truth, as well as a new kind of beauty. In the *Confessions*, the *Dialogues* and the *Rêveries du promeneur solitaire*, Rousseau lucidly analysed the intricacies of his own individuality, in all its strangeness and all its reality.

NOTES

1 *La Nouvelle Héloïse*, Pt I, Letter vii, ed. D. Mornet (Paris, 1925), vol. II, p. 25.

2 *Lettres . . . sur la Nouvelle Héloïse*. Voltaire, *Mélanges* (Pléiade, 1961), p. 396. The image which Voltaire finds so funny appears to be borrowed from Psalm 22, v. 14 in the Marot and Bèze translation:

> Las! ma vertu comme eau s'écoule toute:
> De tous mes os la jointure est dissoute:
> Et comme cire en moi fond goutte à goutte
> Mon cœur fâché.

The next verse of this Psalm suggests the idea of death with which the passage ends:

> Tu m'as fait prêt d'être au tombeau couché
> Réduit en cendre.

There are various other Biblical echoes in the passage. 'Je gémis, je souffre . . .' resembles Psalm 6, v. 6–7: 'Je me suis travaillé en mon gémissement, je baigne ma couche toutes les nuits, je trempe mon lit de mes larmes. Mon regard est tout défait de chagrin, il est envieilli à cause de ceux qui me pressent' (*Ancien Testament*, Amsterdam, 1710). 'Un pain gagné . . . insipide' sounds like an allusion to *Proverbs*, XV, 17: 'Better is a dinner of herbs where love is than a stalled ox and hatred therewith'. Julie and Saint-Preux, both Protestants, may be assumed to know their Bible just as Rousseau did. The Biblical echoes serve to make Saint-Preux's appeal seem lofty, virtuous, and the will of God.

3 *N.H.*, Pt I, xxii, ed. cit., vol. II, p. 73.

4 Ibid., xxvi, pp. 95–6. Rousseau stated that he himself, despite his low rank and birth, was worthy of attention because he felt and thought deeply: 'Or les âmes ne sont plus ou moins illustres que selon qu'elles ont des sentiments plus ou moins grands et nobles, des idées plus ou moins vives et nombreuses . . . . Dans quelque obscurité que j'aie pu vivre, si j'ai pensé plus et mieux que les rois, l'histoire de mon âme est plus intéressante que celle des leurs' (*La première rédaction des 'Confessions'*, ed. Th. Dufour, *Annales Jean-Jacques Rousseau*, IV (1908), p. 5.)

5 *N.H.*, Pt I, xii, ed. cit., p. 51.

6 Ibid., Pt II, ii, p. 250.

7 *Discours sur l'Inégalité*, note (i). In a paper which he read to the Institut on 22 Fructidor, An IV (8 September 1796) the celebrated Idéologue doctor Cabanis (from whom Stendhal derived some of his ideas), maintained that romantic love was a disease of the Ancien Régime, and had no place in a bourgeois republic: '[l'amour] tel qu'on le dépeint, et que la société le présente en effet quelquefois, l'amour est sans doute fort étranger au plan

primitif de la nature. Deux circonstances ont principalement contribué, dans les sociétés modernes, à le dénaturer par une exaltation factice: je veux dire d'abord, ces barrières mal-adroites que les parents ou les institutions civiles prétendent lui opposer, et tous les autres obstacles qu'il rencontre dans les préjugés relatifs à la naissance, au rang et à la fortune . . .: je veux dire en second lieu, le défaut d'objets d'un intérêt véritablement grand, et le désœuvrement général des classes aisées dans les gouvernements monarchiques; à quoi l'on peut ajouter encore les restes de l'esprit de chevalerie, fruit ridicule de l'odieuse féodalité, et cette espèce de conjuration des gens à talents pour diriger toute l'énergie humaine vers des dissipations qui tendaient de plus en plus à river pour toujours les fers des nations. . . . Sous le régime bienfaisant de l'égalité, sous l'influence toute-puissante de la raison publique, libre enfin de toutes les chaînes dont l'avaient chargé les absurdités politiques, civiles ou superstitieuses, étranger à toute exagération, à tout enthousiasme ridicule, l'amour sera le consolateur, mais non l'arbitre de la vie; il l'embellira, mais il ne la remplira point. Lorsqu'il la remplit, il la dégrade, et bientôt il s'éteint lui-même dans les dégoûts.' *Œuvres philosophiques de Cabanis*, ed. C. Lehec et J. Cazeneuve (Paris, 1956), vol. 1, pp. 313–14. The *Rapports du physique et du moral de l'homme*, from which this passage is taken, was published in Paris in 1802 and 1805.

8 *N.H.*, Pt I, xxiii, ed. cit., p. 87. Presumably remorse at having disposed of his own children in the Foundlings Home prevented Rousseau from mentioning parenthood in this dream of conjugal bliss.

9 Ibid., pp. 81–3. Cf. the Montagnons described in the *Lettre à d'Alembert*, ed. M. Fuchs (Genève, 1948), pp. 80–6. A favourite entertainment of this happy community is the vociferous singing of the Protestant Psalms in four-part setting (p. 82).

10 In G. Chinard's Introduction to Morelly, *Le Code de la Nature* (Paris, 1950), p. 52.

11 *Œuvres* (Bibliothèque de la Pléiade, 1935), pp. 769, 785. The *Supplément* was first published in 1796.

12 For the internal chronology of the novel, see Mornet's edition, vol. I, pp. 313–17.

13 Ibid., Pt III, xx, vol. III, pp. 90–1.

14 Ibid., Pt II, iii, vol. II, pp. 257–8.

15 Ibid., Pt V, vii, vol. IV, p. 136.

16 Ibid., Pt V, xii, Pt VI, iii, vol. IV, pp. 160, 199.

17 Ibid., Pt VI, ii and viii, vol. IV, pp. 183, 263.

18 Ibid, xii, p. 333.

19 But the *Lettres écrites de la montagne* were written in 1764, the *Projet de Constitution pour la Corse* in 1765, and the *Considérations sur le Gouvernement de Pologne* in 1771–2.

X · Rousseau (1712–1778)

FROM *Du Contrat social* (published 1762)
(Book III, ch. xv)

C'est le tracas du commerce et des arts, c'est l'avide intérêt du gain, c'est la mollesse et l'amour des commodités, qui changent les services personnels en argent. On cède une partie de son profit pour l'augmenter à son aise. Donnez de l'argent, et bientôt vous aurez des fers. Ce mot de *finance* est un mot d'esclave, il est inconnu dans la Cité. Dans un Etat vraiment libre, les citoyens font tout avec leurs bras, et rien avec de l'argent; loin de payer pour s'exempter de leurs devoirs, ils payeraient pour les remplir eux-mêmes. Je suis bien loin des idées communes: je crois les corvées moins contraires à la liberté que les taxes.

Mieux l'Etat est constitué, plus les affaires publiques l'emportent sur les privées, dans l'esprit des citoyens. Il y a même beaucoup moins d'affaires privées, parce que la somme du bonheur commun fournissant une portion plus considérable à celui de chaque individu, il lui en reste moins à chercher dans les soins particuliers. Dans une Cité bien conduite chacun vole aux assemblées; sous un mauvais Gouvernement nul n'aime à faire un pas pour s'y rendre, parce que nul ne prend intérêt à ce qui s'y fait, qu'on prévoit que la volonté générale n'y dominera pas, et qu'enfin les soins domestiques absorbent tout. Les bonnes lois en font faire de meilleures, les mauvaises en amènent de pires. Sitôt que quelqu'un dit des affaires de l'Etat: *Que m'importe?* on doit compter que l'Etat est perdu.

L'attiédissement de l'amour de la patrie, l'activité de l'intérêt privé, l'immensité des Etats, les conquêtes, l'abus du Gouvernement, ont fait imaginer la voie des députés ou représentants du peuple dans les assemblées de la nation. C'est ce qu'en certains pays on ose appeler le Tiers Etat. Ainsi l'intérêt particulier de deux ordres est mis au premier et second rang; l'intérêt public n'est qu'au troisième.

Ed. C. E. Vaughan (Manchester, 1918), pp. 82–3.

The word *finance*, which Rousseau says would be unknown in a free society, meant money, the tax-farming system, and financiers generally.

From the *Discours sur les sciences et les arts* onwards, Rousseau inveighed against riches, luxury and the cult of material progress. In contrast to the liberal economic theorists of the century, who tended to identify liberty and the common good with the rights of the individual to make money freely, Rousseau saw in private property the source of wickedness and social oppression:

> Avant que ces mots affreux de tien et de mien fussent inventés; avant qu'il y eût de cette espèce d'hommes cruels et brutaux qu'on appelle maîtres, et de cette autre espèce d'hommes fripons et menteurs qu'on appelle esclaves; avant qu'il y eût des hommes assez abominables pour oser avoir du superflu pendant que d'autres hommes meurent de faim; avant qu'une dépendance mutuelle les eût tous forcés à devenir fourbes, jaloux et traîtres, je voudrais bien qu'on m'expliquât en quoi pouvaient consister ces vices, ces crimes qu'on leur reproche avec tant d'emphase. On m'assure qu'on est depuis longtemps désabusé de la chimère de l'âge d'or. Que n'ajoutait-on encore qu'il y a longtemps qu'on est désabusé de la chimère de la vertu?[1]

Had he so desired, Rousseau could have accepted the patronage of rich men and the whole philosophe party, and become at least as affluent as the much less talented writer Marmontel, who – by intelligent cultivation of the right people – had amassed for himself by the age of fifty a capital of 130,000 livres, all safely invested.[2] Rousseau reviled the rich, and opted for comparative poverty. Like one of the Old Testament prophets whose writings he knew so well, he cried woe upon a whole corrupt, unjust, materialistic society. The philosophes looked forward to a happier era of ever-increasing commercial, industrial and scientific progress. Rousseau foresaw only the horrors which the era of self-seeking individualism was to bring:

> Mécontent de ton état présent, par des raisons qui annoncent à ta postérité malheureuse de plus grands mécontentements encore, peut-être voudrais-tu pouvoir rétrograder; et ce sentiment doit faire l'éloge de tes premiers aïeux, la critique de tes contemporains, et l'effroi de ceux qui auront le malheur de vivre après toi.[3]

There were many eighteenth-century writers – Fénelon, Foigny, Vairasse, Meslier, Morelly, Mably, Restif de la Bretonne and others – who, with varying degrees of seriousness, described imaginary communist societies, based largely on agriculture, and free from the moral and social evils of contemporary France. (Gracchus Babeuf, the first modern communist who actually tried to take over power, was sent to the guillotine in 1797 by the Republican heirs of the philosophes.[4]) But Rousseau, in spite of his nostalgia for the early stage of society when men lived 'libres, sains, bons et heureux autant qu'ils pouvaient l'être par leur nature',[5] deemed it impossible to retrogress to a state of nature in which property did not exist. In his article on Political Economy, published in the same year as the *Discours sur l'inégalité*, he pronounced property to be the most sacred of all rights – more important even than liberty.[6] The ideal state – the *Cité* – outlined in *Du Contrat social* seems to require property as a qualification for full citizenship[7]; but it is a state in which trade, commerce and industry are minimal, and no citizens are very rich or very poor:

> Voulez-vous donc donner à l'Etat de la consistance, rapprochez les degrés extrêmes autant qu'il est possible: ne souffrez ni des gens opulents ni des gueux. Ces deux états, naturellement inséparables, sont également funestes au bien commun; de l'un sortent les fauteurs de la tyrannie, et de l'autre les tyrans.[8]

Liberty and equality can only exist if the size and economy of a state are such that ordinary citizens, instead of paying taxes to support soldiers and legislators, can themselves defend their country and make its laws. Compulsory manual labour, willingly undertaken by all able-bodied men, would promote patriotism and equality between citizens.[9] Commercial success and material comfort are incompatible with civic liberty.

One of the many paradoxes in Rousseau, the solitary introspective who gloried in his own individuality, is his belief that happiness is best found in communal activity, not in private preoccupations. A yearning for acceptance into a closely-knit fellowship of free citizens was one of the ways by which this expatriate social misfit, sick in body and mind, sought escape from dissatisfaction with himself and society, and *Du Contrat social* is, to some extent, a projection of such yearnings. Sparta was one of his ideals:

> C'est à Sparte que, dans une laborieuse oisiveté, tout était plaisir et spectacle; c'est là que les plus rudes travaux passaient pour des récréations, et que les moindres délassements formaient une instruction publique; c'est là que les citoyens, continuellement assemblés, consacraient la vie entière à des amusements qui faisaient la grande affaire de l'Etat, et à des jeux dont on ne se délassait qu'à la guerre.[10]

One of his earliest recollections was of a popular celebration in Geneva, when the army, officers and men alike, drank and danced in the street with the citizenry:

> Mon père, en m'embrassant, fut saisi d'un tressaillement que je crois sentir et partager encore. 'Jean-Jacques, me disait-il, aime ton pays.

Vois-tu ces bons Genevois; ils sont tous amis, ils sont tous frères; la joie et la concorde règnent au milieu d'eux' . . . Non, il n'y a de pure joie que la joie publique, et les vrais sentiments de la Nature ne règnent que sur le peuple.[11]

In his ideal *Cité*, liberty and happiness would merge into the State, since the State consists of individuals – virtuous, high-minded, predominantly peasant proprietors – bound together by common consent, into a Sovereign People responsible for its own laws and deciding its policies by majority vote at open-air assemblies of all citizens:

> Le souverain, n'ayant d'autre force que la puissance législative . . ., et les lois n'étant que des actes authentiques de la volonté générale, le souverain ne saurait agir que quand le peuple est assemblé.

It is in countries like France, Rousseau maintains, where the people have not the will to assume sovereignty, that individualism and inequality flourish, and freedom does not exist:

> Le peuple assemblé, dira-t-on, quelle chimère! C'est une chimère aujourd'hui; mais ce n'en était pas une il y a deux mille ans. Les hommes ont-ils changé de nature?
>
> Les bornes du possible, dans les choses morales, sont moins étroites que nous ne pensons: ce sont nos faiblesses, nos vices, nos préjugés, qui les rétrécissent. Les âmes basses ne croient point aux grands hommes: de vils esclaves sourient d'un air moqueur à ce mot de liberté.[12]

The only delegation of authority which Rousseau permits the sovereign (that is, the community of citizens) is in the appointment of executive officers responsible for ensuring that the laws are carried out. All power to make or change laws must reside in the assembly of the whole sovereign people. The executive (which Rousseau calls 'le gouvernement') is merely an agent of the legislative assembly, even in times of grave emergency when, by the will of the people, 'on nomme un chef suprême, qui fasse taire toutes les lois et suspende un moment l'autorité souveraine'.[13] Unlike Montesquieu and Voltaire, Rousseau disapproves of the English system, where the legislative authority is delegated by the people to their representatives in Parliament:

> Toute loi que le peuple en personne n'a pas ratifiée est nulle; ce n'est point une loi. Le peuple anglais pense être libre, il se trompe fort: il ne l'est que durant l'élection des membres du parlement; sitôt qu'ils sont élus, il est esclave, il n'est rien. Dans les courts moments de sa liberté [i.e. at election-times] l'usage qu'il en fait mérite bien qu'il la perde.[14]

The reference to the traditional French representative system of the

Estates General, and 'ce qu'en certains pays on ose nommer le Tiers
Etat' (i.e. the commons – the other two Estates were the clergy and the
nobles) is one of those inflammatory remarks which Rivarol had in
mind when he said 'Rousseau a des cris et des gestes dans son style.
Il n'écrit pas, il est toujours à la tribune.'[15] It heralds the revolutionary
threat made by the abbé Sieyès in 1788:

> Qu'est-ce que c'est le tiers état? Tout. Qu'est-ce qu'il a été jusqu'ici?
> Rien. Qu'est-ce qu'il va devenir? Quelque chose.[16]

It is often alleged that *Du Contrat social* advocates a totalitarian
subordination of the individual to the collectivity. The book does,
indeed, contain some potentially sinister observations: 'L'aliénation
totale de chaque associé avec tous ses droits à toute la communauté';
'Quiconque refusera d'obéir à la volonté générale y sera contraint
par tout le corps: ce qui ne signifie autre chose sinon qu'on le forcera
d'être libre'; 'Qui veut la fin veut aussi les moyens, et ces moyens sont
inséparables de quelques risques, même de quelques pertes'; 'Sa vie
n'est plus seulement un bienfait de la nature, mais un don conditionnel
de l'Etat'.[17] Deviousness and ambiguity, to the point of dishonesty,[18]
were at least as characteristic of Rousseau as was his search for the
truth, so that when he qualifies some of his enormities, it is often difficult
to discover where he stands. Thus, he will not say plainly that any
citizen can exercise his natural liberty and leave the country whenever
he so desires.[19] The provision for executing atheists – itself disingenuously
phrased – in the civil religion chapter of *Du Contrat social* is refuted in
La Nouvelle Héloïse, but in terms even more horrifying:

> Si j'étais magistrat, et que la loi portât peine de mort contre les athées,
> je commencerais par faire brûler comme tel quiconque en viendrait
> dénoncer un autre.[20]

Yet, though it cannot be denied that Rousseau's theories about capital
punishment, virtue, patriotism and dictatorship provided Robespierre
with a ready-made justification for the Terror, this is no reason for
viewing Rousseau as the forerunner of twentieth-century régimes
incomparably more evil than anything the eighteenth century could
conceive. And *Du Contrat social* also contains texts proving that the
free, sovereign collectivity in which citizens have chosen to merge their
isolated independence does not, and must not, control all spheres of
private activity:

> Il s'agit donc de bien distinguer les droits respectifs des citoyens et
> du souverain [i.e. the citizens as a body], et les devoirs qu'ont à

remplir les premiers en qualité de sujets, du droit naturel dont ils doivent jouir en qualité d'hommes.

Le droit que le pacte social donne au souverain . . . ne passe point, comme je l'ai dit, les bornes de l'utilité publique. 'Dans la république, dit le Marquis d'Argenson, chacun est parfaitement libre de faire ce qui ne nuit pas aux autres.' Voilà la borne invariable; on ne peut la poser plus exactement.[21]

The whole book is inspired by Rousseau's passionate concern for personal freedom:

Renoncer à sa liberté, c'est renoncer à sa qualité d'homme, aux droits de l'humanité, même à ses devoirs. Il n'y a nul dédommagement possible pour quiconque renonce à tout. Une telle renonciation est incompatible avec la nature de l'homme; et c'est ôter toute moralité à ses actions que d'ôter toute liberté à sa volonté.[22]

And, constantly, he affirms that if liberty is endangered or destroyed by tyrants, usurpers or wicked men, the people have the right to seize power through revolution:

Il . . . se trouve quelquefois dans la durée des Etats des époques violentes où les révolutions font sur les peuples ce que certaines crises font sur les individus, où l'horreur du passé tient lieu d'oubli, et où l'Etat, embrasé par les guerres civiles, renaît pour ainsi dire de sa cendre, et reprend la vigueur de la jeunesse en sortant des bras de la mort. Telle fut Sparte au temps de Lycurgue; telle fut Rome après les Tarquins; et telles ont été parmi nous la Hollande et la Suisse après l'expulsion des tyrans.[23]

Of course, the philosophe apologists for *le luxe* were quite right in thinking that human progress in the eighteenth and nineteenth centuries depended on ever-increasing trade, profit and production, and that the amassing of wealth by individuals was essential for such progress. Rousseau's dreams of high-minded small-holders and village craftsmen deciding the affairs of petty states[24] under an oak-tree were, patently, unrealistic. His theory of the general will as the expression of upright, simple men who placed the common good above their private or group interests, and unquestioningly accepted what was decided by the majority vote of their equally patriotic fellows, clearly does not fully correspond to political or economic reality. Indeed, if the Marxist exegetes are correct, Rousseau's whole notion of simple virtue and small incomes is in itself a partisan view, with Rousseau the spokesman for the petty bourgeois and artisan classes, hostile to the privileges of the nobility and the ambitions of the ascending bourgeoisie.[25]

Yet the greatness of *Du Contrat social* does derive in part from its lucid realism. Rousseau points out that the finest constitutional systems are derisory if the will to make them work is lacking in the individuals of whom a society is comprised. He sees no grounds for believing that men will continuously, over a long period, manage to subdue their selfishness, cupidity and lust for power.[26] He bids us aim at reforms which are possible, but he knows that all plans for Utopia are doomed to failure:

> Tout ce qui n'est point dans la nature a ses inconvénients, et la société civile plus que tout le reste.[27]

Two centuries of critical writings have failed to establish incontrovertibly what, precisely, *Du Contrat social* says, and what value its pronouncements have.[28] All that the reader can do is to study it as honestly and thoroughly as possible, and then interpret it according to his own prejudices. But it is because the problems it raises have no ultimate solution that *Du Contrat social* remains a key text of political philosophy. It places before us, with unflinching brutality, the inescapable question: how much private liberty must we surrender if we hope to participate in a just social order? It continues to ask us whether, in serving the Mammon[29] of profit or productivity, we are, necessarily, promoting the public good. Even the nostalgia for an earlier world, which Rousseau knew could never be regained, is still very much with us. The theme 'peut-être voudrais-tu pouvoir rétrograder' appears in many guises today, from commuters' cottages to anarchist manifestoes.

NOTES

1 *Discours sur les Sciences et les Arts: Dernière réponse à M. Bordes, Œuvres complètes*, Pléiade (Paris, 1964), III, p. 80. But in *Du Contrat social*, Ch. 1, Rousseau no longer maintains that evil and oppression came into the world with property: 'Comment ce changement s'est-il fait? Je l'ignore.' H. Guillemin uses this sentence to suggest that Rousseau did not reject the Christian doctrine of the Fall of Man. (*Annales J.-J. Rousseau, XXX*, 1943–5.)

2 Marmontel, *Mémoires* (Paris, 1819), II, pp. 96ff.

3 *Discours sur l'Inégalité*, ed. Vaughan, *Political Writings*, I, p. 142.

4 On the links between Babeuf and nineteenth-century socialists, see J. McManners, *Lectures on European History 1789–1914* (Oxford, 1966), pp. 103–4.

5 *Discours sur l'Inégalité*, Pt II (ed. cit., p. 175).

6 *Political Writings*, ed. Vaughan, I, p. 259: 'Il est certain que le droit de propriété est le plus sacré de tous les droits des citoyens, et plus important, à certains égards, que la liberté même: soit parce qu'il tient de plus près à la conservation de la vie; soit parce que, les biens étant plus faciles à

usurper et plus pénibles à défendre que la personne, on doit plus respecter ce qui peut se ravir plus aisément; soit enfin parce que la propriété est le vrai fondement de la société civile, et le vrai garant des engagements des citoyens: car, si les biens ne répondaient pas des personnes, rien ne serait si facile que d'éluder ses devoirs et de se moquer des lois.' For Rousseau's development to an almost socialist theory in his *Projet pour la Corse* and the *Considérations sur le Gouvernement de Pologne*, see *Political Writings*, II, pp. 303–4, 337–8, 477–9. On property and the evils of money, as on most other problems, Rousseau gives no single, clear, consistent solution. In the *Considérations* he warns against drawing extremist consequences from any of his statements: 'Il ne faut pas outrer mes maximes au delà de mes intentions et de la raison . . .; je n'entends proscrire ni l'argent ni l'or, mais les rendre moins nécessaires; et faire que celui qui n'en a pas soit pauvre, sans être gueux. Au fond, l'argent n'est pas la richesse, il n'en est que le signe; ce n'est pas le signe qu'il faut multiplier, mais la chose représentée' (ibid. II, p. 480).

7 Ed. cit., p. 101.

8 Ibid., p. 45. Cf. p. 20., n.

9 The paradoxical remark about *corvées* in the passage is one of the many instances where Rousseau tells his French contemporaries that they are slaves because they are more interested in their own ease and comfort than in public service. Not, of course, that Rousseau approves of the forced labour exacted from the French peasants; the Swiss type of *corvée* which he recommends for Corsica and Poland (*Political Writings*, II, pp. 338–9, 478, 481) is an honourable patriotic duty in which the leading magistrates do not disdain to partake. This conception of Rousseau's is not utterly fantastic: still today, prominent and respected citizens of the island of Sark opt to work on the roads for a specified period during the winter as an alternative to paying a tax.

10 *Lettre à M. d'Alembert sur les spectacles*, ed. M. Fuchs (Geneva, 1948), p. 179.

11 Ibid., pp. 181–3. Cf. pp. 80–3, his evocation of the egalitarian, psalm-singing Montagnons.

12 *Du Contrat social*, ed. cit., pp. 78–9.

13 Ibid., pp. 48, 81, 89, 109.

14 Ibid., p. 83. For a summary of Rousseau's varying views on England, 'nation personnellement animée contre moi, et dont on n'a jamais cité aucun acte de justice contre son propre intérêt', see *Confessions*, ed. Jacques Voisine (1964), pp. 209–10. As the century progressed, and especially by the time of the American War of Independence, praise for the English constitution became the sign of – relatively – conservative views. The criticism of the English parliamentary system in *Du C. S.* had, however, already been made in an English book – *An Estimate*, published in 1757 by the Revd John Brown, Fellow of St John's College, Cambridge, and Vicar of Newcastle-upon-Tyne. This work, which declared England to be dissolute, decadent, ruined, and ripe for conquest by the more vigorous French, appeared in French translation at The Hague in 1758: *Les Mœurs Anglaises, ou Appréciation des Mœurs et des Principes qui caractérisent actuellement la Nation Britannique*. Pages 88–93 of the translation deal with electoral and

parliamentary corruption: 'Ce sont les élections pour le parlement qui
deviennent la pomme de discorde entre les grands et les riches du pays
. . . chacun voulut avoir part au gâteau. . . . Ainsi, à la fin s'est formée
cette grande chaîne d'intérêts politiques et personnels. Ainsi, du misérable
savetier dans le moindre bourg elle s'est étendue jusqu'au premier ministre
du royaume.' This is the antithesis of what Rousseau understands by the
General Will. 'Le docteur Brown' is mentioned by Rousseau's former friend
Mably in his anti-English *Observations sur le Gouvernement des Etats-Unis
d'Amérique*, but there is already evidence of Brown's influence in Mably's
Entretiens de Phocion, of 1763.

15 *Esprit de Rivarol*, ed. Fayol et Chênedollé (Paris, 1808), p. 123.

16 See *Du Contrat social*, ed. cit., p. 151.

17 Ibid., pp. 13, 16, 29.

18 See, for example, his treatment of the Gospels and the Eucharist in *Emile*,
ed. F. and P. Richard (Paris, s.d.), pp. 379–81. Of course, in his simultaneous
refusal either to believe or disbelieve in traditional Christian doctrine,
Rousseau pointed the way to some aspects of twentieth-century religious
thought.

19 *Du Contrat social*, ed. cit., pp. 89, 93.

20 Bk V, Ch. 5, ed. D. Mornet (Paris, 1925), vol. IV, p. 103.

21 *Du Contrat social*, ed. cit., pp. 25, 122. See also Franz Haymann, *La lo
naturelle chez Rousseau, Annales J.-J. Rousseau*, vol. 30, 1943–5.

22 *Du Contrat social*, ed. cit., p. 8.

23 Ibid., p. 38. Cf. pp. 74, 88, and *Discours sur l'Inégalité, Political Writings*,
I, pp. 183, 194. But there is no general agreement among critics that Rousseau
approved of revolution. His own temperament was a blend of pugnacity
and submissiveness. Of the civil disputes in Geneva in 1767 he remarks:
'Peut-être ne serait-il pas à désirer que j'en fusse l'arbitre; je craindrais que
l'amour de la paix ne fût plus fort dans mon cœur que celui de la liberté'
(*Political Writings*, II, p. 183).

24 Rousseau thought, however, that small states could band together in a
federal republic (*Du Contrat social*, ed. cit., p. 85).

25 E.g. J.-L. Lecercle, in his edition of the *Discours sur l'Inégalité* (Les Classiques du Peuple, Editions Sociales, Paris, 1965), p. 9.

26 *Du Contrat social*, ed. cit., p. 91.

27 Ibid., p. 84.

28 See J. McManners, *The Social Contract and Rousseau's Revolt against
Society* (Leicester University Press, 1968, 25 pp.), for an account of various
contradictory interpretations made by critics between 1950 and 1966.

29 'Car il s'agit de convaincre tous ceux qui ne jurent que par Mammon'
(*Political Writings*, I, p. 333).

XI · De Belloy (1725–1775)

FROM *Le Siège de Calais* (performed 1765)
(Act IV, scene iv)

Act IV takes place in an underground prison in the Governor's Palace at Calais, in the year 1347. Eustache de Saint-Pierre is mayor of the city; Amblétuse is a burgher. Aliénor is daughter of the comte de Vienne, Governor of Calais. Harcourt is a renegade French noble, now general of the English Army. Edouard is King Edward III of England, who has ordered the execution of six burghers. Valois is Philippe de Valois, King of France.

SAINT-PIERRE, *à part*.
Inspire mieux mon maître, ô puissance céleste!
Et défends sa bonté d'un conseil si funeste!
  (*A Aliénor*)
Partez, opposez-vous à ce dangereux soin;
Qu'on permette ma mort: l'Etat en a besoin.
Vous voyez cette guerre, en disgrâces féconde,
De nos fameux débris couvrir la terre et l'onde:
Chez les Français toujours l'excès de sentiment
Augmente le bonheur, rend le malheur plus grand.
Peu faits aux longs revers, las de voir leur courage
Servir à leur défaite et hâter leur naufrage,
Dans un dépit amer, hélas! ils ont pensé
Que le siècle est déchu, que leur règne est passé.
Mais qu'il s'élève enfin, dans cette erreur commune,
Une âme inébranlable aux coups de l'infortune,
Digne de nos aïeux et de ces temps si chers
Où les lis florissants ombrageaient l'univers,
Et vous verrez soudain partout ce peuple avide
Saisir, suivre, égaler son audace intrépide.
Devenus ses rivaux de ses admirateurs,
Son noble enthousiasme embrasera les cœurs.
Indignés d'avoir pu désespérer d'eux-même,
Ils forceront le sort par leur constance extrême,
Et peut-être à l'Etat rendront un plus beau jour
Que ces jours qu'ils croyaient regretter sans retour.
Voilà de notre mort les fruits inséparables;
Notre sang va partout enfanter nos semblables.

AMBLÉTUSE, *à Aliénor.*
Bien plus, si du destin les nouvelles rigueurs
Chez nos neveux un jour ramenaient nos malheurs,
Du héros de Calais l'impérieux exemple,
Que la gloire à leurs yeux offrira dans son temple,
Jusques au fond des cœurs attendris et confus
Ira chercher l'honneur, éveiller les vertus;
Et dans les citoyens, du rang même où nous sommes,
Déployer le génie et l'âme des grands hommes.
C'est ainsi qu'un mortel, surpassant ses souhaits,
Par une belle mort se survit à jamais,
Et qu'après un long cours de siècles et d'années,
De sa patrie encore on fait les destinées.

ALIÉNOR, *à part.*
O courage! ô vertu! dont l'héroïque ardeur,
Etonnant la raison, s'empare de mon cœur!
Ils font presque approuver à mon âme ravie
Et désirer pour eux ce trépas que j'envie.
Valois leur devra tout; et souvent, en effet,
Le sort des souverains dépend d'un seul sujet.
Harcourt trahit son prince, et d'Artois l'abandonne;
Un maire de Calais raffermit sa couronne.
Quelle leçon pour vous, superbes potentats!
Veillez sur vos sujets dans le rang le plus bas:
Tel qui sous l'oppresseur, loin de vos yeux, expire,
Peut-être quelque jour eût sauvé votre empire.
(*Aux bourgeois.*)
Malheureux! fiez-vous aux fureurs d'Edouard:
Les offres de Valois arriveront trop tard.

> *Théâtre des auteurs du second ordre. Tragédies,* tome VI
> (Paris, 1808), pp. 137–9.

It was a seventeenth-century aristocrat, François de Salignac de la Mothe-Fénelon, archbishop of Cambrai, who in 1714, the year before Louis XIV's death, announced to the Academy that French tragedy was no longer convincing. But instead of realising that the genre was dead, he suggested that it could be revived by liberating it from its artificial style and rigid versification, and infusing into it the edifying nobleness and republican simplicity which had characterised the tragedies of the Ancients.[1] During the whole of the century, unavailing attempts were made, by theorists and dramatists, to give tragedy new life. It was not obvious to the immediate heirs of the Grand Siècle culture that even modified versions of the forms used by Corneille and Racine were not a medium in which the confused and conflicting aspirations of the new era could find valid expression. Tragedy retained its prestige. It was the way to fame for actor and poet alike.

Crébillon responded to the growing public taste for strong emotion by depicting horrors and atrocities. As La Chaussée put it, in his 'Epître de Clio' of 1731:

> Mais tu connais sa valeur poétique:
> D'un nouveau genre inventeur dramatique,
> Quand il lui plaît, Melpomène en fureur
> Répand l'effroi, l'épouvante et l'horreur,
> Fait ruisseler le sang avec les larmes,
> Dans la terreur nous fait trouver des charmes
> Que jusqu'alors les timides rimeurs
> N'ont point eu l'art d'ajuster à nos mœurs.

Crébillon's glory was officially recognised in the 1740s, when Mme de Pompadour became his patroness at Court. Doubtless she was edified by the hymn to French virtue in his *Catalina*, of 1748:

> Notre unique vertu n'est pas notre valeur,
> Nous aimons la justice autant que la candeur.
> Quoique enfant de la guerre, allaité sous les tentes
> Le Gaulois n'eut jamais que des mœurs innocentes.
>
> (Act III, sc. 2)

It was partly because of Crébillon's success at Versailles, and his own disfavour there, that Voltaire in 1750 went to Berlin, hoping that the less frivolous Prussian court would be more propitious to his muse. For it was as an epic and tragic poet that Voltaire, at this date, was chiefly famous. A brilliant pupil of his Jesuit school-masters, Voltaire exemplified the theories of Father C. Porée, who produced at the college of Louis-le-Grand in 1726 a ballet called 'L'Homme instruit par le spectacle, ou le théâtre changé en école de vertu'.[2] The 'virtue' which Voltaire's tragedies preached was, of course, the philosophe gospel of tolerance, liberty and 'bienfaisance'. Already in the preliminary discourse to *Alzire*, in 1736, he stated:

> On trouvera dans presque tous mes écrits cette humanité qui doit être le premier caractère d'un être pensant; on y verra . . . le désir du bonheur des hommes, l'horreur de l'injustice et de l'oppression; et c'est cela seul qui a jusqu'ici tiré mes ouvrages de l'obscurité où leurs défauts devaient les ensevelir.

More action on the stage, greater realism, elegant adaptations of some

K

less barbaric features of Shakespeare, a wider range of subject-matter – these were ways in which Voltaire brought novelty to tragedy. His choice of new subjects was, indeed, remarkable:

> Pour donner au public un peu de ce neuf qu'il demande toujours, et que bientôt il sera impossible de trouver, un amateur du théâtre a été forcé de mettre sur la scène l'ancienne chevalerie, le contraste des Mahométans et des Chrétiens, celui des Américains et des Espagnols, celui des Chinois et des Tartares. Il a été forcé de joindre à des passions si souvent exprimées, des mœurs que nous ne connaissions pas sur la scène.[3]

Whatever his deficiencies as a tragedian, Voltaire had spent his youth among cultivated survivors from the days of Racine, and did feel himself to be in direct line of descent from the great men of the seventeenth century. He also had a dramatic sense, great skill in versification, creative ability, and the passionate conviction that his taste and his message were both the true ones. Not all would-be heirs of Racine possessed these advantages. Marmontel describes his own youthful attempts to be a tragic poet:

> Les sujets donnés par l'histoire me semblaient épuisés; je trouvais tous les grands intérêts du cœur humain, toutes les passions violentes, toutes les situations tragiques, en un mot, tous les grands ressorts de la terreur et de la compassion employés avant moi par les maîtres de l'art. Je me creusai la tête pour inventer une action nouvelle et hors de la route commune.[4]

The result, *Les Funérailles de Sésostris*, was a failure. Marmontel freely admitted it: 'des combats de générosité et de vertu n'avaient rien de tragique'. Though he wrote other plays, for the most part he pursued his literary ambitions in less exacting genres. But tragedies went on being written, and the public went on acclaiming them.

Pierre-Laurent Buirette, who called himself de Belloy, achieved one of the biggest dramatic successes of the century with *Le Siège de Calais*.[5] The first performance, on 15 February 1765, brought him an unparalleled ovation; on 21 February there was a performance at Court, then two further ones; the King gave him a gold medal and allowed the tragedy to be dedicated to him; by royal command, on 12 March there was a free performance for the poor at the Comédie Française, with wine and money distributed to the audience, who danced on the stage at the end of the play amid effusions of national brotherhood and cries of 'Vive le Roy et M. de Belloy'. Three dukes were present, and the Paris coalmen complete with drums. Performances were ordered for the troops in garrison towns. A deputation from Calais presented the author with honorary citizenship of the town, and a gold snuff-box from the Governor. When, in 1772, after further tragedies, Belloy was elected to the Academy in succession to the Prince de Clermont, Voltaire wrote: 'c'est une belle époque pour la littérature quand un simple fils d'Apollon succède à un prince du sang'.

It is obvious from our passage that *Le Siège de Calais* did not rise to fame by reason of its lyric qualities. The syntax is inelegant: 'Un plus beau jour que ces jours que. . . .' The sense is not immediately clear: 'Devenus ses rivaux de ses admirateurs' means 'will seek to emulate the hero they admire.' Rhymes are dragged in. The imagery is banal. The characters do not come alive. Even the plot is tedious and contrived. The actual story, based on Froissart, is moving and dramatic: Edward III of England, enraged at the citizens' long resistance and refusal to surrender until overcome, demands the execution of six burghers as an example to other towns. The willing victims are the mayor, Eustache de Saint-Pierre, his son, and four kinsmen. Edward finally relents and spares their lives. But Belloy does not announce Edward's demand until Act II, scene iv; the remainder of the play is a jumble of plans to make Edward relent, or to devise some stratagem which will save the six burghers. Only in Act V, scene vi, is the uncertainty resolved. (The 'conseil si funeste' which Saint-Pierre asks Aliénor, the Governor's daughter, to oppose, is a proposal that Valois, the French king, shall surrender a province to ransom them.)

This fake masterpiece was acclaimed because it appealed to the patriotic feeling of the moment, and adroitly flattered King, nobles and bourgeois all at once. Patriotism had won applause on the English stage also. Drury Lane theatre, on 31 December 1759, presented an anti-French pantomime, *Harlequin's Invasion*, written by the grandson of a Huguenot refugee, de la Garrigue. What the complete text was like we do not know, for the author, David Garrick, never had it printed; but the songs, set to music by William Boyce, were published. And so, though Louis XV's threatened invasion of England has faded from memory, some of Garrick's lines have survived to become part of our patriotic folk-lore:

> Heart of oak are our ships,
> Heart of oak are our men:
> We always are ready;
> Steady, boys, steady;
> We'll fight and we'll conquer again and again.

Such stalwart sentiment was not possible in France at the time. Mme de Pompadour's protégé Soubise – Prince de Soubise et d'Epernay, duc de Rohan-Rohan, whose name in France today connotes an onion sauce – suffered one of the most humiliating defeats of the century at Rosbach in November 1757. Leadership was deplorable. The troops' name for the maréchal de Richelieu was 'père la Maraude'. The foreign minister Bernis (the abbé Bernis who wrote pretty verses and was known to Voltaire as Babet la Bouquetière) complained to his successor Choiseul:

> Le public ne s'accoutume point à la honte de cette bataille. . .
> Le grand malheur, c'est que ce sont les hommes qui mènent les affaires, et nous n'avons ni généraux ni ministres. . . . Dieu veuille nous envoyer une volonté quelconque ou quelqu'un qui en ait pour nous.[6]

In 1758 there were English landings at St Malo, St Brieuc and Cherbourg. In 1759 Montcalm was defeated at Quebec. The French fleet was beaten at Quiberon, and things were going badly in India. Belle-Ile was occupied.

Calls to victory were indeed made: in 1762 the ferocious poet Ecouchard Lebrun, son of a prince's valet, heralded Danton and the *Marseillaise* in his *Ode aux Français sur la guerre présente. Par un citoyen:*

> Français, ressaisissez le char de la victoire.
> Aux armes, citoyens! il faut tenter le sort.
> Il n'est que deux sentiers dans les champs de la gloire:
> Le triomphe, ou la mort.
>
>   .   .   .
>
> Soldats! vouez ce glaive aux dangers de la France;
> Ne quittez pas ce fer de carnage altéré,
> Que ce fer n'ait éteint sa soif et sa vengeance
> Dans un sang abhorré.
>
>   .   .   .
>
> Toujours on vit l'audace enchaîner la fortune.
> Faites à la Victoire expier son erreur;
> Dans le sein d'Albion, chez les fils de Neptune,
> Renvoyer la terreur.[7]

But Albion continued to be victorious. By the Treaty of Paris, in February 1763, France signed away the major portion of her colonial empire. Enough was left, however, for foreign trade to flourish, especially the lucrative slave-trade, and the sugar which depended on it. As always, French resilience conquered defeat.

It was to this ardour for national resurgence that Belloy's tragedy appealed. The 'goodness' of the French monarch, to which Saint-Pierre refers, is a central theme of the play. The English King is envious of it in Act III, scene ii. The lady Aliénor touchingly evokes a King who is both father and brother to his subjects:

> Le Français dans son prince aime à trouver un frère,
> Qui né fils de l'Etat en devienne le père.
> L'Etat et le monarque à nos yeux confondus,
> N'ont jamais divisé nos vœux et nos tributs.

Such sentiment did, of course, exist. It is one reason why the sorely provoked French people waited for a century and a half before it followed Cromwell's example and chopped off the head of its lawful sovereign. The title Louis le Bien-aimé bestowed on the victorious Louis XV when he lay ill at Metz in 1744 was not, at that date, ironic. But by the time of our play the love had cooled. It is obvious why Belloy got his gold medal. Unfortunately, Louis's pleasure at these loyal effusions was soon ruined by the rebellion of Mlle Clairon, who played Aliénor in the tragedy. Rejecting a royal command to allow one Dubois to act with her, she was incarcerated in the prison of For-l'Evêque on 16 April. Her liberation on 21 April was accompanied by tumultuous demonstrations in her support, and the occasion was called the Journée du Siège de Calais. Obdurate in her refusal to forgive Louis, she resigned from the Comédie Française and made her way to Ferney, where, on St Clair's day, 1765, Voltaire organised in her honour the *fête champêtre* described in Chapter XVI below.

Aliénor, daughter of the Governor of Calais, expresses Belloy's flattery of the French aristocracy. Her valiant father and the knights have succeeded in rejoining the French lines to carry on the fight. She remains, to inspire the population of the captured city. Fearless, beautiful and tender, she rejects with scorn Edward's invitation to become Vicereine of France, and is at one with the burghers in their self-sacrificial patriotism:

> Dieu! l'admiration a suspendu mes larmes!
> O cœur vraiment français! ô transport plein de charmes!

Gracious and condescending, this *grande dame* is able to realise that a bourgeois mayor is capable of heroism – hence her half-wish that he shall achieve glory by going to the scaffold. Sadly she recalls that two noblemen have caused the disaster. It was Artois (this is not clear in the play, but Belloy explains it all in his Preface) who urged Edward to begin the war. The traitor Harcourt is general of the English force which has captured Calais. But his heart remains French. In full knowledge that it means instant death, he liberates the condemned burghers, and abjures his oath of fidelity to his country's foe. Aliénor then accepts his hand *in extremis*:

> Cher Harcourt, je te rends et te prouve ma foi;
> Je mourrai ton amante et mourrai près de toi.

The aristocracy of France has proved faithful still to its high ideals. The burghers prove even more heroic. Realising that Harcourt had no authority to release them, they voluntarily return to lay their heads on the block. Edward relents, forgives everyone, and renounces the French throne.

By their valour the burghers have saved France. At last, on the stage of the Comédie Française, there is a classical tragedy with bourgeois heroes. Saint-Pierre is the spokesman for the nation as he urges his compatriots to build anew. (His lines 'Mais qu'il s'élève' to 'embrasera les cœurs' are, presumably, an apostrophe to Choiseul, Louis's minister.[8]) Amblétuse reiterates the point: the Burghers of Calais will live in history. Aliénor expounds the lesson: the King's bourgeois subjects are the backbone of France. Of course, there is no criticism of the social structure: the bourgeois unquestioningly accept Aliénor's description of the Third Estate as 'le rang le plus bas'.

War in the eighteenth century was less destructive of civilisation than it later became. In his *Sentimental Journey* Laurence Sterne recounts how, having forgotten both his passport and the fact that England and France were at war, he none the less made his way agreeably to Paris.[9] When peace came in 1763, English visitors to Paris were received with warmth and friendship. (Among them was David Garrick, who called on Mlle Clairon.) And so, to give pleasure all round, Belloy manages to be pro-English too. As Edward is half-French, and his general Harcourt wholly so, the English are not to blame for them. The English knight Sir Walter Manny (in real life he came from Belgium, but this would have made the plot even harder to grasp) is revolted by his half-breed monarch's savagery. The mayor of Calais, though about to be executed by the English, is an ardent Anglophile:

> Nous l'avouerons sans fard, mourant pour les Français,
> Nous espérons laisser des noms chers aux Anglais.
> Plus rivaux qu'ennemis d'un peuple magnanime,
> Notre plus beau laurier, seigneur, est son estime.

The play ends in an Entente Cordiale:

> Grand prince! avec mon roi que de nœuds vous rassemblent!
> Le ciel fit pour s'aimer les cœurs qui se ressemblent.
> Ah! de l'humanité rétablissez les droits!
> A l'Europe, tous deux, faites chérir ses lois;
> Que, par vous, des vertus cette mère féconde [i.e. l'humanité]
> Soit la reine des rois, et l'oracle du monde!

The clergy are not mentioned in the play. Nor is the Parlement de Paris. For the rest, everyone is flattered, except the philosophes. They are denounced as bad Frenchmen and cold-blooded cosmopolitans:

> Je hais ces cœurs glacés et morts pour leur pays,
> Qui, voyant ses malheurs dans une paix profonde,
> S'honorent du grand nom de citoyens du monde,
> Feignent dans tout climat d'aimer l'humanité
> Pour ne la point servir dans leur propre cité;
> Fils ingrats, vils fardeaux du sein qui les fit naître,
> Et dignes du néant par l'oubli de leur être.

It is not surprising that Grimm's *Correspondance littéraire* for February, March and April 1765, savagely attacked the plot, style, treatment and versification of *Le Siège de Calais*. Though the subject was 'beau et national', he wrote, all that Belloy had achieved was to 'avilir la nation par un enthousiasme imbécile'.[10]

Poor Belloy took his play seriously. After all, his friend Ecouchard Lebrun, who was a real poet, wrote for him an *Epître à M. de Belloy, auteur tragique*:

> A l'immortalité quand ils volent ensemble,
> Que deux amis sont fiers d'un nœud qui les rassemble.[11]

Like Racine, Belloy explained in his Preface where, and why, he had departed from history. One of the incidents, he revealed, was modelled on Homer: 'Imitons les anciens en nous occupant de nous-mêmes.' He admitted that Voltaire, 'le Sophocle français', had already used French historical material; but *Le Siège de Calais*, he suggested, was perhaps the first French tragedy based wholly on native historical material and with 'un intérêt national'. It had demonstrated to foreigners that 'la légèreté de notre esprit n'ôte rien de la force de notre âme; et qu'il ne faut qu'une étincelle pour enflammer à l'instant les semences de feu que nous portons au fond du cœur'.

Froissart's account of the Burghers of Calais was already well known in the eighteenth century. Mme de Tencin had used it in 1739 as a minor incident in her short novel *Le Siège de Calais*. Belloy's play ensured the survival of this story, so unflattering to France's hereditary enemy.[12] French interest in pseudo-medieval themes continued to increase. Belloy went on writing tragedies. His *Gabrielle de Vergy*, produced in Paris two years after his death, contained a famous scene in which Gabrielle went mad on discovering that the goblet she was about to quaff contained, not poison, but the bleeding heart of her innocent lover, Raoul de Coucy:

> Il t'arrache à mes mains, objet cher et horrible!
> Eh! quel nouveau forfait a-t-il donc apprêté?
> Isaure, le vois-tu? Ce tigre ensanglanté [i.e. her husband]
> S'acharne à déchirer les restes du carnage.
> Vois ce cœur palpitant que frappe encor sa rage.
> Sous les couteaux tranchants j'entends ce cœur gémir.
> Vois ses lambeaux épars, que Fayel vient m'offrir.
> Arrête, monstre! arrête. Eh quoi! tes mains fumantes
> Osent porter ce cœur sur mes lèvres sanglantes. (Act V, sc. xii)

There were numerous other writers of would-be tragedies: a dreary succession, imitations of imitations, ancient, medieval, Shakespearian, modern; melodramatic, sentimental, philosophe, political. Step by step, they lead on to the dramas of Victor Hugo. Not that this is anything in their favour. Marie-Joseph Chénier made a stir in November 1789 with his *Charles IX ou la Saint-Barthélemy*, which he claimed to be the first real 'tragédie nationale'. The official Republican propagandists of the 1790s called for a freer, purer, sterner classical tragedy, modelled on the Ancients, which would reflect and inspire the onward march of the people liberated from the odious yoke of tyrant, priest and noble. By 1799, there was general agreement that this recipe for the rebirth of tragedy had produced no great play. Then, for Napoleon's imitation Louis XIV court, bedizened imitations of imitation Racine were provided. The very names provoke a yawn: Raynouard, Baour-Lormian, Luce de Lancival. The industry continued under Louis XVIII and after. Chateaubriand spent twenty years on his biblical tragedy *Moïse*, begun in 1811. Classical tragedy was still the genre ambitious young writers like Balzac aspired to excel in. The Republican bourgeois went on liking it because it was Voltairian and safe. Some Royalists attacked it because it was associated with Voltaire. Ponsard's classical tragedy *Lucrèce* was the great dramatic success of 1843, the year which saw the failure of Hugo's *Les Burgraves*, and – according to the traditional histories of literature – the end of Romanticism.

It is easy to scorn the men of the eighteenth century who failed to see

that classical tragedy was a fossilised genre.[13] It is more difficult to
decide which of the art-forms practised today are in a similar position.

NOTES

1 *Lettre à l'Académie*, ed. M. Roux. Classiques Larousse, s.d., pp. 48–55.
2 On le père Porée, see Y. Belaval, *L'Esthétique sans paradoxe de Diderot*
 (Paris, 1950), pp. 16–19.
3 *Les Scythes*, Préface. For Voltaire's dramatic theories, see F. Vial et L. Denise,
 Idées et doctrines littéraires du XVIIIᵉ siècle (Paris, 1930), pp. 182–208.
4 *Mémoires* (Paris, 1819), vol. I, p. 203.
5 Erich Zimmermann, *P.-L. Buirette de Belloy, sein Leben und seine Tragödien*
 (Leipzig, 1911), gives a balanced and informative account of Belloy. Belloy's
 dedication to the King, his Preface, and historical notes, are given in the
 1765 Paris edition, and in the Glasgow edition of the same year. An English
 translation, in blank verse, was published in Dublin.
6 P. Sagnac, *La Formation de la société française moderne* (Paris, 1946), vol. 2,
 p. 159.
7 P. D. E. Lebrun, *Œuvres*, ed. P. L. Ginguené (Paris, 1811), vol. 1, pp. 221–9;
 Ch. Lenient, *La Poésie patriotique en France dans les temps modernes* (Paris,
 1894), vol. 2, pp. 62–5.
8 Cf. Voltaire's flattery of Choiseul in *Ode à la Vérité* of 1766: 'Imitons les
 mœurs héroïques/De ce ministre des combats/Qui, de nos chevaliers antiques
 /A le cœur, la tête et le bras;/Qui pense et parle avec courage,/Qui de la
 Fortune volage/Dédaigne les dons passagers,/Qui foule aux pieds la calomnie,
 Et qui sait mépriser l'envie/Comme il méprise les dangers.' (Lenient, op. cit.,
 p. 83.) Voltaire was pleased with Choiseul for his part in the expulsion of the
 Jesuits and the rehabilitation of Calas.
9 *Sentimental Journey* (Oxford, 1927), pp. 85–6: 'I had left London with so
 much precipitation, that it never enter'd my head that we were at war with
 France: and had reach'd Dover, and look'd through my glass at the hills
 beyond Boulogne, before the idea presented itself . . .'
10 On cosmopolitanism, see R. Pomeau, *L'Europe des lumières. Cosmopolitisme
 et unité européenne au XVIIIᵉ siècle* (Paris, 1966).
11 *Œuvres*, ed. Ginguené, vol. II, p. 157.
12 Belloy toned down the story by having the Burghers in chains, and not, as
 in Froissart, with a halter round their necks. (Already in Froissart they were
 to be decapitated, not hanged.) On medievalism in eighteenth-century
 France, see R. Lanson, *Le Goût du Moyen Age en France au XVIIIᵉ siècle*
 (Paris, 1926), and L. Gossman, *Medievalism and the Ideologies of the
 Enlightenment* (Baltimore, 1968). Professor Gossman examines the connection between medieval scholarship in the century and the provincial
 noblesse de robe.
13 See George Steiner, *The Death of Tragedy* (London, 1961), pp. 193–7, for
 possible reasons why tragedy could not flourish in eighteenth-century
 Europe.

XII · Voltaire (1694-1778)

FROM *Pot-Pourri* (published 1765)

Je contais ces choses, il y a quelques jours, à M. de Boucacous, Languedocien très chaud et huguenot très zélé. *'Cavalisque!* me dit-il, on nous traite donc en France comme les Turcs; on leur refuse des mosquées, et on ne nous accorde point de temples! – Pour des mosquées, lui dis-je, les Turcs ne nous en ont encore point demandé, et j'ose me flatter qu'ils en obtiendront quand ils voudront, parce qu'ils sont nos bons alliés; mais je doute fort qu'on rétablisse vos temples, malgré toute la politesse dont nous nous piquons: la raison en est que vous êtes un peu nos ennemis. – Vos ennemis! s'écria M. de Boucacous, nous qui sommes les plus ardents serviteurs du roi! – Vous êtes fort ardents, lui répliquai-je, et si ardents que vous avez fait neuf guerres civiles, sans compter les massacres des Cévennes. – Mais, dit-il, si nous avons fait des guerres civiles, c'est que vous nous cuisiez en place publique; on se lasse à la longue d'être brûlé, il n'y a patience de saint qui puisse y tenir: qu'on nous laisse en repos, et je vous jure que nous serons des sujets très fidèles. – C'est précisément ce qu'on fait, lui dis-je; on ferme les yeux sur vous, on vous laisse faire votre commerce, vous avez une liberté assez honnête. Voilà une plaisante liberté! dit M. de Boucacous; nous ne pouvons nous assembler en pleine campagne quatre ou cinq mille seulement, avec des psaumes à quatre parties, que sur le champ il ne vienne un régiment de dragons qui nous fait rentrer chacun chez nous. Est-ce là vivre? Est-ce là être libre?'

Alors je lui parlai ainsi: 'Il n'y a aucun pays dans le monde où l'on puisse s'attrouper sans l'ordre du souverain; tout attroupement est contre les lois. Servez Dieu à votre mode dans vos maisons; n'étourdissez personne par des hurlements que vous appelez *musique*. Pensez-vous que Dieu soit bien content de vous quand vous chantez ses commandements sur l'air de *Réveillez-vous, belle endormie?* Et quand vous dites avec les Juifs, en parlant d'un peuple voisin:

> Heureux qui doit te détruire à jamais!
> Qui, t'arrachant les enfants des mamelles,
> Ecrasera leurs têtes infidèles!

Dieu veut-il absolument qu'on écrase les cervelles des petits enfants? De plus, Dieu aime-t-il tant les mauvais vers et la mauvaise musique?'

M. de Boucacous m'interrompit, et me demanda si le latin de cuisine de nos psaumes valait mieux.

> *Mélanges*, ed. J. van den Heuvel. Bibliothèque de la Pléiade
> (Paris, 1961), pp. 723–4.

Voltaire, the apostle of deism and tolerance, the enemy of Christian dogma, the would-be destroyer of the Church of Rome, was born and educated a Catholic. It was as an outraged Catholic that he quarrelled with the English Quaker Edward Higginson for rejecting the sacrament of baptism.[1] He built a Catholic church for his tenants at Ferney. He was loud in his praises of good parish priests. And his last battle, fought on his death-bed, was to try and secure for himself burial in consecrated Catholic ground.

Those Anglicans in the eighteenth century and later, who have liked to imagine that, except for one consonant, the Gallican Church is much the same thing as their own, were, and are, mistaken. None the less, Englishmen old enough to remember the distrust that Church felt for chapels in the days before paganism and ecumenical enlightenment descended on the land may, possibly, have some inkling of what French Catholics, and Voltaire, felt about those of their countrymen who worshipped outside the national religion, whose seminaries and headquarters were in foreign countries, and who had borne arms against the King. Certainly, those of us not brought up on a metrical version of the Psalms can sympathise with the Voltaire who asked

> Ne valait-il pas mieux réciter les psaumes en latin que de faire chanter aux femmes, dans l'église, les psaumes impertinents de Marot et de Bèze:
>
> > Seigneur, je n'ai point le cœur fier,
> > Je n'ai point le regard trop haut,
> > Et plus grand qu'il ne me faut,
> > Je n'ai rien voulu manier.[2]

In 1765, when he published in his *Nouveaux Mélanges III* the scurrilously anti-Christian and anti-clerical Punch and Judy show which he entitled *Pot-Pourri*, Voltaire felt himself entitled to a little fun at the expense of Huguenot zealotry. For in his *Nouveaux Mélanges II*, of the same year, had appeared a supplement to his *Traité sur la Tolérance* – the *Article nouvellement ajouté* – in which he celebrated two victories. French Jesuits, who persecuted Jansenists, had been involved also in the persecution of Protestants, and in the criminally foolish Revocation of the Edict of Nantes. Now, in 1764, the Jansenistic Parlement had suppressed the Jesuit Order in France, and Voltaire was pushing the sale of d'Alembert's

> excellent livre intitulé *Sur la destruction des Jésuites en France*, ouvrage impartiel, parce qu'il est d'un philosophe, écrit avec la finesse et l'éloquence de Pascal, et surtout avec une supériorité de lumières qui n'est pas offusquée, comme dans Pascal, par des préjugés qui ont quelquefois séduit de grands hommes.[3]

And on 9 March 1765, after a three-year publicity campaign organised by Voltaire, the Paris courts had announced that the Protestant Jean Calas was innocent of the murder for which in 1762 he had been tortured and executed at Toulouse:

> Ce fut dans Paris une joie universelle: on s'attroupait dans les places publiques, dans les promenades; on accourait pour voir cette famille si malheureuse et si bien justifiée; on battait des mains en voyant passer les juges, on les comblait de bénédictions. Ce qui rendait encore ce spectacle plus touchant, c'est que ce jour, neuvième mars, était le jour même où Calas avait péri, trois ans auparavant.[4]

Consequently, our passage shows Voltaire in a gay, sprightly, light-hearted, ironic mood. The 'things' he has been telling Boucacous are (1) that on the stock-exchanges of Amsterdam, London, Hamburg, Danzig, Venice even, adherents of fifty-three different religions trade together with the utmost amity; (2) that the Turkish authorities accord full official honours to the Greek Orthodox Patriarch in Constantinople. Boucacous is one of those comic names Voltaire is so adept at inventing: it suggests a billy-goat and sounds ludicrously authentic: Bonafous, Boucicaut, Boucaut, Boucoune, Boucoiran all exist in Languedoc. When preparing his *Siècle de Louis XIV* Voltaire may even have come across the letter which the Maréchal de Montrevel, commander of the troops sent to suppress the Protestant rebellion in Languedoc, had written in 1703 to the Minister of War about the surrender of 'un de leurs chefs, nommé Boucarut'.[5] *Cavalisque* is a Languedoc expression of scorn. Hot-headed Protestant military gentlemen from Languedoc continued to attract attention in Voltaire's time, and serve in the Army: in 1756 there had been a plan (thwarted by the pious Mme de Pompadour) to raise a Regiment of Protestant Dragoons with the pro-Protestant Prince de Conti as Colonel. The accusation that the Protestants are 'un peu nos ennemis' is a fair one. Though, after the Wars of Religion, the Huguenots had become pacific subjects of the King (as Voltaire says in the *Siècle de Louis XIV*, 'ils se firent même un mérite de rester tranquilles au milieu des factions de la Fronde'), some of the refugees after 1685 had allied themselves with foreign powers. The Maréchal de Schomberg, a former officer in the French Army, helped to defeat Louis's troops at the Battle of the Boyne, and the refugee Pastor Jurieu was an organiser and instigator of anti-French activity. Then, in 1702, brutal persecution goaded Languedoc peasants into the savage guerrilla uprising known as the Camisard rebellion, which held down an army of 60,000 Royalist troops, and, though it was suppressed, made the Paris authorities for the remainder of the Ancien Régime tremble at any mention of Southern Protestant unrest. (Voltaire's interest in this rebellion was not merely historical: the Camisard commander, Jean Cavalier, had emigrated to Holland, where he succeeded Voltaire in the affections of Olympe Dunoyer, the 'Pimpette' whom Voltaire sought to marry at The Hague in 1713.)

The frivolous tone Voltaire adopts in the passage belies his passionate nature and the deep sympathy he felt for the persecuted Protestants. Their sufferings moved him to pity and rage: he denounced the fanaticism which aimed at extirpating them. The early Protestants, he declares, were agents of human progress:

> Ne dissimulons point que, malgré leurs erreurs, nous leur devons le développement de l'esprit humain, longtemps enseveli dans la plus épaisse barbarie.

He praises the virtue of the Waldensian heretics martyred at Mérindol and Cabrières in 1545:

> Ces peuples, jusqu'alors inconnus, avaient tort, sans doute, d'être nés vaudois; c'était leur seule iniquité. Ils étaient établis depuis trois cents ans dans des déserts et sur des montagnes qu'ils avaient rendus fertiles par un travail incroyable. Leur vie pastorale et tranquille retraçait l'innocence attribuée aux premiers âges du monde . . . on les égorgea comme des animaux fugitifs qu'on tue dans une enceinte.

Only after years of suffering were the Protestants themselves infected by the savagery of their persecutors:

> La secte s'était multipliée à la lueur des bûchers et sous le fer des bourreaux; la rage succéda à la patience; ils imitèrent les cruautés de leurs ennemis: neuf guerres civiles remplirent la France de carnage.

So was it again in the Camisard revolt: 'Les camisards agirent en bêtes féroces; mais on leur avait enlevé leurs femelles et leurs petits:

ils déchirèrent les chasseurs qui couraient après eux.'[6] M. de Boucacous compresses such sentiments into the ironic remark 'c'est que vous nous cuisiez'. For Voltaire, jubilant at the Calas victory, believes that tolerance for Protestants, though not, of course, for Jesuits, is well-nigh achieved, if only the Huguenots will show some tact and not ask for too much at a time. Though the 'attroupements' in Paris on 9 March 1765 had delighted Voltaire, the Huguenot *assemblées du désert* – huge open-air services held in defiance of the law which forbade heretic worship – did not. M. de Boucacous's laconic description of the assemblies as 'quatre ou cinq mille *seulement*', with a thousand or more voices for each of the four parts (Superius, Contra, Tenor, Bassus), adds to the comic tone of the text; but Voltaire, like the civil and military authorities, regarded such tumultuous psalm-singing with apprehension. From the sixteenth century onwards, the Protestant martyrs had sung psalms on the scaffold or at the stake. So had the pastors who still, in the civilised reign of Louis XV – in 1719, 1728, 1739, 1746, 1752, 1754 – were executed for defying the law by ministering to their flocks. The last of these executions was that of a twenty-six-year-old pastor named Rochette, hanged at Toulouse in February 1762. Like his predecessors, Pastor Rochette went to his death singing 'La voici, l'heureuse journée'; a considerable body of troops had been brought into the town to prevent disorder. Psalm-singing had been a potent weapon of the Camisards: from Psalm 68, *Exurgat Deus* (called by nineteenth-century French Protestants *La Marseillaise des Huguenots*), they drew strength to fight the enemies of God's people:

> Que Dieu se montre seulement
> Et on verra soudainement
> Abandonner la place,
> Le camp des ennemis épars,
> Et ses haineux de toutes parts
> Fuir devant sa face.
> Dieu les fera tous s'enfuir,
> Ainsi qu'on voit s'évanouir
> Un amas de fumée;
> Comme la cire auprès du feu,
> Ainsi des méchants devant Dieu
> La force est consumée.

These sounds, reverberating from the rocks of the Cévennes, filled the King's troops with terror: 'Quand ces diables-là se mettaient à chanter leur bougresse de chanson, nous ne pouvions plus être maîtres de nos gens; ils fuyaient comme si tous les diables avaient été à leurs trousses.'[7]

Obviously, there is a case for Voltaire's objection to the potential mob violence wanted by M. de Boucacous, whose litotes is so amusing. But Voltaire is blind, in this passage as elsewhere, to what the Psalter is really about. It is not important whether the metrical version is, or is not, doggerel; what matters is that the Psalms are noble, and that in them, through two centuries of oppression, the Huguenots found spiritual sustenance and the strength to resist. Voltaire also was a resister. He, too, was noble in fighting for the truth as he saw it:

> Je vois qu'aujourd'hui, dans ce siècle qui est l'aurore de la raison, quelques têtes de cette hydre du fanatisme renaissent encore . . .; quiconque recherchera la vérité risquera d'être persécuté. Faut-il rester oisif dans les ténèbres? ou faut-il allumer un flambeau auquel l'envie et la calomnie rallumeront leurs torches? Pour moi, je crois que la vérité ne doit pas plus se cacher devant ces monstres que l'on ne doit s'abstenir de prendre de la nourriture dans la crainte d'être empoisonné . . .[8]

or, more succinctly:

> celui qui connaît la vérité et ne la dit pas est un pitoyable drôle.[9]

In addition, he was Voltaire the mocker, the permanent *enfant terrible*, the 'Jean qui pleure et qui rit', the spiteful buffoon dancing with rage in his night-shirt[10] and patently incapable of the sustained dignity and seriousness necessary to write a real tragedy. To this Voltaire, the Psalms of David, whatever the translation or music, were an object of derision: the whole Old Testament, ancestor of the New, was hateful to him as the source of superstition, fanaticism, persecution. Calvin, the burner of Servetus, was as vile to him as any Romish Inquisitor; and Bèze, translator of the Psalms, was Calvin's odious successor:

> Bèze et Calvin sortent de leurs tombeaux;
> Leur voix terrible épouvante les sots:
> Ils ont crié d'une voix de tonnerre
> *Persécutez!* c'est là leur cri de guerre.[11]

That is why Voltaire jocularly refers to Boucacous's psalms as 'deafening howls', and is unable to resist a jest about 'Réveillez-vous, belle endormie'. It is indeed a very comic picture that Voltaire conjures up of a Calvinist Chapel congregation, incongruously bellowing the metrical version of the Ten Commandments:

> Oyons la loi que de sa voix
> Nous a donnée le créateur,
> De tous hommes législateur, etc.

to an air associated by the ungodly with such verses as:

> Mais la belle s'est endormie,
> Entre les bras de son amant;
> Et celui-ci qui la regarde,
> En lui voyant ses yeux mourants, etc.[12]

Voltaire found it so funny that he repeated it two years later, in his mock-heroic poem *La Guerre Civile de Genève*:

> Pour tout plaisir Genève psalmodie
> Du bon David les antiques concerts,
> Croyant que Dieu se plaît aux mauvais vers.
> (Ces vers sont dignes de la musique; on y chante les commandements
> de Dieu sur l'air *Réveillez-vous, belle endormie*.)[13]

Unfortunately, the French Protestant scholar O. Douen, who last century investigated the popular airs on which the French Psalter based some of its tunes, found no trace whatsoever of the Ten Commandments ever being sung, in Geneva or France, to any tune resembling that of *Réveillez-vous. . . .*[14] Now when there is a choice between believing a member of the Eglise Réformée de France and believing a ribald, antireligious joke of Voltaire, one would be ill-advised to believe Voltaire. For, as he wrote to Thiriot in 1736:

> Le mensonge n'est un vice que quand il fait du mal; c'est une très grande vertu quand il fait du bien. Soyez donc plus vertueux que jamais. Il faut mentir comme un diable, non pas timidement, non pas pour un temps, mais hardiment et toujours.[15]

Jokes that made fanatics look ludicrous were unquestionably good and virtuous.

Because of his virulent hatred of Holy Writ, Voltaire is unable to share the taste, so widespread in his age, for verse translations of the Psalms. Protestant Psalms were, indeed, forbidden – men singing them in groups were in danger of being sent to the galleys – but Catholic versions were encouraged. Already in 1649 Antoine Godeau, bishop of Grasse and Vence, published a *Paraphrase des Psaumes de David*, aimed at turning Catholics into psalm-singers too:

> Ceux dont nous déplorons la séparation de l'Eglise, ont rendu la version dont ils se servent célèbre par les airs agréables que de doctes musiciens y mirent, lorsqu'ils furent composés. Les savoir par cœur est parmi eux comme une marque de leur Communion; et à notre grande honte, aux villes où ils sont en grand nombre, on les entend retentir dans la bouche des artisans, et à la campagne dans celle des laboureurs; tandis que les Catholiques sont ou muets, ou chantent des chansons deshonnêtes.

If only, the bishop suggested, some skilful musician could adapt popular melodies to his Psalms, so that they could replace 'tant de paroles ou vaines ou dangereuses, qui reçoivent jusqu'à cette heure tous les ornements de la musique'.[16] Among Godeau's many imitators was a protégé of Mme de Maintenon, the abbé Simon-Joseph Pellegrin, author of *Les Psaumes de David mis en vers sur les plus beaux airs* (1705) and *Cantiques spirituels* (1706). According to Voltaire, Pellegrin's sacred songs could be heard on the lips of the merry French peasantry:

> leur voix fausse et rustique
> Gaiement de Pellegrin détonne un vieux cantique.
> La paix, le doux sommeil, la force, la santé,
> Sont le fruit de leur peine et de leur pauvreté.

In a note of 1752, Voltaire maintains that

> L'abbé Pellegrin a fait des cantiques de dévotion sur les airs du Pont-Neuf; c'est là qu'on trouve, à ce qu'on dit:
> 'Quand on a perdu Jésus-Christ,
> Adieu, paniers, vendanges sont faites.'[17]
> Ces cantiques ont été chantés à la campagne et dans des couvents de province.

Alas for Voltaire's veracity: some of Pellegrin's hymns *are* set to the air *Adieu, paniers*; but these words nowhere form part of the text. What can be found there are two *cantiques*, *En quoi consiste la véritable dévotion*, and *Sur la vie mortelle de Jésus-Christ*, set to the air of *Réveillez-vous, belle endormie!* [18]

There were at the very least sixty French poets in the eighteenth century who translated psalms. The anti-*philosophe* N. J. L. Gilbert, in his *Ode imitée de plusieurs psaumes* of 1780, managed not only to suggest Chénier and Lamartine, but even to supply a half-line for Baudelaire:

> Soyez béni, mon Dieu, vous qui daignez me rendre
> L'innocence et son noble orgueil;
> Vous qui, pour protéger le repos de ma cendre,
> Veillerez près de mon cercueil.
>
> Au banquet de la vie, infortuné convive,
> J'apparus un jour, et je meurs:
> Je meurs, et sur ma tombe, où lentement j'arrive,
> Nul ne viendra verser des pleurs.
>
> Salut, champs que j'aimais, et vous, douce verdure,
> Et vous, riant exil des bois!
> Ciel, pavillon de l'homme, admirable nature,
> Salut pour la dernière fois!

L

> Ah! puissent voir longtemps votre beauté sacrée
> Tant d'amis sourds à mes adieux!
> Qu'ils meurent pleins de jours! que leur mort soit pleurée!
> Qu'un ami leur ferme les yeux!

Voltaire had great difficulty himself in avoiding the office of court psalmist to Mme de Pompadour. For reasons unknown (public approval? the King's religious scruples? sex-appeal?) this lady in 1756 made a show of piety, fasted thrice weekly during Lent, and, with the Duc de la Vallière as her intermediary, commissioned the poet Voltaire to translate the Psalms for her. If Condorcet is to be believed, she promised to make Voltaire a cardinal as a reward for his services.[19] No psalms were forthcoming; but Voltaire did make what he called a *Précis* of *Ecclesiastes* and the *Song of Songs*. In his Preface to the *Ecclésiaste*, he explains his departures from the sacred text as an attempt to 'y mettre une liaison nécessaire pour nous, et un ordre qui était inutile à l'Esprit Saint'. The result sounds like a slightly more respectable Chaulieu:

> Que les plaisirs de la table,
> Les entretiens amusants,
> Prolongent pour nous le temps;
> Et qu'une compagne aimable
> M'inspire un amour durable,
> Sans trop régner sur mes sens.

The King read it; but the Parlement de Paris in September condemned it to be 'lacéré et brûlé au pied du grand escalier du Palais' by the executioner. In the 1761 edition of the *Précis du Cantique des Cantiques*, a *Lettre de M. Eratou* (how surprising that M. de Voltaire still made anagrams on his plebeian name Arouet) states that, though the original is too obscene for modern ears, the 'spirit of the text' has been preserved. (It, also, would not have disgraced the Société du Temple.)

> Paix du cœur, volupté pure,
> Doux et tendre emportement,
> Vous guérissez ma blessure.
>
> . . .
>
> Fuyons la superbe ville:
> Le village est plus tranquille;
> Et la nature et l'amour
> L'ont choisi pour leur asile.[20]

Psalms had been very much in Voltaire's mind in 1760. On 10 March, Jean-Jacques LeFranc, marquis de Pompignan, author of *Poésies sacrées*, had attacked the *Encyclopédie* and the philosophes in his reception speech at the Academy. In May, he fled from Paris to his native Languedoc: Voltaire had been ordered by his doctor 'to hunt the Pompignan an hour or two every morning for the sake of exercise'. In other words, he assailed the wretched man with a series of lampoons: *Les QUAND, Les POUR, Les QUE, Les QUI, Les QUOI, Les OUI, Les NON, Les CAR, Les Ah! Ah! Moïse LeFranc de Pompignan.* Mockery of his Psalm translations was part of the attack:

> Quoi! dans les odes hébraïques
> Qu'il translata si tristement. (*Les QUOI*)

> . . .

> Oui, ses psaumes sont un ouvrage
> Qui nous fait bâiller longuement (*Les OUI*)

> . . .

> Récitez les psaumes pénitentiaux, et ne les translatez point en vers plus durs et plus chargés d'épithètes que votre *Didon* (*Les CAR*).[21]

One of the Psalms the hapless Pompignan had translated was *Super flumina Babylonis*:

> Puissent tes Palais embrasés
> Eclairer de tes Rois les tristes funérailles;
> Et que sur la pierre écrasés
> Tes enfants de leur sang arrosent tes murailles.[22]

So it is not surprising that Voltaire should include Psalm 137 in his diatribe against his imaginary but not untypical Languedoc Protestant, Boucacous. Of course, the end of this Psalm *is* so barbaric that one can forgive Voltaire for not having learned, while he was in England, to appreciate its stylistic merits:

> O daughter of Babylon, who art to be destroyed: happy shall he be that rewardeth thee as thou hast served us. Happy shall he be that taketh and dasheth thy little ones against the stone.

There were, however, two things which, with all his Protestant Geneva friends, he could easily have discovered. The first is that even Calvin was worried by its sentiment, and explained it as an example of the statement in Matthew VII, 2, 'comme quand le Seigneur prononce que de telle mesure qu'un chacun aura usé envers les autres, il lui sera aussi mesuré'. The second is that, in 1693, a commission in Geneva decided to eliminate from those psalms used in worship 'toutes les phrases qui rappellent trop les malédictions des Juifs contre leurs ennemis'.[23] But it would spoil Voltaire's propaganda if he asked Boucacous whether the lines he quotes were in fact ever sung by the

Huguenots. It was, however, careless of Voltaire to choose his example of bad verse from the translation of the Psalms prepared by a distinguished founder-member of the French Academy. The Marot and Bèze version of Psalm 137, which appears in the French Huguenot psalters up to 1678, ends:

> Heureux celui qui viendra arracher
> Les tiens enfants de ta mamelle impure
> Pour les froisser contre la pierre dure.

What Voltaire quotes is Psalm 137 as it appears in the French Protestant Psalter of 1679: *Les Psaumes en vers français. Retouchés sur l'ancienne version de Cl. Marot et Th. de Bèze. Par M. V. Conrart. Conseiller et Secrétaire du roi.* Conrart was the first Secrétaire perpétuel of the Academy, and held the office until his death in 1675. He was accepted as an arbiter of literary taste and an authority on style and language, even though he published little and was mocked by Boileau for his 'prudent silence'. It is probable that he himself only translated the first fifty psalms, which appeared separately in 1677. Nevertheless, the complete 1679 Psalter appeared under his name, and – like his cousin and friend bishop Antoine Godeau – he undoubtedly approved of metrical psalms. If Voltaire had mentioned the source of his quotation, his readers might have asked themselves whether the taste of Voltaire and his philosophe God was necessarily superior to that of the Secretary of the French Academy during the greatest period of French classicism.

There *was* something wrong with the taste of the Voltaire who could dismiss the Vulgate version of the Psalms as mere 'latin de cuisine': the numerous versifiers of the century who tried to translate psalms had, in this respect, more appreciation of poetry than he. But none of his faults can detract from the perfection of 'Dieu veut-il absolument qu'on écrase les cervelles des petits enfants?', where Voltaire's anti-clerical rage and his obsession with the ludicrous and the incongruous are transmuted into an expression of horror at all massacres and bloodthirsty systems.

Thirty-five years of pacific conduct by the French Protestants[24] had been rewarded in 1752 with a new wave of persecution: the galleys, imprisonment, hangings, forced conversions, the kidnapping of Protestant children. The Assembly General of the French clergy in 1758 reaffirmed its opposition to toleration of heretics. Calas's execution was followed in 1764 by the death sentence *in absentia* on the Protestant Sirven, also at Toulouse. In 1765, the Tour de Constance at Aigues-

Mortes still contained Protestant women captives, faithful to their watch-word: *Résistez*. Though the authorities rarely chose to apply it in full, the 1724 Royal Declaration against Protestants remained in force. The pretence still was that the R.P.R. (Religion prétendue réformée) no longer existed – only its former members, who were now Catholic, and liable to savage penalties if they relapsed into heresy.

Tolerance, however, or a growing distaste for religious zeal, was gaining ground. Though, in the authorities' opinion, the nation would not accept complete religious equality for Protestants, it was becoming generally agreed that they should have the right to exist, the right to marry as non-Catholics, and the right to leave property to their children who would no longer be considered bastards. Public worship, and admission to offices of state, were another matter. It is this limited tolerance which Voltaire promises to Boucacous in *Pot-Pourri*:

> Mais enfin, nous sommes la religion dominante chez nous; il ne vous est pas permis de vous attrouper en Angleterre: pourquoi voudriez-vous avoir cette liberté en France? Faites ce qu'il vous plaira dans vos maisons, et j'ai parole de M. le gouverneur et de M. l'intendant qu'en étant sages vous serez tranquilles: l'imprudence seule fit et fera les persécutions. Je trouve très mauvais que vos mariages, l'état de vos enfants, le droit de l'héritage, souffrent la moindre difficulté. Il n'est pas juste de vous saigner et de vous purger parce que vos pères ont été malades; mais que voulez-vous? Ce monde est un grand Bedlam, où des fous enchaînent d'autres fous.

On the whole, this tolerance was already being achieved as he wrote. Choiseul in Paris had no wish to persecute: the Governor of Languedoc, and the Intendant, gladly collaborated with him in avoiding strife. Here and there, sporadically, the penal laws continued to be applied; it was 'une atmosphère de tolérance de fait, mitigée de temps en temps de quelques sanctions rigoureuses, prises au hasard pour rappeler l'illégalité oubliée de la R.P.R.'.

For Cévenol peasants and some Languedoc country gentry, this tacit right to exist was not enough. They wanted public worship, or, failing that, the illegal *assemblées du désert*. Respectable, middle-class Protestants, especially those in Paris and the north of France, shared Voltaire's distaste for such uncouth activities. Edifying readings in the drawing-room, pious meditations, little private services after dinner organised by the ladies, an ethical code, and the knowledge that one did not share antiquated Papist superstition – this was what much middle-class French Protestantism appears to have consisted of in the late 1760s. Even pastors such as Paul Rabaut in Nîmes – reasonably safe now in their emergence from clandestinity and well paid by their bourgeois flock – tended to prefer collaboration with the civil authorities to the turbulent and ill-bred zealotry of Huguenot yokels. Civil rights, and private worship in buildings devoid of any external religious signs, was all that Pastor Jean-Paul Rabaut-Saint-Etienne, the future Girondin, tried to secure from the central government. Quietly but effectively, powerful persons such as M. de Malesherbes were doing their best for liberty. Protestant bankers and merchants, with their links in Geneva, London, Holland, Germany, continued to make money. 'Foreign' Protestant communities flourished in French commercial cities. Voltaire's Protestant friends the Tronchins, of Geneva, occupied an increasingly prominent position in Paris society of the 1760s: J. R. Tronchin was a fermier-général, and Dr T. Tronchin, surgeon to the King's cousin, was, according to Grimm, 'l'homme le plus à la mode qu'il y ait actuellement en France'. Between Voltairian deism, 'enlightened' bourgeois Protestantism, and the free-masonry which many French Protestants resorted to as a substitute for the public worship forbidden them, the difference was imperceptible. M. de Boucacous, the fire-eating squireen from Languedoc, belonged to a vanished age of barbarism. Voltaire could mock him with a clear conscience: he, and his psalms, and his ex-Camisard terrorists and his Babylonian captivity had little to do with the *haute bourgeoisie protestante* that M. de Voltaire frequented.

But still, the old prejudices remained. The last three years of Louis XV's reign saw a new persecution of Protestants in Marseilles: Saint-Florentin, minister for religious affairs, said that it was done 'as a matter of principle'. Louis XVI could not bring himself to undo the work of Louis le Grand, and restore the Edict of Nantes. In the 1770s Voltaire was still writing to pastors, whom he assured of his efforts to help 'citizens whom he regards as his brothers, although he shares neither their opinions nor those of their persecutors'. He expressed his earnest desire to live long enough 'to see the end of all these horrors destructive of society and of reason'.

His wish was not granted. Only in 1787 did the King sign the Edict of Tolerance, granting Protestants civil rights, civil marriage and freedom to engage in trades and professions.

NOTES

1 *Lettres philosophiques*, ed. Lanson (Paris, 1930), vol. 1, p. 20: 'In a violent passion he said, I lied – which I put up patiently, till he, becoming cooler, desired to know why I should impose upon a stranger. . . . He replied, our Bible was falsely translated, and done by heretics.' (Higginson's own account of the incident.)

2 *Œuvres*, ed. Moland, vol. 32, p. 586. In the 1679 Huguenot Psalter, Psalm 131 (Domine, non est exaltatum cor) was given a revised form: 'Seigneur, je n'ai point l'esprit vain,/Je n'aspirai jamais trop haut;/Et je n'eus jamais le défaut/ De tenter un trop grand dessein.'

3 *Traité sur la Tolérance. Mélanges*, Pléiade ed., p. 647. On the expulsion of the Jesuits from France, see Sagnac, *La Formation de la société française moderne* (Paris, 1946), vol. 2, pp. 132–5.

4 *Traité sur la Tolérance*, ed. cit., p. 649. On the Calas case, see D. D. Bien, *The Calas Affair* (Princeton, 1960). Professor Bien says that 'Protestantism had a bloody, unsavoury past' in France (p. 52) and that the alliance between Voltaire and the Protestants was 'unnatural' (p. 25). He states that the conviction of Calas was a judicial error, but seeks to exculpate the Toulouse judges by asserting that Calas has never been proved innocent of the murder. Professor Bien's main thesis is that the verdict must be interpreted against the background of war, economic crisis, social unrest, and the judges' views about Protestants as rabble-rousers, fanatics who were disobedient to the King, scornful of authority, and instigators of revolt. He traces a connection between the price of corn at Toulouse in 1761 and the preceding years, and the fact that, in March 1762, the peaceful, respectable citizen Calas was racked, forcibly filled with water, broken on the wheel, strangled, his corpse burned, and the ashes thrown to the wind. As Diderot remarked: 'C'est une belle chose que la science économique, mais elle nous abrutira.'

5 C. Devic and J. Vaissette, *Histoire générale du Languedoc* (Toulouse, 1876), vol. 14, p. 1755.

6 *Traité sur la Tolérance*, ed. cit., pp. 573–5; *Œuvres*, ed. Moland, vol. 24, p. 571 ('Remarques pour servir de supplément à l'*Essai sur les Mœurs*').

7 E. G. Léonard, *Histoire Générale du Protestantisme* (Paris, 1964), III, pp. 18ff. For the economic and psychological causes of the Camisard rebellion, see E. Leroy Ladurie, *Les Paysans de Languedoc* (Paris, 1966), pp. 605–29.

8 *Le Philosophe ignorant, Mélanges*, ed. cit., pp. 929–30.

9 Quoted by A. Delattre, *Voltaire l'impétueux*, ed. R. Pomeau (Paris, 1957), p. 49.

10 Voltaire's poem 'Jean qui pleure et qui rit' (1772) is in vol. 9 of Moland. The night-shirt incident is related in Marmontel's *Mémoires*, vol. I, pp. 230–1.

11 *Guerre civile de Genève*, Ch. IV, Moland, vol. 9, p. 541.

12 H. Davenson, *Le Livre des chansons. Introduction à la chanson populaire française*, 3ᵉ édition (Neuchâtel, Paris, 1955), pp. 286–8, 515.

13 *Guerre civile de Genève*, Ch. I, ibid., p. 516.

14 O. Douen, *Clément Marot et le Psautier Huguenot* (Paris, 1878), vol. 1, p. 730.

15 Quoted by A. Delattre, op. cit., pp. 41–2.

16 *Paraphrase des Psaumes de David*. Par Antoine Godeau. Evêque de Grasse et Vence. Paris, 1649. Préface.

17 *Discours en vers sur l'homme, Mélanges*, ed. cit., pp. 213, 1371.

18 Douen, op. cit., p. 695.

19 *Œuvres*, Moland, vol. I, p. 241. See also *Psaumes* in *Tableau Général*, vol. 52.

20 Ibid., vol. 9, pp. 481–506.

21 *Les Quand, Mélanges*, ed. cit., pp. 369–78, and Marmontel, *Mémoires*, vol. I, p. 375.

22 *Poésies Sacrées* de Monsieur L* F*** (Paris, 1753), p. 38.

23 Douen, op. cit., pp. 31, 525.

24 On French Protestantism in the second half of the eighteenth century, see E. G. Léonard, op. cit., and *Mon Village sous Louis XV, d'après les Mémoires d'un Paysan* (Paris, 1941); R. Stephen, *Histoire du Protestantisme français* (Paris, 1961); H. Lüthy, *La Banque Protestante en France de la Révocation de l'Edit de Nantes à la Révolution* (Paris, 1959); P. Grosclaude, *Malesherbes. Témoin et interprète de son temps* (Paris, 1961); M. Richard, *La Vie quotidienne des Protestants sous l'Ancien Régime* (Paris, 1966).

XIII · Voltaire (1694–1778)

FROM *Lettre au Docteur Pansophe* (published 1766)

'Au nom de la sainte vertu, Amen. Comme ainsi soit, mes frères, que j'ai travaillé sans relâche à vous rendre sots et ignorants, je meurs avec la consolation d'avoir réussi, et de n'avoir point jeté mes paroles en l'air. Vous savez que j'ai établi des cabarets pour y noyer votre raison, mais point d'académie pour la cultiver: car, encore une fois, un ivrogne vaut mieux que tous les philosophes de l'Europe. N'oubliez jamais mon histoire du régiment de Saint-Gervais, dont tous les officiers et les soldats ivres dansaient avec édification dans la place publique de Genève, comme un saint roi juif dansa autrefois devant l'arche. Voilà les honnêtes gens. Le vin et l'ignorance sont le sommaire de toute la sagesse. Les hommes sobres sont fous; les ivrognes sont francs et vertueux. Mais je crains ce qui peut arriver, c'est-à-dire que la science, cette mère de tous les crimes et de tous les vices, ne se glisse parmi vous. L'ennemi rôde autour de vous; il a la subtilité du serpent et la force du lion; il vous menace. Peut-être, hélas! bientôt le luxe, les arts, la philosophie, la bonne chère, les auteurs, les perruquiers, les prêtres et les marchands de mode vous empoisonneront et ruineront mon ouvrage. O sainte vertu! détourne tous ces maux! Mes petits enfants, obstinez-vous dans votre ignorance et votre simplicité; c'est-à-dire, soyez toujours vertueux, car c'est la même chose. Soyez attentifs à mes paroles; que ceux qui ont des oreilles entendent. Les mondains vous ont dit: Nos institutions sont bonnes; elles nous rendent heureux; et moi, je vous dis que leurs institutions sont abominables et les rendent malheureux. Le vrai bonheur de l'homme est de vivre seul, de manger des fruits sauvages, de dormir sur la terre nue ou dans le creux d'un arbre, et de ne jamais penser. Les mondains vous ont dit: Nous ne sommes pas des bêtes féroces; nous faisons du bien à nos semblables; nous punissons les vices, et nous nous aimons les uns les autres; et moi, je vous dis que tous les Européens sont des bêtes féroces ou des fripons, que toute l'Europe ne sera bientôt qu'un affreux désert; que les mondains ne font du bien que pour faire du mal; qu'ils se haïssent tous et qu'ils récompensent le vice. O sainte vertu! Les mondains vous ont dit: Vous êtes des fous; l'homme est fait pour vivre en société, et non pour manger du gland dans les bois; et moi, je vous dis que vous êtes les seuls sages, et qu'ils sont fous et méchants; l'homme n'est pas plus fait pour la société, qui est nécessairement l'école du crime, que pour aller voler sur les grands chemins. O mes petits enfants, restez dans les bois, c'est la place de l'homme. O sainte vertu! Emile, mon premier disciple, est selon mon cœur; il me succédera. Je lui ai appris à lire et à écrire, et à parler beaucoup; c'en est assez pour vous gouverner. Il vous lira quelquefois la Bible, l'excellente histoire de Robinson Crusoé, et mes ouvrages; il n'y a que cela de bon.'

> *Mélanges*, ed. J. van den Heuvel. Bibliothèque de la
> Pléiade (Paris, 1961), pp. 855–7.

Voltaire was a great comic genius who can still make his readers laugh. This passage typifies the verve, fantasy, sprightliness and glee with which he misrepresents his victims and transmogrifies them into permanent figures of fun. Le Docteur Pansophe is Jean-Jacques Rousseau in London, in the spring of 1766. (Dr is Voltairian shorthand for ludicrous medieval theologians, pretentious Germanic pedants and the ignorant, interfering clerics of the Sorbonne alias the Non-sober; Pansophe means all-wise.) Voltaire imagines him setting up as a revivalist preacher for the back-to-nature, noble-savage cult, taking his converts to graze in Hyde Park or rootle for acorns in Windsor Forest. His mission accomplished, his disciples restored to the state of brute beasts, Jean-Jacques, conscious that death is nigh, will crawl to his flock on all fours. He delivers them this sermon. As the sermon ends, he expires:

> Mes petits enfants, je vous répète encore ma grande leçon, bannissez d'entre vous la raison et la philosophie, comme elles sont bannies de mes livres. Soyez machinalement vertueux; ne pensez jamais, ou que très rarement; rapprochez-vous sans cesse de l'état des bêtes, qui est votre état naturel. A ces causes, je vous recommande la sainte vertu. Adieu, mes petits enfants; je meurs. Que Dieu vous soit en aide! Amen.

The summary of Rousseauism provided by Voltaire[1] is, of course, a caricature. But his mockery is effective because each of his points can be substantiated by passages in Rousseau which, taken out of context, are more outrageous than wise. Rousseau had said that 'l'homme qui pense est un animal dépravé'. He had attacked arts, science, learning, luxury, priests, philosophes, and the whole of modern society. He had equated sobriety with vice, cunning, treachery and deceit, and wine-bibbing with sincerity, open-heartedness, stupidity, goodness:

> Mais enfin, le goût du vin n'est pas un crime, il en fait rarement commettre, il rend l'homme stupide et non pas méchant. . . . Généralement

parlant, les buveurs ont de la cordialité, de la franchise; ils sont presque tous bons, droits, justes, fidèles, braves et honnêtes gens, à ce défaut près.[2]

The drunken caperings of the Régiment de Saint-Gervais are a curious exemplar for civic fraternity.[3] (King David leaping and dancing before the Lord – II Samuel, ch. vi – makes an apt parallel with psalm-singing Geneva; though, of course, the real reason why Voltaire brings in David is that he likes to ridicule this 'adulterous murderer', ancestor of the Messiah.) *Robinson Crusoe* was much admired by Rousseau:

> Je hais les livres; ils n'apprennent qu'à parler de ce qu'on ne sait pas. ... Puisqu'il nous faut absolument des livres, il en existe un qui fournit, à mon gré, le plus heureux traité d'éducation naturelle. Ce livre sera le premier que lira mon Emile; seul il composera durant longtemps toute sa bibliothèque, et il y tiendra longtemps une place distinguée. ... Quel est donc ce merveilleux livre: Est-ce Aristote? est-ce Pline? est-ce Buffon? Non, c'est Robinson Crusoé.[4]

The various echoes from the Gospels that occur in the passage ('He that hath ears to hear, let him hear', etc.) are appropriate to a sermon. They also recall the accusation made by Voltaire, sixteen months earlier, that in his blasphemous pride and madness Rousseau had compared himself to Jesus Christ.[5]

Spontaneous effervescence of humour for its own sake does occur in Voltaire, especially in his correspondence. But the irony of the *Lettre au Docteur Pansophe* is, in a literal sense, deadly. The double mention of Jean-Jacques dying is more than a joke, more even than the expression of a subconscious desire: Voltaire passionately wants to have Rousseau silenced, whether by prison, mad-house, suicide or public executioner. In the *Sentiment des Citoyens* (December 1764) Voltaire had written:

> On a pitié d'un fou; mais quand la démence devient fureur, on le lie. La tolérance, qui est une vertu, serait alors un vice

and had gone on to accuse Rousseau of blasphemy, hypocrisy, apostasy, calumny. The *Sentiment* not only reveals Rousseau's bitter secret, the abandoning of his children in the Foundlings Home; it affirms that he has venereal disease and that he killed the mother of his wretched mistress. He is a dangerous agitator bent on causing armed strife in Geneva. The Genevan authorities must threaten him with death:

> S'il a cru que nous tirerions l'épée pour le roman d'Emile, il peut mettre cette idée dans le nombre de ses ridicules et de ses folies. Mais il faut lui apprendre que si on châtie légèrement un romancier impie, on punit capitalement un vil séditieux.[6]

The *Lettre au Docteur Pansophe* continues the attack in a lighter vein. It is succeeded in November 1766 by the *Lettres de Voltaire à M. Hume*:

> Il a mis le trouble dans sa patrie avant d'en sortir, comme un incendiaire qui s'enfuit après avoir allumé la mèche. Celui-là, certes, a eu raison qui a dit que Jean-Jacques descendait en droite ligne du barbet de Diogène accouplé avec une des couleuvres de la Discorde. . . . On peut, sur le fumier où il est couché et où il grince des dents contre le genre humain, lui jeter du pain s'il en a besoin; mais il a fallu le faire connaître, et mettre ceux qui peuvent le nourrir à l'abri des morsures.

La Guerre Civile de Genève, begun early in 1767, likewise vituperates against 'le roux Rousseau, de fureur hébété', and his bed-mate Thérèse Levasseur, 'Vachine, sa gaupe'. The main charge here is that Rousseau is an ungrateful cur, full of hatred for his benefactors and for all mankind:

> Il tient beaucoup du naturel d'un chien,
> Il jappe et fuit, et mord qui le caresse.[8]

Why does M. de Voltaire, the man of taste, the successor of Racine, demean himself by such scurrilities? The immediate occasion of the *Sentiment des Citoyens* was Rousseau's *Lettres écrites de la Montagne* (November 1764). In the fifth of these letters, Rousseau regrets that Voltaire did not use his influence to prevent the decree issued by the Geneva Petit Conseil for the burning of *Emile* and the arrest of Jean-Jacques. In mock Voltairian style (Voltaire returns the compliment in the *Lettre au Docteur Pansophe*), Rousseau writes the speech which he thinks Voltaire ought to have made in his favour:

> 'Moi-même, enfin, si je ne raisonne pas, je fais mieux; je fais raisonner mes lecteurs. Voyez mon chapitre des Juifs: voyez ce même chapitre plus développé dans le *Sermon des Cinquante*. Il y a là du raisonnement, ou l'équivalent, je pense. Vous conviendrez aussi qu'il y a peu de *détour*, et quelque chose de plus que des *traits épars et indiscrets*.
>
> Nous avons arrangé que mon grand crédit à la Cour et ma toute-puissance prétendue vous serviraient de prétexte pour laisser courir en paix les jeux badins de mes vieux ans: cela est bon, mais ne brûlez pas pour cela des écrits plus graves: car alors cela serait trop choquant.
>
> J'ai tant prêché la tolérance! Il ne faut pas toujours l'exiger des autres et n'en jamais user avec eux. Ce pauvre homme croit en Dieu? passons-lui cela, il ne fera pas secte. Il est ennuyeux? Tous les raisonneurs le sont. . . . Croyez-moi, laissons raisonner ceux qui nous laissent plaisanter; ne brûlons ni gens, ni livres, et restons en paix, c'est mon avis.' Voilà, selon moi, ce qu'eût pu dire d'un meilleur ton M. de Voltaire, et ce n'eût pas été là, ce me semble, le plus mauvais conseil qu'il aurait donné.[9]

In other words, Rousseau denounces Voltaire as the author of the anonymous *Sermon des Cinquante*, and insinuates to the Genevan authorities, on whose good-will Voltaire is so dependent for his comfort and safety, that Voltaire is an atheist.

Now, the *Sermon des Cinquante*, published in 1749 and again in about 1762, is Voltaire's most virulent attack on the Bible and Christianity. In it he vilifies the Old Testament as a series of horrors, iniquities, abominations and obscenities, and the New Testament as an odious and puerile tissue of lies, fraud, deceit and imposture. He sneers at Christ:

> Il y eut toujours chez les Juifs des gens de la lie du peuple qui firent les prophètes pour se distinguer de la populace: voici celui qui a fait le plus de bruit, et dont on a fait un Dieu.

He presents Christian doctrine as extravagant, blasphemous superstition, and the history of Christianity as a history of war, bloodshed, fanaticism and subversion:

> Cette secte se partage en une multitude de sectes: dans tous les temps on se bat, on s'égorge, on s'assassine. A chaque dispute, les rois, les princes sont massacrés.
>
> Tel est le fruit, mes très chers frères, de l'arbre de la croix, de la potence qu'on a divinisée.
>
> Voilà donc pourquoi on ose faire venir Dieu sur la terre! pour livrer l'Europe pendant des siècles au meurtre et au brigandage.[10]

It is easy to understand why Joseph de Maistre anathematised Voltaire and those who read him with pleasure:

> L'admiration effrénée dont trop de gens l'entourent est le signe infaillible d'une âme corrompue. Qu'on ne se fasse point illusion: si quelqu'un, en parcourant sa bibliothèque, se sent attiré vers les *Œuvres de Ferney*, Dieu ne l'aime pas.[11]

But it is also easy to understand why Voltaire wanted to silence the Rousseau who divulged such dangerous secrets. In spite of his money, his prestige, and the facilities for avoiding arrest which his frontier residences afforded him, Voltaire's blasphemies, if publicly proven to be by Voltaire, were enough to send him to the stake. The repression by the Parlement de Paris of the philosophes' enemies, the Jesuits, in no way implied that the Parlement would leave anti-Christian propagandists unpunished. In June 1762 it had issued an arrest-warrant against Rousseau, for the irreligious *Emile* which he had been so inconsiderate as to publish under his own name. Though the authorities proceeded against him with an easy-going dilatoriness not unusual in the decaying monarchy, and inconceivable in efficient police states, it was none the less made clear to Rousseau that only by escaping from France could he save his skin.[12] The chevalier de la Barre did not manage to flee the country: though he was a well-connected nobleman, the Parlement de Paris in June 1766 confirmed the death-sentence imposed upon him for blasphemies trivial in comparison with those in Voltaire's *Sermon des Cinquante*.[13]

Rousseau's fears that his own life was in danger from his enemies were not without substance:

> Sitôt qu'on m'apprête des prisons, des bourreaux, des chaînes, quiconque m'accuse est un délateur; il sait qu'il n'attaque pas seulement l'auteur, mais l'homme; . . . ce n'est plus à ma seule réputation qu'il en veut, c'est à mon honneur, à ma liberté, à ma vie.[14]

Faced with arrest in France and Switzerland, his *Lettres écrites de la Montagne* burned even by the Protestant Dutch, he sought asylum in England, under the guidance and protection of David Hume, 'le bon David', the friend and ally of the philosophes. They arrived in London on 13 January 1766. The publication there in April of the *Lettre au Docteur Pansophe* proved to Rousseau that he was still within reach of his enemies.[15] By June, he was accusing Hume of the vilest treachery: one of Hume's crimes against him was the circumstances in which Hume had recommended him for a secret pension from King George III. Hume sent his account of the quarrel to d'Holbach and d'Alembert, who touched it up and had it translated into French. English and French versions of it were on sale by November. The *Exposé succinct de la contestation qui s'est élevée entre M. Hume et M. Rousseau* depicts Rousseau as a base ingrate who hates his benefactor and who, in his pride and madness, imagines that the whole world is conspiring against him. It concludes with an affirmation of the philosophe party's solidarity against Rousseau the renegade:

> Non est ille qualem speravimus; simus nos quales fuimus, ei dissimiles.
> Seneca, *De Beneficiis*, lib. VII, cap. 29.[16]

The philosophes knew that Rousseau had just begun work on his memoirs. The accusations in the *Exposé succinct* that he was both a deliberate liar and so crazed that he could not distinguish between fact and fiction were a defence, in advance, against the blackening of their names which they assumed the *Confessions* would contain. And, as Rousseau himself observed,[17] once it was established that he was mad, his allegations that they persecuted him could be dismissed as lunacy.

One school of Rousseau criticism presents him as a Defender of the

Faith against the atheist materialists. Already in 1797 Chateaubriand called him 'the apostle of God and of morality'.[18] According to M. Henri Guillemin, Rousseau was hounded by the philosophes because he preached an almost Christian doctrine:

> Et parce que ce livre (*La Nouvelle Héloïse*) est un immense plaidoyer pour l'ordre, parce que le mariage y est tenu pour un sacrement, parce que l'amour n'y trouve de grandeur que s'il dépasse l'appétit des sens, parce que la vie entière y est décrite comme un travail d'accomplissement, parce que Dieu y est présent d'un bout à l'autre, il soulèvera contre lui l'exécration des philosophes.[19]

In M. François Mauriac's view, he was the chief witness for God in the despicable eighteenth century:

> Après tous les crimes qu'il avoue, cet homme n'en demeure pas moins, dans le siècle de Voltaire, l'avocat misérable de Dieu. Dans un temps où l'indulgente pensée voltairienne avait rang de philosophie, il était juste que le surnaturel fût défendu par ce maniaque, par ce fou. Si nous cherchons au XVIIIᵉ siècle l'héritier de Bossuet, nous n'en trouvons aucun autre que le promeneur solitaire. Voilà vraiment l'époque de la grande humiliation catholique! ... Enfin rendons-lui cette justice: aussi éloigné qu'il soit du véritable christianisme, il a confessé le Christ devant les hommes, et cela aussi lui sera compté.[20]

It is true that Rousseau speaks of Christ as his master, and (in the Fourth of his *Lettres écrites de la Montagne*) claims that all his works 'respirent le même amour pour l'Evangile, la même vénération pour Jésus-Christ'. He retained a deep-rooted attachment to the Church in which he had been nurtured:

> la communion protestante qui tire son unique règle de l'Ecriture Sainte et de la raison . . ., une religion raisonnable et sainte qui, loin d'abrutir l'homme, l'ennoblit et l'élève, qui ne favorisant ni l'impiété ni le fanatisme, permet d'être sage et de croire, d'être humain et pieux tout à la fois.[21]

Instinctively and emotionally, Rousseau felt himself within the Christian fold, whereas Voltaire, at any rate until late in his life, was hysterically hostile to Christianity. Undoubtedly, Rousseau's pro-Christian arguments in *Emile* were one of the reasons why Voltaire hated him.

Nevertheless, though in the *Profession de foi du vicaire savoyard* Rousseau refused to deny the divinity of Christ, the authenticity of the Gospels, or the holy mystery of the Eucharist,[22] he also refused to accept them. Like his instructress Mme de Warens, who 'croyait tout autrement que l'Eglise, toujours en s'y soumettant'[23], Rousseau gave positive intellectual assent to very little apart from God and an ethical system with divine sanctions. It was not because of its arguments *for* Christianity that *Emile* was condemned in Geneva, Berne and Holland, as well as in Paris. There is little that is specifically Christian in the sentimental Christ portrayed by Rousseau in the Third of the *Lettres*:

> je ne puis m'empêcher de dire qu'une des choses qui me charment dans le caractère de Jésus n'est pas seulement la douceur des mœurs, la simplicité, mais la facilité, la grâce, et même l'élégance. . . . Il était à la fois indulgent et juste, doux aux faibles et terrible aux méchants. Sa morale avait quelque chose d'attrayant, de caressant, de tendre, il avait le cœur sensible, il était homme de bonne société. Quand il n'eût pas été le plus sage des mortels, il en eût été le plus aimable.

It was such a dechristianised Christ that Voltaire himself, from the mid-1760s onward, began to find attractive, and of whom he, also, wrote: 'Je vous prends pour mon seul maître.'[24] In spite of differences in emphasis, and their temperamental incompatibility, Rousseau and Voltaire shared the same deist creed. Voltaire spoke the truth in the *Lettre au Docteur Pansophe* when he affirmed 'j'ai fait de mon mieux pour défendre la cause de Dieu'.[25] He worshipped the Supreme Being; he preached a 'Dieu rémunérateur et vengeur'; he denounced atheism as intellectually untenable and destructive of all social order.[26] Steadfast in his belief that the Universe was created and sustained by God, the giver of eternal laws unalterable, and, in the last resort, unfathomable by man, Voltaire rejected out of hand any facts which seemed to conflict with this belief, and scathingly attacked those scientific theories of the age which viewed Nature as a self-sufficient, self-modifying force. 'Tout ce qui prête à la nature une activité quelconque lui est suspect *a priori*, parce que donner à la nature ou à l'homme c'est ôter à Dieu. Une conclusion s'impose et elle ne surprendra que ceux qui méconnaissent le caractère religieux de sa pensée: si Voltaire a mis tant d'acharnement à combattre une philosophie et une science qui promettaient à l'homme la connaissance du monde, c'est parce qu'il défendait sa foi.'[27] If belief in God and morality were enough to make a man hated by the philosophes, Voltaire would have aroused stronger reactions from his followers than the tolerant distaste which some of the more radical of them felt for that bigoted old deist.[28] But of course, no antireligious test was imposed upon those who wished to associate themselves with the Encyclopédistes. The memoirs of the abbé Morellet describe how he and the abbé Galiani defended the cause of God at the discussion-groups organised by their friend, 'Monsieur et cher athée' the baron d'Holbach.

It was not because he fervently and instinctively adhered to a 'modernist' form of Protestantism that the philosophes attacked Jean-Jacques Rousseau; it was because he spurned and attacked them. He not only quarrelled with them individually: from his first *Discours*[29] onwards, he equated them, as a group, with all that he thought most evil in the civilisation which they were successfully persuading enlightened despots to modernise and improve, but which he rejected as doomed and damned. Rousseau's literary genius which brought him a European reputation, and his spell-binding charm still perceptible to the modern reader, made him the more dangerous an adversary. Voltaire meant what he said in the *Lettre au Docteur Pansophe* when he accused Rousseau of assassinating the movement to which he owed his life and liberty:

> Il y a dix siècles, vous auriez été . . . brûlé ou pendu, ainsi que quantité d'honnêtes gens qui cultivent aujourd'hui les lettres en paix, et avouez que le temps présent vaut mieux. C'est à la philosophie que vous devez votre salut, et vous l'assassinez: mettez-vous à genoux, ingrat, et pleurez sur votre folie. Nous ne sommes plus esclaves de ces tyrans spirituels et temporels qui désolaient toute l'Europe; la vie est plus douce, les mœurs plus humaines, et les Etats plus tranquilles.[30]

Above all it was because he was a renegade from the party[31] that the philosophes' hatred of Rousseau was so virulent:

> O comme nous aurions chéri ce fou, s'il n'avait pas été faux frère.[32]

The famous statement of Voltaire: 'I disapprove of what you say, but I will defend to the death your right to say it' has not, unfortunately, been located in his published works. It appears to have been invented in 1907 by a man called Tallentyre.[33] Voltaire mostly harassed to the death those who offended him. But he was something of a poet as well as a machine for mocking the enemies of liberalism. Jubilant at the destruction of the Jesuits in France, he writes in *Pot-Pourri*:

> O mes frères les Jésuites! vous n'avez pas été tolérants, et on ne l'est pas pour vous. Consolez-vous; d'autres à leur tour deviendront persécuteurs, et à leur tour ils seront abhorrés.[34]

Is it perhaps himself that he has in mind here, and the aggressively confident philosophe movement? Or had he prophetic, as well as poetic gifts? At any rate, it is not inconceivable that he was being sincere when he stated:

> Nous sommes tous pétris de faiblesses et d'erreurs; pardonnons-nous réciproquement nos sottises, c'est la première loi de la nature.[35]

M

NOTES

1 Voltaire denied having written the *Lettre au Docteur Pansophe*. H. Roddier, *J.-J. Rousseau en Angleterre au XVIII* siècle. *L'Œuvre et l'homme* (Paris, 1950), pp. 286–7, gives reasons for believing that it is by Voltaire, and describes it as 'digne de sa meilleure plume'.

2 *Lettre à d'Alembert*, ed. M. Fuchs (Genève, 1948), pp. 146–7. Cf. *La Nouvelle Héloïse*, Pt I, xxiii, ed. Mornet, vol. II, p. 83.

3 *Lettre à d'Alembert*, ed. cit., pp. 181–2.

4 *Emile*, ed. F. et P. Richard (Paris, Garnier), pp. 210–11.

5 *Sentiment des Citoyens*. Voltaire, *Mélanges* (Pléiade), p. 716. Voltaire's accusation is based on the last paragraphs of Rousseau's *Lettres écrites de la montagne*, Letter I.

6 *Sentiment des Citoyens*, ed. cit., pp. 715–18.

7 *Mélanges* (Pléiade), p. 875.

8 Voltaire, *Œuvres*, ed. Moland, vol. IX, pp. 533–45.

9 *Lettres écrites de la montagne*, Letter V. *Œuvres complètes*, Pléiade (Paris, 1964), vol. III, pp. 799–800. The *détour* and *traits épars et indiscrets* refer to a passage from J.-R. Tronchin's *Lettres écrites de la campagne* which Rousseau quoted earlier in Letter V: 'Y a-t-il parité entre des livres où l'on trouve des traits épars et indiscrets contre la religion et des livres où, sans détour, sans ménagement, on l'attaque dans ses dogmes, dans sa morale, dans son influence sur la société?' Rousseau's *Lettres* were a riposte to Tronchin's.

10 *Mélanges* (Pléiade), pp. 253–70.

11 *Soirées de Saint-Pétersbourg*, ed. L. A. de Grémilly (Paris, 1960), p. 116. The *Soirées* were first published in 1821.

12 Rousseau, *Confessions*, ed. J. Voisine (Paris, 1964), pp. 676–93.

13 See above, Ch. VIII, note 12.

14 *Lettres écrites de la montagne*, Letter I. Ed. cit., vol. III, p. 693.

15 'Le noble objet de ce spirituel ouvrage est de m'attirer le mépris et la haine de ceux chez qui je me suis réfugié. Je ne doutai point que mon cher patron [Hume] n'eût été un des instruments de cette publication' (*Exposé succinct de la contestation qui s'est élevée entre M. Hume et M. Rousseau. Œuvres complètes de J.-J. Rousseau. Nouvelle Edition*, 1793, vol. 27, p. 85).

16 For the Hume–Rousseau quarrel, the various lampoons on Rousseau in the London press, and Rousseau's mad journey, in fear of his life, from Wootton (near Ashbourne in Derbyshire) to Spalding, then Dover and France, in May 1767, see H. Roddier, op. cit., pp. 259–306. H. Guillemin, *Les Philosophes contre Jean-Jacques. 'Cette affaire infernale'. L'Affaire J.-J. Rousseau–Hume* (Paris, 1942) maintains that Rousseau was right in believing that the philosophes deliberately lured him to England in order to ruin his reputation. M. Roddier does not consider that M. Guillemin has proved his case. M. Jacques Voisine, in his edition of the *Confessions* (p. 210, n.) points out that Rousseau did get a pension from George III, and that a portrait of the King adorned Rousseau's apartment in the rue Plâtrière.

17 H. Guillemin, op. cit., p. 336.

18 *Essai sur les révolutions. Œuvres complètes* (Paris, Garnier, s.d.), vol. 1, p. 583.

19 *Annales J.-J. Rousseau*, XXX, p. 229.

20 *Trois grands hommes devant Dieu* (Paris, 1947), p. 49. M. Mauriac goes on to mention St Benoît-Joseph Labre (1748–83, canonised 1883). Like Rousseau, Labre tramped the roads and fled from eighteenth-century civilisation. 'Benedict Labre, a symbol of the poor man, stands for all the poverty of the eighteenth century' (A. de la Gorce, *St Benedict Joseph Labre*, Sheed & Ward, London, 1952, p. 89). Voltaire's views on canonising filthy, idle tramps are expressed in the article *Superstition* of the *Dictionnaire philosophique*.

21 *Nouvelle Héloïse*, Pt. VI, xi, ed. Mornet, vol. IV, pp. 296, 309.

22 *Emile*, ed. cit., pp. 360–83.

23 *Confessions*, ed. Voisine, p. 265.

24 *Religion II* of the *Questions sur l'Encyclopédie*. See R. Pomeau, *La Religion de Voltaire* (Paris, 1957), p. 375.

25 *Mélanges* (Pléiade), p. 850.

26 On Voltaire's religious beliefs, see R. Pomeau, op. cit., and Voltaire, *Histoire de Jenni*, ed. J. H. Brumfitt and M. I. Gerard Davis (Oxford, 1960), pp. xxviii–xlviii.

27 Jacques Roger, *Les Sciences de la vie dans la pensée française du XVIIIe siècle* (Paris, 1963), p. 748. Professor John Weightman, on the other hand, assigns little importance to the religious faith of either Voltaire or Rousseau: 'Although scientific evolutionism was not yet fully established, the major thinkers of the French Enlightenment foresaw, or sensed, its implications. Montesquieu, Voltaire, Diderot and Rousseau, all of whom had some knowledge of science, were in a sense sociologists, trying to understand human life as a dynamic process in time, and as a secular process, which cannot be accounted for in religious terms, and more especially not in terms of the Christian revelation. This is true, I think, of Voltaire and Rousseau who were technically deists, and not agnostics or atheists. Their deism, although they themselves may sincerely have believed in it, was only a kind of surface dressing over what is essentially a secular enquiry into the nature of man and human history' ('The Concept of the Avant-Garde', *Encounter*, July 1969, p. 9).

28 On Voltaire and Diderot, see J. Fabre, *Lumières et Romantisme* (Paris, 1963), pp. 1–18.

29 *Discours sur les Sciences et les Arts*, ed. G. R. Havens (New York, London, 1946), pp. 132–3: '. . . cette foule d'Ecrivains obscurs et de Lettrés oisifs, qui dévorent en pure perte la substance de l'Etat. Que dis-je; oisifs? et plût-à-Dieu qu'ils le fussent en effet! Les mœurs en seraient plus saines et la société plus paisible. Mais ces vains et futiles déclamateurs vont de tous côtés, armés de leurs funestes paradoxes; sapant les fondements de la foi, et anéantissant la vertu. Ils sourient dédaigneusement à ces vieux mots de Patrie et de Religion, et consacrent leurs talents et leur Philosophie à détruire et avilir tout ce qu'il y a de sacré parmi les hommes. Non qu'au fond ils haïssent ni la vertu ni nos dogmes; c'est de l'opinion publique qu'ils sont ennemis; et pour les ramener aux pieds des autels, il suffirait de les reléguer parmi les Athées.' Cf. *Nouvelle Héloïse*, ed. cit., vol. II, pp. 334–6; *Emile*, ed. cit., pp. 322–4.

30 *Mélanges* (Pléiade), p. 851.

31 Rousseau in 1755 was still calling Voltaire 'notre chef'. In his letter of 17 June 1760 informing Voltaire 'je ne vous aime point, Monsieur', 'Je vous hais, enfin, puisque vous l'avez voulu', Rousseau speaks of the 'applaudissements que je vous ai prodigués' (*Confessions*, ed. Voisine, pp. 1085, 637. On Diderot and Rousseau, see J. Fabre, op. cit., Ch. 2, 'Deux frères ennemis'.

32 Quoted by R. Naves, *Le Goût de Voltaire* (Paris, s.d.), in his discussion of Voltaire's attitude to Rousseau, pp. 365–7. Letter to Damilaville, 31 July 1762 (Moland, vol. 42, p. 192).

33 See *Oxford Dictionary of Quotations*, under 'Voltaire'.

34 *Mélanges* (Pléiade), p. 723.

35 *Dictionnaire philosophique*, article 'Tolérance'.

XIV · Diderot (1713–1784)

FROM *Essais sur la peinture* (written 1765–6)

Je vois une haute montagne couverte d'une obscure, antique et profonde forêt. J'en vois, j'en entends descendre à grand bruit un torrent, dont les eaux vont se briser contre les pointes escarpées d'un rocher. Le soleil penche à son couchant; il transforme en autant de diamants les gouttes d'eau qui pendent attachées aux extrémités inégales des pierres. Cependant les eaux, après avoir franchi les obstacles qui les retardaient, vont se rassembler dans un vaste et large canal qui les conduit à une certaine distance vers une machine. C'est là que, sous des masses énormes, se broie et se prépare la subsistance la plus générale de l'homme. J'entrevois la machine, j'entrevois ses roues que l'écume des eaux blanchit; j'entrevois, au travers de quelques saules, le haut de la chaumière du propriétaire: je rentre en moi-même, et je rêve.

Sans doute la forêt qui me ramène à l'origine du monde est une belle chose; sans doute ce rocher, image de la constance et de la durée, est une belle chose; sans doute ces gouttes d'eau transformées par les rayons du soleil, brisées et décomposées en autant de diamants étincelants et liquides, sont une belle chose; sans doute le bruit, le fracas d'un torrent qui brise le vaste silence de la montagne et de sa solitude, et porte à mon âme une secousse violente, une terreur secrète, est une belle chose!

Mais ces saules, cette chaumière, ces animaux qui paissent aux environs; tout ce spectacle d'utilité n'ajoute-t-il rien à mon plaisir? Et quelle différence encore de la sensation de l'homme ordinaire à celle du philosophe! C'est lui qui réfléchit et qui voit, dans l'arbre de la forêt, le mât qui doit un jour opposer sa tête altière à la tempête et aux vents; dans les entrailles de la montagne, le métal brut qui bouillonnera un jour au fond des fourneaux ardents, et prendra la forme, et des machines qui fécondent la terre, et de celles qui en détruisent les habitants; dans le rocher, les masses de pierre dont on élèvera des palais aux rois et des temples aux dieux; dans les eaux du torrent, tantôt la fertilité, tantôt le ravage de la campagne, la formation des rivières, des fleuves, le commerce, les habitants de l'univers liés, leurs trésors portés de rivage en rivage, et de là dispersés dans toute la profondeur des continents; et son âme mobile passera subitement de la douce et voluptueuse émotion du plaisir au sentiment de la terreur, si son imagination vient à soulever les flots de l'océan.

C'est ainsi que le plaisir s'accroîtra à proportion de l'imagination, de la sensibilité et des connaissances. La nature, ni l'art qui la copie, ne disent rien à l'homme stupide ou froid, peu de chose à l'homme ignorant.

Qu'est-ce donc que le goût? Une faculté acquise, par des expériences réitérées, à saisir le vrai ou le bon, avec la circonstance qui le rend beau, et d'en être promptement et vivement touché.

Œuvres esthétiques, ed. P. Vernière (Paris, 1959), pp. 737–

Diderot, like Rousseau, enjoyed going for long country walks. Though, as the son of a small master cutler, he regarded the peasants with an amused superiority, he genuinely appreciated rustic scenes. He had a sense of affinity with hill, rock and water, and especially with the Marne – the river that rises near his native town of Langres, that flows by Isle-sur-Marne where his mistress Sophie Volland spent her absences from Paris, and that curves in a huge sweep a hundred metres below the village of Chennevières, near which lay the baron d'Holbach's château of Grandval, in the present *département* of Val-de-Marne. He writes to Sophie of his feeling for her and for nature:

> Après dîner . . . nous avons tenté une longue promenade, quoique la terre fût molle, et que le ciel, qui se chargeait vers le couchant, nous menaçât d'un orage.
>
> Je les ai revus, ces côteaux où je suis allé tant de fois promener votre image et ma rêverie, et Chennevière qui couronne la côte, et Champigny qui la décore en amphithéâtre, et ma triste et tortueuse compatriote, la Marne.

But Diderot did not restrict himself to romantic meditations or communings with the forces of nature during the cross-country excursions he made with his host, d'Holbach, during his visits to Grandval. They used the time to discuss a whole range of Encyclopaedic topics:

> Entre trois et quatre, nous prenons nos bâtons et nous allons nous promener; les femmes de leur côté, le Baron et moi du nôtre. Nous faisons des tournées très étendues. Rien ne nous arrête, ni les coteaux, ni les bois, ni les fondrières, ni les terres labourées. Le spectacle de la nature nous plaît à tous deux. Chemin faisant, nous parlons ou d'histoire, ou de politique, ou de chimie, ou de littérature, ou de physique, ou de morale. Le coucher du soleil et la fraîcheur de la soirée nous rapprochent de la maison, et nous n'y arrivons guère avant sept heures.[1]

The selected passage, which may well contain echoes of such a conversation, illustrates two aspects of Diderot: the analytic thinker, and the man of sentiment and imagination. The logical construction of the first three paragraphs, and their generalised definitions (e.g. bread is 'la subsistance la plus générale de l'homme'; ploughs are 'des machines qui fécondent la terre'; guns 'celles qui en détruisent les habitants') contrast with the expressions of emotion in the passage. The antitheses between the wild beauties of nature and the purposes for which man can harness or utilise them, symbolise the other theme of the passage, which is the function of feeling and ratiocination in aesthetics.

The industrialisation of the countryside is hardly a poetic subject in England, where, since the eighteenth century, nature-lovers have inveighed against the desecration of solitudes.[2] But, of course, Diderot was writing before the industrial revolution came to France. Water-wheels, which were still the main motive-power for machinery, readily fit into a description of cascades and torrents, with the poetic contrast between the evanescent diamonds of sun-flecked spray and the enduring rock, so permanent by the standards of the awe-struck beholder, but itself subject to erosion and decay.[3] Even Stendhal sees something impressive in a factory powered by water:

> A peine entre-t-on dans la ville que l'on est étourdi par le fracas d'une machine bruyante et terrible en apparence. Vingt marteaux pesants, et retombant avec un bruit qui fait trembler le pavé, sont élevés par une roue que l'eau du torrent fait mouvoir. . . . Ce travail, si rude en apparence, est un de ceux qui étonnent le plus le voyageur qui pénètre pour la première fois dans les montagnes qui séparent la France de l'Helvétie.[4]

And after all, the mills, mines and foundries known to Diderot were too small to cause any vast disfigurement of the landscape. Even Jean-Jacques Rousseau experienced a certain pleasure at finding a stocking-factory on a Swiss mountain:

> Surpris et curieux, je me lève, je perce à travers un fourré de brous-sailles du côté d'où venait le bruit, et dans une combe à vingt pas du lieu même où je croyais être parvenu le premier, j'aperçois une manu-facture de bas. . . . Mon premier mouvement fut un sentiment de joie de me retrouver parmi les humains où je m'étais cru totalement seul.[5]

Nevertheless, Diderot's insistence on *utility* does seem to be an expression of that bourgeois commercial spirit against which the Romantics railed. His tone here is very different from that of the escapist Stendhal, who deplores the exploitation of nature for profit, and makes his hero Julien reject a lucrative partnership in a timber-business in order to follow anachronistic dreams which eventually lead him to death on the scaffold:

Rien ne put vaincre la vocation de Julien. Fouqué finit par le croire un peu fou. Le troisième jour, de grand matin, Julien quitta son ami pour passer la journée au milieu des rochers de la grande montagne. Il retrouva sa petite grotte, mais il n'avait plus la paix de l'âme, les offres de son ami la lui avaient enlevée. Comme Hercule, il se trouvait non entre le vice et la vertu, mais entre la médiocrité suivie d'un bien-être assuré et tous les rêves héroïques de sa jeunesse.[6]

But if there is something smug and Philistine about Diderot the bourgeois, the pompous writer of hollow and pretentious plays, there is also Diderot the poet and dreamer who, like so many of the Romantics after him, saw in middle-class values the very negation of art:

Le goût des beaux-arts suppose un certain mépris de la fortune, je ne sais quelle incurie des affaires domestiques, un certain dérangement de cervelle, une folie qui diminue de jour en jour. On devient sage et plat. . . . On disserte, on examine, on sent peu, on raisonne beaucoup, on mesure tout au niveau scrupuleux de la logique, de la méthode et même de la vérité; et que voulez-vous que des arts, qui ont tous pour base l'exagération et le mensonge, deviennent parmi les hommes sans cesse occupés de réalités et ennemis par état des fantômes de l'imagination, que leur souffle fait disparaître? C'est une belle chose que la science économique, mais elle nous abrutira.[7]

There is even evidence of a Romantic Diderot who sought to soothe his cares by surrendering to the apathetic peace of nature

qui lui répète à voix basse et sans cesse, qui lui murmure à l'oreille: demeure en repos, demeure en repos, reste comme tout ce qui t'environne, dure comme tout ce qui t'environne, jouis doucement comme tout ce qui t'environne, laisse aller les heures, les journées, les années, comme tout ce qui t'environne, et passe comme tout ce qui t'environne; voilà la leçon continue de la nature.[8]

Romanticism, however, was not merely a matter of laments, escapism and melancholia: there was a vigorous, positive Romanticism, full of exhilaration at man's victories over nature and the assertion of his own independence. This Romanticism of striving, liberation and progress, which inspires much of Hugo, is expressed by Shelley, the disciple of the Encyclopédistes, in his *Queen Mab*, of 1812:

> Nature, impartial in munificence,
> Has gifted man with all-subduing will.
> Matter, with all its transitory shapes,
> Lies subjected and plastic at his feet,
> That, weak from bondage, tremble as they tread.
>
> .   .   .
>
> Ah me! a pathless wilderness remains
> Yet unsubdued by man's reclaiming hand.[9]

It underlies Faust's dying speech, as he glories in his achievement of wresting fruitful land from the sea:

> Green fields and fruitful; men and cattle hiving
> Upon this newest earth at once and thriving,
> Settled at once beneath this sheltering hill
> Heaped by the masses' brave and busy skill.
> With such a heavenly land behind this hedge,
> The sea beyond may bluster to its edge
> And, as it gnaws to swamp the work of masons,
> To stop the gap one common impulse hastens.
> Aye! wedded to this concept like a wife,
> I find this wisdom's final form:
> He only earns his freedom and his life
> Who takes them every day by storm.[10]

It is some such vision of man's mastery over the elements that Diderot has in mind when, comparing 'la sensation de l'homme ordinaire à celle du philosophe',[11] he pictures to himself the ships, storms, molten metals, wars, temples, palaces, harvests and merchant-adventurers penetrating into the remotest parts of continents as yet unexplored.

The pleasurable terror which Diderot twice mentions in the passage is elaborated in the *Pensées détachées sur la peinture*:

> Le grand paysagiste a son enthousiasme particulier; c'est une espèce d'horreur sacrée. Ses antres sont ténébreux et profonds; ses rochers escarpés menacent le ciel; les torrents en descendent avec fracas, ils rompent au loin le silence auguste de ses forêts. L'homme passe à travers de la demeure des démons et des dieux. . . . C'est là que le philosophe, assis ou marchant à pas lents, s'enfonce en lui-même. Si j'arrête mon regard sur cette mystérieuse imitation de la nature, je frissonne.[12]

The demons and deities here stand, primarily, for Diderot's sense of the mysteriousness of artistic creation. They doubtless reflect, also, primitive folk beliefs, still not far below the surface in the eighteenth century. But, in addition, the terror Diderot experiences is (like the feet trembling as they tread in *Queen Mab*), the obverse side of his elation at man's temerity in striving to impose his will upon the universe. For, in spite of the comfortable doctrines about the beneficial results of freedom and the providential identity of self-interest with the common good, Diderot knows that human energy, like the swollen torrent laying waste the countryside, can have destructive as well as creative results. None the less, he steadfastly admires human enterprise, so much more grandiose than the blind forces of nature when man's achievements are contrasted with his puny resources:

c'est sans contredit une grande chose que cet univers; mais, quand je le compare avec l'énergie de la cause productrice, si j'avais à m'émerveiller, c'est que son œuvre ne soit pas plus belle et plus parfaite encore. C'est tout le contraire, lorsque je pense à la faiblesse de l'homme, à ses pauvres moyens, aux embarras et à la courte durée de sa vie et à certaines choses qu'il a entreprises et exécutées.[13]

In the 1780 edition of Raynal's *Histoire philosophique* – that corporate philosophe manifesto published under the name of Raynal, but in which Diderot and his colleagues had a hand – there is a hymn of praise ascribable to Diderot, a kind of atheist *Te Deum* glorifying man's dominion over nature, whether for good or for bad:

Car, que ne peuvent point les nations actives et industrieuses? Par elles des régions qu'on croyait inhabitables sont peuplées. Les terres les plus ingrates sont fécondées. Les eaux sont repoussées, et la fertilité s'élève sur le limon. Les marais portent des maisons. A travers des monts entr'ouverts, l'homme se fait des chemins. Il sépare à son gré ou lie les rochers par des ponts qui restent comme suspendus sur la profondeur obscure de l'abîme, au fond duquel le torrent courroucé semble murmurer de son audace. Il oppose des digues à la mer et dort tranquillement dans le domicile qu'il a fondé au-dessous des flots. Il assemble quelques planches sur lesquelles il s'assied; il dit aux vents de le porter à l'extrémité du globe et les vents lui obéissent. Homme quelquefois si pusillanime et si petit, que tu te montres grand et dans tes projets et dans tes œuvres! Avec deux faibles leviers de chair, aidés de ton intelligence, tu attaques la nature entière et tu la subjugues. Tu affrontes les éléments conjurés, et tu les asservis. Rien ne te résiste, si ton âme est tourmentée par l'amour ou le désir de posséder une belle femme que tu haïras un jour, par l'intérêt ou la fureur de remplir tes coffres. . . . Si tu fais de grandes choses par passion, tu n'en fais pas de moindres par ennui. Tu ne connaissais qu'un monde. Tu soupçonnas qu'il en était un autre. Tu l'allas chercher et tu le trouvas. Si la hardiesse de tes entreprises m'en dérobe quelquefois l'atrocité, je suis toujours également confondu, soit que tes forfaits me glacent d'horreur, soit que tes vertus me transportent d'admiration.[14]

There is obviously a relationship between Diderot's ideas on art and his views about man's role in nature and society. The Diderot who sees landscape as a 'spectacle d'utilité' is the careful, calculating bourgeois, the respectable sage of *Le Philosophe*[15] who is proud to be 'pétri, pour ainsi dire, avec le levain de l'ordre et de la règle'. To this Diderot, taste is a matter of judgment, experience, analysis, and art is a methodical reproduction of reality, static and rational in its processes. But there is also the audacious Diderot for whom commerce means exploration and heroic endeavour, Diderot the enthusiast, the advocate of energy and action, the visionary who sees mankind as 'porté dans l'océan sans bornes des fantaisies d'où l'on ne se retire plus',[16] the diviner of those seething forces which were shortly to burst forth and transform the world. For him, art and the appreciation of art imply frenzy, dynamism, and transports of terror or delight.

This duality makes it extremely difficult to interpret or assess the complexities of Diderot's aesthetics.[17] Thus, the simple statement that art copies nature is contradicted by remarks elsewhere in his work, as, for example, in the *Pensées détachées sur la peinture*:

> Eclairez vos objets selon votre soleil, qui n'est pas celui de la nature; soyez le disciple de l'arc-en-ciel, mais n'en soyez pas l'esclave.[18]

Yet, in requiring the artist to impose his private vision upon external reality, Diderot still seems to regard the artist as part of nature's creative process.[19] The identification of 'le beau' with 'le bon' and 'le vrai' occurs frequently in Diderot's writings. Yet he also admires the grandiose effects of the imagination, and finds a potential source of sublimity in crime:

> C'est une belle chose que le crime et dans l'histoire et dans la poésie, et sur la toile et sur le marbre.[20]

And in spite of his constant emphasis on inspiration and enthusiasm, his ultimate ideal, for artist and spectator alike, appears to be deep insight, guided and controlled by calm, rational judgment:

> Le grand homme ... se possédera au milieu des plus grands dangers; il jugera froidement, mais sainement. Rien de ce qui peut servir à ses vues, concourir à son but ne lui échappera. On l'étonnera difficilement.[21]

But this Olympian quiet is not the quality most apparent in his own best works.

The social and political ideas of Diderot, notwithstanding his excitable temperament, his exultation at human progress since the Renaissance, his plans for reform and his sporadic flashes of Utopian anarchism,[22] can hardly be described as revolutionary. He was, after all, the willing pensioner of the Czarina Catherine the Great, in whom he admired 'l'âme de César avec toutes les séductions de Cléopâtre'.[23] But as far as literature was concerned, he saw renewal as possible only through violence. He considered that great lyric poetry – which his theories heralded and which his own prose on occasion so closely resembled – was impossible in the social conditions of the old monarchy:

Quelle sera donc la ressource d'un poète, chez un peuple dont les mœurs sont faibles, petites et maniérées; où l'imitation rigoureuse des conversations ne formerait qu'un tissu d'expressions fausses, insensées et basses; où il n'y a plus ni franchise, ni bonhomie; où un père appelle son fils monsieur, et où une mère appelle sa fille mademoiselle; où les cérémonies publiques n'ont rien d'auguste; la conduite domestique, rien de touchant et d'honnête; les actes solennels, rien de vrai?[24]

Only during and after some bloody cataclysm, he averred, would there be an outpouring of the poetic spirit, and the creation of a new literature:

La poésie veut quelque chose d'énorme, de barbare et de sauvage. C'est lorsque la fureur de la guerre civile ou du fanatisme arme les hommes de poignards, et que le sang coule à grands flots sur la terre, que le laurier d'Apollon s'agite et verdit. Il en veut être arrosé. Il se flétrit dans les temps de la paix et du loisir. . . .
Quand verra-t-on naître des poètes? Ce sera après les temps de désastres et de grands malheurs; lorsque les peuples harassés commenceront à respirer. Alors les imaginations, ébranlées par des spectacles terribles, peindront des choses inconnues à ceux qui n'en ont pas été les témoins.[25]

Chénier and Chateaubriand were soon to fulfil his prophecy.

NOTES

1 Lettres à Sophie Volland, ed. A. Babelon (Paris, 1938), vol. I, pp. 116, 59–60 (25 September 1760, 1 October 1759). Cf. pp. 39, 53–4, 76–7, 178–9; and J. Seznec, Diderot: Sur l'art et les artistes (Paris, 1967), pp. 154–6.
2 See W. G. Hoskins, The Making of the English Landscape (London, 1955), pp. 166–7. In a poem written about 1785, Anna Seward of Lichfield lamented the violation of Coalbrookdale, in Shropshire, by the Darbys' ironworks. Arthur Young, however, in the 1770s, had found the noise, machinery, flames and smoke 'altogether sublime'. The artist Joseph Wright of Derby saw a romantic beauty in Arkwright's cotton mill by night. This picture, painted in 1789, is reproduced in M. Levey, Rococo to Revolution (London, 1966), p. 101.
3 On factories and machinery in France, see R. Mousnier, Progrès scientifique et technique au XVIIIᵉ siècle (Paris, 1958), and G. V. Taylor, 'Types of Capitalism in Eighteenth-Century France' (English Historical Review, vol. 79, 1964, pp. 478–97). Though the comte de Buffon's ironworks at Montbard employed 400 men in 1767, most ironworks were tiny rural enterprises, employing only 6 to 20. Newcomen pumping-engines were common in French mines by the 1750s, but Watt and Boulton's steam-engine pump was not introduced until the 1770s. At the end of the Ancien Régime there were only 8 cotton spinning mills in France equipped with modern English machinery and less than 20 well-equipped calico works. The marquis Jouffroy

d'Abbans designed a paddle-steamer which he demonstrated on the Saône at Lyons in 1783, the year before Diderot's death.

Diderot on a number of occasions uses rock as a symbol of change and decay in the whole of nature. E.g. J. Seznec, op. cit., pp. 170–1 (*Salon de 1767*).

4 *Le Rouge et le Noir*, Ch. 1.

5 *Les Rêveries du Promeneur Solitaire*, VII.

6 *Le Rouge et le Noir*, Ch. I and XII. Cf. *La Chartreuse de Parme*, Ch. II: 'Le lac de Côme, se disait-elle, n'est point environné, comme le lac de Genève, de grandes pièces de terre bien closes et cultivées selon les meilleures méthodes, choses qui rappellent l'argent et la spéculation. Ici, de tous côtés, je vois des collines d'inégales hauteurs couvertes de bouquets d'arbres plantés par le hasard et que la main de l'homme n'a point encore gâtés et forcés à *rendre du revenu*.' In his 'pursuit of happiness' (was this phrase from the American Declaration of Independence of 4 July 1776 the source of Stendhal's famous *chasse au bonheur?*) and his detestation of Romantic transcendental mysticism, Stendhal, the disciple of the Idéologues, is himself very much a man of the eighteenth century. But one of the forms his 'Romanticism' takes is an escape into an idealised eighteenth century of wit, cynicism, and scorn for the bourgeois's worship of money. M. de la Mole in *Le Rouge et le Noir*, Mosca in *La Chartreuse de Parme*, and Leuwen père in *Lucien Leuwen*, are all three inhabitants of Stendhal's imaginary eighteenth century.

7 J. Seznec, op. cit., p. 89 (*Salon de 1769*).

8 *Lettres à Sophie Volland*, ed. cit., II, pp. 274–5.

9 *The Complete Poetical Works of P. B. Shelley*, ed. T. Hutchinson (Oxford, 1905), pp. 781, 799. Cf. ibid., pp. 10–11, *The Dæmon of the World*, Part II: 'All things are void of terror: man has lost/His desolating privilege, and stands/An equal among equals: happiness/And science dawn though late upon the earth;/Peace cheers the mind, health renovates the frame;/ Disease and pleasure cease to mingle here,/Reason and passion cease to combat there;/Whilst mind unfettered o'er the earth extends/Its all-subduing energies, and wields/The sceptre of a vast dominion there.' Even the poet Delille, in *Les Jardins* (Chant III) saw man's conquest over the elements as a source of lyricism: 'A l'aspect de ces flots qu'un art audacieux/ Fait sortir de la terre et lance jusqu'aux cieux,/L'homme se dit: "C'est moi qui créai ces prodiges."/L'homme admire son art dans ces brillants prestiges.'

10 Goethe, *Faust*, II. Teil, Fünfter Akt, Grosser Vorhof des Palasts. According to some commentators, the passage is an example of Goethe's irony. Translation by Louis Macneice and E. L. Stahl (London, 1965), p. 287.

11 Cf. Rousseau, *La Nouvelle Héloïse*, I, xii (ed. Mornet, Paris, 1925, II, p. 47): J'ai toujours cru que le bon n'était que le beau mis en action. . . . Il suit de cette idée que le goût se perfectionne par les mêmes moyens que la sagesse, et qu'une âme bien touchée des charmes de la vertu doit à proportion être aussi sensible à tous les autres genres de beautés. On s'exerce à voir comme à sentir, ou plutôt une vue exquise n'est qu'un sentiment délicat et fin. C'est ainsi qu'un peintre à l'aspect d'un beau paysage ou devant un beau tableau

s'extasie à des objets qui ne sont pas même remarqués d'un spectateur vulgaire.'

12 Diderot, *Œuvres esthétiques*, ed. P. Vernière (Paris, 1959), p. 772.

13 J. Seznec, op. cit., p. 36 (*Salon de 1767*).

14 Raynal, *Histoire philosophique et politique des établissements et du commerce des Européens dans les deux Indes* (Genève, Pellet, MDCCLXXX), Livre 6, Ch. xxvi, pp. 111–12. Rousseau had already drawn up a similar catalogue of human achievement in the *Discours sur l'inégalité*, note *i*: 'Quand, d'un côté, l'on considère les immenses travaux des hommes, tant de sciences approfondies, tant d'arts inventés, tant de forces employées, des abîmes comblés, des montagnes rasées, des rochers brisés, des fleuves rendus navigables, des terres défrichées, des lacs creusés, des marais séchés, des bâtiments énormes élevés sur la terre, la mer couverte de vaisseaux et de matelots. . . .' But Rousseau sees it all as foolish pride and a source of miseries.

15 *Le Philosophe*, ed. H. Dieckmann (St. Louis, 1948), p. 54, *Encyclopédie* version.

16 *Supplément au voyage de Bougainville*, IV, *Suite du dialogue*.

17 For Diderot's writings on aesthetics, and a discussion of his ideas, see: Diderot, *Les Salons* (*Textes choisis*), *Essais sur la peinture, Pensées détachées*, ed. R. Desné (Paris, 1955); *Œuvres esthétiques*, ed. P. Vernière (Paris, 1959); *Sur l'art et les artistes*, ed. J. Seznec (Paris, 1967); Y. Belaval, *L'Esthétique sans paradoxe de Diderot* (Paris, 1950); J. Seznec, *Essais sur Diderot et l'antiquité* (Oxford, 1957); J. Ehrard, *L'Idée de nature en France dans la première moitié du XVIIIᵉ siècle* (Paris, 1963), pp. 317–28; P. Francastel, 'L'Esthétique des Lumières', pp. 332–57 of *Utopie et institutions au XVIIIᵉ siècle*, ed. Francastel (Paris, La Haye, 1963).

18 P. Vernière, op. cit., p. 771.

19 See J. Roger, *Les Sciences de la vie dans la pensée française du XVIIIᵉ siècle* (Paris, 1963), pp. 775–6.

20 J. Seznec, *Diderot: Sur l'art et les artistes*, p. 125. Cf. ibid, p. 48, and Y. Belaval, op. cit., pp. 72–3. For a discussion of the unresolved problems raised in *Le Neveu de Rameau*, see R. Laufer, *Style rococo, style des 'lumières'* (Paris, 1963), pp. 127–32; J.-M. Goulemot, M. Launay, *Le Siècle des lumières* (Paris, 1968), pp. 134–40.

21 *Le Rêve de d'Alembert*, ed. J. Varloot (Paris, 1962), p. 81.

22 E.g. 'Voulez-vous que je vous dise un beau paradoxe? C'est que je suis convaincu qu'il ne peut y avoir de vrai bonheur pour l'espèce humaine que dans un état social où il n'y aurait ni roi, ni magistrat, ni prêtre, ni lois, ni tien, ni mien, ni propriété mobilière, ni propriété foncière, ni vices, ni vertus; et cet état social est diablement idéal' (*Textes politiques*, ed. Y. Benot (Paris, 1960), p. 56; Assézat, VI, p. 439).

23 *Lettres à Sophie Volland*, Hambourg, 30 mars, 1774, ed. cit., II, p. 252.

24 *De la poésie dramatique* (1758), Vernière, op. cit., p. 262.

25 Ibid., pp. 261–2.

XV · Beaumarchais (1732–1799)

FROM *Les Deux Amis ou Le Négociant de Lyon* (performed 1770)
(Act I, scene xi)

(The scene is the drawing-room of the house jointly occupied by Aurelly – a rich silk-manufacturer who has just been made a noble – and by his friend Mélac père, who is *Receveur Général des Fermes* (tax collector) at Lyons. It is ten o'clock on the morning before Quarter Day (*le paiement*). Aurelly's cashier has just informed Mélac that legal formalities, consequent upon the sudden death of the Paris banker with whom Aurelly had deposited 1,100,000 livres, will make it impossible for Aurelly to pay the 600,000 livres due from him, next day. The news of his impending bankruptcy and public disgrace has not yet been broken to Aurelly.)

AURELLY, *gaiement*. – Je t'ai bien désiré tout à l'heure à l'Intendance, tu m'aurais vu batailler . . .

MÉLAC PÈRE – Contre qui?

AURELLY. – Ce nouveau Noble, si plein de sa dignité, si gros d'argent et si bouffi d'orgueil qu'il croit toujours se commettre lorsqu'il salue un Roturier.

MÉLAC PÈRE, *distrait*. – Moins il y a de distance entre les hommes, plus ils sont pointilleux pour la faire remarquer.

AURELLY. – Celui-ci, qui jusqu'à l'époque de mes Lettres de Noblesse ne m'avait jamais regardé, s'avise de me complimenter aujourd'hui d'un ton supérieur: 'Je me flatte, m'a-t-il dit, que vous quittez enfin le commerce avec la roture.'

MÉLAC PÈRE, *à part*. – Ah! Dieux!

AURELLY. – Quoi?

MÉLAC PÈRE, *s'efforçant de rire*. – Je crois l'entendre.

AURELLY. – 'Au contraire, Monsieur, ai-je répondu; je ne puis mieux reconnaître le nouveau bien que je lui dois qu'en continuant à l'exercer avec honneur.'

MÉLAC PÈRE, *embarrassé*. Ah! mon ami! le Commerce expose à de si terribles revers!

AURELLY. – Tu m'y fais songer: l'Agent de Change ne s'explique pas; mais, à son air, je gagerais que le paiement ne se passera pas sans quelque Banqueroute considérable.

MÉLAC PÈRE. – Je ne vois jamais ce temps de crise sans éprouver un serrement de cœur sur le sort de ceux à qui il peut être fatal.

AURELLY. – Et moi, je dis que la pitié qu'on a pour les fripons n'est qu'une misérable faiblesse, un vol qu'on fait aux honnêtes gens. La race des bons est-elle éteinte pour . . .?

MÉLAC PÈRE. – Je ne parle point des fripons.

AURELLY, *avec chaleur*. – Les malhonnêtes gens reconnus sont moins à craindre que ceux-ci: l'on s'en méfie; leur réputation garantit au moins de leur mauvaise foi.

MÉLAC PÈRE. – Fort bien; mais . . .

AURELLY. – Mais un méchant qui travailla vingt ans à passer pour honnête homme porte un coup mortel à la confiance quand son fantôme d'honneur disparaît: l'exemple de sa fausse probité fait qu'on n'ose plus se fier à la véritable.

MÉLAC PÈRE, *douloureusement*. – Mon cher Aurelly, n'y a-t-il donc point de faillites excusables? Il ne faut qu'une mort, un retard de fonds, il ne faut qu'une Banqueroute frauduleuse un peu considérable, pour en entraîner une foule de malheureuses.

AURELLY. – Malheureuses ou non, la sûreté du commerce ne permet pas d'admettre ces subtiles différences, et les faillites qui sont exemptes de mauvaise foi ne le sont presque jamais de témérité.

MÉLAC PÈRE. – Mais c'est outrer les choses que de confondre ainsi . . .

AURELLY. – Je voudrais qu'il y eût là-dessus des lois si sévères qu'elles forçassent enfin tous les hommes d'être justes.

MÉLAC PÈRE. – Eh! mon ami, les lois contiennent les méchants sans les rendre meilleurs, et les mœurs les plus pures ne peuvent sauver un honnête homme d'un malheur imprévu.

AURELLY. – Monsieur, la probité du Négociant importe à trop de gens pour qu'on lui fasse grâce en pareil cas.

> *Théâtre complet*, ed. Maurice Allem. Bibliothèque de la
> Pléiade (Paris, 1949), pp. 100–2.

> Que me font à moi, sujet paisible d'un Etat Monarchique du dix-huitième siècle, les révolutions d'Athènes et de Rome? Quel véritable intérêt puis-je prendre à la mort d'un tyran du Péloponnèse? . . . Qu'est-ce que l'intérêt? C'est le sentiment . . . qui nous met en place de celui qui souffre, au milieu de sa situation . . . Ce sentiment est dans le cœur de tous les hommes, il sert de base à ce principe certain de l'Art, qu'il n'y a ni moralité ni intérêt au Théâtre sans un secret rapport du sujet dramatique à nous.

In these sentences from his *Essai sur le genre dramatique sérieux*, which appeared in 1767 shortly after his play *Eugénie*, Beaumarchais states why he thinks that the *drame bourgeois* – the new form of play which had grown up alongside attempts to reform classical tragedy and comedy – was suited to the age. Ten years earlier, Diderot had provided both the theory for the genre, in his treatises *Dorval et Moi* and *De la poésie*

PLATE V   F. Boucher (1703–70): *Paysage avec moulin* (1743)

PLATE VI   C.-J. Vernet (1714–89): *La Tempête* (1777)

dramatique, and the models, in *Le Fils Naturel* and *Le Père de Famille.*
Though many people in the century had serious reservations about it –
Diderot himself eventually pronounced all *drames bourgeois* to be
'détestables'[1] – they went on being written, acted and applauded.
Apart from Sedaine's *Le Philosophe sans le savoir,* they are, to modern
taste, dreary, tedious, ludicrously sentimental: the most interesting
thing about the genre is why it failed to achieve what its theory promised. Why, indeed, was it not possible to write a genuinely realistic
drama, which would reflect or interpret the moral, social, intellectual
and artistic struggles of the age, and – like Racine and Molière – remain
valid for posterity? And how was it that a century famous for its wit,
gaiety and liveliness, could find delectation in drab, platitudinous
sermonising which seems more appropriate to a Victorian Sabbath
than to the sprightly era of the philosophes? It is not that amusing
men chose amusing genres, and only dullards the *drame.* Diderot's
letters and philosophical writings, his fiction and his works about art
and literature, are still exciting: it is his two *drames* which are soporific.
Beaumarchais's *Eugénie* and *Les Deux Amis* are leaden: his two real
comedies remain exemplars of eighteenth-century vivacity.

To a very considerable extent, *Les Deux Amis* is realistic. The stage
directions:

> Le théâtre représente un Salon; à l'un des côtés est un clavecin ouvert
> avec un pupitre chargé de musique. Pauline en peignoir est assise
> devant; elle joue une pièce. Mélac (fils), debout à côté d'elle, en léger
> habit du matin, ses cheveux relevés avec un peigne, un violon à la
> main, l'accompagne. La toile se lève aux premières mesures de l'andante

or,

> André, en papillottes et en veste du matin, un balai de plumes sous
> son bras, entre, regarde de côté et s'en retourne

give an illusion of life. Technical terms about finance (*agent de change,
suspendre ses paiements, négocier des effets, bordereau, titres*), and everyday
details about forwarding goods on the Paris mail-coach:

> la diligence part cette nuit; vous pourrez y placer le caisson . . . S'ils
> font les difficiles, ils ont un ballot à moi, votre argent prendra sa place:
> il est plus pressé que mon envoi

provide an atmosphere of authenticity. The prose style, as our extract
shows, sounds almost like a real conversation. Aurelly's talk is pompous,
complacent, sententious; but that is not out of place in a leading citizen
of a provincial textile town.[2] As turgid moralising and improving

N

maxims are common in the memoirs and correspondence of the time, they presumably did occur in bourgeois speech too. Aurelly's economic status is described precisely: he has expanded the family business into which he married, and now:

> je fais battre journellement deux cents métiers dans Lyon. Le triple de bras est nécessaire aux apprêts de mes soies. Mes plantations de mûriers et mes vers [silk-worms] en occupent autant. Mes envois se détaillent chez tous les marchands du Royaume; tout cela vit, tout cela gagne, et l'industrie portant le prix des matières au centuple . . . (Act II, sc. x).

His rise was typical of Lyons in the eighteenth century: the annual value of silk manufactured there rose from 46,000,000 livres in 1752 to 60,000,000 in the 1770s; by 1777 there were more than 11,000 looms in the town. Since there was no University, Parlement or Provincial Estates at Lyons, and next to no ancient nobility – a pamphlet of 1774 stated that 'cette ville, qui n'a d'existence que par le commerce, ne doit s'illustrer que par lui' – the bourgeois had no rivals. Aurelly's pride at being a manufacturing wholesale merchant (*négociant*), not a retailer, was that of his counterparts in real life: an article in the *Journal de Lyon*, in 1786, pointed out the difference between

> un marchand et un négociant: celui-là n'est renfermé que dans de petites vues mercantiles; les sous s'attachent à son âme et y portent une rouille grossière. L'autre étend ses regards partout, au-delà des mers, et, entouré de grandes entreprises, son caractère nécessairement contracte de la noblesse et de l'élévation.[3]

A very successful businessman at Lyons could expect to become ennobled: at least forty-two of them were during the century. And, contrary to what was customary at Bordeaux, Nantes, and many other commercial cities, newly ennobled Lyons bourgeois normally carried on in business as a matter of course.[4] The *nouveau noble* whom Aurelly met at the Intendant's palace would therefore, if a Lyonnais, have been anomalous: Beaumarchais introduces him to stress the irony between Aurelly's impending ruin and his resolve to continue in commerce. (The Intendant himself, who does not appear in the play, was Jacques de Flesselles – very popular with the leading citizens, whom he entertained magnificently. He was promoted Prévost des Marchands at Paris in 1788; on 14 July 1789 he was killed by the mob, and his head carried round the streets on the end of a pike.) Though Lyons was no longer the important financial centre it had been in 1709, at the time of Samuel Bernard's crash there, the 'paiements de Lyon' – the solemn assembly each quarter-day before the Prévost des Marchands – remained famous in France.[5] Even the heroic devotion of one friend for another, which the play purports to be about, is almost credible when set in Lyons, a city of mystical fervour as well as of money-making. The concept of friendship was important there: Lyons Masonic lodges in the 1770s bore such names as Parfaite Amitié, Les Vrais Amis, Sincère Amitié, Parfaite Réunion. Not that freemasonry inclined the silk-manufacturers to *philosophie*: though they believed in progress, they tended, on the whole, to view Voltaire and the Encyclopédistes as potentially dangerous to morals, religion and the social order.[6] It is thus appropriate for Aurelly to denounce the philosophes:

> Les voilà donc, ces Philosophes! Ils font indifféremment le bien ou le mal, selon qu'il sert à leurs vues! Vantant à tout propos la vertu, dont ils se moquent, et ne songeant qu'à leurs intérêts, dont ils ne parlent jamais! Comment un principe d'honnêteté les arrêterait-il, eux qui n'ont jamais fait le bien que pour tromper impunément les hommes? (Act III, sc. ii).

Les Deux Amis was a failure in Paris; it had to be withdrawn after ten performances: but it was successful in provincial cities, including Lyons,[7] perhaps because, whatever its faults, the play authentically portrays a commercial milieu.

The plot, much less of an imbroglio than that of *Le Mariage de Figaro*, is not devoid of dramatic tension and interest.

Since Aurelly will soon be solvent again, Mélac père secretly lends Aurelly's cashier half a million livres from the tax money, which is not yet due to be handed over. Unexpectedly, the *fermier général* Saint-Alban arrives in Lyons, and demands the cash forthwith. Rather than see his friend and benefactor Aurelly go bankrupt, Mélac conceals the loan and allows Aurelly and Saint-Alban to think him an embezzler. Marriage between Mélac fils and Pauline, Aurelly's semi-legitimate daughter, seems impossible, particularly since it appears that Saint-Alban will demand Pauline's hand as the price for not ruining Mélac père. But the cashier reveals Mélac père's heroic devotion; Saint-Alban advances the money needed for Aurelly's debts, and renounces Pauline; all ends in effusions of love, happiness and virtue. Beaumarchais himself thought that *Les Deux Amis* was very well constructed. Certainly, it is not through weakness of dramatic technique that it is a poor play.[8]

If he had chosen to write a gay, cynical comedy about swindlers, there is every reason for thinking that he would have succeeded. There were models. *Le Banqueroutier*, a 'comédie italienne' of 1687 by A. M.

de Fatouville, depicts a recently ennobled financier, Persillet, who goes bankrupt in order to give his daughter a dowry, his son a dukedom, and himself two fine houses:

> Je crois qu'un bon père de famille est obligé en conscience de faire banqueroute au moins une fois dans la vie pour l'avantage de ses enfants.[9]

This farce, still readable in parts, must have been known to Beaumarchais. (It is followed, in the standard eighteenth-century edition of the *Comédie italienne*, by a play called *La Précaution inutile*, which is the sub-title Beaumarchais chose for *Le Barbier de Séville*.) Then, of course, there is Lesage's *Turcaret*. In *Les Deux Amis*, on the other hand, the characters are virtuous. They merely have foibles, like Aurelly's irascible pomposity and Mélac fils's excessive excitability. But after all, there are good, tender, loving creatures in *Andromaque* and *Bérénice*. 'Bonté' is prominent in Marivaux's comedies, which are none the less good theatre. Gide was mistaken in making fine sentiments responsible for bad literature. Certainly, Diderot's cynical and unedifying comedy *Est-il bon? est-il méchant?* is as lively and entertaining as his two virtuous *drames* are dull.[10] But in the short story *Les Deux Amis de Bourbonne*, that Diderot wrote partly as a riposte to *Les Deux Amis*, he movingly portrays the self-sacrifice of an unfortunate peasant to the widows and children of two men who gave their lives to save his. And this short story is a masterpiece of realism, free from cant, hypocrisy and falseness.

According to Diderot in *Les Deux Amis de Bourbonne*, true friendship is virtually impossible for the monied classes:

> Félix était un gueux qui n'avait rien; Olivier était un autre gueux qui n'avait rien; dites-en autant du charbonnier, de la charbonnière, et des autres personnages de ce conte; et concluez qu'en général il ne peut guère y avoir d'amitiés entières et solides qu'entre des hommes qui n'ont rien.[11]

A hard saying, but Beaumarchais does not prove it untrue. All five main characters in his play revel in virtue and abnegation. Mélac père accepts dishonour and ruin to save Aurelly from death by bankruptcy; Pauline (partly modelled on her namesake in *Polyeucte*) is willing to sacrifice dowry and happiness to save the father of her beloved Mélac fils; Saint-Alban pulls strings, sacrifices his love and risks a fortune, to make her happy; Mélac fils (he, too, is 'Cornelian', in his quarrel with Aurelly) is prepared to die silently of a broken heart in the pursuance of his filial obligations; Aurelly, the embodiment of commercial probity, tries to save Mélac even though convinced that he is an embezzler, then vies with him in altruism. But it is all false. According to Beaumarchais's theory in his *Essai sur le genre dramatique sérieux*, the businessmen and Inspectors of Taxes in the audience should be able to identify themselves with the play. But they cannot in any genuine sense do so: they know that sacrificing honour, life and fortune to friends is not the way affairs are in fact conducted. Even within the play itself the sacrifices are semi-spurious: too much of the pathos is caused by coincidence and misunderstandings. Mélac does not foresee any real danger in lending the money:

> Mon cœur se déchire. Si je dispose un moment en sa faveur des fonds qu'on me laisse . . . Après tout, ils ne courent aucun risque. (*Il soupire*) (Act. II, sc. iv).

Saint-Alban, when standing surety for the money, knows that Aurelly's funds are only temporarily blocked:

> SAINT-ALBAN – Aurelly, rendez-moi votre mandat, je pars; soyez tranquille. Vos effets de Paris me seront remis promptement ou je supplée à tout.
> AURELLY – De vos biens?
> SAINT-ALBAN – Puissent-ils être toujours aussi heureusement employés! Vous m'avez appris comme on jouit de ses sacrifices. En vain je vous admire, si votre exemple ne m'élève pas jusqu'à l'honneur de l'imiter. Nous compterons [i.e. settle accounts] à mon retour. (*Chacun exprime son admiration.*) (Act V, sc. xi.)

In Balzac's novel *César Birotteau* the pompous bankrupt shopkeeper achieves heroic virtue because he suffers and dies in the struggle to pay his debts. Beaumarchais's smug message to his bourgeois audience is that wealth, happiness, virtue, altruism, safety and self-satisfaction are all comfortably compatible.

Like so much eighteenth-century literature this play is conformist. Beaumarchais's battles with authority, and his literary masterpieces, are post-1770. At the time of *Les Deux Amis* he was court favourite of the King's four ugly daughters, and a protégé of Pâris-Duverney, the rich financier and army contractor. Like Aurelly, he had become a noble: for 85,000 livres, largely borrowed from Duverney, he had bought the title of *secrétaire du roi*, that *savonnette à vilain* which gave privileged status immediately, and full, hereditary nobility after twenty years' tenure.[12]

When revealing to his daughter Pauline the circumstances of her birth, Aurelly denounces the cruel pride of backward country aristocrats:

La fille d'un Gentilhomme (peu riche à la vérité) m'avait permis de
l'obtenir de ses parents: ma demande fut rejetée avec dédain. Dans
le désespoir où ce refus nous mit, nous n'écoutâmes que la passion.
Un mariage secret nous unit. Mais la famille hautaine, loin de le
confirmer, renferma cette malheureuse victime, et l'accabla de tant de
mauvais traitements, qu'elle perdit la vie en la donnant à une fille . . .
que les cruels dérobèrent à mes yeux. (Act III, sc. v.)

And he is somewhat patronising to Mélac père, a provincial nobleman
who, when he was a penniless ex-officer, had the good sense to accept
the bourgeois job which Aurelly found for him.[13] But there is nothing
in the least subversive or revolutionary in Aurelly's determination to
continue in commerce though ennobled, or in his assertion that
merchants do as much for France as the *noblesse d'épée*:

L'utilité dont nos vertus et nos talents sont pour les autres est la
balance où je pèse leur mérite . . . Et tout l'or que la guerre disperse,
Messieurs, qui le fait rentrer à la paix? Qui osera disputer au Commerce
l'honneur de rendre à l'Etat épuisé le nerf et les richesses qu'il n'a
plus? Tous les Citoyens sentent l'importance de cette tâche: le
Négociant seul le remplit. Au moment que le Guerrier se repose, le
Négociant a l'honneur d'être à son tour l'homme de la Patrie.
(Act II, sc. x.)

The *lois de dérogeance*, which deprived of his rank any noble who engaged
in retail trade or failed to 'vivre noblement', remained in force; but from
the time of Richelieu and Colbert it had been the policy of the Bourbons
to try and persuade new nobles *not* to renounce commerce, and to
encourage the old nobility to engage in it:

In the seventeenth and eighteenth centuries one of the most interesting
aspects of royal policy towards the nobility had in fact been the repeated
invitations addressed to its more impoverished members to imitate the
example of their British, Dutch and Italian counterparts by becoming
a *noblesse commerçante*.[14]

A royal *arrêt du conseil* of 30 October 1767 specifically reaffirmed the
right of nobles to engage in wholesale trade, and announced a special
octroi of two *lettres de noblesse* per year to honour prominent négociants.
(This was in addition to the other methods of acquiring nobility –
purchase of office, service as *échevin*, etc.) Opposition to a commercial
nobility came from new nobles themselves, anxious to assimilate with
the old nobility; from the Merchant Guilds, which felt themselves
belittled and feared unfair aristocratic competition; from the Physiocrats,
who put agriculture before commerce; and from much of the old
nobility.[15]

Some modern historians question the traditional view that the nobles paid derisory amounts in taxation, quite out of keeping with their taxable capacity. It is argued that privileges existed for other classes too (certain *villes libres* such as Lyons and Paris enjoyed certain immunities); that the nobles' exemption from the *taille* tended 'to be more in the nature of a fringe benefit of which the actual financial advantage would vary according to local circumstances and of which the cost to the Treasury was inconsiderable'; that nobles did pay the *vingtième* from 1750 onwards; that some peasants were cleverer at tax evasion than some aristocrats; and that 'the French nobility appears to have borne a relatively heavier burden of taxation than the British nobility of the period.'[16] Be that as it may – and it is odd that the French nobles themselves were so unaware that their privileges were so piffling – one would still expect any serious problem-play of the 1770s to say something about the injustices of the tax-system, and the attempts, throughout the century, to reform it. But all that *Les Deux Amis* says about tax-payers is that those connected with the silk industry cheerfully pay sums which are assessed according to their profits in free enterprise:

> Tout cela vit, tout cela gagne, et, l'industrie portant le prix des matières au centuple, il n'y a pas une de ces créatures, à commencer par moi, qui ne rende gaiement à l'Etat un tribut proportionné au gain que son émulation lui procure. (Act II, sc. x.)

By no means all *fermiers-généraux* were the blood-suckers that popular tradition and the Revolutionary Tribunal accused them of being. But Beaumarchais makes their office as edifying as it was lucrative. Saint-Alban, just and punctilious in his duties, acts nobly and generously. Mélac père had apparently accepted the post of *receveur-général* because it offered opportunities to do good:

> Plus l'abus d'un métier est facile, moins il faut l'être au choix des gens qui doivent l'exercer; et qui sait, dans celui-ci, le bien qu'un homme vertueux peut faire, tout le mal qu'il peut empêcher? (Act II, sc. v.)

His emotional son is overjoyed at being promised the succession. The liberal economist Jean-Baptiste Say, born at Lyons in 1767, wrote of that city as he had known it in his boyhood:

> Vous dites que le luxe fait vivre des ouvriers: oui, mais comment les fait-il vivre? Avez-vous visité la ville de France que le luxe faisait le plus travailler, Lyon? Avez-vous vu, dans le temps où l'ouvrage allait le mieux, ces misérables ouvriers: hâves, maigres, déguenillés, entassés dans des maisons à huit étages, pêle-mêle avec leurs femmes, leurs

enfants, leurs métiers [looms], leurs parents malades? Si au lieu de faire des brocards d'or, ils avaient fabriqué de bons draps, ils auraient eu de bons habits.[17]

Not a tear is shed in the play over these problems. Pauline does bestow some of her pin-money on the poor, and the manuscript version of the play ends by giving to the poor the money intended for a fête to celebrate Aurelly's ennoblement. But there is no suggestion that anything might be wrong with the social order. The answer to such demagogues as Rousseau (and the only joke in the play) is supplied by the simpleton servant André:

> Euh! que je voudrais bien! Je voudrais bien que chacun ne fût pas plus égaux l'un que l'autre. Les Maîtres seraient bien attrapés! . . . Oui! et mes gages, qui est-ce qui me les payerait? (Act IV, sc. i.)

Beaumarchais did well to disclaim any interest in the revolutions of Athens and Rome. For it was from these that the pre-revolutionary reformers, to a large extent, drew their vision of a happier world. The makers of the French Revolution saw themselves as heirs of the ancient republicans: in life, if not in literature, they created real epics, real dramas, of the conquering bourgeoisie. The Beaumarchais of *Les Deux Amis*, a time-serving pseudo-gentleman, offers nothing more revolutionary than the suggestion that illegitimate children, because of a 'préjugé respectable', are perhaps treated with undue harshness.[18]

The works of Diderot which are still alive today explored genuine problems about man, nature, art and society. Partly because of the censorship – obviously it was impossible to present on the stage ideas like those for which he had already been sent to gaol – and partly because, in all probability, Diderot himself in the 1750s considered the speculations of 'advanced' intellectuals unsuitable for the public at large, his *drames bourgeois*, like Beaumarchais's, evade real issues. In light comedy that might have been an advantage. But Diderot aspired to lay bare the 'misérables conventions qui pervertissent l'homme', and shock the nation into true humanity:

> Il est une impression plus violente encore, et que vous concevrez, si vous êtes nés pour votre art, et si vous en pressentez toute la magie: c'est de mettre un peuple comme à la gêne [on the rack]. Alors les esprits seront troublés, incertains, flottants, éperdus; et vos spectateurs, tels que ceux qui, dans les tremblements d'une partie du globe, voient les murs de leurs maisons vaciller, et sentent la terre se dérober sous leurs pieds.[19]

All that he and his imitators in fact achieve in the *drame bourgeois* is to indulge the audience with complacent thrills of moral self-righteousness.[20] They deal in an illusory virtue, free from effort or disturbing ideas. And that, rather than because of any technical weakness, is why the plays are bad.

Eighteenth-century French bourgeois could write brilliantly when criticising institutions, and when depicting polite society. As we saw in the previous chapter, they had begun to sense the grandeur of man's domination over nature. Rousseau showed future generations how to explore the private worlds of bourgeois individualism. What the age did not achieve was an artistically valid depiction of an ambitious but non-revolutionary middle class, exemplifying those public and private virtues which – in contrast to the alleged thriftless immorality of aristocrats and the lower orders – the bourgeois liked to believe were the hall-mark of their class.

But perhaps this was an impossible task in France. The arch-bourgeois Balzac condemned the money-making society which he recreated. Stendhal fled from it. The bourgeois *rentier* Flaubert spent his days pretending that art and the middle class were incompatible. Zola – whether genuinely or hypocritically is a matter of opinion – believed not in the bourgeoisie but in what he imagined to be socialism.

NOTES

1 *Est-il bon? Est-il méchant?* Act I, sc. x (*Œuvres*, ed. Assézat, VIII, p. 156). On the *drame bourgeois*, see F. Gaiffe, *Le Drame en France au XVIIIe siècle* (Paris, 1907).
2 Beaumarchais eliminated from his final version some of the more exaggerated elements, e.g. 'Homme rare et sublime, en qui la philosophie n'a point éteint la sensibilité, conservez votre place' (Beaumarchais, *Théâtre*, Pléiade, 1949, p. 625). But even apostrophes like this were used on solemn occasions: they can still be heard today, from the lips of university vice-chancellors conferring honorary degrees.
3 L. Trénard, *Lyon de l'Encyclopédie au Préromantisme* (Paris, 1958), pp. 22–3; 58–65; 85.
4 Guy Richard, 'La Noblesse commerçante à Bordeaux et à Nantes au XVIIIe siècle' (*L'Information historique*, 1958, pp. 185–90, 201); 'A propos de la noblesse commerçante de Lyon au XVIIIe siècle' (*L'Information historique*, 1959, pp. 156–61).
5 H. Lüthy, *La Banque protestante en France de la Révocation de l'Edit de Nantes à la Révolution*, vol. I, 1959, pp. 51–5.
6 Trénard, op. cit., pp. 76, 178, 206. Voltaire had many useful friends in Lyons, but so had Rousseau, who had lived there. Aurelly's diatribe against the philosophes reads like some of Rousseau's attacks.

7 R. Pomeau, *Beaumarchais, l'homme et l'œuvre*, 1956, pp. 32, 127; *Théâtre*, Pléiade, p. 548; Trénard, op. cit., p. 157.

8 Letter of 22 November 1779 (Pléiade, p. 548).

9 *Le Théâtre italien de Gherardi* (Paris, 1741), vol. I, p. 421.

10 Baudelaire considered *Est-il bon? est-il méchant?* a good play, and tried unsuc-cessfully to have it produced at Paris (Diderot, *Œuvres*, ed. Assézat, vol. VIII, pp. 140–1).

11 *Œuvres romanesques*, ed. P. Bénac (Paris, 1959), p. 792.

12 Pomeau, op. cit., pp. 14–15, 34–5. On the office of *secrétaire du roi*, see F. Bluche, *Les Magistrats du Parlement de Paris au XVIIIᵉ siècle* (Paris, 1960), pp. 112–15.

13 Act II, sc. v.

14 A. Goodwin, 'French Eighteenth Century Nobility', p. 398 (*Bulletin of the John Rylands Library*, vol. 47, Manchester, 1965, pp. 382–403).

15 P. Sagnac, *La Formation de la société française moderne*, vol. 2, p. 107; M. Reinhard, 'Elite et Noblesse dans la seconde moitié du XVIIIᵉ siècle' (*Revue d'histoire moderne et contemporaine*, vol. III, 1956, pp. 5–37); G. Richard, 'Les Corporations et la noblesse commerçante en France au XVIIIᵉ siècle' (*L'Information historique*, 1957, pp. 185–9). For a summary of the abbé G. F. Coyer's celebrated work *La Noblesse commerçante* (Londres et Paris, 1756), see R. Mauzi, *L'Idée du bonheur au XVIIIᵉ siècle*, 1960, pp. 276–7. Reinhard considers that the idea of a commercial nobility was 'morte née', and that, in spite of the policy of ennobling business men and 'hommes à talents', 'les rois avaient manqué une occasion, l'une des dernières, d'adapter le régime aux temps nouveaux' (p. 35). G. Richard, however, points out that nobles did business under a *prête-nom*, or as major share-holders of companies without their names being published: he maintains that, by the end of the monarchy, the nobility were on the way to controlling heavy industry (mines, iron, steel, chemicals).

16 A. Goodwin, op. cit., pp. 386–7. Professor Goodwin largely accepts the conclusions of Miss C. B. A. Behrens, 'Privileges and taxes at the end of the Ancien Régime', published in the *Economic History Review* in 1963.

17 *Olbie, ou Essai sur les moyens de réformer les mœurs d'une nation*, Paris, An VIII (1799–1800), note V, p. 126.

18 Act IV, sc. x. Illegitimacy was one of the themes of the Second Empire bourgeois drama which, like that of the eighteenth century, dealt in moral platitudes and left untouched fundamental social, political, and economic problems.

19 Diderot, *De la poésie dramatique* (*Œuvres esthétiques*, ed. P. Vernière, 1959, pp. 195, 197–8).

20 Cf. Diderot's remarks in the *Salon de 1767*: 'Nous allons au théâtre chercher de nous-mêmes une estime que nous ne méritons pas, prendre bonne opinion de nous; partager l'orgueil des grandes actions que nous ne ferons jamais. . . . Le poète, le peintre, le statuaire, le comédien, sont des charlatans . . . en un mot, les plus séduisants des flatteurs'. *Salons*, ed. J. Seznec et J. Adhémar (Oxford, 1963), vol. III, p. 143.

XVI · Delille (1738–1813)

FROM *Les Jardins* (published 1782)
(Chant I)

J'applaudis l'orateur dont les nobles pensées
Roulent pompeusement, avec soin cadencées:
Mais ce plaisir est court. Je quitte l'orateur
Pour chercher un ami qui me parle du cœur.
Du marbre, de l'airain, qu'un vain luxe prodigue,
Des ornements de l'art, l'œil bientôt se fatigue;
Mais les bois, mais les eaux, mais les ombrages frais,
Tout ce luxe innocent ne fatigue jamais.
Aimez donc des jardins la beauté naturelle;
Dieu lui-même aux mortels en traça le modèle.
Regardez dans Milton, quand ses puissantes mains
Préparent un asile aux premiers des humains:
Le voyez-vous tracer des routes régulières,
Contraindre dans leurs cours des ondes prisonnières?
Le voyez-vous parer d'étrangers ornements
L'enfance de la terre et son premier printemps?
Sans contrainte, sans art, de ses douces prémices
La nature épuisa les plus pures délices.
Des plaines, des coteaux le mélange charmant,
Les ondes à leur choix errantes mollement,
Des sentiers sinueux les routes indécises,
Le désordre enchanteur, les piquantes surprises,
Des aspects où les yeux hésitaient à choisir,
Variaient, suspendaient, prolongeaient leur plaisir.
Sur l'émail velouté d'une fraîche verdure,
Mille arbres, de ces lieux ondoyante parure,
Charme de l'odorat, du goût et des regards
Elégamment groupés, négligemment épars,
Se fuyaient, s'approchaient, quelquefois à leur vue
Ouvraient dans le lointain une scène imprévue;
Ou, tombant jusqu'à terre, et recourbant leurs bras,
Venaient d'un doux obstacle embarrasser leurs pas;
Ou pendaient sur leur tête en festons de verdure,
Et de fleurs, en passant, semaient leur chevelure.

Dirai-je ces forêts d'arbustes, d'arbrisseaux,
Entrelaçant en voûte, en alcôve, en berceaux,
Leurs bras voluptueux et leurs tiges fleuries?
  C'est là que les yeux pleins de tendres rêveries,
Eve à son jeune époux abandonna sa main,
Et rougit comme l'aube aux portes du matin.
Tout les félicitait dans toute la nature,
Le ciel par son éclat, l'onde par son murmure.
La terre en tressaillant ressentit leurs plaisirs;
Zéphire aux antres verts redisait leurs soupirs;
Les arbres frémissaient, et la rose inclinée
Versait tous ses parfums sur le lit d'hyménée.
  O bonheur ineffable! O fortunés époux!
Heureux dans ses jardins, heureux qui, comme vous,
Vivrait loin des tourments où l'orgueil est en proie,
Riche de fruits, de fleurs, d'innocence et de joie!

Œuvres complètes (Paris, 1865) p. 12.

The word Paradise, which the Greeks borrowed from the Persians, meant a park. When Voltaire quoted Genesis II, xv, at the end of *Candide,* and bade his contemporaries cultivate their garden, an earthly paradise seemed to him as unattainable as the Eden to which successive generations nostalgically looked back. What he meant was that hard work and goodwill could make society less hideous. But for Voltaire the garden was more than a symbol. As squire of Ferney, he not only engaged in reformist propaganda and good estate management. He also enjoyed the pleasures of his superbly situated park. His protégé Florian – 'le gentil Florianet' – describes a fête Voltaire gave at Ferney on St Clair's day, 12 August 1765, in honour of the actress Mlle Clairon, recently released from her Paris prison. There was song, a firework display in the gardens, Tokay wine, supper beneath a canopy of flowers, dancing all night, and then the view of the Alps at dawn:

Ferney est entouré de montagnes couvertes de neige en tout temps; dès que les premiers rayons du soleil viennent les frapper, on voit l'or se répandre lentement et par degrés sur les sommets glacés que l'œil peut à peine mesurer; cette vive lumière descend des montagnes pour venir éclairer un pays superbe, et se réfléchir dans un lac qui couvre sept lieues d'étendue. Le chant des oiseaux qui saluent le jour, le bruit et les chansons des paysans qui vont couper les épis qu'ils ont fait éclore, le coup d'œil d'un fleuve majestueux qui sort en bouillant du lac, et roule avec impétuosité une onde assez rapide pour ne pas se mêler à ses eaux: une ville bâtie sur ses bords et qui repose la vue: tel est le spectacle dont on pouvait jouir dans les jardins de Ferney: tout le monde l'admira, et fut se coucher.[1]

The artificiality implicit in the style of Florian's passage typifies much eighteenth-century landscape description. Delille himself, as Marie-Joseph Chénier pointed out, had little real contact with the fields:

> Sous son maigre et joli pinceau
> La nature est naine et coquette;
> L'habile arrangeur de palette
> N'a vu, pour son petit tableau,
> Les champs qu'à travers sa lorgnette,
> Et par les vitres du château.[2]

The civilised townsman's longing for country pleasures was, of course, already a theme of ancient literature:

> O rus, quando ego te aspiciam? quandoque licebit
> Nunc veterum libris, nunc somno et inertibus horis,
> Ducere sollicitae jucunda oblivia vitae?[3]

It was in part through literary influences, including that of the seventeenth-century imitation shepherd Des Yveteaux, that Chaulieu sought happiness in a country retreat. In 1769 Saint-Lambert, author of the descriptive poem *Les Saisons*, listed among the poets who had influenced him Theocritus, Horace and Virgil; his German–Swiss contemporaries Haller and Gessner; the pastoral poet Ambrose Philips (Namby-Pamby was how his own contemporaries referred to this rival of Pope), and James Thomson, on whose *Seasons* Saint-Lambert's poem is modelled.[4] From England, too, came the fashion for the asymmetrical type of garden which rich French landowners were beginning to prefer.[5]

Love of nature was more, however, than literary reminiscence or an imported fashion. For Rousseau, it was part of his condemnation of an irremediably evil civilisation:

> plus [les nations] s'approchent de la nature, plus la bonté domine dans leur caractère; ce n'est qu'en se renfermant dans les villes, ce n'est qu'en s'altérant à force de culture, qu'elles se dépravent . . . Heureux, mon jeune ami, le pays où l'on n'a pas besoin d'aller chercher la paix dans un désert! Mais où est ce pays?

Certainly not France; so he dreamed of escape to a Swiss lake, to the Wolmar household with its secret garden, or to a country cottage of his own:

> Sur le penchant de quelque agréable colline bien ombragée, j'aurais une petite maison rustique, une maison blanche avec des contrevents verts; et quoique une couverture de chaume soit en toute saison la meilleure, je préférerais magnifiquement, non la triste ardoise, mais la tuile, parce qu'elle a l'air plus propre et plus gai que le chaume, qu'on

ne couvre pas autrement les maisons de mon pays, et que cela me
rappellerait un peu l'heureux temps de ma jeunesse.[6]

For Diderot in 1757, hill, stream and forest were the background and
inspiration for a new type of philosopher-poet, possessed by forces as
chaotic and irrational as those of nature herself:

C'est ici qu'on voit la nature. Voici le séjour sacré de l'enthousiasme.
Un homme a-t-il reçu du génie? il quitte la ville et ses habitants. Il
aime, selon l'attrait de son cœur, à mêler ses pleurs au cristal d'une
fontaine . . . à fouler d'un pied léger l'herbe tendre de la prairie . . .
à fuir au fond des forêts. Il aime leur horreur secrète. Il erre. Il
cherche un antre qui l'inspire . . . Bientôt ce n'est plus un frémissement;
c'est une chaleur forte et permanente qui l'embrase, qui le fait haleter,
qui le consume, qui le tue; mais qui donne l'âme, la vie à tout ce
qu'il touche. Si cette chaleur s'accroissait encore, les spectres se
multiplieraient devant lui. Sa passion s'élèverait jusqu'à la fureur.
Il ne connaîtrait de soulagement qu'à verser au dehors un torrent
d'idées qui se pressent, se heurtent et se chassent.[7]

According to Saint-Lambert, country life attracted many because of the
relief it offered from the routine pleasures of a rationalistic society:

Dans les siècles de discussion et de raison . . . quand les plaisirs du
luxe sont réduits à leur juste valeur, . . . on sent davantage le prix de la
vie champêtre; on sait mieux ce qu'on doit à l'agriculture; ses occupations sont honorées; la paix, l'innocence qui les accompagnent sont
regrettées. Des sybarites, ennuyés de leurs vices et de leurs intrigues,
aiment à voir l'homme simple et sans artifice découvrant sa manière
de sentir et de penser. Ils aimeraient les tableaux de la campagne, quand
ils n'auraient que le mérite de présenter des objets nouveaux.[8]

The rich art-patron Watelet, creator of one of the most famous *jardins
anglais* of the century, maintained that all the talk about nature was, in
many instances, pure affectation and hypocrisy – one of the 'enthou-
siasmes joués qui deviennent si communs et si épidémiques parmi nous
. . . la prétention de sentir vivement et de s'exprimer d'une manière
distinguée'. Though he himself tried to persuade the idle rich – 'des
oisifs victimes de l'ennui, qui s'efforcent de le fuir et le portent partout
avec eux' – to take up landscape-painting as a hobby, he affirmed that
even professional French landscape painters were loath to go out
into the wilds, 'car, ressemblant en cela à nos possesseurs de biens de
campagne, ils n'ont pas d'attrait réel pour les beautés et les mœurs
champêtres'. The artificial ruins and imitation cottages which landowners dotted about their parks were, in Watelet's opinion, proof of
spurious, or even callous sentiment:

Le luxe personnel veut jouir à son gré des contrastes qui lui font mieux
sentir les avantages qu'il possède, ou bien . . . dédaignant et redoutant
la peine d'aller observer les cabanes véritables, qui n'inspirent, par
l'état de leurs habitants, que des sentiments pénibles, aime mieux en
former des représentations, qui laissent l'âme des riches dans la
tranquillité.[9]

Whether love of nature was affectation or not, the interest in estate
management was in many cases undoubtedly real. It was not only that
the Physiocrat theorists proclaimed the land to be the prime source of a
nation's wealth. It was a profitable source for individuals too. With the
end of the war in 1763 began a period of agricultural prosperity which,
in spite of fluctuations and bad years, meant higher prices, higher rents,
higher feudal dues, for the landlords. More land was brought into cultivation; commons were enclosed; new crops, fertilisers and techniques
were introduced. Progressive nobles set about exploiting their properties
with the utmost efficiency; urban bourgeois saw profit as well as gentlemanly status in acquiring country estates; rich peasants increased their
riches.[10] If all this capital investment brought scant benefit to the mass
of the peasantry, their poverty at least afforded writers an opportunity
to sentimentalise about the *bienfaisance* of the landlords. The rich nobleman in Saint-Lambert's *Saisons* finds moral satisfaction in employing
pauper labour:

> Moi, je vis chaque instant croître mon opulence,
> Je pus laisser sans crainte agir ma bienfaisance.
>
> .   .   .
>
> Il faut rendre meilleur le pauvre qu'on soulage,
> C'est l'effet du travail en tout temps, à tout âge.
> On vit dans mon château la veuve et l'orphelin
> Ourdir et préparer et la laine et le lin.
> Les vieillards, par des soins, par des travaux faciles,
> Pouvaient jouir encor du plaisir d'être utiles.[11]

Delille even invents a use for dead peasants: country gentlemen whose
estates contain no tomb of relative or friend to weep over can keep themselves supplied with the pleasures of Melancholy by erecting memorials
to rustics:

> Ah! si d'aucun ami vous n'honorez la cendre,
> Voyez sous ces vieux ifs la tombe où vont se rendre
> Ceux qui, courbés pour vous sur des sillons ingrats,
> Au sein de la misère espèrent le trépas.
>
> .   .   .

Pour consoler leur vie, honorez donc leur mort.

. . .

Tracez-y les vertus et les pleurs du hameau:
Qu'on y lise: *Ci-gît le bon fils, le bon père,*
Le bon époux. Souvent un charme involontaire
Vers les enclos sacrés appellera vos yeux.[12]

Farming by verse brought more than sentimental satisfactions to Delille himself. He published his verse translation of Virgil's *Georgics* in 1769, when, as his 'Discours Préliminaire' stated, interest in agriculture had already developed into 'le ridicule de l'agromanie'. Hailed as 'le Virgile français', he was able to abandon his post as schoolmaster in the former Jesuit college at Amiens for one in Paris; in 1774 he was elected to the Academy, then to the chair of Latin poetry at the Collège de France; he was appointed to a canonry at Moissac, and, through the good offices of the duc d'Artois (the future Charles X), was given the abbey of Saint-Séverin, which brought him a country residence and 30,000 livres per year.[13] In 1774, with his *Epître sur le luxe*, he turned to economics for a topic. The following passage exhorts 'un gros millionnaire' – a plebeian who has bought an estate – to do something about his starving tenants and the flight from the land:

Vois-tu, près de tes parcs, sous ton château superbe,
Ces spectres affamés qui se disputent l'herbe?
Vois-tu tous ces vassaux, filles, femmes, enfants,
De ton domaine ingrat abandonner les champs?
Sois homme: par tes dons retiens ce peuple utile,
Laisse-lui quelque épi du champ qu'il rend fertile;
Et que ses humbles toits, réparés à tes frais,
Pardonnent à l'orgueil de tes riches palais.[14]

Les Jardins, ou L'art d'embellir les paysages, on the other hand, is a tribute to rich landowners who have spent fortunes laying out gardens:

L'art des jardins, qu'on pourrait appeler le luxe de l'agriculture, me paraît un des amusements les plus convenables, je dirais presque les plus vertueux, des personnes riches. Comme culture, il les ramène à l'innocence des occupations champêtres; comme décoration, il favorise sans danger ce goût des dépenses qui suit les grandes fortunes; enfin il a, pour cette classe d'hommes, le double avantage de tenir à la fois aux goûts de la ville et à ceux de la campagne. Ce plaisir des particuliers s'est trouvé joint à l'utilité publique: il a fait aimer aux personnes opulentes le séjour de leurs terres. L'argent, qui aurait entretenu les artisans du luxe, va nourrir les cultivateurs; et la richesse retourne à sa véritable source. De plus, la culture s'est enrichie d'une foule de plantes et d'arbres étrangers aux productions de notre sol, et cela vaut bien tout le marbre que nos jardins ont perdu.[15]

PLATE VIIa   J.-P. de Loutherbourg (1740–1812): *La Latière* (1766)

PLATE VIIb   E. Aubry (1745–81): *L'Amour paternel* (*c.* 1774)

PLATE VIII J.-L. David (1748–1825): *Le Premier consul franchissant
le mont Saint-Bernard* (1800)

All this doubtless explains why Delille thought it worth while to write *Les Jardins*, and why, in 1782, he found a publisher and a public. It tells us nothing about the poem itself.

In the lines preceding our extract, Delille had described the splendours of Versailles, declining to compare it to the English style attributed to the gardener William Kent:

> Je ne décide point entre Kent et Le Nôtre.

Then he gives his real preference. Though his use of a line of Jean Racine (line 4 is a quotation from *Bérénice*, Act I, sc. iv) illustrates the similarities between the late eighteenth-century idiom and that of the classicists, the grandiose stateliness of Versailles had lost its appeal. Already in the 1760s Louis XV and his mistresses had opted for the illusion of freedom, naturalness and informality provided by the Petit Trianon.[16] By 1780, Marie-Antoinette was constructing a *jardin anglais*, in which she was soon to install the mock peasant paraphernalia of Le Hameau. Even informal gardens, as Delille admits in Canto II of his poem, may become a bore:

> L'habitude bientôt a flétri vos bocages.
> Souvent quand l'étranger jouit de vos ombrages,
> Déjà leur possesseur languit sans intérêt.

But not the garden in our extract, for it is Eden – a Louis XVI Eden, full of the restlessness which, as Professor Mauzi points out, was one of the ingredients in the eighteenth-century recipe for happiness.[17] Thus, the streams are *errantes*; the eye does not know on what to settle; the trees offer both the static perspectives of a landscape painting and the sinuous movements of a group of dryads; the earth itself quivers in sympathy with the lovers' embrace. Such features, and the insistence on curved lines instead of symmetrical patterns, had since early in the century characterised the rococo style.[18] In Julie's Elysium also, straight lines were banished .[19] The quest for movement, the dislike of geometrical constraint, was, it would seem, part of a general desire for freedom. Delille's association of the two concepts in Canto I:

> Mais si du mouvement notre œil est enchanté,
> Il ne chérit pas moins un air de liberté

is made more explicit in Canto IV:

> Pas un arbre au cordeau n'osa désobéir;
> Tout s'aligna, partout, en deux rangs étalées,
> S'allongèrent sans fin d'éternelles allées.
> Autre temps, autre goût, enfin le parc anglais

O

> D'une beauté plus libre avertit le Français.
> Dès lors on ne vit plus que lignes ondoyantes,
> Que sentiers tortueux, que routes tournoyantes.

Delille's actual rhythms exemplify the freedom – within an accepted traditional order – to which the age aspired. Though 'Des sentiers sinueux les routes indécises' is a long way yet from Verlaine's

> Chanson grise
> Où l'Indécis au Précis se joint

Delille's alexandrines are well on the way to such flexibility as the Romantic poets practised. (Mornet counted one 'coupe nettement irrégulière' every 192 lines in Racine, every 86 in Lebrun, every 28 in Delille, every 15 in Hugo's *Les Feuilles d'automne*.[20]) There are no examples in our extract of those spectacular metrical irregularities which, with the 'harmonie imitative' that Delille was so proud of, from time to time intensify the sensory impact of his verse. One had occurred a few lines earlier, describing the fountains of Versailles, where the observer sees

> . . . ces fleuves suspendus,
> En gros bouillons d'écume à grand bruit descendus
> Tomber, se prolonger dans des canaux superbes.

His immediate source for the description of Eden is Book IV of *Paradise Lost*, which was available to him in the prose translation of his friend Louis Racine, published in 1755. In a note, Delille explains that, though the *jardin anglais* probably originated in China, some Englishmen attribute it to Spenser and Milton:

> j'ai préféré l'autorité de Milton, comme plus poétique. D'ailleurs, j'ai cru qu'on verrait avec plaisir toute la magnificence du plus grand roi du monde [i.e. Louis XIV], tous les prodiges des arts, mis en opposition avec les charmes de la nature naissante, l'innocence des premières créatures qui l'embellirent, et l'intérêt des premières amours.[21]

Not that he is much interested in the theological aspects of Eden – the last three lines of our extract seem to envisage the abolition of original sin for garden-lovers.[22] Religion is little in evidence anywhere in *Les Jardins*. But after all, the abbé was not a priest: all that was required of him for his benefice was minor orders and a pretence of celibacy. What he coyly terms 'l'intérêt des premières amours' was a theme particularly relished by those eighteenth-century circles in which all fleshly pleasures were available except those of inexperience. Adam and Eve had for such readers the same appeal as Chérubin in *Le Mariage de*

Figaro (1778), Cécile and Danceny in *Les Liaisons dangereuses* (1782), or *Paul et Virginie* (1787). It can hardly be claimed that Delille achieves the serene, majestic sensuousness with which Milton enfolds

> the loveliest pair
> That ever since in love's embraces met.

Lines like

> Le désordre enchanteur, les piquantes surprises

are more suggestive of Crébillon *fils* than of Eden before the Fall. (It was, indeed, as much to achieve piquancy as to avoid 'ignoble' words that Delille evolved those elaborate periphrases for which he is so famous, but of which our passage is free.[23]) All the same, the last ten lines are genuine poetry. They prove that Delille was more than the clever versifier, the ingenious contriver of pretty artificialities, which, since the days of his imitators the Romantic poets, is what he has been chiefly remembered for.[24] In his *Observations* on Saint-Lambert's *Saisons*, Diderot complained that the verses were as sober as Saint-Lambert himself:

> Ce qui lui manque? C'est une âme qui se tourmente, un esprit violent, une imagination forte et bouillante, une lyre qui ait plus de cordes.

In his essay *Sur les femmes*, of 1772, Diderot speaks of a poetry which is linked to uncontrolled forces of the body and of the sub-conscious:

> Rien de plus contigu que l'extase, la vision, la prophétie, la révélation, la poésie fougueuse et l'hystérisme.[25]

By eighteenth-century standards of that sort, Delille's poetry was antiquated before it was printed. None the less, the last ten lines of the passage point the way to some aspects of Lamartine and Hugo. They do more than that. By their music and imagery, and so, by the intensiveness of their sensuous appeal, they remain alive today.

The last line ends Canto I of the poem in the 1782 edition. Unfortunately, Delille added to it. By 1801, he has introduced a merchant who, like Rousseau, is dreaming of a house in the country:

> A son triste bureau le marchand sédentaire,
> Lassé de ses calculs, lassé de son comptoir,
> D'avance se promet un champêtre manoir,
> Rêve ses boulingrins, ses arbres, son bocage,
> Et d'un verger futur se peint déjà l'image.

Here we are back at a level which sociological explanations of literature can deal with confidently.

NOTES

1 *Mémoires d'un jeune Espagnol* (Paris, 1812), pp. 18–23. Florian adopted a mock-Spanish disguise for this autobiography of his youth, and called Ferney Fernixo. His description of the view is not altogether accurate. Voltaire gives an account of the fête in a letter to the duc de Richelieu, 23 August 1765: 'J'ai reçu Madlle Clairon, comme vous le vouliez, et comme elle le mérite. Elle a été honorée, fêtée, chantée. Il ne lui a manqué que la petite attention dont vous l'honorâtes il y a quelques années; mais il n'y a pas moyen que je sois aussi poli que vous' (*Voltaire's Correspondence*, ed. Besterman, LIX, p. 34).

2 *Œuvres posthumes* (Paris, 1824), p. 350. This epigram is not directed at *Les Jardins* of 1782, but at the anti-republican sentiments of the poems Delille wrote while an émigré. The republican philosophes began to attack him in 1799 in their journal *La Décade philosophique* (An VII, 10 Fructidor, p. 440), when they thought that he was about to publish his poem *La Pitié* in Germany.

3 Horace, *Satires*, II, vi, 60–3: 'O ma chère maison des champs! quand vous reverrai-je? quand pourrai-je dans cet heureux asile, passant tour à tour de la lecture des livres des anciens aux douceurs de l'oisiveté et d'un tranquille sommeil, oublier toutes les tracasseries de cette vie agitée et tumultueuse?' (trans. by Féletz in *Œuvres complètes d'Horace*, Classiques Garnier, n.d., p. 260).

4 Saint-Lambert, *Les Saisons* (Paris, 1823), pp. i–v.

5 On the English garden in France, see D. Mornet, *Le Romantisme en France au XVIIIᵉ siècle* (Paris, 1912), pp. 15–18, 30–42, 62–4, 112–14, 120–22, 242–5, 271–5; Marguerite Charageat, *L'Art des jardins* (Paris, 1962), pp. 160–70.

6 *Émile*, ed. F. et P. Richard (Paris, 1951), pp. 439, 600, 606. Julie's private garden is described in *La Nouvelle Héloïse*, IV, xi (ed. Mornet, vol. III, pp. 223–47).

7 *Œuvres esthétiques*, ed. P. Vernière (Paris, 1959), pp. 97–8 (*Entretiens sur 'Le Fils naturel'*).

8 Ed. cit., p. iv.

9 *Dictionnaire des Arts de peinture, sculpture et gravure par M. Watelet* (Paris, 1792), II, pp. 162–3, 248–53; IV, pp. 8–21. Claude-Henri Watelet (1718–86) was Receveur Général des Finances de la Généralité d'Orléans. His garden, Moulin-Joli, on the banks of the Seine near Paris, is described by Delille in Canto III of *Les Jardins*. Watelet excluded Poussin and Claude Le Lorrain from his condemnation of French landscape painters on the grounds that they were almost Italian. He preferred Gessner to French descriptions of nature: 'O mon ami! C'est près de vous, c'est sur les bords des eaux limpides et ombragées de ce beau lac où vous avez guidé nos pas, qu'il faut étudier avec vous l'originalité piquante, simple et touchante des beautés de la nature . . . vous charmez les sens et vous consolez de leurs peines et de leurs maux ceux qui s'occupent de vos ouvrages'. For an account of Watelet's *Essai sur les jardins* (1774), see R. Mauzi, *L'Idée du bonheur au XVIIIᵉ siècle*, pp. 369–72.

10 Sagnac, op. cit., II, pp. 216–19; 227–8; 240–4; P. de Saint Jacob, *Les Paysans de la Bourgogne du Nord* . . . (Paris, 1960), pp. 353–500. The area of land under cultivation seems to have declined after the late 1770s, and there was an exodus of peasants to the towns (Saint Jacob, pp. 502, 527). G. Lizerand, *Le Régime rural de l'ancienne France* (Paris, 1942), pp. 165–7, gives examples of the rise in the cost of leases. On the 'feudal reaction' – 'l'élévation arbitraire des droits existants et surtout . . . le rétablissement de droits tombés en désuétude', see H. Sée, *La France économique et sociale au XVIIIᵉ siècle*, pp. 30, 31, 52. Professor A. Goodwin (*Bulletin of the John Rylands Library*, Manchester, 1965, 47, pp. 388–91) considers that the feudal reaction has been exaggerated, that peasant discontent was directed at least as much against urban financial interests in the country, and that 'the traditional picture of an impoverished provincial nobility eking out a proud but wretched existence on the proceeds of feudal dues seems hardly more than a literary travesty'. Professor Albert Soboul, on the other hand, thinks that the feudal reaction was important.

11 Op. cit., p. 142.

12 *Les Jardins*, Chant IV.

13 Vedad Zeki Örs, *Jacques Delille* (Zürich, 1936), pp. 14–36. There is a place called Saint-Séverin, which had an abbey, in Charente-Maritime.

14 *Œuvres* (Paris, 1865), p. 858.

15 From the Preface to *Les Jardins*.

16 On the style and social significance of the Petit Trianon, see A. Dupront, *Les Lettres, les sciences, la religion et les arts dans la société française de la deuxième moitié du XVIIIᵉ siècle* (C.D.U., Paris, 1963), Fascicule IV, pp. 309–11.

17 R. Mauzi, *L'Idée du bonheur au XVIIIᵉ siècle* (Paris, 1960), pp. 386–513. Pp. 330–85 are on immobility and repose. Martin, in *Candide*, 'conclut que l'homme était né pour vivre dans les convulsions de l'inquiétude, ou dans la léthargie de l'ennui' (Ch. 30, *Conclusion*).

18 A. Dupront, op. cit., Fasc. III, 222–35. See also S. Fiske Kimball, *The Creation of the Rococo* (Philadelphia, 1943).

19 *La Nouvelle Héloïse*, ed. cit., III, p. 239: 'La nature emploie-t-elle sans cesse l'équerre et la règle? . . . l'homme de goût . . . ne donnera à rien de la symétrie; elle est ennemie de la nature et de la variété'. Cf. Marcel Proust, *A la recherche du temps perdu*, ed. Pléiade, I, 11: 'ma grand'mère . . . parcourait les allées détrempées – trop symétriquement alignées à son gré par le nouveau jardinier dépourvu du sentiment de la nature'.

20 Mornet, op. cit., p. 237.

21 The Chinese influence on gardening is mentioned in *La Nouvelle Héloïse*, loc. cit., p. 240. On the evolution of eighteenth-century English gardens, see Edward Hyams, *The English Garden* (London, 1964) and Christopher Hussey, *English Gardens and Landscape 1700–1750* (London, 1967). The description of the Garden of Eden in our extract follows fairly closely that in *Paradise Lost*, Book IV, which Delille presumably read in Louis Racine's translation. Racine states, in a note: 'Milton rabaisse ici les travaux de nos jardiniers, parce que la nature est plus habile.' (*Œuvres de Louis Racine*, Paris, 1808, III, p. 326).

22 To enjoy the fourfold riches mentioned in the last line, the financier Nicolas Beaujon in 1773 spent one million livres on a mansion in the Champs Elysées; he then constructed, nearby, what he called his Chartreuse or Hermitage. This had an English garden, a chapel, mill, farm-yard, billiard rooms, classical urns, a chaplain-librarian, richly clad footmen, and rare wines including some from South Africa (C. Kunstler, *La Vie quotidienne sous Louis XVI* (Paris, 1950), p. 218).

23 In the Preliminary Discourse to his *Georgics*, Delille says of *le style noble*: 'Le destin de notre langue ressemble assez à celui de ces gentilshommes ruinés qui se condamnent à l'indigence de peur de déroger'. In Canto III of *Les Jardins* he urges gentlemen 'D'ouvrir vos parcs au bœuf, à la vache féconde/Qui ne dégradent plus ni vos parcs ni mes vers'.

24 V. Klemperer, in *Delilles "Gärten": Ein Mosaikbild des 18. Jahrhunderts* (*Sitzungsberichte der Deutschen Akademie der Wissenschaften zu Berlin*, Klasse für Sprachen, Literatur und Kunst, 1953, Nr. 2, Berlin, 1954), presents a convincing 'rehabilitation' of Delille as a poet, as well as an assessment of his ideological position.

25 *Œuvres*, Assézat, vol. V, p. 250; vol. II, p. 255.

XVII · Restif de la Bretonne (1734–1806)

FROM *Monsieur Nicolas ou Le Cœur humain dévoilé:* Première Epoque (published 1796)

Arrivé le soir, je soupais seul, et dès le matin je faisais sortir le troupeau. Il prospérait entre mes mains; je ne le ramenais que rassasié, et grâce à Friquette, les loups n'en diminuaient pas le nombre; cette excellente gardienne poursuivait quelquefois à elle seule deux loups et les obligeait à fuir. Ce qu'il y a de singulier, c'est que moi, qui craignais les chiens jusqu'à la pusillanimité, j'attaquais les loups en téméraire; je les poursuivais sans aucune autre arme que des pierres que je lançais contre eux; et comme j'étais preste à la course, je les harcelais, les fatiguais, et souvent je les blessais à sang.

Vis-à-vis les vignes de Mont-Gré, derrière le bois du Bout-Parc, était un vallon plus solitaire, où je n'avais encore osé pénétrer; la haute lisière du bois lui donnait quelque chose de sombre qui m'effrayait. Le quatrième jour après les vendanges de Nitry, je me hasardai à y passer avec tout mon troupeau. Il y avait, au fond du vallon, sur le bord d'une ravine, des buissons pour mes chèvres, avec une pelouse où mes génisses pouvaient paître comme dans le Grand-Pré. En me voyant là, j'éprouvai une secrète horreur, causée par les contes d'excommuniés changés en bêtes que me faisait Jacquot, mais cette horreur n'était pas sans plaisir. Mon quadruple troupeau paissait; les cochons trouvaient en abondance une espèce de carotte sauvage, que les paysans nomment échavie, et ils labouraient la terre, tandis que les plus gros, et surtout leur mère, s'avançaient du côté du bois. Je les suivais pour les empêcher d'y entrer, lorsque j'aperçus, sous un vieux chêne à glands, un énorme sanglier. Je tressaillis d'horreur et de plaisir, car cet animal augmentait l'aspect sauvage qui avait tant de charmes pour moi. Je m'avançai le plus qu'il me fut possible. Le fier animal m'aperçut et, dédaignant un enfant, il continua de se rassasier. Par un heureux hasard, la truie était en chaleur; elle s'approcha du sanglier qui courut à elle dès qu'il la sentit. J'étais ivre de joie du spectacle qu'ils m'offrirent, et je retins mes trois chiens en laisse pour ne pas troubler le sanglier. Dans le même moment parurent un lièvre et un chevreuil: je me croyais transporté dans le pays des Fées; je respirais à peine. Je m'écriais inarticulément, quand un loup parut. Je fus obligé de lâcher mes chiens contre cet ennemi public; la crainte qu'il n'attaquât le troupeau détruisait le charme de sa présence, car tous ces animaux sauvages augmentaient à mes yeux celui de cette solitude. Mes chiens effrayèrent et lièvre, et chevreuil, et sanglier; tout disparut et rentra dans les bois; mais le charme resta. Il fut même augmenté par une belle huppe qui vint se percher sur deux gros poiriers dont les paysans appellent le fruit poires de miel, parce qu'elles sont si douces et si sucrées dans leur maturité que les guêpes et les abeilles les dévorent. Je connaissais déjà ce fruit; les parents de mon ami Etienne Dumont avaient un poirier de miel au bas d'un champ très voisin de la maison paternelle, et il m'avait quelquefois mené en manger les poirettes tombées. Mais que je trouvais celles-ci délicieuses, à moi, et dans une terre de liberté! Ajoutez qu'elles étaient plus mûres, mieux nourries, et que je n'en avais obligation à personne, car les poiriers étaient dans la pelouse inculte qui bordait la ravine. J'admirai la huppe, oiseau que je voyais pour la première fois; je mangeai des poires et j'en remplis mes poches afin de régaler mes jeunes frères et sœurs.

> *L'Œuvre de Restif de la Bretonne*, ed. H. Bachelin (Paris, 1932). *Monsieur Nicolas*, I, pp. 48–9.

Amid all the urbane idylls, pastorals, georgics and bucolics, Restif de la Bretonne[1] brings to his contemporaries impressions of the country-side that he knew and loved when a boy on his father's farm in Burgundy. Edmond, the semi-autobiographical hero of *Le Paysan perverti* (1775) has settled in Paris, but longs for the land:

> Ce matin, cher Pierre, mes larmes coulaient de mes yeux comme deux fontaines, en me remémorant une veille de Fête-Dieu où j'étais allé faner seul du sainfoin dans notre vallée du Vau-de-Lannard: que j'étais heureux! Tout était pour moi un sujet de plaisir; le temps demi-sauvage qu'il faisait, le cri du cul-blanc [stone-chat or wheatear] solitaire, l'herbe même, l'herbe fleurie des côteaux avait une âme qui parlait à la mienne.[2]

In *La Vie de mon père* (1778), Restif has recorded some authentic aspects of Ancien Régime country life: the patriarchal existence of a prosperous farmer, the village community, the seasonal routine of ploughman, vine-grower and harvester, the breaking-in of uncultivated land, the payment of tithes, taxes and feudal dues. The passage selected – if we are to believe what Restif has said a few pages earlier – was written in 1784, and describes an early October day in 1745, when he was a shepherd boy nearly eleven years old.[3] Not a real shepherd boy, however; he was looking after the flock, with his parents' permission, because he wanted to, and the regular shepherd, his friend Jacquot, was away on a pilgrimage. Beneath the apparent genuineness of his descriptions, there are signs of literary artifice and sentimental embellishment. The herd which Nicolas brings back to La Bretonne each evening consists of heifers (*génisses* is used here in its proper sense, and not as a 'noble' word for *vaches*), sheep, goats and pigs. The three dogs are called Pinçard, Babillard and Friquette. Friquette is described in *La Vie de mon père* as 'une chienne rouge demi-levrette . . . beaucoup moins grande qu'un mâtin ordinaire', highly intelligent and faithful, with a place in the affection of her master Edmond Restif immediately after Flamand his horse and Germain his ploughman. Jacquot had set out in the week before 21 September to walk to St Michael's Mount in Brittany – a pilgrimage undertaken by all the village boys of 15 or 16: 'Un garçon qui n'avait pas été à Saint-Michel était regardé comme un couard, un poltron.' (The girls went to Sainte-Reine, at Whitsun.) Though it is now a week after Michaelmas, Jacquot is still away: his father, Blaise the tiler, has stoically assumed 'qu'il était . . . péri en s'exposant témérairement à passer au pied du Mont Saint-Michel à la marée montante'. Nicolas had just been singing to himself a song about Jacquot, to the tune of 'la complainte des Pèlerins de Saint-Jacques, que j'avais entendu chanter à des mendiants'; now, in the lonely valley under the wood, he recalls Jacquot's ghost-stories. He had already felt eerie, going by the field of

> Jean Simon le mansier, ou le faiseur de manses. C'était un homme à qui la religion avait tourné la tête, par la crainte de l'enfer. Il avait cessé d'aller à la messe, il travaillait le dimanche et les fêtes à ses vignes. Il faisait des manses, ou petites boules de terre argileuse, pour éloigner le diable qui lui apparaissait sous la forme d'une araignée.

Nicolas's superstitious fears turn to thrilled excitement as he watches the wild boar inseminate his sow. Restif's sexual obsessions – a dominating theme of his works, and the reason why Victorian critics neglected him[4] – came to him early: he claims, in *Monsieur Nicolas*, that at the age of ten and a half he was already a prey to 'cet indomptable érotisme qui tourmentera les plus belles années de ma vie'.[5] Eroticism, rather than the arrival of a hare and a roebuck, is the reason for his ecstasy.

Fairyland, to which he compares the scene, was still able to attract some eighteenth-century readers. Mornet lists 46 volumes of fairy stories printed between 1741 and 1758, and 24 between 1765 and 1780.

Saint-Lambert says that belief in fairies and ghosts still existed in the country districts:

> De l'antique féerie on raconte une histoire;
> L'orateur, qui la croit, l'atteste et la fait croire.
> Un spectre, dit l'un d'eux, paraît vers le grand bois;
> Le jour de la tempête on entendit sa voix.[6]

Restif's use of *le pays des fées* appears, therefore, to be perfectly natural in the context, and without any of the artificiality which the word Fairyland has in modern English. The arrival of the wolf, the unleashing of the dogs, the flight of the four wild animals, are recounted undramatically because his mind is still on the mating scene. His lack of fear, explained by the fact that Friquette can deal with wolves, is made more credible by the mention of his childish terror of other dogs. Though he says that the spell remained unbroken after the disappearance of the wild animals, the remainder of the passage is on a level which would normally be expected in a little boy's narrative. The unconvincing explanation of why *poires de miel* are so called has the authentic touch of children's logic; apart perhaps from the phrase 'maison paternelle', the sentence about Etienne Dumont might come straight from a school exercise today. So might the twelve words on the hoopoe: the absence of any description makes this recollection from childhood the more convincing. The last three sentences are natural enough, even though there are echoes of Rousseau. Filling his pockets with the pears he could not eat must be true. And the present for the younger children is a proof that he has left infancy behind him.

The passage is a delightfully fresh piece of writing, unselfconsciously naïve, as remote from the ironic wit of Montesquieu and Voltaire as it is from the turgid moralising and sanctimonious *bienfaisance* in which the century, and Restif himself, so often indulged. Closer to the soil than the rustic novels of George Sand, it carries the reader into a world where ancient traditions had not yet become fossilized into folklore. Though it lacks the intense poetic sensuousness of Restif's fellow-Burgundian Colette,[7] it does convey the wonder and delight of a real child discovering nature and his own emotions.

The simultaneous presence of wild boar, hare, roebuck, wolf, and then the hoopoe, suggests literary arrangement rather than a single event; but it is not impossibly miraculous. There is nothing whatever wrong about the hoopoe. It is seen north of the Mediterranean provinces, but only rarely. Its appearance is so striking that a child could not fail to remember it:

When it is seen, however, it is easily recognised by its lovely cinnamon-pink plumage, which is barred across the wings, lower back and tail, with black and white. It has a large, deep pink Cockatoo-like crest, also barred with black, which can be raised and lowered at will, and a long, thin, slightly curved bill.

As it migrates to Africa in September or October, its sudden arrival near Sacy a week after Michaelmas day is plausible. The noise made by Nicolas and his dogs would not have frightened it: 'It is very unsuspecting and tame to human beings.'[8]

P. de Saint Jacob's study of the North Burgundian peasants, based on first-hand material but not the novels of Restif, confirms some details in the passage. The wolf, 'cet ennemi public', still was a menace: a bounty was paid on each wolf's head handed in. Shepherds and their dogs did deal with them. Wild boar did ravage the fields, and domestic swine also sometimes: these last 'tiennent encore du sanglier'. So the mating of sow and wild boar may well have happened. Shepherds, like Jacquot, did talk of spirits: 'En communion intime avec la nature, ils savent beaucoup de choses, et se disent volontiers sorciers'. After 29 August (the Beheading of St John the Baptist), restrictions on grazing rights were largely lifted. And after harvest, wild fruit was gathered: 'Quand la chose est permise, les pauvres gens, les enfants, vont ramasser les poires et pommes sauvages, les prunelles au long des haies. On maraude aussi, près des arbres des vignes.'[9]

The peasant word *échavie* (Old French *eschevis*, *eschervis*, Modern French *chervis*) also takes the reader straight into the country. One would look in vain for such touches in Marivaux or Laclos. But the distinction made between the narrator and the peasants reminds us not only that Nicolas is the son of a prosperous farmer, not a farm labourer, but that Restif himself had long since abandoned the fields for Paris. Edmond, the *Paysan perverti*, might feel nostalgia for the farm, but he was determined not to live there:

> J'ai résolu de me fixer à Paris: depuis que j'ai goûté de ce délicieux séjour de la liberté, la province me paraît insupportable.[10]

For all its authentic detail and closeness to nature, our passage is another literary pastoral, not a reproduction of actual reality.

Life for Burgundian peasants in 1745 did not consist of idyllic rapture and *poires de miel*. In 1738, the road corvée was introduced, making peasants liable to twenty days of compulsory unpaid road-work a year, up to a distance of two and a half leagues from their village. With France at war from 1740 to 1748, a lot of road-work was required. Saint-Lambert describes how disastrous it was when the *corvée* was imposed during a fine spell at harvest time. The winter of 1740-1 had caused another of the periodic famines; the price of grain rose; poor day-labourers were 'hors d'état de vivre'. Between 1740 and 1744 disease was rife among cattle and horses: in 1743 the number of cattle declined by 50 per cent.[11] There may be an echo of this in the fact that Nicolas's flock contained goats, sheep and pigs: the number of sheep rose as a consequence of the loss of cattle. Otherwise, there is no indication at all in the passage of any rural distress. This of course is perfectly natural: one would not expect a boy of ten to realise the economic situation. But the year 1784, when Restif says he wrote the passage, was also one of misery for Burgundian peasants: cattle-plague from 1782 onwards, the *corvée*, then the winter of 1784-5, one of the harshest since 1709. Saint Jacob describes the villagers of Lucy-sur-Cure, in the Auxerrois:

> Les habitants disent qu'ils ont été obligés 'pour pouvoir subsister de prendre pour toute nourriture de l'herbe cuite à l'eau sans sel; cette ressource leur ayant manqué l'année, la plupart d'entre eux avaient été forcés d'y substituer des chardons, qu'il était résulté de tant de maux et de misères une maladie épidémique'. Le curé confirme les déclarations des habitants.[12]

And in 1796, when Restif printed the book, it could still not be said that the new, non-feudal landowners had made life conspicuously easier for the peasantry.

What Restif gives us in *Monsieur Nicolas* and in *La Vie de mon père* is not reality, but an idealised, sentimentalised account of life in the household of a *laboureur*: that is, a yeoman who owned his own horses, oxen, and farm equipment, and either owned or rented (or both) enough land to keep his family. Though the small or unsuccessful *laboureur* might suffer the same ills as the peasant, the *gros laboureur*, the *coq de village*, rich enough to benefit from the new techniques and the agricultural expansion, was often hand in glove with the large landowners, and himself an encloser of commons and exploiter of the impoverished peasantry.[13] Edmond Restif, in *La Vie de mon père*, is notary for the village, judge for the local seigneur, the father of the vicar and of the curate in a neighbouring parish, a friend and confidant of the saintly M. de Caylus, bishop of Auxerre. The book makes it clear that he is no landless labourer. When soldiers have commandeered his horses, the officer apologises: 'Nous vous avons pris pour un simple paysan.'[14] Edmond is proud to be a husbandman; he quotes what his own father told him:

L'art le plus digne de l'homme, c'est l'agriculture: tous les autres sont appuyés sur lui; les richesses ne sont richesses qu'autant qu'il les réalise: restons à la source; elle est plus pure que le ruisseau. Il est noble d'exercer l'art duquel dépendent tous les autres.[15]

He is equally proud of what he considers to be his middle-class status:

Le roturier est l'homme par excellence: c'est lui qui paie les impôts; qui travaille, ensemence, récolte, commerce . . .; la classe du milieu, la classe précieuse, si chérie des bons rois, voilà celle où je désire de vivre et de mourir.[16]

He has improved his lands by his skill and enterprise; he has added to them by purchase; he travels to Paris to find the best market for his wines. If he does not make a fortune, it is only because he deliberately chooses to practise Christian charity instead.[17]

Up to a point, the portrait is convincing. Restif's father may well have been, in fact, almost as virtuous and high-minded as Restif portrays him. After all, Restif himself, in a very different way, was a most unusual type of man too. Often, the emotional scenes in the book ring true. Occasionally – as, for example, in the description of Anne-Simon Restif's death – Restif approaches a genuine pathos which allows us to understand why the eighteenth century so enjoyed emotionalism. But all too frequently he luxuriates in religious and moral mawkishness.[18] Poverty, starvation, distress are mentioned – but only in order to show how the capable and virtuous Edmond, the saintly, charitable clergy, even the local tax-collector, bring relief and prosperity to the sufferers. Edmond is the heaven-sent saviour of his people:

'Mon cher Edmond! je vois par ce qui t'arrive, que c'est Dieu lui-même qui inspire les pères, lorsqu'ils commandent à leurs enfants. . . . Quel avantage pour ce pays, que ton digne père, inspiré de Dieu, t'ait rappelé dans ta patrie, pour y exercer ces précieux talents, d'où dépend le bien-être de toute une grande paroisse! . . . Ton grand-père, mon honorable oncle, s'appelait l'*Homme juste*; tu le fais revivre, et l'épithète qui sort de la bouche d'un chacun dès qu'on t'a nommé, c'est l'*Honnête homme*! Ah! mon ami, mon cher cousin! le beau titre, si volontairement et si librement donné par tout un pays, à un homme qui ne compte pas encore trente-six ans! Béni sois-tu, Edmond! Béni soit le père qui t'a rappelé parmi nous, et Dieu l'en récompense! Bénie soit la mère qui t'a nourri et qui t'a élevé dans l'amour du travail et du devoir, en te donnant son cher et précieux exemple!'

J'ai rapporté ici cette tendre effusion d'un cœur vertueux, pour couronner dignement cet article des travaux rustiques de mon père. Mais la récompense la plus flatteuse pour lui et la plus digne de son

cœur, ç'a été de laisser en mourant la paroisse florissante et les habitants
en général, qu'il avait trouvés mendiant leur pain, les plus à leur aise
de tous les environs.[19]

This quasi-canonisation by Restif of his father makes it plain that *La Vie
de mon père* is not intended as a typical picture of village life generally.
And the stylistic flaws in the book are evidence of a certain basic falseness. Much of the detail does seem authentic. Some of the characters
have the stamp of life. The relative prosperity and progress of French
agriculture between 1730 and 1770 did benefit *gros laboureurs* such as
Edmond.[20] Nevertheless, as a general assessment of peasant life in the
eighteenth century, *La Vie de mon père* is patently unreliable.

Saint Jacob gives a very different account of rural Burgundy on the
eve of the Revolution:

> En dehors de l'échec d'une réforme fiscale rejetée par les privilégiés,
> le malaise rural de 1789 semble ainsi sorti d'une triple origine:
> offensive capitaliste qui a largement détruit le vieil organisme terrien
> où le paysan sans argent pouvait vivre malgré tout, grâce au bail en
> nature, aux biens et aux droits collectifs; redoutable décimation du
> troupeau, qui emporte les dernières ressources; récession économique
> qui montre toute la fragilité du *boom* physiocratique et rend méchants
> les marchands fermiers, la petite bourgeoisie rurale, désespérés du
> faible profit que leur créent la baisse des grains et la mévente. . . . Sous
> ces multiples causes, un prolétariat a grandi au village. Sans argent,
> sans bétail, sans terres rentables, diminué dans son pouvoir d'achat
> qui a faibli de 80% en un demi-siècle, il cherche ses adversaires.[21]

Obviously, the hoopoes and fairy deer that Restif wrote about in our
passage from *Monsieur Nicolas* have little to do with life in the 1780s.
A truer picture is given by the townsman André Chénier, who wrote
literary pastorals and bucolics:

> France, ô belle contrée, ô terre généreuse,
> Que les dieux complaisants formaient pour être heureuse,
>
> .   .   .
>
> J'ai vu dans tes hameaux la plaintive misère,
> La mendicité blême et la douleur amère.
> Je t'ai vu dans tes biens, indigent laboureur,
> D'un fisc avare et dur maudissant la rigueur,
> Versant aux pieds des grands des larmes inutiles,
> Tout trempé de sueurs pour toi-même infertiles,
> Découragé de vivre, et plein d'un juste effroi
> De mettre au jour des fils malheureux comme toi;
> Tu vois sous les soldats les villes gémissantes;
> Corvées, impôts rongeurs, tributs, taxes pesantes,

Le sel, fils de la terre, ou même l'eau des mers,
Source d'oppressions et de fléaux divers.

.   .   .

O sainte égalité! dissipe nos ténèbres,
Renverse les verrous, les bastilles funèbres.

('Hymne à la Justice', 1787)

Any account of eighteenth-century French peasants must include
the farmer's wife whom Arthur Young met on the road from Châlons-
sur-Marne to Metz on 12 July 1789, two days before the storming of
the Bastille:

> I was joined by a poor woman who complained of the times, and that it
> was a sad country; demanding her reasons, she said her husband had
> but a morsel of land, one cow, and a poor little horse, yet they had a
> *franchar* (42 lb.) of wheat, and three chickens, to pay as a quit-rent to
> one Seigneur; and four *franchar* of oats, one chicken and 1 sou to
> pay to another, besides very heavy tailles and other taxes . . . It was
> said, at present, that 'something was to be done by some great folks
> for such poor ones, but she did not know who nor how, but God send
> us better, *car les tailles et les droits* [feudal dues] *nous écrasent*'. This
> woman, at no great distance, might have been taken for sixty or seventy,
> her figure was so bent, and her face so furrowed and hardened by
> labour, but she said she was only twenty-eight.[22]

NOTES

1 Nicolas Edme Restif, or Rétif (1734–1806) took the name 'de la Bretonne'
  from La Bretonne, the farm at Sacy, near Auxerre, in Burgundy, where he
  was brought up. His father was Edme or Edmond Restif (1692–1764). Edme
  is the shortened form of Edmond: St Edmund of Abingdon died in Burgundy
  in 1240, and his body was enshrined above the high altar in the abbey church
  at Pontigny, where it still is today. Pontigny is about 20 miles North of
  Sacy.
    I have referred to the author as Restif or Restif de la Bretonne. By
  Nicolas I mean the hero of the book *Monsieur Nicolas*, which purports to be
  autobiographical. I refer once to 'Edmond, the hero of *Le Paysan perverti*',
  and once to 'Edmond, the *Paysan perverti*': this is a fictional character in
  the work *Le Paysan perverti*, who none the less possesses some things in
  common with Restif. By Edmond Restif, Edmond, and Restif's father, I
  mean the character in *La Vie de mon père*, which according to Restif
  is a true biography.
2 *L'Œuvre de Restif de la Bretonne*, ed. H. Bachelin (Paris, 1931), vol. VI,
  p. 11.
3 *Monsieur Nicolas*, 1883, Paris edition, pp. 129–34. (The Bachelin edition of
  Monsieur Nicolas is an abridged text.)

4 Lanson, *Histoire de la littérature française*, 12th edition, p. 679, gives him four lines and a footnote: 'Je ne le nommerais pas sans le réalisme intime et sérieux de quelques parties de *Monsieur Nicolas*'.

5 Ed. Bachelin, p. 27.

6 *Les Saisons* (ed. Paris, 1823), p. 137.

7 Saint-Sauveur-en-Puisaye, which Colette describes in *La Maison de Claudine* and in *Sido*, is about 28 miles from Restif's village of Sacy.

8 S. Durango, *Les Oiseaux* (Paris, s.d.), pp. 53, 160; S. Vere Benson, *The Observer's Book of British Birds* (London, n.d.), p. 109.

9 P. de Saint Jacob, *Les Paysans de la Bourgogne du Nord au dernier siècle de l'ancien régime* (Paris, 1960), pp. 273–82.

10 Ed. H. Bachelin, vol. VI, p. 173.

11 Saint Jacob, op. cit., pp. 295–9.

12 Ibid., p. 479. The tax on salt (*la gabelle*) was harshly enforced. Cf. 'Hymne à la Justice', below.

13 A. Davies, *The Origins of the French peasant revolution of 1789*, *History*, vol. XLIX (1964), pp. 29–40; Saint Jacob, op. cit., pp. 516–29; M. Bloch, *Les Caractères originaux de l'histoire rurale française* (Paris, 1952), pp. 194–9.

14 *La Vie de mon père* (Librairie Hachette, 1963), p. 103.

15 Ibid., p. 83.

16 Ibid., p. 80.

17 E.g. ibid., p. 108: when he bought a piece of land, 's'apercevant déjà que les terres augmentaient peu à peu de valeur, il ajoutait au prix, ce que l'héritage aurait valu de plus dans dix ans. Ensuite, si c'était un pauvre homme, il lui faisait présent quelques jours après la vente, de deux ou trois boisseaux de grain pour lui et pour ses bestiaux. Aussi, tout ce qui se trouvait à vendre lui était-il offert, avant qu'on pensât à d'autres.' Restif does not say how much land his father monopolized by this method, or how accurate his forecasts were of the rise in land values.

18 The descriptions of the household prayers at 5 a.m., and the evening prayers and Bible reading ('il commençait par la Genèse et lisait avec onction trois ou quatre chapitres' – ibid., p. 151 and pp. 53, 215) could come straight from a pietistic English Victorian family magazine. The Restif family had been Protestant in the sixteenth century, and were now Jansenist Puritans. Greuze's picture of a paterfamilias reading from the Bible was exhibited in the 1750s.

19 Ibid., p. 99. Restif also compares his father to the heroes of the ancient Roman Republic (p. 113).

20 See R. Mandrou, *La France au XVIIᵉ et XVIIIᵉ siècles* (Paris, 1967), pp. 124–32 ('L'Essor du XVIIIᵉ siècle: 1730–70, l'amorce d'une transformation structurelle').

21 Op. cit., pp. 571–2. Cf. A. Davies, op. cit.; G. Walter, *Histoire des paysans en France* (Paris, 1963), pp. 313–45.

22 *Travels in France* (London, 1909), pp. 197–8.

XVIII · André Chénier
(1762–1794)

Versailles (written 1793)

O Versaille, ô bois, ô portiques,
Marbres vivants, berceaux antiques,
Par les Dieux et les rois Elysée embelli,
A ton aspect, dans ma pensée,
Comme sur l'herbe aride une fraîche rosée,
Coule un peu de calme et d'oubli.

Paris me semble un autre empire,
Dès que chez toi je vois sourire
Mes pénates secrets couronnés de rameaux;
D'où souvent les monts et les plaines
Vont dirigeant mes pas aux campagnes prochaines,
Sous de triples cintres d'ormeaux.

Les chars, les royales merveilles,
Des gardes les nocturnes veilles,
Tout a fui; des grandeurs tu n'es plus le séjour.
Mais le sommeil, la solitude,
Dieux jadis inconnus, et les arts, et l'étude
Composent aujourd'hui ta cour.

Ah! malheureux! à ma jeunesse
Une oisive et morne paresse
Ne laisse plus goûter les studieux loisirs.
Mon âme, d'ennui consumée,
S'endort dans les langueurs. Louange et renommée
N'inquiètent plus mes désirs.

L'abandon, l'obscurité, l'ombre,
Une paix taciturne et sombre,
Voilà tous mes souhaits. Cache mes tristes jours,
Et nourris, s'il faut que je vive,
De mon pâle flambeau la clarté fugitive,
Aux douces chimères d'amours.

P

L'âme n'est point encor flétrie,
La vie encor n'est point tarie,
Quand un regard nous trouble et le cœur et la voix.
Qui cherche les pas d'une belle,
Qui peut ou s'égayer ou gémir auprès d'elle,
De ses jours peut porter le poids.

J'aime; je vis. Heureux rivage!
Tu conserves sa noble image,
Son nom, qu'à tes forêts j'ose apprendre le soir;
Quand, l'âme doucement émue,
J'y reviens méditer l'instant où je l'ai vue,
Et l'instant où je dois la voir.

Pour elle seule encore abonde
Cette source, jadis féconde,
Qui coulait de ma bouche en sons harmonieux.
Sur mes lèvres tes bosquets sombres
Forment pour elle encor ces poétiques nombres,
Langage d'amour et des Dieux.

Ah! témoin des succès du crime,
Si l'homme juste et magnanime
Pouvait ouvrir son cœur à la félicité,
Versailles, tes routes fleuries,
Ton silence, fertile en belles rêveries,
N'aurait que joie et volupté.

Mais souvent tes vallons tranquilles,
Tes sommets verts, tes frais asiles,
Tout à coup à mes yeux s'enveloppent de deuil.
J'y vois errer l'ombre livide
D'un peuple d'innocents, qu'un tribunal perfide
Précipite dans le cercueil.

Œuvres complètes, ed. G. Walter. Bibliothèque de la
Pléiade (Paris, 1950), pp. 183–5.

In the fragment 'O mon fils, mon Hermès, ma plus belle espérance',
Chénier imagines a future age when French is a dead language, and his
poem *Hermès* is being read by some scholar:

alors peut-être un sage,
Près d'une lampe assis, dans l'étude plongé,
Te retrouvant poudreux, obscur, demi-rongé,
Voudra creuser le sens de tes lignes pensantes.[1]

Let us consider what the *Ode à Versailles* might convey to such a
reader, sufficiently versed in French to know what *portiques* and

berceaux mean here,[2] but ignorant of French history and Chénier's biography. The poem describes the desolation of some royal abode, forsaken by its Gods and by its court, but whose trees and forests console the young poet who has sought *calme et oubli* in a secluded house overlooking the avenues of elms and the countryside, where he walks. Some sort of school (an art school?) seems to be installed in the palace.[3] The poet himself has renounced study and the desire for fame. Apathetic and dejected, his sole intent (but this a strong one, expressed in four nouns, two adjectives and one verb – stanza 5) is to lie low, miserably, and, if fate wills, survive. Life is bearable to him there, even in his sick and dejected state, because he visits a beautiful woman. The fugitive is also a lover (not more than *doucement ému*, it is true); the woods of Versailles are an extension of his beloved's presence. She has restored to him his poetic fertility: it is in the shady groves, where he meditates upon her, that his lines take shape. Set among the arbours are Gods, marble statues which adorn this Elysium. Though 'Tout a fui', to the poet these Gods are still alive; his verse is in their language, the language of Versailles before it was forsaken; his lines are not mere harmonies of gloom and solitude, the private outpourings of a timid lover. If life and love were all that mattered, he could be happy amid the tranquil beauty of Versailles. But he cannot surrender himself to joy when some public evil is predominant. Versailles is connected in his mind with some monstrous injustice, some slaughter of innocents. He is on the side of the victims. When he thinks of this horror, his self-pitying langour and his amorous delight are of no consequence. The marble statues of Gods lose their power. The poet does not appear to believe in any other religion. All that remains to him is the consciousness that, though evil triumphs, he is *juste et magnanime*.

To sense the greatness of this poem, and to realise how its shape and significance are determined by the interplay between the poet's own emotions and some social cataclysm that engulfs them, it is not necessary to know why he was a despondent fugitive, what the *royales merveilles* were, why they had ceased to exist, which Gods the statues represented, who the Criminals were, or how iniquitous the Perfidious Tribunal was. It is even less important to inquire into the identity of the lady, and the nature of their embraces, if any. The poem might well have a greater impact, and so be closer to life, if it were not explained in terms of its original historical context, but left unlocalised, and applicable to all just men hiding from bloody tyrannies. If any reader is deaf to the *sons harmonieux* and *nombres poétiques* which the poet claims to employ, it is unlikely that historical exegesis could make him receptive to Chénier's rhythm and music.

For the twentieth-century reader, however, Versailles cannot be merely an indeterminate poetic symbol: it implies certain things in history, and our judgment on them. Curiosity impels us to discover what period at Versailles the poem refers to, and then – whether or not some aesthetic theory condemns such questions as idle and impure – to consider how far our appreciation of the poem is affected by Chénier's attitude to the historical events.

From 1794 to 1918 to write about Versailles was, in part, to 'tell sad stories of the death of kings'. Proust intones its sentimental connotation for the 1890s:

> Je ne voudrais pas vous prononcer ici après tant d'autres, Versailles, grand nom rouillé et doux, royal cimetière de feuillages, de vastes eaux et de marbres, lieu vraiment aristocratique et démoralisant . . .[4]

Among the 'tant d'autres' Proust presumably included Delille:

> O Versaille! ô regrets! ô bosquets ravissants,
> Chef-d'œuvre d'un grand roi, de Le Nôtre, et des ans!
> La hache est à vos pieds, et votre heure est venue.
> Ces arbres, dont l'orgueil s'élançait dans la nue,
> Frappés dans leur racine, et balançant dans l'air,
> Leurs superbes sommets ébranlés par le fer,
> Tombent, et de leurs troncs jonchent au loin ces routes
> Sur qui leurs bras pompeux s'arrondissaient en voûtes:
> Ils sont détruits ces bois, dont le front glorieux
> Ombrageait de Louis le front victorieux,
> Ces bois où, célébrant de plus douces conquêtes,
> Les arts voluptueux multipliaient les fêtes.[5]

The incantatory charm of these lines evokes the passing of a civilisation, the fleetingness of human existence. But they come from the 1782 edition of *Les Jardins*. This threnody was not occasioned by some act of revolutionary vandalism; merely by a routine tree-felling operation under the monarchy. The passage expresses none of the horror and despair present in Chénier's Ode, which in some ways closely resembles it. Delille may well be intimating that, like felled trees, the whole society which Versailles symbolises is due for replacement. But the tone of the passage is one of elegiac resignation: no convulsions have yet disrupted the old order, and its laureate, Delille, remains a dispassionate spectator of its placid decay.

Chénier, on the other hand, was ill at ease under the Ancien Régime. The unhappiness from which he suffered had social as well as physical and sentimental causes.[6] In spite of rich, aristocratic friends who welcomed him into their pleasant society, and the title of Chevalier de Saint-André which he bestowed upon himself, he lacked birth and money. Like Figaro,[7] the most he could become at the London embassy was a hired employee of the aristocrat ambassador. The abbé Delille did very well out of the corruption and injustice of the 1780s: his safe, alluring verses brought him fame, money, comfort, and a mistress-housekeeper to beguile his mercenary celibacy. For Chénier, a professional literary career was unacceptable in a society which, he asserts, wanted its writers to 'revêtir d'expressions éblouissantes et recherchées des pensées fausses ou frivoles, ou point de pensées du tout': letters could not be, as they were in the Ancient Republics, *augustes*, *sacrées*, *citoyennes*.[8] The despair and the vituperation which are so marked a feature of his counter-revolutionary poems are already present in the poems written before the Revolution. 'Aujourd'hui qu'au tombeau je suis prêt à descendre' (1783?), and 'O nécessité dure! ô pesant esclavage!' (1788 or 1789) both toy with the idea of death. Already by 1782, in the 'Épître à Le Brun et à Brazais', he declaims about the grandeur of ancient republican poets who defied oppressors:

> Vous tous dignes enfants de la patrie antique,
> Je vous vois tous amis, entourés de bourreaux,
> Braver du scélérat les indignes faisceaux,
> Du lâche délateur l'impudente richesse,
> Et du vil affranchi l'orgueilleuse bassesse.
> Je vous vois, au milieu des crimes, des noirceurs,
> Garder une patrie et des lois et des mœurs.[9]

The 'Hymne à la Justice' of 1787 denounces the same evils in the France of Louis XVI: brigands athirst for blood, executioners, oppressors, vile delators, pitiless nobles,

> Et les crimes puissants qui font trembler les lois.

In disgust, he contemplates emigrating to the United States:

> Non, je ne veux plus vivre en ce séjour servile;
> J'irai, j'irai bien loin me chercher un asile
>
> .   .   .
>
> Où, loin des ravisseurs, la main cultivatrice
> Recueillera les dons d'une terre propice;
> Où mon cœur, respirant sous un ciel étranger,
> Ne verra plus de maux qu'il ne peut soulager.[10]

P2

By 1791 everything politically necessary to sweep away such ills had, in his opinion, been done. Feudal privileges were abolished, a constitutional monarchy instituted, all citizens enjoyed the same civil rights, and those with the requisite property qualifications could take part in elections. A public career was now open to Chénier, as literary spokesman for the Feuillants – the conservative-liberal monarchists who, in December 1791, were the largest group in the Legislative Assembly. His devotion to liberty and the new constitution was sincere and profound. So was his detestation of demagogues, popular violence and threats to middle-class interests:

> Mais au peuple surtout sauvez l'abus amer
> De sa subite indépendance.
> Contenez dans son lit cette orageuse mer.
> Par vous seuls dépouillé de ses liens de fer,
> Dirigez sa bouillante enfance.
> Vous les lois, le devoir, et l'ordre, et l'équité
> Guidez, hélas! sa jeune liberté.
> Gardez que nul remords n'en attriste la fête.[11]

In February 1792 he published an article calling for the extermination of Jacobinism. Everyone except scoundrels and imbeciles was aware, he wrote,

> que ces clubs sont et seront funestes à la liberté; qu'ils anéantiront la constitution; que la horde énergumène de Coblentz [i.e. the émigrés threatening to invade France] n'a pas de plus sûrs auxiliaires; que leur destruction est le seul remède aux maux de la France; et que le jour de leur mort sera un jour de fête et d'allégresse publique. Ils crient partout que la patrie est en danger; cela est malheureusement bien vrai; et cela sera vrai tant qu'ils existeront.[12]

By the end of July, he realised that the 'moderate' party for which he fought had been defeated. Disillusioned and embittered, he challenged the Girondins to kill him:

> Parmi les auteurs de suppléments, il en est sans doute plusieurs, mais au moins un, dont les méchants, heureux, n'intimideront jamais ni le cœur ni la bouche; qui, dans les cachots et sous le fer des bourreaux, ne cesserait pas d'en appeler aux lois, aux autorités légitimes, à la justice, à l'humanité, et à dévouer à l'exécration publique les tyrans déguisés sous le nom de patriotes; qui est prêt à mourir pour cette doctrine impudemment traitée de parricide; et qui mourra content de n'avoir plus sous les yeux l'avilissement d'une grande nation, réduite par ses fautes à choisir entre Coblentz et les jacobins, entre les Autrichiens et Brissot.[13]

In August 1792 the King was deposed; between 2 and 9 September approximately fourteen hundred prisoners were massacred in Paris; on 21 September a republic was proclaimed. Louis was executed on 21 January 1793. Shortly after, Chénier withdrew to a house in the rue de Satory at Versailles, and wrote the Ode in the autumn of that year. Versailles provided him with a refuge from the 'autre empire' – the revolutionary rulers in Paris, whom he had wished to exterminate. It also allowed him to escape into dreams of the pre-revolutionary era when, in spite of 'les crimes puissants qui font trembler les lois', peace and beauty were still to be found. The form of his poem reflects the seventeenth-century classicism which Versailles typifies. The statues of the Gods recall his own self-identification with Greece: in the 'Ode à Versailles' he is still a disciple of the Ancients.[14] But his walks through the Versailles woods, and the situation of his 'pénates rustiques', are constant reminders that he is in peril of his life.

The *belle* in stanza 6 was Mme Françoise Lecoulteux, who had withdrawn from Paris to her château at Voisins, three miles north of Versailles. Her husband and her father were arrested in August 1793, and imprisoned in December. Lecoulteux & Cie, one of the three largest Paris banking houses, had been involved during the autumn of 1792 in the Spanish ambassador's attempt to bribe Danton and smuggle Louis XVI to England. Chénier himself was almost certainly implicated in this conspiracy.[15] Thus, the idyll with Fanny had poignant political undertones.

The sinister note in the final stanza is no poetic fiction. In 1791 the Constituent Assembly had set up a High Court in Orléans to deal with political cases. On 2 September 1792, fifty-three royalists awaiting trial by this Court (they included two bishops, a commander of the King's Guard and an ex-Minister for War) were removed, on orders from Paris, by a revolutionary agitator known as Fourier l'Américain, a former rum distiller from San Domingo. On 9 September the convoy of carts, military escort and six field-guns arrived at Versailles, where there were between five and six thousand young Army volunteers awaiting posting to the front. The mayor of Versailles implored Fourier to avoid the town centre, or to use the escort to protect the prisoners. Fourier did not comply. Only nine prisoners, in the carts at the rear of the column, escaped with their lives. Some forty-four were put to the sword. The butchery took place by the junction of the rue de l'Orangerie and the rue de Satory. The mayor fainted at the sight. There followed the usual scene of heads on pikes: methods of execution under the Most Christian Kings had accustomed the public to the dismembering of corpses.

> La scène se passait à quelques pas de l'endroit où, trois ans auparavant, l'Assemblée constituante avait inauguré ses travaux, au milieu d'un beau rêve de fraternité. Les canons placés en tête du convoi étaient arrêtés au pied des cent marches de l'escalier qui monte au château, entre le miroir paisible où la pièce d'eau des Suisses reflète les arbres de Satory et les rectangles, bien disciplinés, de l'Orangerie. Le majestueux décor combiné par Louis XIV pour l'apothéose de la monarchie servait de décor à l'égorgement de ses derniers défenseurs.[16]

These were the *ombres livides* which haunted Chénier in his little house with an orchard at number 69 rue de Satory (later rue du Maréchal Joffre), a few hundred yards from the junction with the rue de l'Orangerie.

As the comte Joseph de Maistre and the vicomte de Chateaubriand show in our next chapter, there are circumstances which explain, even though they do not excuse, the atrocities committed by the revolutionary terrorists. No such considerations influence Chénier. The 'Ode à Versailles' is the work of a virulent anti-Jacobin, not of a historian. It is also the work of a brave man who would not submit. He had already attacked in the press those whom he regarded as betrayers of liberty. It was not possible for him to publish the testimony which he wrote during the last year of his life:

> Et un nommé A.C. fut un des cinq ou six que ni la frénésie générale, ni l'avidité, ni la crainte, ne purent engager à ployer le genou devant des assassins couronnés, à toucher des mains mouillées de meurtres, et à s'asseoir à la table où l'on boit le sang des hommes.[17]

Chénier remains an exemplar of writers who resist.

For Chénier, a poem contained 'thoughts'; it had a 'subject'; it was 'about' something. He intended that posterity should understand what he said, and, in the case of his political poems, share his feelings. Thus, in a fragment of vituperation against those revolutionaries who watched executions for pleasure, he writes:

> Pour moi, j'ai voulu que leur noble mémoire
> Allât faire vomir un jour
> L'érudit qui lira cet hymne de leur gloire,
> Monument d'estime et d'amour.[18]

In trying to see what the 'Ode à Versailles' meant in the terms of its historical context, we are, therefore, doing what Chénier hoped that his readers in future centuries would do. What may at first sight seem cold, formalistic, pseudo-romantic rhetoric, is shown to be an intensely dramatic expression of personal emotion. Mawkish touches like 'gémir auprès d'elle' become less unacceptable. The conventional line:

Son nom, qu'à tes forêts j'ose apprendre le soir

reveals its full resonance. It is borrowed from Virgil's First Eclogue:

Nos patriae fines et dulcia linquimus arva.
Nos patriam fugimus: tu, Tityre, lentus in umbra
Formosam resonare doces Amaryllida silvas.[19]

For Chénier, who in 1787 had contemplated going to America, it was now too late to flee the shores of his *douce patrie*: captured émigrés were now guillotined as traitors. And *in umbra* but not *lentus*, in the shadow but not at ease, he had good reason to translate 'resonare doces' by 'j'ose apprendre le soir'.

Chénier was picked up by the police on 7 March 1794. He was guillotined in July.

NOTES

1 Chénier, *Poems*, Selected and edited by F. Scarfe (Oxford, 1961), p. 96.
2 Portique: 'espace long ou circulaire, dont la couverture est soutenue par des colonnes. On fait des portiques de treillage pour la décoration des jardins' (Littré). Berceau: 'treillage en voûte'.
3 On 10 June 1793, the Convention decreed that furnishings, etc., in the *repaire de la tyrannie* should be sold by auction. The sale began on 25 August 1793, and lasted for a year. A school was established in part of the buildings. A. Decaux, *La Belle Histoire de Versailles* (Paris, 1962), p. 258.
4 Proust, *Les Plaisirs et les Jours*, 1896 (Gallimard ed., Paris, 1924, p. 176).
5 *Les Jardins* (Paris, Reims, MDCCLXXXII), Chant II, p. 36. Delille makes a little joke about how naked the Gods feel, now that the trees which shrouded them have gone:

Ces dieux, dont le ciseau peupla ces verts portiques,
D'un voile de verdure autrefois habillés,
Tout honteux aujourd'hui de se voir dépouillés,
Pleurent leur doux ombrage; et, redoutant la vue,
Vénus même une fois s'étonna d'être nue.

Proust, op. cit., p. 173, plays with the same idea: 'Les statues qui sur nos places publiques effrayent comme des folles, rêvent ici dans les charmilles comme des sages sous la verdure lumineuse qui protège leur blancheur.' To Chénier, the Gods were not a subject for detached *badinage*, but an expression of the Greek culture from which he claimed descent.
6 Chénier, *Œuvres complètes*, Pléiade, ed. G. Walter (Paris, 1950), p. 624: 'Choqué de voir les lettres si prosternées et le genre humain ne pas songer à relever sa tête, je me livrai souvent aux distractions et aux égarements d'une

jeunesse forte et fougueuse; mais toujours dominé par l'amour de la poésie, des lettres et de l'étude, souvent chagrin et découragé par la fortune ou par moi-même, toujours soutenu par mes amis . . . '. He would have liked a safe private income:

> Heureux qui, se livrant aux sages disciplines,
> Nourri du lait sacré des antiques doctrines,
> Ainsi que de talents a jadis hérité
> D'un bien modique et sûr qui fait la liberté.

(Scarfe, ed. cit., p. 53.)

7 Beaumarchais, *Le Mariage de Figaro*, Act. III, sc. v; Act V, sc. iii.
8 Walter, ed. cit., pp. 622–3.
9 Ibid., pp. 144–5.
10 Scarfe, ed. cit., pp. 82–3.
11 'Le Jeu de Paume', Scarfe, ed. cit., p. 85. Cf. (Walter, ed. cit., p. 581) his definition of a sansculotte:

> C'est celui
> Qui n'a rien; mais qui veut avoir le bien d'autrui.

On the Feuillants, see A. Goodwin, *The French Revolution* (London, 1953), pp. 106–14, 123, 138.

12 *Journal de Paris*, No. 57, Dimanche, 26 Février 1792, Supplément, No. 19, p. 4; Walter, ed. cit., p. 279. The *Journal de Paris* charged a fee for publishing articles in its Supplements. It is assumed, though not proved, that Chénier's articles were paid for by members of the Feuillant party. (See Scarfe, *A. Chénier. His Life and Work* (Oxford, 1965), pp. 246–7.)
13 Walter, ed. cit., p. 357. J.-P. Brissot (1754–93) was a Girondin leader.
14 The poem contains reminiscences of the Greek Anthology and of Virgil.
15 Scarfe, *Life*, pp. 282–6; 315. On Lecoulteux et Cie, see H. Lüthy, *La Banque protestante en France*, vol. 2 (Paris, 1961), p. 142. The Lecoulteux were a Rouen Catholic family.
16 E. Seligman, *La Justice en France pendant la Révolution*, 2ᵉ édition (Paris, 1913), vol. 2, p. 274. See also H. Caron, *Les Massacres de Septembre* (Paris, 1935), pp. 382–6.
17 Walter, ed. cit., p. 581.
18 'Iambes, La Guillotine.' Scarfe, ed. cit., pp. 100–1.
19 Virgil, *Bucolics*, Eclogue I, lines 3–5. The émigré wit Rivarol made a macabre parody of line 3: 'Nos patriae funes et lampada linquimus alta' ('Lov'd frontier posts once sadden'd exiles' plight, Now hangman's lamp-posts urge our fearful flight.' – tr. E.G.M.)

XIX · Chateaubriand (1768–1848)

FROM the *Essai historique, politique et moral, sur les révolutions anciennes et modernes, considérées dans leurs rapports avec la Révolution française.* Dédié à tous les partis (published 1797)

Attaquée par l'Europe entière, déchirée par des guerres civiles, agitée de mille factions, ses places frontières ou prises ou assiégées, sans soldats, sans finances, hors un papier discrédité qui tombait de jour en jour, le découragement dans tous les états, et la famine presque assurée : telle était la France, tel le tableau qu'elle présentait à l'instant même qu'on méditait de la livrer à une révolution générale. Il fallait remédier à cette complication de maux ; il fallait établir à la fois par un miracle la république de Lycurgue chez un vieux peuple nourri sous une monarchie, immense dans sa population et corrompu dans ses mœurs, et sauver un grand pays sans armées, amolli dans la paix et expirant dans les convulsions politiques, de l'invasion de cinq cent mille hommes des meilleures troupes de l'Europe.

Ces forcenés seuls pouvaient en imaginer les moyens, et, ce qui est encore plus incroyable, parvenir en partie à les exécuter : moyens exécrables sans doute, mais, il faut l'avouer, d'une conception gigantesque. Ces esprits raréfiés au feu de l'enthousiasme républicain et, pour ainsi dire, réduits par leurs scrutins épuratoires* à la quintessence du crime, déployèrent à la fois une énergie dont il n'y a jamais eu d'exemple et des forfaits que tous ceux de l'histoire mis ensemble pourraient à peine égaler.

Ils virent que pour obtenir le résultat qu'ils se proposaient les systèmes reçus de justice, les axiomes communs d'humanité, tout le cercle des principes adoptés par Lycurgue, ne pouvaient être utiles, et qu'il fallait parvenir au même but par un chemin différent. Attendre que la mort vînt saisir les grands propriétaires, ou que ceux-ci consentissent à se dépouiller, que les années déracinassent le fanatisme et vinssent changer les costumes et les mœurs, que des recrues ordinaires fussent envoyées aux armées, attendre tout cela leur parut douteux et trop long ; et comme si l'établissement de la république et

* On sait que les jacobins expulsaient à certaines époques périodiques tous ceux de leurs membres soupçonnés de modérantisme ou d'humanité, et on appelait cela un scrutin épuratoire. (Note de Chateaubriand.)

la défense de la France, pris séparément, eussent été trop peu pour
leur génie, ils résolurent de tenter les deux à la fois.

Les gardes nationales étant achetées, des agents placés à leurs
postes dans tous les coins de la république, le mot communiqué aux
sociétés affiliées, les monstres se bouchant les oreilles, ou s'arrachant,
pour ainsi dire, les entrailles de peur d'être attendris, donnèrent
l'affreux signal qui devait rappeler Sparte de ses ruines. Il retentit
dans la France comme la trompette de l'ange exterminateur: les
monuments des fils des hommes s'écroulèrent, et les tombes s'ouvrirent.

Œuvres complètes (Paris, Garnier Frères, s.d.), vol. I,
pp. 305–6.

When he began work on the *Essai sur les Révolutions* in 1794, at the
age of twenty-six, Chateaubriand already possessed considerable experience of social change. The younger son of a country noble who had made
a slender fortune in maritime enterprises which included the slave-
trade, he grew up in a feudal atmosphere, was presented at Court,
granted a commission in the Army, and accepted for membership of
the celibate and very rich order of the Knights of Malta. The Revolution
ended his hopes of privileged affluence. It was not the abolition of
aristocratic prerogative which disenchanted him with the Revolution,
however, but the spectacle of political murders in the streets. In 1791
he sailed for America, where he learned about modern democracy as
well as about the immensity of nature and the customs of Redskins.
News of the King's arrest at Varennes brought him home: though
without sympathy for authoritarian monarchy, his duty as an officer
was to defend his sovereign. In July 1792 he joined the Army of the
Princes, which was invading France for the purpose of re-establishing
royal power. In September – during the days when in Paris the alleged
potential Royalist fifth column was being massacred – he was wounded
at the siege of Thionville, and honourably discharged. Weak from wounds
and smallpox, he made his way to Ostend, and thence by sea to his uncle
in Jersey. Still a sick man, he arrived in London in May 1793, dependent
on what he could earn or on émigré relief funds. In 1794 he heard that
his brother had been guillotined – along with Malesherbes, who had been
the friend of Rousseau, the champion of Protestant emancipation, and
the defence counsel at Louis's trial. The *Essai* was published in London
on 18 March 1797.

The passage deals with France between 1792 and 1794. In April
1792, the Legislative Assembly went to war with Austria and Prussia.
In July, the Duke of Brunswick's manifesto threatened Paris with fire

and slaughter if any harm befell the royal family. On 1 September, the Prussians captured Verdun. The massacres in Paris followed. On 20 September the Revolutionary armies defeated the Prussians at Valmy. In December 1792, the Convention offered military support to all peoples aspiring to liberty, and began to annex frontier territories. The execution of the King provoked a coalition against France: soon the only European countries not at war with it were Turkey, Switzerland and Scandinavia. In March 1793, General Dumouriez was defeated in Belgium, and went over to the enemy. Royalist revolts broke out in the Vendée and elsewhere. The Girondins, defeated in Paris, took up arms in the provinces. By June sixty *départements* were hostile or in rebellion against the Jacobin government. The harvests from 1791 to 1793 were bad. *Assignats*, the new paper currency, had lost 50 per cent of their nominal value by February 1793. Yet the Convention drew up the Constitution de l'An I, which provided for universal manhood suffrage, liberty, happiness, and various social welfare measures. In August 1793 this Constitution, duly approved by a referendum, was placed in an ark of cedar-wood at the feet of the President of the Convention. In October a revolutionary dictatorship was proclaimed for the duration of the war. *Représentants en mission* were posted to the provinces and armies; Jacobin societies were officially recognised; terror was instituted as a means of defeating enemies of the Republic. It is estimated that from May 1793 to July 1794, there were between thirty-five and forty thousand victims, of whom about half were peasants or proletarians. The 'levy in mass' raised an army of over one million, from a total population of about twenty-five million inhabitants; supplies and funds were made available; the nation was organised for victory. In June 1794, the Austrians were defeated at Fleurus, in Belgium. Robespierre, no longer necessary or tolerable, was replaced by a less sanguinary régime, free also from the suspicion of economic egalitarianism. The era of European conquest by French armies had begun. It was to last until 1814.[1]

Chateaubriand was in no way original in realising that there was a connection between the invasion of France by counter-revolutionary armies, the Terror, and the upsurge of energy which saved the Republic from defeat. The same idea is expressed by Joseph de Maistre in his *Considérations sur la France*, written independently of Chateaubriand's *Essai*, and published a few weeks before it:

Qu'on y réfléchisse bien, on verra que le mouvement révolutionnaire une fois établi, la France et la monarchie ne pouvaient être sauvées

que par le jacobinisme. . . . Or, comment résister à la coalition? Par
quel moyen surnaturel briser l'effort de l'Europe conjurée? Le génie
infernal de Robespierre pouvait seul opérer ce prodige. Le gouvernement révolutionnaire endurcissait l'âme des Français, en la trempant
dans le sang: il exaspérait l'esprit des soldats, et doublait leurs forces
par un désespoir féroce et un mépris de la vie, qui tenait de la rage.
L'horreur des échafauds poussant le citoyen aux frontières, alimentait
la force extérieure, à mesure qu'elle anéantissait jusqu'à la moindre
résistance dans l'intérieur. Toutes les vies, toutes les richesses, tous
les pouvoirs étaient dans les mains du pouvoir révolutionnaire; et ce
monstre de puissance, ivre de sang et de succès, phénomène épouvantable qu'on n'avait jamais vu, et que sans doute on ne reverra jamais,
était tout à la fois un châtiment épouvantable pour les Français, et
le seul moyen de sauver la France.[2]

The Revolution, in de Maistre's view, was inflicted by God upon the
whole French people to punish it for its sins. The Jacobins, hellish in
their blasphemous cruelties, were instruments of Providence: France,
purified and regenerated, its frontiers intact as a result of Jacobin
exertions, should now call back its divinely appointed monarch.

Chateaubriand has no such mysticism in his *Essai*, but explains in
purely human terms how the Ancien Régime dug its own grave:

A voir ainsi le monarque [Louis XV] endormi dans la volupté, des
courtisans corrompus, des ministres méchants ou imbéciles, le peuple
perdant ses mœurs; les philosophes les uns sapant la religion, les
autres l'Etat; des nobles ou ignorants ou atteints des vices du jour;
des ecclésiastiques à Paris la honte de leur ordre, dans les provinces
pleins de préjugés, on eût dit d'une foule de manœuvres s'empressant
à l'envi de démolir un grand édifice.[3]

The end of our passage has a biblical ring, but it does not invoke the
deity. In using the philosophes' word *fanatisme* instead of *religion* or
christianisme in the third paragraph, Chateaubriand is perhaps
unconsciously revealing that, at this period of his life, he is an unbeliever.
Though later in the *Essai* he refutes the philosophes' anti-Christian
arguments, he is unconvinced by his own refutations. One of the final
chapters of the book bears the title, 'Quelle sera la religion qui rempla-
cera le christianisme'.

Comparisons between modern and ancient history had been common throughout the century. The twenty or so books on the French
Revolution published between 1789 and 1793 contained copious allu-
sions to Greco-Roman history.[4] It was, therefore, natural that Chateaubriand should base his work on parallels between France and Antiquity.
Sparta, and its legislator Lycurgus, had been prominent in political

thought of the century from Montesquieu onwards.[5] Chateaubriand himself, like so many of his contemporaries, had liked to dream of himself as a citizen of an ancient republic:

Et moi aussi je voudrais passer mes jours sous une démocratie telle que je l'ai souvent rêvée, comme le plus sublime des gouvernements en théorie; et moi aussi j'ai vécu citoyen de l'Italie et de la Grèce; peut-être mes opinions actuelles ne sont-elles que le triomphe de ma raison sur mon penchant. Mais prétendre former des républiques partout, en dépit de tous les obstacles, c'est une absurdité dans la bouche de plusieurs, une méchanceté dans celle de quelques-uns.[6]

The respects in which the Jacobins tried to imitate the Spartans and build a republic of virtuous citizens were, according to Chateaubriand: the destruction of commerce; the extirpation of literature; the institution of republican schools, meals in common, and political clubs; the compulsory marriage of female aristocrats to 'citizens'; the requisitioning of property; the preparation of agrarian laws. On each of these items he would have been able to produce some sort of evidence. The reference in paragraph 3 to the seizure of large estates presumably refers to the sequestration of émigrés' lands, and the decree of February 1794 (not, in fact, carried out to any appreciable extent) which ordered the property of enemies of the republic to be devoted to needy citizens. How far the Jacobins interfered with commerce, and anticipated modern socialist measures, is still debated by economic historians.[7]

Lois agraires – a phrase which in the Ancient Roman jargon of the times meant communism – were abhorrent to the Convention, which in March 1793 introduced the death penalty for 'quiconque proposera ou tentera d'établir des lois agraires ou toutes autres lois ou mesures subversives des propriétés territoriales, commerciales ou industrielles'.[8] The 'socialist' *enragés* were sent to the guillotine by Robespierre in 1794, just as were the communist Babeuf and his confederates by the Directoire in 1797.[9] Robespierre specifically denied any intention of trying to fit France into a Spartan mould. He did, however, remark that French women, like Spartan women, had given birth to heroes.[10]

Chateaubriand himself lost patience with these tedious parallels, which he came to regard as futile and pointless.[11] This may be one reason why he never published the second volume of the *Essai*. He wrote the *Essai*, he tells us, with dogged application at a time when he was very productive: 'J'ai souvent écrit douze ou quinze heures sans quitter la table où j'étais assis, raturant et recomposant dix fois la même page.'[12] It is for the most part the work of an apprentice, not the magician in words which he was to become. Like that of many writers of the revolutionary period, his style is in places bare, violent, frenzied, pseudo-epical, declamatory. For this very reason, it conveys to the modern reader something of the unreal, melodramatic atmosphere of the time: Chateaubriand is aware that he is recording one of the turning-points in history:

> Où sont ces petits esprits qui calculent pertinemment ce qu'on aurait dû faire par ce qu'on a fait jadis, qui ne voient dans la lutte actuelle que des batailles perdues ou gagnées, et non le génie de la France dans les convulsions d'une crise amenée par la force des choses, déchirant, comme l'Hercule d'Œta, ceux qui osent l'approcher, lançant leurs membres ensanglantés sur les plaines cadavéreuses de l'Italie et de la Flandre, et s'apprêtant à tourner sur lui-même des mains forcenées? On pourrait soupçonner qu'il existe des époques inconnues, mais régulières, auxquelles la face du monde se renouvelle. Nous avons le malheur d'être nés au moment d'une de ces grandes révolutions: quel qu'en soit le résultat, heureux ou malheureux pour les hommes à naître, la génération présente est perdue: ainsi le furent celles du Ve et du VIe siècle, lorsque tous les peuples de l'Europe, comme des fleuves, sortirent de leur cours.[13]

This sense of belonging to a doomed generation heightened in the exiled, impoverished Chateaubriand that unassuageable, aimless yearning which he had already felt as an adolescent in the woods of Combourg. He sensed all the misery which the revolution had brought into being, shared in the aspirations of his contemporaries for a better order of things, yet was unable to believe that human frailty and sinfulness could attain to any ideal form of society:

> Eh! malheureux, nous nous tourmentons pour un gouvernement parfait, et nous sommes méchants! Nous nous agitons aujourd'hui pour un gouvernement parfait, et nous sommes vicieux! bon, et nous sommes méchants! ... Nous nous agitons aujourd'hui pour un vain système, et nous ne serons plus demain! Des soixante années que le ciel peut-être nous destine à traîner sur ce globe, nous en dépenserons vingt à naître, et vingt à mourir, et la moitié des vingt autres s'évanouira dans le sommeil. Craignons-nous que les misères inhérentes à notre nature d'homme ne remplissent pas assez ce court espace, sans y ajouter des maux d'opinion? Est-ce un instinct indéterminé, un vide intérieur que nous ne saurions remplir, qui nous tourmente? Je l'ai aussi sentie, cette soif vague de quelque chose. Elle m'a traîné dans les solitudes muettes de l'Amérique et dans les villes bruyantes de l'Europe; je me suis enfoncé pour la satisfaire dans l'épaisseur des forêts du Canada, et dans la foule qui inonde nos jardins et nos temples. Que de fois elle m'a contraint de sortir des spectacles de nos cités, pour aller voir le soleil se coucher au loin sur quelque site sauvage! que de fois,

échappé à la société des hommes, je me suis tenu immobile sur une grève solitaire, à contempler durant des heures, avec cette même inquiétude, le tableau philosophique de la mer![14]

The *Essai* ends with a grandiose, melodic description of moonlight in the Canadian woods, and one of those sentences that reverberate into endless desolation:

Auprès tout était silence et repos, hors la chute de quelques feuilles, le passage brusque d'un vent subit, les gémissements rares et interrompus de la hulotte; mais au loin, par intervalles, on entendait les roulements solennels de la cataracte de Niagara, qui dans le calme de la nuit se prolongeaient de désert en désert, et expiraient à travers les forêts solitaires.[15]

If this were all Chateaubriand stood for, he would have his place in literary history as a founder of French romantic melancholia, a stylist who gave a new music to the language. But there is more to Chateaubriand than melodious despair. The *Essai sur les Révolutions* testifies, for example, to his fervent love of freedom. Though it maintains that the ideals of republicanism were impossible to achieve at the time, the *Essai* is in no way an apology for absolutism. In the 1826 Preface to the work, he asserts that enemies of freedom have still not forgiven him for 'l'amour de la liberté qui respire dans cet ouvrage'.[16] A man of the right, he upheld certain principles more often associated with the left:

L'*Essai* fit du bruit dans l'émigration: il était en contradiction avec les sentiments de mes compagnons d'infortune; mon indépendance dans mes diverses positions sociales a presque toujours blessé les hommes avec qui je marchais. J'ai tour à tour été le chef d'armées différentes dont les soldats n'étaient pas de mon parti: j'ai mené les vieux royalistes à la conquête des libertés publiques, et surtout de la liberté de la presse, qu'ils détestaient; j'ai rallié les libéraux au nom de cette même liberté sous le drapeau des Bourbons qu'ils ont en horreur.[17]

Throughout his political battles, Chateaubriand the disillusioned life-hater, the faithful knight-errant of the Bourbon dynasty which he knew to be anachronistic, was aware that a vigorous new era of democracy, industry and science had emerged from the chaos of revolutionary wars. In that stupendous proto-Proustian work[18] which he entitled *Mémoires d'Outre-Tombe*, his main interest is in himself; his only real antidote to nihilism and despair lies in his Christian faith which, eventually, he had learned to rely on. But the work also makes positive affirmations about progress, liberty, social justice – those other aspects of romanticism which he shares with Lamartine, Hugo and Michelet, and which derive from the Enlightenment. In 1833, Chateaubriand remained conscious that evils which the Jacobins had so signally failed to eradicate still awaited a remedy:

> Dans la vallée du Rhône, je rencontrai une garçonnette presque nue, qui dansait avec sa chèvre; elle demandait la charité à un riche jeune homme bien vêtu qui passait en poste, courrier galonné en avant, deux laquais assis derrière le brillant carrosse. Et vous vous figurez qu'une telle distribution de la propriété peut exister? Vous pensez qu'elle ne justifie pas les soulèvements populaires?[19]

Like Robespierre, he rejected *lois agraires* as a solution. But he looked forward to a regenerated society in which the ideals of Christianity and of 1789 would coincide:

> Loin d'être à son terme, la religion du libérateur entre à peine dans sa troisième période, la période politique, *liberté, égalité, fraternité*. L'Evangile, sentence d'acquittement, n'a pas été lu encore à tous; nous en sommes encore aux malédictions prononcées par le Christ: 'Malheur à vous qui chargez les hommes de fardeaux qu'ils ne sauraient porter, et qui ne voudriez pas les avoir touchés du bout du doigt.'[20]

Chateaubriand himself mocked the celebrity of *Atala*,[21] and denounced the fatuous, self-indulgent morbidity of *René*: 'si *René* n'existait pas, je ne l'écrirais plus; s'il m'était possible de le détruire, je le détruirais.'[22] It would, of course, be erroneous to exaggerate the positive, vigorous, aspects of his personality, and to forget that, throughout his life, he continued to be René. Nevertheless, he was by no means René only, and nothing more. Various features of his manifold greatness are already visible in the *Essai sur les Révolutions*, that 'livre de doute et de douleur'[23] written by a counter-revolutionary aristocrat who believed in liberty.

NOTES

1 J. Godechot, *Les Révolutions (1770–1789)*, Nouvelle Clio (Paris, 1963), pp. 157–75; 315–27; A. Goodwin, *The French Revolution* (London, 1953), Ch. VIII–X.

2 *Considérations sur la France* par M. le comte Joseph de Maistre (Lyon; Paris, 1852), pp. 20–1.

3 *Essai sur les révolutions. Œuvres complètes de Chateaubriand* (Paris, Garnier Frères, s.d.), vol. 1, p. 585.

4 P. Christophorov, *Sur les pas de Chateaubriand en exil* (Paris, 1960), pp. 78–93.

5 For Montesquieu and Sparta see Montesquieu, *Œuvres complètes*, Pléiade (Paris, 1951), Index, under 'Lacédémone', 'Lycurgue', 'Sparte', 'Spartiates'.

6 *Essai*, ed. cit., p. 465.

7 J. Godechot, op. cit., pp. 328–31 (arguments of Cobb, Rudé and Soboul).
8 M. Leroy, *Histoire des idées sociales en France* (Paris, 1946), vol. I, p. 257.
9 Ibid., pp. 270–99; J. McManners, *Lectures on European History 1789–1914* (Oxford, 1966), pp. 96–104.
10 Robespierre, *Textes choisis*, ed. J. Poperen, vol. III (Paris, 1958), p. 116; p. 156 ('Sparte brille comme un éclair dans des ténèbres immenses'); p. 179.
11 *Essai*, ed. cit., pp. 393, 615.
12 *Mémoires d'Outre-Tombe*, Pléiade, vol. I (Paris, 1966), p. 383.
13 *Essai*, ed. cit., pp. 367–8.
14 Ibid., p. 465.
15 Ibid., p. 626.
16 Ibid., p. 257.
17 *Mémoires d'Outre-Tombe*, ed. cit., vol. I, p. 383.
18 On Chateaubriand as a predecessor of Proust, see *A la recherche du temps perdu*, Pléiade, vol. III (Paris, 1954), p. 919 and Index.
19 *Mémoires d'Outre-Tombe*, ed. cit., vol. II (Paris, 1964), p. 765.
20 Ibid., p. 932.
21 Ibid., vol. I, pp. 444–6.
22 Ibid., p. 462.
23 Ibid., p. 398.

XX · Madame de Staël (1766–1817)

FROM *De la littérature considérée dans ses rapports avec les institutions sociales* (published 1800)
(Seconde partie, ch. IX)

J'ai tenté de montrer avec quelle force la raison philosophique, malgré tous les obstacles, après tous les malheurs, a toujours su se frayer une route, et s'est développée successivement dans tous les pays, dès qu'une tolérance quelconque, quelque modifiée qu'elle pût être, a permis à l'homme de penser. Comment donc forcer l'esprit humain à rétrograder, et lors même qu'on aurait obtenu ce triste succès, comment prévenir toutes les circonstances qui pourraient donner aux facultés morales une impulsion nouvelle? On désire d'abord, et les rois mêmes sont de cet avis, que la littérature et les arts fassent des progrès. Or, ces progrès tiennent nécessairement à toutes les pensées qui doivent mener la réflexion beaucoup au-delà des sujets qui l'ont fait naître. Dès que les ouvrages de littérature ont pour but de remuer l'âme, ils approchent nécessairement des idées philosophiques, et les idées philosophiques conduisent à toutes les vérités. Quand on imiterait l'inquisition d'Espagne et le despotisme de Russie, il faudrait encore être assuré que dans aucun pays de l'Europe, il ne s'établira d'autres institutions; car les simples rapports de commerce, même lorsqu'on interdirait les autres, finiraient par communiquer à un pays les lumières des pays voisins.

Les sciences physiques ayant pour but une utilité immédiate, aucun gouvernement ne veut ni ne peut les interdire; et comment l'étude de la nature ne bannirait-elle pas la croyance de certains dogmes? comment l'indépendance religieuse ne conduirait-elle pas au libre examen de toutes les autorités de la terre? On peut, dira-t-on, réprimer ces excès sans entraver la raison. Qui réprimera ces excès? – le gouvernement. – Peut-il jamais être considéré comme une puissance impartiale? et les bornes qu'il voudra poser aux recherches de la pensée ne seron-telles pas précisément celles que les esprits ardents voudront franchir?

Ed. Paul van Tieghem (Genève–Paris, 1959), vol. 2,
pp. 420–1

'L'entreprise est laborieuse et les rieurs ne sont pas pour nous.' This is what a Catholic priest says, in letter LXI of the *Lettres persanes*, about the clergy's task of converting polite Parisian society to Christian beliefs. From the 1720s onwards, the philosophe propagandists had on their side the advantages of wit, novelty and aggressiveness, so that even within the Church and nobility they found adherents to help them in their campaign for progress. By the 1760s, they had evidence that their proposals for replacing 'prejudice' by 'liberty' could actually be carried out. Of course, the philosophes denied any absolute meaning to the word 'liberty': since any action is necessarily determined by the whole chain of circumstance in which the doer of the action finds himself, unconditional freedom to act would be miraculous, and therefore unnatural. As Voltaire put it:

Il n'y a rien sans cause. Un effet sans cause n'est qu'une parole absurde. Toutes les fois que je veux, ce ne peut être qu'en vertu de mon jugement bon ou mauvais; ce jugement est nécessaire, donc ma volonté l'est aussi. En effet, il serait bien singulier que toute la nature, tous les astres obéissent à des lois éternelles, et qu'il y eût un petit animal haut de cinq pieds qui, au mépris de ces lois, pût agir comme il lui plairait au seul gré de son caprice. Il agirait au hasard, et on sait que le hasard n'est rien. Nous avons inventé ce mot pour exprimer l'effet connu de toute cause inconnue . . . Etre véritablement libre, c'est pouvoir. Quand je peux faire ce que je veux, voilà ma liberté; mais je veux nécessairement ce que je veux; autrement je voudrais sans raison, sans cause, ce qui est impossible. Ma liberté consiste à marcher quand je veux marcher et que je n'ai point la goutte. Ma liberté consiste à ne point faire une mauvaise action quand mon esprit se la représente nécessairement mauvaise; à subjuguer une passion quand mon esprit m'en fait sentir le danger, et que l'horreur de cette action combat puissamment mon désir.[1]

For the most part, however, the philosophes saw no incompatibility between their denial of free will and their pursuit of 'liberty' in a social and political sense. Indeed, the very laws of nature, it seemed to some of them, had determined that thought, speech, property and trade should be 'free', and that this freedom, subject only to such restraints as society should consider necessary for its smooth running, would allow man to attain a degree of happiness denied to him by illiberal, and therefore unnatural governments.

Their belief in progress and happiness did not mean that the philosophes were all blind optimists, devoid of objective common sense. Voltaire, who more than any other man in the century campaigned for liberty, was under no illusions about human wickedness:

'Croyez-vous, dit Candide, que les hommes se soient toujours mutuellement massacrés comme ils font aujourd'hui? qu'ils aient toujours été
menteurs, fourbes, perfides, ingrats, brigands, faibles, volages, lâches,
envieux, gourmands, ivrognes, avares, ambitieux, sanguinaires,
calomniateurs, débauchés, fanatiques, hypocrites et sots? – Croyez-
vous, dit Martin, que les éperviers aient toujours mangé des pigeons
quand ils en ont trouvé? – Oui, sans doute, dit Candide. – Eh bien!
dit Martin, si les éperviers ont toujours eu le même caractère, pourquoi
voulez-vous que les hommes aient changé le leur? – Oh! dit Candide,
il y a bien de la différence, car le libre arbitre . . .'²

Though the atheist determinist Diderot hailed American liberty as a
model for all mankind, he saw change and decay, not continual progress,
as an ineluctable law of nature:

Puissent ces braves Américains . . . reculer, au moins pour quelques
siècles, le décret prononcé contre toutes les choses de ce monde; décret
qui les a condamnées à avoir leur naissance, leur temps de vigueur,
leur décrépitude et leur fin!³

Yet for all their doubts and difficulties, and their controversies one with
another, the philosophes believed that the human mind, unaided by any
revealed religious dogma, could arrive at some limited aspects of truth,
and that this truth could be used for the betterment of humanity.
In 1805 that remarkably liberal priest the abbé Morellet (who numbered
among the crimes and errors of the revolution the suppression of his own
life-fellowship at the Sorbonne) defined the philosophe faith to which
he himself unshakeably adhered:

Cette ardeur de savoir, cette activité de l'esprit qui ne veut pas laisser
un effet sans en chercher la cause, un phénomène sans explication,
une assertion sans preuves, une objection sans réponse, une erreur sans
la combattre, un mal sans en chercher le remède, un bien possible sans
tâcher d'y atteindre; c'est ce mouvement général des esprits qui a
marqué le 18ᵉ siècle et qui fera à jamais sa gloire.⁴

The ideals of the French Revolution had been based on the belief
that society was a human institution which human beings could change,
control and improve. In his *Catéchisme du citoyen français*, published in
1793, the philosophe Volney asserted that the laws of social morality
could be determined scientifically, that progress was as possible in society
as it was in the physical sciences, and that 'nous portons en nous le
germe de toute vertu, de toute perfection'.⁵ In 1793 also, the marquis
de Condorcet completed the main philosophe manifesto on progress –
the *Esquisse d'un tableau historique des progrès de l'esprit humain*. All
human error, Condorcet maintained, is due to ignorance of the laws of

nature, including that 'loi générale du monde moral' which, in a free
society, ensures that private self-interest, rightly understood, shall
coincide with the common good:

> Ainsi, l'homme doit pouvoir déployer ses facultés, disposer de ses
> richesses, pourvoir à ses besoins, avec une liberté entière. L'intérêt
> général de chaque société, loin d'ordonner d'en restreindre l'exercice,
> défend au contraire d'y porter atteinte.

All nations will soon approach the degree of civilisation reached by
'les peuples les plus éclairés, les plus libres, les plus affranchis de préjugés, tels que les Français et les Anglo-Américains'. Slavery and 'notre
mépris sanguinaire pour les hommes d'une autre couleur' will disappear;
European colonists, ceasing to be monopolist brigands, will spread
enlightenment and liberty in Africa and Asia, which consequently will
develop more rapidly than did Europe itself. In order that food and
goods may be produced, toil must remain the lot of 'la classe la plus
nombreuse et la plus active de nos sociétés', but thrift, encouraged by
insurance companies and mutual benefit societies, privately or publicly
run, will save them from destitution in sickness or old age, and their
children will go to the same schools, and speak the same standard
language, as children of the rich. Economic, social and intellectual
inequality will diminish, without disappearing. The standard of living
will rise: 'chaque génération . . . est appelée à des jouissances plus
étendues'. As science develops, new methods of food production and
preservation will be available to feed the growing population, until
eventually, 'si on suppose . . . que les progrès de la raison aient marché
de pair avec ceux de la science', birth-control methods will stabilise the
population at the level best suited to the happiness and well-being of
the earth's inhabitants. Eugenics may produce a higher breed of man.
With a properly organised educational system, moral progress will keep
pace with scientific progress, because all normal men possess within them

> ces principes d'une justice rigoureuse et pure, ces mouvements
> habituels d'une bienveillance active, éclairée d'une sensibilité délicate
> et généreuse, dont la nature a placé le germe dans tous les cœurs, et
> qui n'attendent, pour s'y développer, que la douce influence des
> lumières et de la liberté.

Wars, like murders, may from time to time occur, but only as rare and
exceptional atrocities. The 'perfectibilité indéfinie de l'espèce humaine'
is a fact; whatever the temporary setbacks, mankind is 'marchant d'un
pas ferme et sûr dans la route de la vérité, de la vertu et du bonheur'.[6]
Unfortunately, when he was writing this blueprint for twentieth-

century Western democracy, Condorcet was in hiding from the police of the revolution. He was eventually arrested on 27 March 1794, and found dead in his cell next morning. Though his politics were of the sort which Chénier and Malesherbes considered dangerously demagogic, Condorcet, too, disapproved of certain revolutionary excesses, and had voted against the death-sentence on the King. It would be difficult to formulate any definition of the word 'counter-revolutionary' if this term is to include all those who were opposed to, or denounced by, any of the revolutionary governments from 1790 onwards. Robespierre, after guiliotining men who were to the left of himself and men who were to the right, was himself guillotined by 'conservatives' who none the less had cogent reasons for opposing a Bourbon restoration. Napoleon himself remained in many respects 'l'homme de la révolution', even when, as Wordsworth inelegantly put it:

> finally to close
> And seal up all the gains of France, a Pope
> Is summoned in, to crown an Emperor –
> This last opprobrium, when we see a people,
> That once looked up in faith, as if to Heaven
> For manna, take a lesson from the dog
> Returning to his vomit.[7]

By any definition, on the other hand, Joseph de Maistre was an opponent of the revolution. His *Considérations sur la France*, published at Basle in 1797, declaimed against liberalism and the republic in the name of religion, monarchy, and common sense. Man in his fallen state is a creature of sin; violence, bloodshed and destruction are laws of nature; therefore the ideas of the Enlightenment are criminal lunacy:

> Il n'y a que violence dans l'univers; mais nous sommes gâtés par la philosophie moderne, qui a dit que *tout est bien*, tandis que le mal a tout souillé, et que, dans un sens très vrai, *tout est mal*, puisque rien n'est à sa place. . . . *Tous les êtres gémissent* (Saint Paul aux Romains, VIII, 22 et suiv.) et tendent, avec effort et douleur, vers un autre ordre de choses.

Providence permits the innocent to suffer in expiation for the sins of the guilty. The Revolution was divine chastisement for the wickedness of the Ancien Régime, and in particular, for the moral degradation of the aristocracy. The revolutionaries themselves were satanic:

> Français, c'est au bruit des chants infernaux, des blasphèmes de l'athéisme, des cris de mort et de longs gémissements, c'est à la lueur des incendies, sur les débris du trône et des autels, arrosés par le sang du meilleur des rois et par celui d'une foule innombrable d'autres

victimes; c'est au mépris des mœurs et de la foi publique, c'est au milieu de tous les forfaits, que vos séducteurs et vos tyrans ont fondé ce qu'ils appellent *votre liberté.*

Condorcet was a dangerous dreamer:

> Ne donnons pas dans les rêves de Condorcet, de ce philosophe si cher à la révolution, qui employa sa vie à préparer le malheur de la génération présente, léguant bénignement la perfection à nos neveux.

In God's good time, all human suffering will be used by Eternal Love to wipe out the Principle of Evil. Frenchmen meanwhile, eschewing philosophy and liberalism, must trust to instinct and tradition, and reinstate Throne and Altar:

> Peuple français, ne te laisse point séduire par les sophismes de l'intérêt particulier, de la vanité ou de la poltronnerie. N'écoute pas les raisonneurs: on ne raisonne que trop en France, et *le raisonnement en bannit la raison.* Livre-toi sans crainte et sans réserve à l'instinct infaillible de ta conscience . . . Rappelle ton souverain.[8]

Similar denunciations, but without Maistre's mysticism, were uttered by the royalist wit Rivarol, who referred to the Declaration of the Rights of Man as 'la préface criminelle d'un livre impossible'.[9] The philosophes considered his tract *De la philosophie moderne*[10] so dangerous that in 1799 they printed a long refutation of it in their periodical *La Décade philosophique.*[11] The philosophes of the Ancien Régime, Rivarol argues, gave birth to a poisonous, brutish, murderous, fanatical progeny who, by their dissolvent analysis, have broken the laws of God and man, and produced chaos, death, annihilation. Lovers of every country and race but their own, they have sacrificed the present generation to some chimerical future:

> Tuteurs hypocrites, ils ont aimé les pauvres et les nègres, de toute leur haine pour les blancs et les riches. Législateurs cosmopolites, ils ont ri des droits de la propriété, des alarmes de la morale, des douleurs de la religion, des cris de l'humanité.

All they have achieved is 'un labyrinthe au fond d'un abîme':

> Philosophie moderne! où nous as-tu conduits, et à qui nous as-tu livrés? Sont-ce là tes saturnales, tes triomphes et tes orgies? Sombre nuit apparue au nom de la lumière; vaste tyrannie, au nom de la liberté; profond délire, au nom de la raison! Sanglants outrages, insultes recherchées, affronts inhumains, on ne saurait vous peindre trop fidèlement pour être utile, ni trop vous atténuer pour être cru.

Even the worst and most superstitious religion is socially more useful than philosophy, because only religion can achieve the 'miracle of

Q

obedience' necessary to hold in check 'cette masse inculte d'hommes qui ne comprennent que les harangues des passions'.

> C'est la religion qui attache la multitude à de saines idées, qui la rassemble sans danger, qui lui prêche l'égalité et la fraternité sans erreur et sans crime.

Without religion, society cannot subsist:

> En un mot, la philosophie divise les hommes par les opinions, la religion les unit dans les mêmes dogmes . . .; il y a donc un contrat éternel entre la politique et la religion. TOUT ETAT, si j'ose le dire, EST UN VAISSEAU MYSTERIEUX DONT LES ANCRES SONT DANS LE CIEL. Le vrai philosophe qui entend ce mystère, laisse la foi à la place de la science, et la crainte à la place de la raison, parce qu'il ne peut se charger de l'éducation du peuple, ni courber par l'habitude, ou élever par le perfectionnement des facultés, les esprits et les cœurs d'une multitude destinée au travail et aux sensations, et non au repos et au raisonnement.[12]

Royalist propaganda of this sort did not succeed in abolishing the Republic: regicide politicians, purchasers of the nationalised Church lands, and the revolutionary armies which had to put to flight the armies of the princes, were not yet ready, in 1799, to invite King Louis XVIII to the throne of his fathers. Instead, they put in power General Bonaparte, so that he could bring peace and order to France, and prevent the restoration of aristocratic and clerical privilege and property. Mockery of the out-of-date philosophes and their tedious if not criminal successors could, however, safely be indulged in by those who, having done well out of the revolution, were in no mood for any recrudescence of Jacobin egalitarianism. General Bonaparte himself, in spite of his philosophe friends and his membership of their *Institut*, quickly set about restoring the Gallican church on his own terms and as an instrument of his own power. It was now the turn of the Ideologues – the bourgeois–republican disciples of Voltaire, Condillac, Helvétius and the Encyclopédistes – to go on the defensive, and to accept the fact that 'the laughs were not on their side'. It must be admitted that the writings of the latter-day Voltairians are not, for the most part, very scintillating. Rivarol had remarked of Condorcet that 'il écrit avec de l'opium sur des feuilles de plomb'.[13]

Mme de Staël does not seek to deny or minimise the crimes of the revolution:

> Nous avons vu des cruautés sans nombre, presque dans le même temps commises et oubliées! Et c'est la plus grande, la plus noble, la plus fière des pensées humaines, la république, qui a prêté son ombre

à ces forfaits exécrables! Ah! qu'on a de peine à repousser ces tristes rapprochements, toutes les fois que le cours des idées ramène à réfléchir sur la destinée de l'homme, la révolution nous apparaît![14]

She is aware that the theory of human perfectibility is derided by many, and 'combattu par quelques penseurs'.[15] When she sent her manuscript to press in time for its publication in April 1800, she already knew that General Bonaparte might impose on France a régime of 'servitude et silence'. But she remains firm in her conviction that mankind has progressed, and will continue to do so. She rejects the view that civilisations must inevitably decay:

> Une des causes de la destruction des empires dans l'antiquité, c'est l'ignorance de plusieurs découvertes importantes dans les sciences. . . . La décadence des empires n'est pas plus dans l'ordre naturel, que celle des lettres et des lumières.[16]

The atrocities of the revolutions were not a sign that Europe has returned to barbarism, but merely that the civilisation of the upper classes had not yet been made available to 'les hommes de la classe du peuple' who had seized power:

> Il faut que l'éducation des vainqueurs se fasse, il faut que les lumières qui étaient renfermées dans un très petit nombre d'hommes s'étendent fort au-delà, avant que les gouvernants de la France soient tous entièrement exempts de vulgarité et de barbarie.[17]

The whole of the book is devoted to showing what progress has been achieved since the early Greeks; the author's aim is to encourage her disillusioned contemporaries not to yield to political or intellectual reaction.[18]

De la littérature was almost complete when Bonaparte seized power on the 18 Brumaire (9 November 1799), and it is not known what alterations she made to it after that date. But, whether it was originally so intended or not, our passage is, in effect, addressed to the Premier Consul of the French Republic, imploring him not to suppress liberty in France, and warning him that to abolish it, he would have to reduce the nation to 'la servitude et l'avilissement le plus absolu'.[19] Unless genuine literature, art and science are stamped out completely, and all contact with civilised foreign nations cut off, 'les esprits ardents' will continue to seek liberty and oppose tyranny.

By progress in literature, Mme de Staël does not mean that greater beauty will be attained, 'parce qu'il est impossible, je le répète, de dépasser une certaine borne dans les arts'.[20] The progress she has in mind consists of 'la connaissance du cœur humain et de la morale qui lui est propre'.[21] This is the substance of literature and the arts; consequently, to be something more than sterile imitation of existing models, art must be linked to 'idées philosophiques', that is, to the free pursuit of truth. She does not specify the 'certains dogmes' which she considers incompatible with modern science.[22] Most probably, she means everything in Christianity not acceptable by a Voltairian or Rousseauistic deist. For Mme de Staël remains a daughter of the Enlightenment, an enemy of 'les défenseurs des préjugés, des doctrines superstitieuses, des privilèges oppressifs'.[23] Some religion, however, is necessary to modern man, 'tous les jours plus aride, tous les jours plus à plaindre'. Some sort of non-dogmatic protestantism was what she would have liked to see adopted as the official religion of France, because

> La réformation est l'époque de l'histoire qui a le plus efficacement servi la perfectibilité de l'espèce humaine. La religion protestante ne renferme dans son sein aucun germe actif de superstition, et donne cependant à la vertu tout l'appui qu'elle peut tirer des opinions sensibles. Dans les pays où la religion protestante est professée, elle n'arrête en rien les recherches philosophiques, et maintient efficacement la pureté des mœurs.[24]

The essentials of a religion are that it will 'lier la morale à l'idée d'un Dieu, sans que jamais ce moyen puisse devenir un instrument de pouvoir dans la main des hommes'. Without freedom to question and oppose authority, whether of Church, State, party, or public opinion, there can be no intellectual or social progress.[25] Independent thought is incompatible with despotism.[26]

Unlike Condorcet, Mme de Staël does not describe the bliss which will be enjoyed by the nations of critically minded, well-educated republican philosophes, when the social sciences have been rationally and methodically developed and applied.[27] She appears to accept the liberals' hopes of a secure bourgeois world in which peace and prosperity are the result of trade.[28] But, a disciple also of Rousseau, she refuses to believe that private self-interest must necessarily promote the common good:

> Ce qui nous manque aujourd'hui, c'est un levier pour soulever l'égoïsme: toutes les forces morales de chaque homme se trouvent concentrées dans l'intérêt personnel.[29]

In the last resort, she holds that moral considerations are more important than any others: society must foster and revere the moral sentiments implanted by nature in the heart of man:

> Sans la vertu, rien ne peut subsister, rien ne peut réussir contre elle.

La consolante idée d'une providence éternelle peut tenir lieu de toute autre réflexion; mais il faut que les hommes déifient la morale elle-même, quand ils refusent de reconnaître un Dieu pour son auteur.[30]

She insists that human life and human personality are sacred:

> Enfin ce que la morale de l'évangile et la philosophie prêchent également, c'est l'humanité. On a appris à respecter profondément le don de la vie; l'existence de l'homme, sacrée pour l'homme, n'inspire plus cette sorte d'indifférence politique, que quelques anciens croyaient pouvoir réunir à de véritables vertus.[31]

In the name of human dignity, she demands intellectual and political freedom:

> La philosophie ne rend impropre qu'à gouverner arbitrairement, despotiquement, et d'une manière méprisante pour l'espèce humaine. Il ne faut pas prétendre, en apportant le vieil esprit des cours dans la république nouvelle, qu'il y ait en administration quelque chose de plus nécessaire que la pensée, de plus sûr que la raison, de plus énergique que la vertu.[32]

NOTES

1 *Le Philosophe ignorant*, XIII. *Mélanges*, Pléiade (Paris, 1961), pp. 886–7.
2 *Candide*, Ch. 21.
3 *Essai sur les règnes de Claude et de Néron*, Livre II, LXXIV, in Diderot, *Textes Politiques*, ed. Y. Benot (Paris, 1960), p. 213.
4 *Eloge de Marmontel*, 12 thermidor, an XIII. Marmontel, *Œuvres Complètes* (Paris, 1819), p. vii.
5 G. Chinard, *Volney et l'Amérique* (Baltimore, Paris, 1923), pp. 18–20. Volney also was imprisoned during the Terror, but only for debt (J. Gaulmier, *L'Idéologue Volney*, Beyrouth, 1951, pp. 287–9).
6 *Esquisse*, ed. O. H. Prior (Paris, 1933), pp. 152–4, 162–6, 191–2, 195–228. Condorcet went into hiding in July 1793, and wrote on the MS of the *Esquisse*: 'Terminé ce vendredi 4 octobre 1793'. It was published after the fall of Robespierre.
7 *The Prelude*, Book Eleventh, *France (concluded)*.
8 *Considérations sur la France* par M. le comte Joseph de Maistre (Lyon, Paris, 1852), pp. 1–4, 18, 41–7, 66, 130–1, 146.
9 *Esprit de Rivarol*, ed. Fayol et Chênedollé (Paris, 1808), pp. 149–50.
10 It was published in Hamburg in 1797, under the title of *Discours préliminaire du nouveau dictionnaire de la langue française*. It was officially allowed to be imported to France in 1799.
11 The refutation, by Rœderer, editor of the *Journal de Paris*, appeared in the numbers of *La Décade philosophique* dated 30 fructidor an VII, 10 vendémiaire, 10 brumaire an VIII (i.e. the week before the Dix-huit Brumaire), and was also published as a separate pamphlet, *De la philosophie moderne, ou Examen de la brochure publiée par Rivarol 'Sur la philosophie moderne'* (Paris, an VIII).

12 *Pensées inédites de Rivarol, suivies de deux discours* (Paris, 1836), pp. 173–80, 188–9, 200–1, 209.

13 *Esprit de Rivarol*, pp. xxxvi, 139.

14 *De la littérature*, ed. Paul Van Tieghem (Geneva; Paris, 1959), p. 156.

15 Ibid., pp. 419–20.

16 Ibid., p. 127. For eighteenth-century ideas on progress see: H. Vyverberg, *Historical Pessimism in the French Enlightenment* (Cambridge, Mass., 1958); C. Vereker, *Eighteenth-Century Optimism* (Liverpool, 1967).

17 *De la littérature*, p. 138. The passage is about the Dark Ages, but Mme de Staël applies it (p. 137) to the French revolutionary period.

18 She realises that, in literature, the fashion is now for gloom and despair ('A l'époque où nous vivons, la mélancolie est la véritable inspiration du talent: qui ne se sent pas atteint par ce sentiment, ne peut prétendre à une grande gloire comme écrivain; c'est à ce prix qu'elle est achetée.' Pp. 365–6); but she regards excessive indulgence in woe as destructive of literature ('quand la souffrance est devenue l'état habituel de l'âme, l'imagination perd jusqu'au besoin de peindre ce qu'elle éprouve.' P. 157). Cf. p. 183: 'Ce que l'homme a fait de plus grand, il le doit au sentiment douloureux de l'incomplet de sa destinée'.

19 Ibid., pp. 422–3.

20 Ibid., p. 56.

21 Ibid., p. 102.

22 Mme de Staël was to play a posthumous part in the development of the physical sciences of the twentieth century. Her daughter, Albertine de Staël (1797–1838), in whom Benjamin Constant always took a fatherly interest, married Léonce-Victor, duc de Broglie. Two great-grandsons of this marriage, Maurice, duc de Broglie (1875–1960), and Louis, prince, then duc de Broglie (b. 1892), became distinguished physicists. The latter won the Nobel Prize in 1929.

23 Ibid., p. 368. Cf. p. 133: 'l'indignation qu'inspirent aujourd'hui les crimes et les folies de la superstition'.

24 Ibid., p. 188.

25 Ibid., p. 321: 'La force de l'esprit ne se développe toute entière qu'en attaquant la puissance'. On tyranny of a party (pp. 320–1): 'Le courage peut lutter contre l'ascendant d'une faction dominante; mais l'inspiration du talent est étouffée par elle. La tyrannie d'un seul ne produirait pas aussi sûrement un tel effet. La tyrannie d'un parti prenant souvent la forme de l'opinion publique, porte une atteinte bien plus profonde à l'émulation.'

26 Ibid., p. 319.

27 Ibid., pp. 375–8.

28 Ibid., p. 128: 'Les douceurs de la vie privée, la diffusion des lumières, les relations commerciales établissant plus de parité dans les jouissances, appaiseront par degrés les sentiments de rivalité entre les nations.'

29 Ibid., p. 86.

30 Ibid., p. 388.

31 Ibid., p. 155.

32 Ibid., p. 325.

Index